C000174187

Gladiators

Violence and Spectacle in Ancient Rome

Roger Dunkle

PEARSON
Longman

Harlow, England • London • New York • Boston • San Francisco • Toronto
Sydney • Tokyo • Singapore • Hong Kong • Seoul • Taipei • New Delhi
Cape Town • Madrid • Mexico City • Amsterdam • Munich • Paris • Milan

PEARSON EDUCATION LIMITED

Edinburgh Gate
Harlow CM20 2JE
United Kingdom
Tel: +44 (0)1279 623623
Fax: +44 (0)1279 431059
Website: www.pearsoned.co.uk

First edition published in Great Britain in 2008

© Pearson Education Limited 2008

The right of Roger Dunkle to be identified as author of this work has been asserted by him in accordance with the Copyright, Designs and Patents Act 1988.

ISBN: 978-1-4058-0739-5

British Library Cataloguing in Publication Data
A CIP catalogue record for this book can be obtained from the British Library

Library of Congress Cataloging in Publication Data
Dunkle, Roger.
   Gladiators : violence and spectacle in ancient Rome / Roger Dunkle.
      p. cm.
   Includes bibliographical references and index.
   ISBN 978-1-4058-0739-5
   1. Gladiators—Rome—History. 2. Violence—Rome—History. I. Title.
   GV35.D86 2008
   796'.0937—dc22   2008025904

10 9 8 7 6 5 4 3 2 1
12 11 10 09 08

Typeset in 10/14 pt Galliard by 73
Printed and bound in China
SWTC/01

The publisher's policy is to use paper manufactured from sustainable forests.

Contents

Preface

Take up gladiators as a topic of serious study? Not a chance. That was the way I felt about ten years ago. I had put together a lecture on gladiators that I thought might interest a wider sampling of students in our department and its electives.[1] As far as I was concerned, however, gladiators might serve as a popular and sensationalistic come-on, but I was not prepared to go any further with the topic. My judgement was sincere, but premature. At the same time as I was putting together the lecture, I was teaching a course on ancient sport that focused on the Greek side with only brief forays into the Roman. My experience with the course taught me that Greek athletics were an important key to the understanding of Greek culture, as essential as other traditional subjects such as politics and philosophy. Athletics were not on the margins of Greek culture, but in fact nearer to the centre. Could this also be true of gladiatorial combat and Roman culture? As I began to dig below the flashy surface of things gladiatorial, I found that I could answer yes. It became clear to me that gladiatorial combat was not an exotic sideshow for the Romans, but an entertainment that was integral to their culture, demonstrating important Roman values, a virtual symbol of what it meant to be Roman. In the back of my mind, the idea began to form of a book that could be especially useful to students and the casual reader, and on occasion even to the scholar.

When Pearson asked me to submit a book proposal, I decided that my main concern in such a book would be to get the reader to see the phenomenon of gladiatorial combat as the Romans saw it: its organization, professionalism, competitive qualities, political character, holiday atmosphere, and, of course, its bloody violence. It is difficult for us to judge the Romans fairly in this area since their naïve delight in arena violence with little hint of guilt goes against the grain of modern ethical values. The modern tendency is to decry violence of any kind, but this attitude, which was not shared as dogmatically by the ancients, verges on the hypocritical, given our society's obsession with violence in entertainment. This approach, of course, is not to imply my advocacy of gladiator duels as entertainment, but my desire to set the record straight. On the other hand, as unattractive as arena entertainments are to modern taste, the Romans cannot be dismissed as pure sadists. There are fascinating paradoxes to be found in the sources. The undeniable callousness of the cold-hearted gladiator 'industry' can be countered with the humane side of life and death evident in the gladiator schools. Equally interesting is the coexistence of the Roman contempt for the low social status of gladiators with admiration for the courage these fighters display in the arena. A similar paradox can be found in the staged animal hunts closely associated with gladiator duels, in which the crowd can switch from enjoying the slaughter of wild animals to admiring the intelligence and skills of trained animals without missing a beat. On the other hand, we must be prepared to accept some unpleasant truths about the Romans (and even ourselves). As Professor Heinrich Von Staden once pointed out, scholars cannot ignore aspects of ancient cultures that offend modern sensibilities. They must be fairly evaluated and communicated to interested readers along with the glories of these civilizations.

Another purpose of this book is to de-emphasize (but not ignore) theoretical approaches to the topic, so beloved of scholars. I will discuss and evaluate various existing theories regarding gladiatorial combat in this book, but will add nothing theoretical to the debate. My approach will be to place gladiatorial combat in its cultural context, while giving an historical perspective to the development and decline of gladiatorial combat. The last two chapters of the book will deal with topics that are not usually included, or are merely mentioned in passing, in books that concentrate on gladiators. Chapter 6 deals with the venues of gladiator shows and what it was like to be a spectator at these sites. Chapter 7 is on gladiators in film and is important to this book, because films are probably the most significant source of the modern public's knowledge of gladiators. I will direct the reader's attention to both the virtues and the flaws of the film industry's depiction of gladiators in films over the past eight decades.

In pursuit of my policy of accessibility for the non-professional, I will explain aspects of Roman culture familiar to the scholar, but probably unfamiliar to the average reader, as they come up in the text. I will also translate foreign words and titles of important scholarly works in other languages. Abbreviations of journals and the names of ancient authors and their works are taken from the *Oxford Classical Dictionary*, Liddell and Scott's *A Greek–English Lexicon* (1961 reprint) and *L'Année philologique* (*The Year in Philology*).[2] Where no generally accepted abbreviations exist, I have given the full title of works and on a few occasions have improvised an easily understood abbreviation, for example *RG* for Augustus' *Res Gestae* (*Accomplishments*). Two frequently used abbreviations referring to inscriptions are *CIL* (= *Corpus Inscriptionum Latinarum*, 'Collection of Latin Inscriptions') and *ILS* (= *Inscriptiones Latinae Selectae*, 'Selected Latin Inscriptions'). *AE* stands for *L'Année epigraphique* (*The Year in Epigraphy*). Translations of ancient and secondary sources are my own, except when their source is indicated in the endnotes. When the three official names (*tria nomina*) of a Roman citizen are mentioned, the first (*praenomen*), in accordance with Roman custom, will be abbreviated as in the following examples: Ap. = Appius; Aul. = Aulus; C. = Gaius; D. = Decimus; Cn. = Gnaeus; L. = Lucius; M'. = Manius; N. = Marcus; P. = Numerius; M. = Publius; Q. = Quintus; Ser. = Servius; Sex. = Sextus; Ti. = Tiberius.

I would like to express my appreciation to Pearson for inviting me to submit a book proposal, with special thanks for the invaluable help I received from the editorial staff and freelance editors (in alphabetical order): Mary-Clare Connellan, Natasha Dupont, Ruth Freestone King, Casey Mein, Helen Parry, Mari Shullaw and Debra Weatherley. I must also mention the Interlibrary Loan department at the Brooklyn College Library, without whose help this book would not have been possible. Finally, I would feel remiss if I did not acknowledge my gratitude to scholars who have preceded me and have written so brilliantly on this topic. My debt to them is obvious throughout the book.

I dedicate this book to my wife, Dr Ruth Passweg. She graciously tolerated a husband who, although present in the house, was in effect absent, holing himself up in his office almost every day for three years. Moreover, going beyond any normal call of duty, she tirelessly proofread various versions of the manuscript, created the index and provided the invaluable service of discovering numerous repetitions and inconsistencies in the text.

Publisher's Acknowledgements

The publisher would like to thank the following for their kind permission to reproduce their photographs:

Tarina Peterson: Figure 1; Jona Lendering (www.livius.org): Figure 2; The Ministry for cultural heritage and Environment (Soprintendenza archeologica di Pompei): Figure 3; Museo Archeologico Nazionale, Naples: Figure 4; The Bridgeman Art Library Ltd: Galleria Borghese, Rome, Italy/ Alinari Figure 5; The Art Archive: Museo Nazionale Terme Rome/Gianni Dagli Orti: Figure 6; akg-images Ltd: Gilles Mermet: Figure 8; Corbis: Roger Wood: Figures 7, 9, 10, 11, 17 and 23; Corbis: The Art Archive: Figures 12 and 18; Bridgeman Art Library Ltd: Museo Archeologico Nazionale, Naples, Italy/Giraudon: Figure 13; Kunstsammlungen de Veste Coburg, Germany: Figure 14; Corbis: Bettmann: Figure 15; Scala London: Bildarchiv Preussischer Kulturbesitz, Berlin/Hermann Buresch: Figure 16; Musée départemental de l'Arles antique.: Cl. M. Lacanaud: Figure 19; The Art Archive: Gianni Dagli Orti: Figure 20; The Trustees of The British Museum: Figures 22 and 29; Bridgeman Art Library Ltd: Phoenix Art Museum, Arizona, USA: Figure 24; Corbis: Alinari Archives: Figure 25; Corbis: Vince Streano: Figure 26; Corbis: Bettmann: Figure 27; Scala London: Vatican, Museo Gregoriano Profano: Figure 28.

Every effort has been made to trace the copyright holders and we apologise in advance for any unintentional omissions. We would be pleased to insert the appropriate acknowledgement in any subsequent edition of this publication.

Chapter 1

Cultural Context and Origins of Gladiatorial Combat

On the day before she was to be thrown to the beasts for refusing to sacrifice for the well-being of the emperors, a young Christian woman named Vibia Perpetua had a dream that, like most dreams, was a combination of reality and fantasy with an admixture of incoherency.[1] In her dream, Perpetua is led into the amphitheatre, but not to face the wild beasts. She finds herself facing a frightening Egyptian opponent in a yet undetermined contest and when her seconds strip off her clothes, she has been transformed into a man.

The Egyptian rolls in the dust and Perpetua is rubbed down with oil, both typical preparations for a wrestling match or for the *pankration*, a no-holds-barred contest that is a combination of boxing and wrestling. Then there arrives a gigantic man taller than the walls of the amphitheatre, who is wearing a tunic with two vertical stripes and carries a rod and a green branch on which are golden apples. His dress and rod identify him as a referee of gladiator matches.[2] The branch seems to be a substitution for a palm branch, one of the symbolic prizes given to winners of Greek athletic contests, but also to victorious gladiators. When the official explains the terms of the contest, saying that the winner must slay the opponent with a sword, we are led to expect a gladiatorial match. Once the contest begins, however, the exchange of blows with fists and feet combined with wrestling holds reveals that the contest is the *pankration*. After defeating the Egyptian, Perpetua leaves the arena in triumph through the *Porta Sanivivaria* ('the Gate of Life'), through which victorious gladiators leave the arena. With the typical freedom of a dreamer, Perpetua has merged the *pankration* and gladiatorial combat.[3] For Perpetua, the dream in which she defeats the Egyptian is prophetic of her victory over the Devil (for which the Egyptian is a stand-in), which she will achieve the next day as a martyr when she and her friends are thrown to the wild beasts in the arena.[4] The golden apples attached to the branch are a symbol of immortality, suggesting the eternal life in heaven that Perpetua will win through her martyrdom.[5]

Perpetua's subconscious identification of herself with a pancratiast and a gladiator seems odd. Indeed, Christianity was extremely hostile to all pagan spectacles, especially gladiatorial combat, but in her concluding remarks on her dream, Perpetua glories in her dream victory as a pancratiast/gladiator.[6] Despite official Christian antagonism, the athlete and the gladiator were admired by those Christians who yearned for the crown of martyrdom.[7] These embodiments of masculine energy and power seem to have been inspiring exemplars, particularly for female martyrs, whom even their fellow Christians might expect to be weak in the face of the horrific mental and physical demands of martyrdom. The encyclical letter from the Christians of Vienne and Lyons in Gaul to their fellow Christians in the Near East describes Blandina's famous martyrdom in Lyons (AD 177) in athletic terms, presenting Christ as her athletic model:

> . . . *tiny, weak, and insignificant as she [Blandina] was, she would give inspiration to her brothers [in Christ], for she had put on Christ, that mighty and invincible athlete, and had overcome the Adversary [the Devil] in many contests, and through her conflict had won the crown of immortality.*[8]

As Brent Shaw points out, the athlete and the gladiator, both arena performers, were empowering figures, because of their strength of will and discipline.[9] Christianity was quick to adopt the athlete as a figure to be emulated in a spiritual context. For example, athletic imagery is prominent in advice to prospective martyrs given by Tertullian, a Christian apologist of the second century AD. He presents God and the Holy Spirit as officials in charge of athletes, whose rigorous training is an inspirational model for

Christians preparing for martyrdom. Just like athletes, martyrs must build up their moral strength by strict training to achieve victory. He describes the prison in which martyrs await their ordeal in the arena as a *palaestra* ('athletic training ground').[10] Even more germane to the martyr was the experience of the gladiator who faced the real possibility of death every time he appeared in the arena. The oath taken by volunteer gladiators emphasized the horrific physical trials they will have to endure during their training and in the arena: burning, binding, beating and death by the sword, all of which were especially pertinent to martyrs.[11] It is not surprising that the popular image of the gladiator as a heroic figure of great moral and physical power, willing to suffer wounds and even death in the all-out struggle for victory, found its way into her dream. The dream must have been a source of great comfort in as much as it encouraged her to see her execution in the arena the next day not as a degrading defeat, as her captors hoped, but as a triumphant victory. The ending of her life as a martyr would follow the glorious example of the gladiator. Just as the gladiator was able to transcend and defeat death by courageous behaviour in battle, she would achieve the same result through her martyrdom. In fact, Perpetua prominently displayed two notable characteristics of the gladiator during the tribulations of her last day on earth. As she and her friends were led from the prison to the amphitheatre, Perpetua stared down the hostile crowd that lined their path.[12] An unflinching stare was prized in gladiators because it signified a powerful will to win. In the gladiator school of the emperor Caligula were two gladiators who did not blink no matter what threat they faced and thus were invincible opponents.[13] Perpetua's death also closely followed the gladiatorial tradition. When the crowd protested the order that Perpetua and her friends be put to death out of the sight of the spectators in the *spoliarium*, she and her colleagues were more than happy to display the strength of their faith in the arena.[14] We know that death in the *spoliarium* was a matter of shame for gladiators: Seneca explains that a true gladiator would rather die in the middle of the arena than in the *spoliarium*.[15] An even more significant similarity to the gladiator was Perpetua's conduct when faced with death in the arena. Since the animals were able to kill only two of her Christian colleagues, an apprentice gladiator was assigned the task of executing Perpetua and two other members of her group with a sword. The executions were accomplished efficiently until it came to Perpetua, who was last in line. It seems that the young gladiator was nervous about killing Perpetua because his first blow hit a bone and she had to guide his wavering (*errantem*) sword to her throat. This situation duplicates the scene that Seneca the Younger describes, in which a losing gladiator, who at first had fought tentatively, redeemed himself by calmly accepting his death as decreed by the giver of the games. He offered his throat to his opponent and guided his wavering (*errantem*) sword to its destination.[16]

Although the legacy of the gladiator lay dormant for centuries after the disappearance of gladiatorial combat in late antiquity, it was revived with the excavations of Pompeii beginning in the eighteenth century. The discovery of an amphitheatre, gladiatorial school (with a store of gladiator armour), and numerous inscriptions gives eloquent testimony of how important a role gladiators had played in the life of the town. Popular novels such as Edward Bulwer-Lytton's *The Last Days of Pompeii* (1834) also did much to popularize the gladiator as did Jean-Léon Gérôme's famous painting *Pollice Verso* (1872) (Figure 24 in this volume) that was inspired by the artist's visit to the Naples museum where he saw the gladiatorial armour discovered at Pompeii. This painting became (and still is) immensely popular and has had enormous influence on the depiction of gladiators in film, which itself has turned out to be an even more effective medium for shaping public awareness of, and interest in, the gladiator.[17] In a more popular vein, the last two decades of the nineteenth century saw a craze for all things Roman, especially arena events. Show business promoters such as P. T. Barnum and the Kiralfy brothers cashed in on this fad and presented onstage in America and in England various aspects of Roman life, with a special emphasis on arena events (portrayed harmlessly), to satisfy, like an ancient sponsor of a gladiator show, their audience's 'fascination with blood in the arena'. Imre Kiralfy's *Nero or the Destruction of Rome* (1888) presented depictions of gladiatorial combat and martyrdoms of Christians by wild beasts and other scenes illustrating the decadence of Rome.[18]

In the academic world, scholars took up research on the historical gladiator with enthusiasm. From Germany came a carefully researched account of gladiators and gladiatorial combat in the second volume of Ludwig Friedländer's four-volume work *Darstellungen aus der Sittengeschichte Roms in der Zeit von August bis zum Ausgang der Antonine* (*Representations from the History of Roman Customs in the Period from Augustus to the End of the Antonines*, 1862–71). The contribution of French scholars has been especially notable. The authoritative article of Georges Lafaye on the gladiator in Daremberg and Saglio's *Dictionnaire des antiquités greques et romaines* (*Dictionary of Greek and Roman Antiquities*, 1896) began a tradition that culminated in two magisterial tomes: Louis Robert's *Les Gladiateurs dans l'Orient grec* (*Gladiators in the Greek East*, 1940) and Georges Ville's *La Gladiature en occident des origines à la mort de Domitien* (*The Phenomenon of the Gladiator in the West from its Origins to the Death of Domitian*, 1981). The spate of books on gladiators in English, French and German in the past forty years give further graphic proof of continued scholarly interest in the topic.

Today, the word 'gladiator' is still highly charged; in addition to its literal meaning, it has been applied figuratively to athletes and even practitioners of non-athletic professions, indicating an aggressively courageous nature and a willingness to sacrifice everything in the pursuit of success. There must be very few people today, young or old, who could not explain what a gladiator is and identify his historical context in a general way. The popularity of the gladiator is probably due in great part to his exotic character, originating in an ancient culture in some ways alien to our own that found entertainment in a sport that involved the very real risk of death. Obviously, no civilized country today would tolerate gladiatorial combat. Real swordplay for entertainment runs counter to the ethical concerns of major modern religions and is objectionable on purely human terms. After all, most modern states have outlawed blood sports involving animals, such as bullfights, dogfighting and cockfighting. A question comes to mind: why did the violent and bloody sport of gladiatorial combat achieve great popularity among the ancient Romans, who are credited with bringing civilization to the western world? The answer to this question reveals how much we moderns are both like and different from our cultural ancestors.

First, we must understand the role of gladiatorial combat in ancient Roman culture. There is a letter written by Pliny the Younger (early second century AD) to a friend named Maximus that provides an interesting insight into the place of gladiatorial combat in Roman society:

You were right to promise a gladiatorial show [gladiatorium munus] *to our fellow citizens of Verona, by whom you have long been loved, looked up to and praised. Also, your most beloved and loyal wife came from that city, to whose memory either some building or spectacle and above all, this one [gladiatorial combat], which is especially appropriate to a funeral, was owed. Moreover, this gladiatorial show was requested by so many citizens of Verona that it seemed not resolute but rude to say no. That show reflected outstandingly on your great generosity, through which you displayed your magnanimity. I wish that the African panthers, which you bought in great numbers, had arrived on the appointed day, but although they were detained by the weather, you nevertheless deserve the credit since you were not responsible for your inability to present these animals . . .[19]*

The purpose of this letter is to congratulate Maximus, a wealthy and well-respected member of the aristocracy in Verona, for a gladiator show he has given in memory of his dead wife.[20] Pliny praises gladiatorial combat as 'especially appropriate to a funeral'. This is because gladiator games from the very beginning of their history at Rome were closely associated with funerals. The connection between a gladiator show and honouring the memory of a dead wife might be hard for us to fathom. The presentation of gladiatorial combat was called by the Romans a *munus*, a Latin word that meant 'duty'or 'gift' and by extension 'funeral honours', an obligation performed for, or a gift given to, the dead. Georges Ville says that throughout the Republic the word *munus* had the general meaning of 'spectacle', a show given as a gift to the people by Roman magistrates or even private citizens. Therefore, the word *munus* could also refer to the spectacles called *ludi* in honour of the gods, consisting of entertainments such as theatrical presentations and chariot racing, or to a gladiatorial spectacle, which until the late first century BC was given only in honour of the dead. By the early empire, the primary meaning of *munus* had become 'gladiatorial combat', driving out the general meaning of 'spectacle'. The reason for this was the immense popularity of gladiator games. All spectacles were 'gifts' to the Roman people, but as Ville points out, gladiatorial combat was 'the gift *par excellence* to the people'.[21]

The giver of a *munus*, called either an *editor* or *munerarius*, undertook all the expenses of giving a *munus*, which were considerable. He was under a great deal of pressure to give a worthy show because stinginess in presenting gladiatorial combat could ruin his reputation among his fellow citizens. Therefore, Maximus' *munus* in memory of his wife was not entirely a private affair. He publicly proclaims his devotion to his wife by presenting the *munus* free of charge to his compatriots, who view the *munus* not as a solemn occasion but as an enjoyable entertainment anticipated with pleasure.[22] They in fact had urgently requested him to give the *munus*, fearing that Maximus would choose a duller alternative funeral honour, like the construction of a public building in Verona dedicated to his wife. This would have been a worthy gift to the city to honour his wife, but nowhere near as exciting as a gladiator show. In the cities and towns of Italy, a *munus* was not a common occurrence and thus was eagerly anticipated. The odd combination of funeral ritual and popular entertainment is characteristic of gladiator games in Italy. The earliest evidence of gladiatorial combat is found in tomb paintings of fourth century BC southern Italy, which were no doubt commemorations of combats given at the funeral, although we also hear of gladiatorial combat that served as a diversion at banquets in Campania at the end of the same century.[23] The poet Silius Italicus (first century AD) writes of Campanians livening up their banquets with gladiators 'falling on the drinking vessels and sprinkling the tables with much blood'. He also refers to this party as 'a horrid sight'.[24] The Romans disliked the luxurious lifestyle of the Campanians and no doubt viewed these gladiatorial duels in the midst of dinner as just another of their excesses. Conservatism led the Romans to require a justification for gladiatorial combat beyond mere amusement. Throughout the Republic, the funerals of great men provided a sufficient pretext for gladiatorial combat. It was not until approximately two and a half centuries after the first gladiator duels in Rome that gladiator games could be offered with no other excuse than their entertainment value.

Perhaps the thing that might strike us the most in Pliny's letter is the matter-of-factness displayed by its author in reference to gladiatorial combat as a way of honouring a dead wife.[25] Another example of what might seem to us an incongruous combination is a *munus* given for the birthday of the emperor Vitellius in AD 69.[26] This was a large-scale spectacle with gladiator duels taking place in all 265 districts of the city (probably in open squares).[27] One could argue that a *munus* fitted the mood of a funeral, but in its later history it could celebrate a happy occasion. Perhaps, the strangest of all examples of this Roman attitude towards gladiatorial combat is the depiction of gladiators arming before a contest in the presence of a referee on a mosaic floor from a Roman villa at Bignor in Sussex. On closer inspection, these figures are revealed to have wings, indicating that they are cupids. K. M. Coleman says that in this mosaic, 'the grim reality of arena has been translated into whimsical fantasy'.[28] It would come as much less of a surprise that children played 'gladiators', if this game did not presuppose that parents were willing to take their children to the amphitheatre.[29] We have only one example in the ancient sources of the experience of a child's reaction to events in the arena, that of the future emperor Commodus, who cried and turned away his eyes when he witnessed condemned criminals (*damnati*) thrown to wild beasts. As we shall see later, Commodus soon adjusted to the violence of the arena and even became a performer, fighting as a gladiator and as an animal hunter.

This matter-of-factness, however, should not be taken to mean universal approval of gladiatorial combat by the Romans. Even the gladiator, who generally enjoyed great popularity, was an ambivalent figure, evoking a mixture of condemnation and approval in Roman society. According to Marcus Junkelmann, in the Roman mind the gladiator was at the same time a 'hero and a criminal' and 'a darling of the public and pariah'.[30] Among the senatorial class, we hear of distaste for gladiator shows and spectacles in general, arising from contempt for what some aristocrats considered the entertainment of the masses and of uncultured aristocrats, unworthy of a refined man's interest. For example, Cicero mocks Piso for pretending that he did not attend games on one occasion because he despised spectacles: 'he will leave the games to us idiots'.[31] Cicero in a letter cites his friend Marius' disdain for gladiator games.[32] Marius had left Rome for the country rather than attend the great games of Pompey in 55 BC. Cicero praises Marius' action: '. . . but if you thought these affairs [i.e., gladiator games] ought to be scorned, which everybody else admires . . . I rejoice . . .'.[33] Cicero had once done the same thing as Marius, when he left for the country to avoid having to attend a *munus*.[34] Cicero also provides evidence for ethical objections to gladiatorial combat in his *Tusculan Disputations*. Cicero states that there are some who think this sport is 'cruel and inhuman', but surprisingly he also says that he himself is undecided about this judgement.[35] Despite his lukewarm attitude towards gladiatorial combat, Cicero may have been a more than an infrequent spectator, as his familiarity with gladiators and gladiatorial shows reveals. Towards the end of the second century AD, however, there is evidence of stronger concerns about the morality of gladiatorial combat, no doubt influenced by Greek philosophy.[36] Marcus Aurelius, an emperor with a strong philosophical bent, disliked the bloodshed of gladiatorial combat and therefore did not allow gladiators to use sharp weapons at any show he attended, but instead required them to fight with blunt swords.[37] Aurelius, however, was often away from Rome fighting in defence of the northern frontier, so in his absence gladiatorial combat was most probably conducted in its traditionally bloody way. His objection to gladiatorial combat seems to be echoed in the speech of a senator speaking on behalf of legislation proposed by Aurelius and his son and co-ruler Commodus. The senator strongly supports the proposal to end a tax on the expenditures of sponsors of gladiatorial shows. He condemns revenue coming into the treasury from gladiator games as 'contrary to divine and human law' and 'contaminated with the sprinkling of human blood'.[38] But again, despite these condemnatory words, the senator does not urge the abolition of gladiatorial games. Simply put, his argument is: 'Let the gladiator games go on, but the emperors should not be tainted with unseemly profit'. These objections, however, were expressed by a very small minority of the population and sometimes were not even sincere, in that they were uttered only because the speaker wanted to show his intellectual and moral superiority to the rest of the population. This attitude is similar to that of some intellectuals today who claim they never watch television. Most Romans took to gladiatorial combat the way Americans take pleasure in baseball and Europeans enjoy football. Gladiators were a frequent topic of ordinary conversation. Educated men such as Maecenas and Horace could discuss the relative merits of two gladiators as they rode together in a carriage.[39] Tacitus complains that a passion for gladiators is practically inborn in Romans and dominates the conversations of the young.[40] Whatever aspersions were cast on gladiatorial games, there was never any question of banning them.

At the Veronian *munus*, there must have been bloodshed and perhaps even one or more gladiators lost their lives, not at all what most of us would call a proper honour for a dead wife. Yet Pliny makes clear how appropriate and proper in his view Maximus' *munus* was. Moreover, there could have been more bloodshed than just that from human bodies. Maximus had scheduled a *venatio* ('hunt'), a staged animal hunt in which men fought wild beasts and wild beasts fought each other, along with other entertainments involving animals. By the first century AD, the *venatio*, originally a separate event, had become a regular part of the *munus*. Maximus had gone to the trouble and expense of importing panthers from Africa, which along with other large cats were among the animal superstars of the *venatio*. The mention of bad weather suggests the delay took place at sea. This does not necessarily mean, however, that Maximus cancelled his *venatio*. He might have purchased local animals as an emergency measure, herbivores such as deer, wild horses, asses etc. to be killed in their place. Another typical feature of the *munus* was the execution of convicted criminals and/or prisoners of war, which by our standards would seem to have made Maximus' *munus* an even less appropriate honour for his wife. Pliny makes no mention of executions at Maximus' spectacle. It may have been that, as sometimes happened, no convicts or prisoners of war were available on this occasion.

Origins of gladiatorial combat

The most popular ancient theory about the origin of gladiatorial combat was that it was a form of human sacrifice to the dead. Tertullian sees the *munus* as a duty performed for the dead, arguing for the progress of the ritual from human sacrifice to what he calls a 'more humane atrocity', that is, combat, in which at least one combatant would survive. His tone is sarcastic and hostile, because as a Christian he disliked gladiatorial combat and in fact, all other pagan spectacles.

> *The ancients thought that performing this spectacle was a duty to the dead, after they tempered it with a more humane atrocity. For, once upon a time, since it had been believed that the souls of the dead were propitiated by human blood, having purchased captives or slaves of bad character, they sacrificed them as part of funeral ritual. Later they decided to mask the impiety as entertainment. And so those they had purchased and trained in what arms and in whatever way they could, only that they might learn to be killed, they soon exposed to death on the appointed day of the funeral. Thus, they sought consolation for death in homicide. This was the origin of the* munus.[41]

The theory still has adherents among modern scholars. Allison Futrell, in a recent book, has argued in its favour, joining it with another major theme of gladiatorial combat: Roman power. She alleges that gladiator games were originally human sacrifices to sustain Roman political power.[42] Thomas Wiedemann in his *Emperors and Gladiators*, however, categorically disassociates human sacrifice from Roman funerals: 'there is no evidence at all that the Romans at any period thought that any such human sacrifices were appropriate in connection with funerals'.[43] Wiedemann's observation is supported by another consideration. Gladiators with their intense desire for victory and readiness to accept death only as a last resort did not make good sacrificial victims. One essential requirement of an effective sacrifice was the complicity, either real or fictional, of the victim. Moreover, not every gladiatorial match ended in death; in fact, as we shall see, many did not.[44]

Moreover, Futrell's emphasis on the theme of Roman power is sometimes overstated. She sees the amphitheatre (and the gladiatorial shows held there) as 'a major political tool for Roman control'.[45] Her primary example of this claim is the gladiatorial games given by high priests of the imperial cult throughout Italy and the Roman provinces in both the west and east. Futrell assumes that these games were imposed on the provincials by a totalitarian Roman state.[46] Indeed, the choice of gladiator shows as an adjunct to the worship of the emperor was a statement of loyalty by the provincials and the presentation and viewing of such fights was a clear sign of romanization.[47] The main impetus for the presentation of gladiator games, however, really came from the provincial priests themselves, who, like Roman aristocrats, used the *munus* and other entertainments to advance themselves in the competition for status with other elites in their city and province. These provincial priests presented gladiatorial combat because they knew it would win them the favour of the grateful people.[48] Keith Hopkins argues that the variety of local celebrations of the imperial cult

> *demonstrates that the festivals were not instituted . . . by the dictate of the central government. The varied arrangements reflected local initiatives or competitive innovations rather than imperial decree.*[49]

Likewise, Simon Price sees the adoption of Roman practices (such as gladiator shows) in the Greek east 'as a strategy in the competition for status within the elite'.[50]

One might not fully agree with Futrell's hyperbolic statement that 'the amphitheater was power', but to reject it completely is wrongheaded. One cannot help but think, especially during the Republic when there were constant wars, that spectators at a *munus* were reminded of Roman military success as they watched gladiatorial combat in the amphitheatre, particularly with the appearance of gladiator types called the Samnite, Gaul and Thracian, all recalling one-time enemies of Rome. J. C. Edmondson argues that gladiator games 'repeatedly underlined the centrality of the military ethic at Rome and emphasized the military basis of Rome's world dominance', while Marilyn Skinner nicely sums up the Roman attitude: 'Rooting for the underdog was not a Roman tradition: audiences preferred the psychological security of locating themselves on the winning side'.[51] In fact, a similar interpretation has been suggested for the *venatio*, since many of the animals in the *venatio* came from far-flung parts of the empire.[52] In addition, the *venatio* implied another kind of Roman supremacy: Rome's power over nature.[53] A central theme of Martial's *A Book of Spectacles* is the submission of wild animal nature to the emperor and his empire, as demonstrated by the *venatio* celebrating the inauguration of the Colosseum.

Gladiatorial combat as funeral games

There is little doubt, however, that gladiatorial games, even if they were not strictly speaking human sacrifice, were in origin funeral offerings in honour of the dead.[54] The first gladiatorial combat at Rome was at the funeral of the Roman aristocrat. D. Junius Brutus Pera in 264 BC, presented by his two sons in honour of their father.[55] There are a few other details about this first *munus* at Rome that are worth mentioning. These details are from late sources, but they seem credible. The fourth century AD poet Ausonius writes that the gladiator show for Junius Pera consisted of three pairs of fighters, while Ausonius' contemporary, Servius, notes that these gladiators were 'captives'.[56] They were called *bustuarii*, that is, 'gladiators who fought at the place where the deceased was cremated and buried' (*bustum*).[57] *Bustuarius* was synonymous with *gladiator* and remained in common usage at Rome at least until the time of Cicero.[58] The three pairs seem appropriate for a first-time event with modest beginnings in a modest setting, while the identification of the gladiators as 'captives' at least accords with the fact that captives (that is, prisoners of war) were one of the primary sources of gladiators throughout the history of the games. It would be interesting to know whether these first matches were fights to the death. Because of the lack of evidence, this question is impossible to answer with certainty. Ausonius says that the three pairs of gladiators were sent as a funeral offering at Pera's tomb, perhaps (but not necessarily) suggesting that death was an expected result.[59] The poet, however, is a very late source (about six centuries after the fact) and probably not reliable on this detail. Donald Kyle believes that early gladiators fought to the death.[60] Perhaps he is right, but our first solid evidence of gladiator fights that did not allow a defeated opponent to be spared dates to the late first century BC. I would prefer to think that these first fights in Rome were like the ones that followed them until the end of the Republic: duels that could end in a death, but not necessarily so. A gladiator could achieve victory just by rendering his opponent unable or unwilling to continue. David Potter has suggested that fourth century BC gladiator bouts in southern Italy probably lasted only to the first appearance of blood.[61] If he is correct, these southern Italian fights could have influenced the format of the first duels at Rome.

Greek funeral games

Competition may seem to us a strange way of honouring the dead at a funeral, but there was a long history of agonistic games presented at funerals in Mediterranean culture. As mentioned earlier, fourth century BC tomb paintings in southern Italy provide good evidence of funeral gladiatorial games (along with boxing and chariot racing). Much has been written on the geographical journey of gladiatorial combat to Rome, but there is some disagreement about their ultimate place of origin. The Augustan historian Nicolaus of Damascus says that the Romans 'borrowed this practice from the Etruscans', a non-Italic people, who were Rome's northern neighbour.[62] Ville does not dispute Nicolaus' claim, but points out that the historian does not say that the Etruscans were inventors of gladiatorial combat, just that the Romans took the practice from them and postulates a path from the Osco-Samnite people in southern Italy to Etruria to Rome.[63] Ville's hypothesis has generally won the acceptance of scholars.[64]

There is abundant literary evidence for funeral games in Greece. Certainly, the most famous set of funeral games were those that Achilles presented in honour of his friend Patroclus in the twenty-third book of the *Iliad*. Other legendary Greek heroes such as Oedipus, Pelias, Amarynkeus, Oenomaus, Pelops, Melicertes and Opheltes were reported to have been honoured with funeral games. That this practice was not confined to legend is confirmed by the poet Hesiod's mention of the funeral games for a certain Amphidamas, at which he won a prize for his poetry.[65] Annually repeated athletic games were instituted in honour of deceased Greek military heroes such as Miltiades, Brasidas, Timoleon and Philopoemen. Even groups of warriors could be honoured by similar games such as the *Eleutheria* ('Freedom Festival'), which celebrated the heroism of the Greek dead at Plataea in their victory over the Persians, and the *Epitaphia*, an annual athletics festival honouring the Athenian war dead, as the name suggests.[66] These funeral contests, both legendary and historical, consisted mostly of Greek-style athletics events such as chariot and foot racing, wrestling, boxing, javelin throwing, discus throwing, and jumping, but in Achilles' games for Patroclus there is an armed duel between Ajax and Diomedes that very much resembles a gladiatorial match. Achilles, beseeched by his fellow Greeks, stops the fight when Diomedes seems to be about to wound Ajax in the neck.[67] The input of the Greek soldiers watching this fight directed towards the presiding Achilles anticipates the practice of the Roman arena, in which the crowd communicates by shouts or gestures its will concerning the fate of the losing gladiator to the *editor*. There is, however, an important difference. The Roman crowd was quite willing to tolerate the serious wounding and even death of a gladiator, because these fighters were persons of no status such as convicts, prisoners of war and slaves, whereas Diomedes and Ajax were aristocrats, heroic leaders of Greek contingents at Troy. Mark Golden points out that it is important to notice that the honorands of Greek games were heroes (like Patroclus): 'The contests affirmed [the] special status [of the deceased] at the same time [as] . . . they revealed that of living victors'.[68] This statement could apply equally to the gladiatorial games given at Rome during the Republic, which honoured important men, frequently with distinguished military careers.[69] Wiedemann describes the purpose of these *munera* given as funeral tributes to great men by their sons: 'In the Republic, a private *munus* symbolized the survival of individuals in the memory of their fellow-citizens because of their military virtue'.[70]

Gladiatorial combat as sport

Like the events of Greek funeral games, gladiatorial combat can be seen as athletic competition. Ville writes of the 'agonistic nature' of gladiatorial duels as a competitive sport that went through the process of secularization and professionalization.[71] The average person today would probably not be willing to call gladiatorial combat a sport because of its bloody and sometimes lethal nature. On the other hand, judged by Johan Huizinga's classic definition of play (of which sport is a subcategory), gladiator fights might actually qualify as sport. Huizinga's requirements are that a game must: (1) be voluntary, but with rules, (2) not be ordinary life, but have the illusion of reality, (3) not be serious but be totally absorbing, and (4) be limited by time and place.[72] Requirements 1 and 3 are troublesome in their application to gladiatorial combat. As for 1, we know that there were reluctant gladiators who fought only because they were forced to do so by their slave status but there probably were many slave gladiators who were like other athletes, both ancient and modern, eager to compete and to win.[73] On the other hand, gladiatorial combat had its rules (to be discussed later) that allowed the possibility of avoiding serious bloodshed and death. Moreover, gladiators were given defensive armour sufficient to allow a trained fighter to defend himself effectively, which required a skilled opponent to work hard to overcome. Every measure was taken to ensure a fair fight. That is why Seneca, a great fan of arena events, was so outraged by the sword fights of untrained convicted criminals without defensive armour.[74] He calls these combats pure homicides, in essence denying these contests the status of sport.[75] In the case of requirement 3, it is difficult to call a game that allows death as one of the conditions of victory, not serious. Huizinga, however, does allow an exception for an ancient competition of this sort that applies to gladiatorial combat:

> . . . it would be rash to assert that every use of the word 'play' in connection with serious strife is nothing but poetic license. We have to feel our way into the archaic sphere of thought, where serious combat with weapons and all kind of contests ranging from the most trifling games to bloody and mortal strife were comprised, together with play proper, in a single fundamental idea of a struggle with fate limited by certain rules.[76]

As far as most ancients were concerned, gladiatorial combat was a civilized sport, but in the second century AD games came under attack by Christian apologists. It should be noted, however, that the violence of gladiatorial combat was not the most crucial factor in Christian objections to gladiator games. An even more important issue for Christians was what they believed to be the close association between gladiatorial games and the pagan gods.

The popularity of gladiatorial combat

How could a civilized people enjoy such a sport as gladiatorial combat? First, there is no doubt that there existed a high tolerance of cruelty and violence in Roman society. Life was harsh in Rome, but not untypical of most pre-industrial states. Nevertheless, we must be careful in identifying the roots of this harshness. There were undoubtedly some Romans who were pitiless sadists, as is true of almost every society, but one should keep in mind Keith Hopkins' caveat: '[in the case of the Romans] we are dealing . . ., not with individual sadistic psychopathology, but with a deep cultural difference'.[77] Coleman also warns of the unfairness of sadism as an explanation of the tolerance of gladiatorial combat among the Romans: 'It is crass and unhelpful merely to characterize the Romans as bloodthirsty'. She instead seeks an answer in Roman attitudes towards the classes of men who became gladiators.[78] A. W. Lintott takes a wider view, explaining that the ethical principles of the Mediterranean world, whether Greco-Roman or 'barbarian', were quite different from ours and 'did not place such a high value on human existence in itself as ours do now'.[79] Moreover, Rome was in origin a warrior society and militarism remained a primary characteristic of the Romans throughout their history. War was a high-stakes proposition, both for the Romans and for their opponents. Thousands of Roman soldiers died in Italy and abroad in countless battles. Roman treatment of the enemy could be very harsh, sometimes even involving the slaughter of non-combatants. In Spain, during the second Punic War, Scipio Africanus attacked the town of Iliturgi in Spain (206 BC), which had gone over to the enemy, and his soldiers killed all armed and unarmed citizens alike, including women and infants.[80] In Rome, prisoners of war were often executed in public as a demonstration of Roman power. Even Roman soldiers were subject to harsh penalties. In order to ensure strict military discipline in the Roman army, serious infractions were dealt with ruthlessly. Consider the practice of decimation, in which one soldier out of every ten guilty of dereliction of duty was chosen by lot to be bludgeoned to death by his fellow soldiers.[81] One famous instance of *decimatio* was Crassus' punishment of soldiers who were defeated by an army led by the gladiator Spartacus.[82] The Romans became more and more inured to the harshness of war during the third and second centuries BC when Roman armies were regularly called on to fight wars on an increasingly wider scale in the west (the three major wars against Carthage) and in the Greek east. It is not surprising that gladiatorial combat quickly became a favoured attraction at Rome during this very period.

The harshness of Roman society was evident not only in warfare but also at home in the treatment of slaves. In fact, the cruel punishment of slaves goes a long way to explaining the Roman tolerance of gladiatorial combat. All gladiators by virtue of their profession were the property of their *lanista* (owner/trainer of a gladiator troupe) and thus in effect his slaves. Even a free man who voluntarily agreed to serve as a gladiator became a temporary slave of the *lanista* for an agreed period. According to Roman civil law, 'slaves are considered to be nothings' with absolutely no rights.[83] A slave was legally the property of the master and could be sold by the master, even if it meant that the slave was separated from his or her family.[84] Slaves were usually branded like cattle to indicate their status and the identity of their master. One method of getting rid of an undesirable slave was to sell him to a *lanista*, a punishment for the slave and a profitable deal for the master.[85] Sick and old slaves were abandoned in the same way as some people today rid themselves of an unwanted pet by releasing it far from home.[86] When offences were committed by slaves in the household, the master was the sole judge and jury. For minor offences, flogging was the typical punishment. For serious crimes, the master legally had the power to impose a death penalty, which could take several cruel forms: crucifixion, burning alive, or exposing the slave to wild beasts in the arena (*ad bestias*).[87] The death penalty was sometimes applied to slaves whether they were guilty or not. When a slave committed a crime such as the murder of a master, the custom was that all slaves in the household be executed. During the reign of Nero, Pedanius Secundus, the prefect of the city, was murdered by his own slave. When there was an attempt to carry out this traditional penalty, there was a minor revolt of the common people on behalf of the innocent slaves. The issue reached the floor of the Senate, which was divided over the justice of this penalty. The speech of C. Cassius, who defended the punishment of all slaves on the basis of deterrence, won over the majority. The Senate voted for death to all, but the common people, using stones and torches, interfered with the implementation of the penalty, until Nero provided a contingent of soldiers to lead the condemned to the place of execution.[88]

The harshness of these penalties for slaves seem to stem from the Roman fear of slave revolts, which had been launched with some temporary success twice in Sicily (135–132 BC and 104–101 BC) and once in Italy under the leadership of Spartacus (73–71 BC). The comment of Pliny the Younger (a very humane man) on the ruthless punishment of slaves who had murdered their cruel and sadistic master is telling and representative of the typical Roman attitude in this matter: 'Slaves are ruined not by the judgment of their master, but by their propensity toward crime'.[89] As far as the Romans were concerned, slaves were not capable of moral behaviour, except under compulsion. Slaves were not part of the Roman community; they were disposable people. Orlando Patterson writes about slaves of all cultures and periods: 'The slave was natally alienated and condemned as a socially dead person, his existence having no legitimacy whatever'.[90] They were without the protection of law and were subject to whatever punishments a master wished to impose on them without concern for the suffering involved. Thus, it is not difficult to understand why, given this attitude towards slaves, most Romans saw nothing wrong with gladiatorial combat. The prevailing feeling among Romans was that gladiators, given their background of slavery, crime, or opposition to the Roman state as enemy soldiers, deserved whatever fate they suffered.[91] This was also the Roman attitude towards freemen who volunteered their services as gladiators, willingly accepting a condition equivalent to slavery in what was considered a disgraced profession.

Compassion did exist among the Romans, but their standards in this matter were quite different from ours. The degree of compassion felt by a Roman citizen was determined by the status of the victim. The higher the status, the greater the compassion; the lower the status, the greater the indifference.[92] In fact, not every Roman saw pity as a virtue, particularly in the case of convicted criminals who lost their freedom because of their crimes. Seneca sees pity (*misericordia*) as a vice in opposition to the virtues mercy (*clementia*) and gentleness (*mansuetudo*):

> . . . all good men should display mercy and gentleness, but will avoid pity; for it is the vice of a timid mind succumbing at the sight of another's troubles. And so it is a common vice of every person of the weakest character such as old women and weak women in general, who are moved by the tears of the worst criminals, and if they could, would break open their prison. Pity does not see the cause of their plight, but only the plight itself.[93]

In view of this attitude, the gladiator could not expect much pity from the crowd.

On the other hand, the life of a gladiator did have a positive side for men whose situation was desperate. It offered the hope of survival and a better life, but naturally did not guarantee the achievement of those goals. The possibility existed that the gladiator could achieve some fame and dignity in the arena and even make some money. If he fought well over a period of years and was skilful and lucky enough to survive, he might be granted a full discharge from his obligation to fight in the arena and eventually his complete freedom, resulting in a modified form of citizenship, from which he had been excluded because of his status and profession. Honour was available not only to winning gladiators but also to losers. Wiedemann has turned on its head the usual view of the arena as a place where men progressed only from life to death and reminds us that the reverse was also true. He points out that spectators were witnesses not just of death in the arena but also of life won back by losing gladiators whose efforts had won the approval of the crowd and the *editor*. Even a gladiator whose request for life was denied could achieve some dignity in death.[94] Spectators respected the gladiator who stoically accepted the *editor*'s decision of death and submitted to death by the sword of his opponent. Such a death was honourable, similar to the death of a Roman citizen on the battlefield and thus a kind of redemption from the disgrace (*infamia*) that the gladiator had endured while alive by the mere fact of his occupation.[95]

As a warrior society in origin, Romans were fascinated with martial virtue and the high-risk game of life and death that was war and gladiatorial combat. Wistrand has pointed out that gladiatorial combat demonstrated the most fundamental of all Roman values, *virtus*, a word whose basic meaning is 'manhood', which came to mean 'courage in war'.[96] J. P. Toner sees the gladiator as an archetypical symbol of Roman culture, whose code in extreme situations was either to kill when necessary, or to accept death when inevitable.[97] The Romans cherished legends from their early days in which heroes voluntarily suffered great pain and even death in conflict with the enemy on behalf of their country. Two legends dating from the late sixth century when the Romans were freeing themselves from Etruscan domination are well-known examples. Horatius Cocles all by himself fearlessly defended a bridge across the Tiber against the attacking Etruscans. As he drove the enemy back, the Romans destroyed the bridge and Horatius swam back to the Roman shore.[98] The heroism of Mucius Scaevola is another case in point. He attempted to kill Porsenna, the Etruscan ruler of Clusium, who had besieged Rome in reaction to the Romans' expulsion of their Etruscan king, Tarquinius Superbus, from their city. Porsenna captured Mucius, but the Roman demonstrated his lack of fear by voluntarily inserting his right hand into fire while giving no evidence of the pain he was feeling. Porsenna, admiring his courage, released him.[99] The general Regulus was captured by the Carthaginians in the first Punic War (264–241 BC). They sent him to

Rome to convince his fellow Romans to exchange prisoners, believing that Regulus would argue in favour of the exchange, which would include himself. Regulus did just the opposite. Since he had made a solemn promise to the Carthaginians to return to them, he went back to Carthage and was tortured to death.[100] Perhaps the most inspiring story of heroic courage and self-sacrifice is to be found in the story of the Roman general Decius Mus, who, during the Samnite wars (340 BC), solemnly dedicated his life to the gods in return for victory, an act that the Romans called a *devotio*. He charged on horseback into the midst of the enemy and was killed. This valiant act changed the tide of battle, which ended in a glorious Roman victory.[101] It seems probable that the spectators recognized a connection between gladiatorial combat and real warfare.[102] Wiedemann argues that gladiatorial combat reflected the way Romans fought in battle with its special emphasis on individual hand-to-hand fighting.[103] The Romans even took this emphasis one step further with their practice of resorting to single combat between a Roman champion and an enemy opponent to settle the issue at hand. S. P. Oakley lists over thirty examples of single combat in Republican warfare. (The custom seems to have died out in the early empire.)[104]

Roman intellectuals such as Cicero, Seneca and Pliny the Younger stressed the association between gladiator games and martial virtue, viewing gladiatorial combat as an incitement to *virtus* in the spectators. This theme appears first in Cicero, which consists of an *a fortiori* argument proposing that if gladiators, men of dubious moral character, could display *virtus* in the face of pain and death, then law-abiding freeborn Roman citizens could find no better reason to behave similarly in a similar situation.

> *What blows do gladiators who are either incorrigible criminals or barbarians bear! How they, who have been well trained, prefer to receive a blow than shamefully avoid it! How often it is apparent that they prefer nothing other than to satisfy their master or the people! They, exhausted by their wounds send a message to their masters to find out what they want: if their masters so desire, they are ready to give up and die. [In this situation] has even a mediocre gladiator groaned, what gladiator has ever even changed his expression? What gladiator has either fought or admitted defeat shamefully? What gladiator, when he has lain down in defeat and was ordered to receive the deathblow, drawn back his neck? So effective is the force of practice, preparation and habit.[105]*

In addition to their courage, Cicero notes in the above passage gladiators' almost obsessive devotion to their master, whether the *editor* who had hired their services in the arena or the crowd in the amphitheatre. When a gladiator indicated that he could no longer continue fighting, he had to accept the decision of the *editor* (advised by the crowd) even if it meant submitting to a deathblow from his opponent. A notable example of gladiatorial loyalty outside the arena can be seen in the behaviour of the gladiator troupe that Marc Antony had acquired to fight in a *munus* to celebrate his anticipated victory over Octavian at Actium. After Octavian's victory, all of Antony's allies deserted him except for this troupe. His gladiators, fighting their way south from Cyzicus (on the southern shore of the Sea of Marmara) where they were training for the *munus*, made their way as far as Syria, in the attempt to reach their master in Egypt. Surrounded by the enemy, they sent a message to Antony to come to them, but when he did not answer, they realized that he was dead, and surrendered. Cassius Dio notes the striking contrast between their despised status and their noble behaviour.[106]

At the end of his life, Cicero had an opportunity to follow the gladiatorial model of *virtus* when he was being pursued by Herennius, an assassin whom Antony had assigned to kill him. Although, at first, Cicero tried to escape in his litter, he eventually accepted death by the sword like his ideal gladiator, achieving an honourable death:

> *When Cicero saw Herennius running through the portico, he ordered his servants to set the litter down. He, as he was accustomed, touching his chin with his left hand, stared intently at his slayers. His squalid and unkempt look along with the anxiety on his face caused the bystanders to hide their faces in shame as Herennius killed him. Extending his neck outside the litter, [Cicero] was slain.[107]*

Seneca similarly expresses admiration for the *virtus* of the gladiator, who, even if his performance has not been stellar, willingly faces death at the hands of his opponent as ordered by the *editor*.[108] Stoicism, a philosophy followed by Seneca, promoted the doctrine that *virtus* was more important than life itself, an attitude which characterized the best gladiators.[109] Pliny the Younger, using the same *a fortiori* argument as Cicero, stresses the moral example that gladiators set for spectators. Gladiatorial combat inspires men to incur 'beautiful wounds and to despise death, when the love of glory and desire for victory is seen even in the bodies of slaves and convicted criminals'.[110] Julius Capitolinus, one of the imperial biographers in the late *Historia Augusta* claims that, in the third century AD, emperors began the practice of giving gladiator games and an animal hunt before they led their troops out to war to habituate the soldiers to the sight of wounds and blood.[111] It should be noted, however, that the writers of the *Historia Augusta* did not always employ the highest standards of historical criticism. In fact, Ville argues that this claim is a fiction and really a defence of gladiatorial combat against Christian objections, drawing upon familiar themes from Cicero and Pliny the Younger.[112]

There is also evidence that Roman spectators held the gladiator to a high standard of moral behaviour in the arena. Seneca, citing Cicero, says that spectators became angry with gladiators if they sought to save their own life at all costs and did not accept death when ordered by the *editor*.[113] On the other hand, the courageous fighter evoked a positive response among spectators. Seneca writes of another arena performer, an animal hunter (*venator*):

> *Occasionally, we spectators experience pleasure if a resolutely minded young man, armed with a spear, stands fast before the charge of a wild animal, if he fearlessly endures the attack of a lion and the more courageous he is, the more pleasing is the spectacle.[114]*

There were, however, other less idealistic reasons for the popularity of gladiator shows. One of the early objectives of gladiatorial combat was to humiliate the enemy. The first recorded contact of Rome with gladiators took place in the late fourth century BC in southern Italy after a significant victory of Rome and its Campanian allies over the Samnites (309 BC), a fierce Italic people who had defeated the Romans at Caudine Forks (321 BC), one of Rome's most disastrous losses. In order to commemorate their military victory, the Romans followed their usual custom after a victory. They took the captured gold- and silver-plated shields back to Rome to display in the Forum and to honour their gods as a thanksgiving for victory. Their Campanian allies, however, had a different method of celebrating their conquest, born of 'contempt and hatred' for their neighbours in central Italy. The Campanians held celebratory banquets at which the diners were entertained by gladiatorial combat in which the gladiators were required to wear captured Samnite armour and were called 'Samnites'.[115] This impersonation was intended as the gravest of insults to the defeated enemy. It was almost as if the Campanians had forced the Samnite prisoners of war themselves to entertain them in this way. The comment of a speaker in a rhetorical exercise on two men forced to fight by a rich man for his amusement is relevant here: 'it is the cause of the greatest anguish to suffer a penalty imposed to give pleasure to an enemy. How wretched it is [to suffer] compulsion!'[116] The Romans must have been impressed by these 'Samnite' gladiators, because they foreshadow the later appearance at Rome of various ethnic gladiatorial types derived from the fighting style, armour and weaponry of Roman enemies. Not surprisingly, the two earliest types, most likely dating from the third century BC, were the 'Samnite' and the 'Gaul', both enemies of the Romans.[117] Later, probably in the early first century BC, the *thraex* ('Thracian') appeared after Roman victories in the Mithridatic Wars.[118] These types may have developed from the practice of originally having actual Samnite, Gallic and Thracian prisoners of war fight each other in their characteristic armour for the entertainment of the Romans. Occasionally, enemies of Rome were able to turn the tables and force Romans to fight each other for their entertainment. The rebel Spartacus forced captured Roman soldiers to fight as gladiators for the amusement of himself and his men in return for the shame that they suffered by being compelled to become gladiators.[119] Jewish rebels in Cyrene (North Africa) did the same thing to both Romans and Greeks.[120] Eventually these different gladiator types were impersonated by professional fighters, who were not of Samnite, Gallic or Thracian origin, and had learned these ethnic fighting styles in gladiatorial schools. For example, an inscription points out that a certain Thelyphus, a Samnite gladiator, was a native Thracian.[121] By the late Republic and the early empire, the Roman gladiator began to lose his various ethnic identities. Ethnically neutral gladiator types like the *murmillo*, *secutor*, *retiarius*, *provocator*, *hoplomachus* and *eques* were introduced and the Samnite and the Gaul eventually disappeared in the early empire. The *thraex*, however, endured throughout the history of gladiator games. Perhaps, the disappearance of two of the three ethnic gladiators is a sign that humiliation of enemies was no longer uppermost in the mind of the Romans in the early empire. The degradation of enemies, however, was still at least implicit in so far as prisoners of war were still being forced to fight as gladiators for the entertainment of their conquerors.

My preference, when it comes to explaining the Roman fascination with gladiatorial combat, is not to emphasize one overarching meaning in this sport. The phenomenon is too complex, as we have seen above in the contradictory reactions of contempt and admiration that gladiatorial combat inspired in the Romans.[122] The reasons for the popularity of the *munus* ranged from the morally idealistic to the satisfaction of baser human instincts. Some of the theories advanced by scholars, such as the display of martial virtue and the demonstration of Roman power, have support in the sources and do shed light on the allure of gladiatorial games. Other theories seem less likely. For example, Paul Plass' catharsis hypothesis that the violence of gladiatorial combat homeopathically cleansed the spectators of aggressive impulses, does not make sense in the context of Roman culture.[123] There is no evidence that the Romans ever believed this and, even if indeed they did, it is impossible to prove that it had any positive effect in this regard. As it was, gladiatorial combat did not prevent Roman society from being rife with violence throughout its history.

Without claiming overriding significance, I would like to suggest an additional reason for the hold that gladiatorial combat had on the attention of the Roman world. A passage from Livy provides some evidence on the appeal of gladiator games from the spectator's point of view. The passage describes the introduction of gladiatorial combat in Antioch in the Greek east by the romanized Hellenistic monarch Antiochus Epiphanes (175 BC). Although the audience is Greek, the example can still be applied to the Romans.

> He [Antiochus] gave a gladiatorial munus of the Roman kind that at first produced significant terror among the spectators, who were unused to such a spectacle, rather than pleasure. Then, by giving munera rather often, both the type that lasted until one opponent was wounded and the other kind that required a fight to the death, he made that sort of spectacle familiar and pleasing to the eyes.[124]

The Greek audience naturally was a bit squeamish at first, never having seen such a spectacle before. Nonetheless, Antiochus determinedly habituated his subjects to gladiatorial combat both in its milder and in its most deadly form. The result of this process was that his spectators soon found bloodshed and death pleasing as entertainment: they had learned to enjoy the pleasure of gladiatorial games. In the early days of gladiator games at Rome, Roman audiences no doubt also experienced this transition from terror to pleasure. A speaker of a practice rhetorical exercise says that some Roman spectators felt squeamish and even turned their heads rather than see the wounds of gladiators. This speaker, however, also points out that squeamish spectators learned to tolerate the bloody violence in the arena, when they experienced what we would today call *Schadenfreude* ('joy in another's suffering') in watching gladiators, who in many cases were condemned criminals or prisoners of war, get their just deserts by risking their lives in the arena.[125] A famous example of this transition from horror to pleasure is the experience of a young man named Alypius who, as a Christian, detested gladiatorial shows but was dragged by his friends to a *munus*. When the games began, Alypius shut his eyes tightly to avoid watching the proceedings, but opened them when he heard a huge shout from the crowd in reaction to a gladiator being wounded and falling to the ground. He was immediately intoxicated by the sight of blood. He had quickly learned to appreciate the delights of the amphitheatre, which, according to Alypius' older friend, the Church Father Augustine, seethed 'with monstrous pleasures'.[126] Pliny the Younger emphasizes the pleasures of sights and sounds in the amphitheatre in a more positive way, while Seneca mentions the pleasure of seeing bloodshed.[127] Although Christian writers are hostile witnesses, they were quite familiar with the attraction of gladiatorial games. Cyprian, a third century AD bishop of Carthage, speaks of blood delighting the eyes and points out the ironic purpose of gladiator shows: a man is killed for the pleasure (*voluptas*) of man.[128] The 'delights' of the amphitheatre derive from one of man's most primal experiences: the sight of blood. Moreover, bloodshed and death did not just occur in gladiatorial combat. By the middle of the first century AD, the *munus* had developed into a three-part show: the morning animal hunt (*venatio*), the noonday event (*meridianum spectaculum*) in which criminals guilty of capital crimes were executed in various ways, and the afternoon gladiator show. Claudius was perhaps the greatest fan of the *munus* among all the emperors. He gladly sat through all three parts of the *munus*, even the noonday festival when most spectators left the arena for lunch. Suetonius describes him as 'cruel and bloodthirsty', and Claudius undoubtedly deserved these epithets for his excesses in the amphitheatre, such as ordering gladiators who fell accidentally to be slain. He was especially eager that *retiarii* ('net-men') suffer this fate because they fought with no helmet and Claudius liked to see the expression on their faces when they died.[129] Claudius, however, despite his excesses, was not that different from the average spectator, who enjoyed viewing violent death. Then there was the demand of the Carthaginian crowd to witness the execution of Perpetua noted earlier in this chapter.[130] Tertullian mentions how people who abhorred the sight of a man dead of natural causes, once inside the amphitheatre were fascinated by the sight of mutilated and bloodied corpses. After the show was over, this wish was fulfilled at closer range. It was the custom at Carthage to allow spectators to come down into the arena after the show to view the corpses of those killed in the show and take pleasure in examining their faces close up.[131] This fascination with the bodies of those killed violently was characteristic not just of the Romans. Plato writes of how a certain Leontios, who was ashamed of his strong desire to look at the corpses of executed criminals in a pit outside Athens, finally capitulated to his craving.[132] The desire to view human suffering and death seems to be a universal human trait. Thomas Macaulay records the party atmosphere that surrounded the punishment of those convicted of serious crimes in seventeenth-century England:

> *Gentlemen arranged parties of pleasure to Bridewell on court days for the purpose of seeing the wretched women who beat hemp there whipped. A man pressed to death for refusing to plead, a woman burned for coining [counterfeiting], excited less sympathy than is now felt for a galled horse or an overdriven ox. Fights compared with which a boxing match is a refined and humane spectacle were among the favourite diversions of a large part of the town.*[133]

It comes as something of shock when Macaulay adds that gladiator matches were held in that era (although certainly not with the frequency of ancient Rome).

> *Multitudes assembled to see gladiators hack each other to pieces with deadly weapons, and shouted with delight when one of the combatants lost a finger or an eye.*

Friedländer gives two other examples of gladiator games in Christian Europe, one in fourteenth century Naples and the other in sixteenth century Lyons. The descriptions of these shows quoted by Friedländer reveal fights as violent and lethal as in ancient Rome.[134] Leonard Thompson points out the festivity (picnics and the like) that surrounded public hangings in eighteenth century England and lynchings in twentieth century America.[135] The celebratory ambiance of all these violent entertainments correlates well with the spectators' mood at a *munus* in ancient Rome. A character in Petronius' *Satyricon* talks about his enthusiastic anticipation of an upcoming *munus* and unashamedly reveals its primary attraction: '[the *editor*] will present, with no chance of reprieve, a regular butcher's shop right in the middle of the arena so that every spectator can see all the bloody action'.[136] The Romans seem to have accepted bloodshed in the arena as a morally neutral spectacle. Seneca depicts travellers, eager to return to the city after some time in the country, talking in the same matter-of-fact way about the pleasures of the *munus*: 'Too long our ears have not heard the applause and noise of the crowd; now it is also time to enjoy human blood'.[137] It seems to be a typical assumption that one of the primary reasons one goes to a gladiator show is to witness a death, as is illustrated by the following incident involving the consul L. Quinctius Flamininus (192 BC). Lucius had taken his favourite male prostitute with him to Gaul, leaving Rome just before the presentation of a *munus* that the prostitute had expected to attend. When a Gallic aristocrat showed up at a banquet, Flamininus asked the prostitute if he would like to see this Gaul die since he had missed the gladiator show at Rome. When the prostitute, not taking Lucius seriously, agreed, the consul took a sword and killed the Gaul.[138] Even in the Greek east where there was some resistance to Roman gladiator games, most cities eventually embraced this form of entertainment as a source of pleasure.[139] A character in a story by the Greek author Lucian, a second century AD satirist, writes of the 'delight' (*terpnon*) of the gladiator show he attended, including seeing wild animals speared and pursued by dogs (*venatio*), and convicted criminals in chains being attacked by wild animals.[140] Pliny the Younger speaks of the crowd's enjoyment of the punishment of informers who plagued their fellow citizens with false accusations during the reign of the tyrannical Domitian. The spectators' enjoyment is the satisfaction of justice done, but not of the informers' bloodshed, because Trajan, ever the merciful emperor, had decreed banishment for them. Pliny, however, may be revealing his unspoken desire to have enjoyed the sight of their blood when he mentions that these informers were standing in the blood of convicts executed earlier.[141]

As unattractive to us as the Roman mindset discussed above is, anyone who believes in the importance of history as a tool for understanding the human condition must be careful to avoid self-righteousness in judging the behaviour of societies that have long disappeared. As Walter Pater explains in *Marius the Epicurean* in reference to gladiator shows, every society has its own peculiar moral blindness that is not shared by posterity and exposes the earlier society to anachronistic criticism:[142]

> *That long chapter of the cruelty of the Roman public shows may, perhaps, leave with the children of the modern world a feeling of self-complacency. Yet it might seem well to ask ourselves – it is always well to do so, when we read of the slave-trade, for instance, or of great religious persecutions on this side or on that, or of anything else which raises in us the question, 'Is thy servant a dog, that he should do this thing?' – not merely, what germs of feeling we may entertain which, under fitting circumstances, would induce us to the like; but, even more practically, what thoughts, what sort of considerations, may be actually present to our minds such as might have furnished us, living in another age, and in the midst of those legal crimes, with plausible excuses for them: each age in turn, perhaps, having its own peculiar point of blindness, with its consequent peculiar sin – the touch-stone of an unfailing conscience in the select few.*[143]

E. Gunderson's use of the word 'banality' to describe Roman acceptance of lethal violence as a normal entertainment seems to recall the thesis of Hannah Arendt's *Eichmann in Jerusalem: A Report on the Banality of Evil*: the normality of evil acts in Nazi Germany. Gunderson writes:

> *What is ultimately scandalous about the arena is its banality. The brutality of the games does not express in sublimated form the brutality of civilization: this brutality instead participates in the production and reproduction of social truths with which violence is ultimately in accord.*[144]

One, however, should not apply Arendt's judgement of the Nazis to ancient Rome. The cruelty of the Nazis, unlike that of the Romans, must be judged in the context of more humane values of the twentieth century.

It could be argued that we moderns have less need for real bloodshed and death as entertainment because we have been accustomed to accept realistic substitutions in films, television, websites, video games and so on that cater to a desire for violent and grotesque fantasies.[145] One might object that these substitutions are primarily directed at young males. True enough, but the popularity of such scenes goes beyond this target group and permeates the rest of society. That, at least, is the judgement of the controllers of various media, who generally know their audience well. It is also the conclusion of the news media (which do not target young males), whose 'if it bleeds, it leads' policy can be observed daily on television and in newspapers.[146] It is hard to disagree with K. M. Coleman when she writes of the human psyche's susceptibility to 'the thrill of vicarious pain'.[147] Remember that the difference between the Romans and ourselves on this issue is not the result of a sudden awareness on our part of the need for the more humane treatment of all human beings and animals, but the gradual shift in societal values that has taken place since the industrial revolution. In the matter of watching wild animals being killed for entertainment, modern Americans are not that different from the Romans. Beginning in the mid-1960s, American television viewers clearly enjoyed watching celebrities and famous hunters kill big game such as elephants, lions, rhinoceros and bears.[148] They watched ABC TV's *The American Sportsman* in large enough numbers that the show lasted twenty-two seasons. Although the climate with regard to hunting and the treatment of animals in general has changed to a degree in the early twenty-first century, another big game hunting show remains on the TV schedule in America.[149] Naturally, the wounding and killing of human beings for entertainment is quite another matter, but it should be noted that we still satisfy our natural appetite for viewing bloodshed and violent death not with live action but at one remove thanks to technological advancements.

Chapter 2

Recruitment and Training
of Gladiators

W ho were gladiators? How did they become gladiators? Cicero identifies them as 'either men of no moral worth or barbarians.'[1] What
Cicero means is that they are either criminals convicted of capital crimes
('men of no moral worth') or prisoners of war ('barbarians') taken captive in
one of the countless wars the Romans waged during the Republic and the
empire.[2] The criminals had been condemned in court to live in a gladiator
school (*damnatio ad ludum gladiatorium*), where they would be trained for
a gladiatorial career. This penalty provided a rich resource of recruitment. In
the province of Bithynia (modern north-west Turkey) in the early second
century AD, so many convicts were given this penalty that the gladiator
schools could not accommodate them and they were forced to become
public slaves.[3] Some convicts were sentenced to a school for arena hunters
(*ludus venatorius*), a penalty equivalent to service in the gladiator school,
although the risk of death was probably less.[4] In the category of 'men of no
moral worth', Cicero probably would also include slaves. The ancients
believed that slaves were not capable of moral judgement: a slave's testimony
in court was accepted only if it was given under torture. Slaves were bought

by *lanistae* on the open market and sometimes were sold by their masters directly to *lanistae*, usually as punishment. The future emperor Vitellius once sold a difficult slave to an itinerant *lanista*, but relented just before the man was to appear as a gladiator and gave him his freedom.[5] In fact, a significant number of gladiators were slaves.[6]

The men who fell into the hands of a *lanista* had little control over their destiny. They were the property of the *lanista*, whom the Romans generally considered a heartless seeker of profit.[7] Seneca compares the *lanista* with a slave dealer who fattens up his slaves like cattle and keeps them in good condition to get a better price for them.[8] In one of his letters, Seneca puts the *lanista* in the same class as the pimp (they are both traffickers in human flesh), each a despised outcast from decent society.[9] Under the control of these ruthless owners, gladiators found themselves forced to embrace the life of a gladiator, spending their best years risking serious injury and an early death in the arena. There could be an upside to a career as a gladiator, but it was a long shot. The loss of a match did not automatically mean death. A loser could be granted discharge, which would allow him to come back and fight another day. There was even the possibility of eventual permanent release from the arena for the lucky few. Despite the odds, there were undoubtedly a significant number of gladiators who embraced the terms of their new life as a gladiator. They welcomed the chance to win glory in the arena as a mitigating factor of their slavery.

A good example of gladiator 'recruitment' is the best-known gladiator in both the ancient and the modern world, Spartacus. His rejection of the career that slavery had imposed on him and his desperate fight for freedom is well known from a novel by Howard Fast (Spartacus 1951) and a popular film starring Kirk Douglas based on this novel and directed by Stanley Kubrick (1960). Since the eighteenth century, Spartacus has been used by various novelists, dramatists and film makers to comment on contemporary issues of personal freedom. For example, the revival of Bernard-Joseph Saurin's tragedy *Spartacus* in 1792 gave public voice to the desire for freedom that fuelled the French Revolution. Dr Robert Montgomery Bird's play *The Gladiator* (1831) was a veiled attack on the institution of slavery in America. In early twentieth century Italy, Spartacus was depicted as a symbol of Italian nationalism in Giovanni Enrico Vidali's film *Spartaco o Il gladiatore della Tracia* (1913), based on Raffaello Giovagnoli's epic novel, *Spartaco* (1874).

Howard Fast, in his novel *Spartacus*, made Spartacus into a communist revolutionary intent on making Rome a classless society:

> *The whole world belongs to Rome so Rome must be destroyed and made only a bad memory, and then where Rome was, we will build a new life where all men will live in peace and brotherhood and love, no slaves and no slave masters, no gladiators and no arenas, but a time like the old times, like the golden age. We will build new cities of brotherhood, and there will be no walls around them.*[10]

When the novel reached the screen, Fast's communist message was toned down to make the film acceptable to a mass American audience of the post-McCarthy era. Spartacus became simply a slave trying to lead his army of slaves back to their homelands, symbolically suggesting at the same time contemporary black and Jewish aspirations and in general the uncontroversial ideal of human freedom. The film even appealed to political and religious conservatives of that era by presenting a crucified Spartacus at the end of the film as a Christ figure and by substituting religious piety for class struggle as a motivation for Spartacus' resistance to Roman tyranny. Thus, conservatives were encouraged to see Spartacus as a symbol of America's cold war struggle against godless communist dictatorships.[11]

The views of Spartacus in these and other modern representations are quite different from how this rebel was perceived by the Romans themselves. The Roman author Florus expresses a typical Roman attitude when he cites his disdain for Spartacus' army of slaves led by gladiators in rebellion against their Roman masters. He calls slaves human beings of the lowest type, and adds that their gladiator leaders were the lowest of the low. In the Roman view, the success achieved by Spartacus' army against Roman armies reversed the natural order of things. Roman soldiers, freemen enjoying full citizenship rights, were not supposed to lose to a ragtag collection of slaves, but in a number of embarrassing defeats, they had become prisoners of war and thus objects of contempt.[12] The ultimate in Roman shame was Spartacus' use of four hundred captured Roman soldiers as gladiators at the funeral of a woman said to have committed suicide because she had been raped by a Roman. This event reversed the Roman custom of using slaves like Spartacus and his colleagues to fight at funerals of notable Romans. Now, like a wealthy aristocrat at Rome, a gladiator had become an *editor* of a *munus* with Romans soldiers providing the entertainment.[13]

Spartacus' native land was Thrace, which today cuts across the bound-aries of three modern nations on the north Aegean coast: Greece, Bulgaria and European Turkey. Spartacus had been a mercenary in the Roman army, probably in the First Mithridatic War in the 80s BC, but had deserted and become a bandit. He was captured and, because of his outstanding strength and military experience, was sold to Lentulus Batiatus, a *lanista* who ran a gladiatorial school (*ludus*) in Capua in southern Italy. Since the third cen-tury BC, Roman conquests in the eastern Mediterranean and Aegean areas had provided a steady supply of slaves to Italy, fuelling an agricultural and pastoral economy that produced unparalleled affluence in Italy. Capua, the chief city of Campania, with its excellent soil and the influx of slaves to work the land, enjoyed great prosperity. Cicero says that this affluence fostered an attitude of *luxuria* and *superbia* ('luxury and arrogance') that no doubt played a role in the growth of gladiator shows in that area.[14] The training of slaves as first-class gladiators along with the cost of their armour and main-tenance was indeed an expensive luxury. Campanian gladiators were con-sidered the *crème de la crème* of the profession. Their stellar reputation was still evident in the middle of the third century AD when a *munerarius* in Minturnae (modern Minturno) proudly boasted of having ordered the deaths of 'eleven leading gladiators of Campania' during his *munus*.[15] This boast of the *munerarius* calls attention to how great his costs were in deny-ing eleven appeals for release from such valuable gladiators, for whom he must compensate the *lanista* on top of the considerable rental fee. The *superbia* of the spectators was also engaged by their experience of *Schaden-freude* as they watched men whom they scorned degrade themselves by participating in bloody fights as an entertainment. Appian reports that Spartacus' speech to his fellow gladiators in favour of escape from the *ludus* focused on this very subject: the shame of being put on view for the amuse-ment of others.[16] The same *luxuria* and *superbia* were evident at an even more affluent Rome and not surprisingly helped promote the spectacular growth of gladiatorial games there.

We can only speculate what Spartacus' period of training was like in Batiatus' gladiatorial school in Capua. It was no doubt as thorough and harsh as necessary to prepare the trainees for their violent careers as gladia-tors. There was another reason for their harsh treatment. A substantial num-ber of the trainees were men who, like Spartacus, had been condemned to a gladiator school (*damnati ad ludum*) for some crime. They were prisoners in the school, who had to be carefully supervised and kept under lock and key while they were not training. Plutarch's account notes that the rebellion began when they seized knives and skewers from a kitchen. Although these are not formidable weapons, they seem to have been enough to hold their guards at bay while they escaped. Plutarch goes on to report that they obtained real weapons when they had the good fortune to come upon a wagon full of gladiatorial weapons going to another city. Later, when they seized weapons from Capuan soldiers trying to stop them, they threw away the gladiator arms, which they considered 'dishonorable' and 'barbaric'.[17]

Plutarch, no admirer of Roman gladiatorial combat, criticizes the 'injustice' of these men being forced by their owner to fight as gladiators.[18] As a man well versed in philosophy, his views in this matter were in line with those of some other Greek intellectuals, but differed from those of the rest of Greek society, who, like the Romans, believed that gladiators, as men of low status and worth, deserved whatever fate befell them.[19] The Roman contempt for slaves in general and for gladiators in particular no doubt contributed to the Romans' slowness in realizing that Spartacus and his colleagues, who were disciplined and skilled fighters, posed a greater threat than two earlier slave revolts in Roman Sicily in the previous century. At first, the Roman authorities did not take the runaways seriously, assigning smaller armies under lesser commanders. Their disdain for Spartacus' slave army had led them to react with less than an all-out military effort. After several disastrous Roman losses, however, their contempt was dispelled. Even then the Romans suffered losses. Two Roman armies, each led by one of the two consuls (the chief executive magistrates of Rome) engaged Spartacus' followers and were soundly defeated. The army of the provincial governor of Cisalpine Gaul suffered the same fate. It was only when M. Licinius Crassus, one of the richest men in Rome and a man of great determination, was appointed general that the tide turned. He restored discipline to his army by applying the penalty of decimation to soldiers guilty of cowardice, putting to death fifty out of a five hundred man group. In a final confrontation, Spartacus was killed in battle (his body was not found) and the six thousand captured survivors of his army were crucified along the complete length of the Appian Way from Rome to Capua, a distance of 125 miles. Over this distance, there would have been one cross every 35–40 yards.[20]

What do we know of Spartacus the gladiator? Was he only a gladiator in training or is it possible that he was already a well-known gladiator? The fact that he was housed at a gladiatorial school does not necessarily mean that he was only a trainee; gladiators who had already embarked on their professional careers also lived in these schools. There is a fresco at the entrance to a house in Pompeii that depicts two gladiators on horseback fighting each other.[21] Each gladiator is named on the fresco, although only one name can be made out clearly: Spartaks, an Oscan (the native Italic language of Campania) form of the name Spartacus.[22] Could this be the famous Spartacus or, since Spartacus was a Thracian name, just another Thracian of the same name? Unfortunately, we have no way of telling. All we know is what Plutarch tells us that the gladiators of Batiatus' *ludus* were mostly Thracians and Gauls, so there could easily have been more than one Spartacus in the school.[23]

Volunteer gladiators (*auctorati*)

Although most men became gladiators involuntarily, there were freemen (and later even women) who were willing to assume the life of a gladiator temporarily. Who were these people and what was their motivation to become gladiators? During most of the Republic, there were no doubt enthusiastic young men of the lower classes, seeking fame and fortune in the arena, who volunteered themselves. After all, they had little to lose. The stigma attached to the profession of gladiator, however, seems to have had considerable force in a society preoccupied with social standing and reputation. It kept men from the two upper orders, the senatorial and equestrian classes, from fighting in the arena.[24] This stigma was called *infamia* ('disgrace') a legal penalty that resulted in disqualification from exercising certain citizen rights in the public and private sectors, such as serving in the army, voting for magistrates or on the passage of laws, serving on juries, immunity from physical attacks or corporal punishment, and acting on behalf of another person in court. *Infamia* could be incurred in various ways: for example, a judge accepting bribes, a soldier avoiding his duty or showing cowardice in battle, any conviction in court, bankruptcy.[25] *Infamia* also applied automatically to anyone engaged in certain lines of work. One of these professions was prostitution, which does not come as a surprise, but also included under this censure was any profession connected with entertainment such as acting or fighting as a gladiator or an arena hunter.

Catharine Edwards points out that what these professions had in common was the production of pleasure:

> *In the theaters, arenas, and brothels of Rome, the infamous sold their own flesh (in the case of actors, gladiators, and prostitutes; and the flesh of others, for pimps and trainers of gladiators were also stigmatized). They lived by providing sex, violence, and laughter for the pleasure of the public – a licentious affront to Roman gravitas.* [26]

By the early empire, however, even the threat of *infamia* was not sufficient to deter significant numbers of freemen of any class from becoming a gladiator. The life of a gladiator seems to have been especially appealing to the financially desperate, whose only hope to make some money was to fight for a price in the arena. In fact, becoming a gladiator was one of the most common options of the insolvent. Satirists saw the bankrupt man's choice to become a gladiator as the equivalent of hitting rock-bottom. Horace's victim of insolvency has only three options: to become a gladiator, a professional gardener or a driver of a carriage.[27] Juvenal saw the ultimate fate of a bankrupt as 'resorting to the pot-luck meals of the gladiator school'.[28] We hear of recruiters of gladiators who took advantage of inexperienced young men.[29] These recruiters, looking for handsome and well-built young men with potential as a sword fighter, no doubt painted an overly positive picture of life as a gladiator to entice them. Such young men were not just of the lower classes, but also from the upper orders of society. Many of the elite volunteers, having acquired an addiction to luxury in their upbringing, had managed to impoverish themselves very quickly.[30] A speaker in a rhetorical exercise gives a good account of their plight, disowned by their families for their spendthrift ways and other unacceptable conduct:

> *Young men who come from wealthy families of the highest rank, suddenly separated from not only their wealth but lacking even the basic necessities to sustain life and spirit will not engage in everyday work, not being able to endure the drudgery of labour. Their only alternative is to take on a dangerous occupation that could cost them their life [i.e., become a gladiator].* [31]

The authorities tried to stem through legislation the tide of elites volunteering as gladiators. Suetonius tells us that aristocratic spendthrifts of both upper orders deliberately brought *infamia* upon themselves in other ways so that they could lose their status as members of the senatorial or equestrian orders and thus circumvent the ban against elites fighting as gladiators.[32]

Bankruptcy was not the only reason for signing up as a gladiator. Ville adds love of glory, a longing to engage in combat, and more sinister motives: a taste for killing, sadism and a death wish.[33] Boredom with peace, the desire to avoid the long-term commitment of military service (20 to 25 years) and the need for a new identity have also been suggested.[34] Carlin Barton has argued eloquently for a psychological explanation of the free-born Roman's desire to take up the life of a gladiator. She sees this aspiration as a desperate response to the devastation of the civil wars that brought an end to the Roman Republic.[35] Samuel Dill suggests some shallower reasons for signing up: 'the splendour of arms, the ostentatious pomp of the scene of combat, the applause of thousands of spectators on the crowded benches, [and] the fascination of danger . . .'.[36]

There was a legally prescribed process (*auctoratio*) for free men who desired to become a gladiator. A person who went through this process was called an *auctoratus*, that is, 'one who hires himself out to another for a price'. This process was also available to prospective wild-beast fighters (*bestiarii* and *venatores*). The first step was to declare one's intention to a tribune of the people, who could either approve or disapprove.[37] If approved, the candidate entered into a contract with a *lanista*, or directly with an *editor* of a gladiator show. The latter method was mostly for the upper orders and the commitment was usually for one appearance only. The usual contract specified the amount of money to be paid to the *auctoratus*, the specific length of service as a gladiator and the maximum number of combats required of the *auctoratus*.[38] The contract probably also specified the cost of release from the agreement for the *auctoratus* before its terms were fully met. Just as a slave could buy his own freedom from his master, an *auctoratus* could buy out his contract with the *lanista* or have someone else do it. The rhetorician Quintilian tells a story of a sister who had redeemed her *auctoratus* brother a number of times. Apparently, he would sell himself to a *lanista* whenever he needed money. The sister, disgusted with having to redeem her brother so many times, cut off his thumb while he was asleep to prevent him from fighting again. He took her to court and she expressed her reaction in this way: 'You really deserved to have your hand intact.' Quintilian explains this cryptic statement by adding that the phrase 'so that you could fight [and be killed in the arena]' is understood.[39] Ovid notes that some *auctorati* did not know when to call it a career.[40] The typical Roman attitude towards this business deal between *lanista* and *auctoratus* can be best summed up in Livy's phrase: '[the *auctorati*] put their blood up for sale'.[41] The candidate solemnly swore 'to be burned, bound, beaten and to be put to death by the sword' and to do 'whatever else was ordered', a total dedication of body and mind.[42] The burning, binding and beating were punishments that could be imposed by his superiors in the course of his training or even in the arena, while death by sword refers to the losing gladiator's willingness to accept death at the hands of his opponent if ordered by the *editor* of a *munus*.[43] This oath was most likely sworn only to a *lanista*. Since the commitment on the part of a *lanista* was a substantial one, involving expensive long-term training in a gladiator school, he needed the firmest possible guarantee of the applicant's sincerity and cooperation. This process was not necessary for an equestrian or a senator in good standing, who generally made an agreement with the *editor* (most often the emperor) for one event only and did not require any special training. The last step in the process of becoming an *auctoratus* seems to have been an initiation ritual in the arena in which the *auctorati* were whipped with rods, perhaps while running a gauntlet of veteran gladiators.[44] In the late Republic, large numbers of freeborn men became gladiators, but by the middle of the first century BC, slaves still outnumbered free gladiators.[45]

The gladiator school (*ludus*)

Each *ludus* housed of a troupe of gladiators (*familia gladiatoria*), who were trained in various styles of fighting. (Note that the singular of the word *ludus* denotes a gladiator school whereas the plural *ludi* refers to games celebrated annually in honour of various gods.) Typically, the gladiator school was owned by a *lanista*, often an ex-gladiator, who rented his troupe to givers of gladiator shows. In Capua, however, the owners of major schools that we hear of belong to upper-class Roman families, for example Lentulus Batiatus (Vatia) and Julius Caesar himself. C. Aurelius Scaurus, whose gladiatorial school provided instructors in swordplay to the Roman army in 105 BC, may have been another Roman aristocrat who owned a *ludus* in Capua.[46] Caesar purchased his *ludus* in anticipation of his aedileship in 65 BC during which he planned to offer a grand *munus* to ensure his election to higher office. He maintained ownership of this school even after his election to the praetorship and the consulship. By 49 BC, this school housed perhaps as many as a thousand gladiators.[47] The fact that Caesar held on to a school of this size after his aedileship was undoubtedly a sign of the scale of his political ambitions beyond even the highest magistracies.

The decision of a Roman politician to own his own gladiator troupe may have been made in good part for economic reasons. First, *lanistae* often charged outlandish fees for the use of their gladiators. Moreover, an *editor* renting gladiators from a *lanista* often found himself in a bind in the midst of a *munus*. The purpose of his giving a *munus* in the first place was to please the people to advance his political career. What if the crowd vociferously demanded the death of a defeated gladiator? The *editor* would have to think twice about ordering the death of a defeated gladiator to please the spectators because of a hefty compensation fee due to the *lanista* in this circumstance. According to one legal source, the compensation was legally defined as fifty times the rental price of the gladiator.[48] On the other hand, failure on the part of the *editor* to cater to the desires of the crowd usually meant a damaging loss of favour and respect. Given these considerations, the choice to own a troupe might seem prudent, especially since the surviving gladiators could be sold at a profit after the *munus* or given to friends to strengthen political alliances. The purchase of a gladiatorial school, aside from its political advantages, could be a good investment. Cicero's best friend Atticus, a member of the equestrian order, invested in a *ludus*. In a letter to Atticus, Cicero is quite enthusiastic about the purchase because of the report he has heard about the excellence of Atticus' gladiators. He points out to Atticus that if he had been willing to hire them out for two recent gladiatorial shows, he would have recovered all his costs in purchasing the school.[49] One might justly wonder how the equestrian Atticus performed what is essentially the function of the disgraced *lanista* without incurring *infamia*. Cicero expresses no disapproval at all of Atticus' investment. Perhaps Atticus, like the members of the senatorial class mentioned above, was able to distance himself from this disreputable business by not being involved in the day-to-day affairs of the school and using representatives to run the school for him. Another consideration is that Atticus, already a wealthy man, did not make his living from his investment; his gladiatorial venture may have been, in effect, a hobby. The same justification could be applied to Caesar's owning a *ludus*, but there is a difference. Caesar established his school to train gladiators for his own use and not as an investment. If he occasionally rented out gladiators to other *editores*, he, too, undoubtedly did it through representatives, anticipating the later practice of emperors as owners of imperial gladiator schools.

The training of gladiators

The training of gladiators was serious business; spectators wanted to see gladiators who were experts at their profession and could produce an exciting fight. The instruction they received in gladiatorial schools was famous for its high quality. Christian writers reluctantly praised the discipline that gladiators attained, which enabled them to kill more effectively. The Christian apologist Minucius Felix, in condemning 'the evil pleasures' of Roman games, notes 'the discipline of killing' in the training of gladiators.[50] Cyprian of Carthage makes the point even more forcefully:

> Skill, discipline, art, all enable [a gladiator] to kill. Not only a crime is committed, but it is taught; what can be more inhuman, what can be more repulsive? Instruction makes it possible to kill and once the slaying is accomplished, there is glory.[51]

The satirist Juvenal in the course of his lampoon of a woman who undergoes gladiator training (perhaps in preparation for the arena), gives an idea of what took place on the exercise grounds of the *ludus*. The most basic drill involved attacking a wooden post called a *palus*, on which she inflicted 'wounds' with repeated attacks of a wooden sword and her shield. (Note that the shield could be used as an offensive, as well as a defensive, weapon.) These attacks, however, are not performed in a random fashion, but follow prescribed and systematic directions of a teacher of gladiatorial skills (*doctor* or *magister*) standing nearby. Juvenal calls these directions 'numbers' (*numeri*), which elsewhere are referred to as 'instructions' (*dictata*).[52] Although there is no clear evidence of exactly what these numbers or *dictata* were, in general they must have been a predetermined series of offensive and defensive movements. A speaker in Petronius' *Satyricon* complains of a gladiator who fought only by the numbers, that is, mechanically.[53] Although following these rules too closely might on occasion have resulted in a boring fight, nonetheless the *dictata* represented a crucially important facet of the gladiatorial art and could not be ignored. Julius Caesar urged trainers to impart the *dictata* to his inexperienced gladiators.[54] The following comment by Tertullian reveals that fans were familiar with these *dictata*, and would try to help a gladiator who was not putting them into practice by shouting them from their seats. Sometimes this practice actually helped the gladiator:

> *Not only trainers and those placed in charge urge the best gladiators [to pay attention to the* dictata*] but also the untrained and amateurs [among the spectators] from afar [from their seats], with the result that often the* dictata *suggested by the crowd itself are profitable [to the gladiators].*[55]

Seneca records traditional wisdom regarding defensive techniques. An old Latin proverb warns the gladiator to keep his head about him and observe warnings given by the face, hands and bending of the body of his opponent.[56] Robert points out that skill was even more important for a gladiator than force.[57] Later in their training, gladiators would engage in practice fights with each other, still using the wooden sword. At the most advanced stage of their training, gladiators practised with opponents, using real weapons.[58]

A description of a training session for new recruits (both soldiers and gladiators) written by Vegetius, a fourth century AD author, gives us more details. In this account, Vegetius looks back to the training techniques of the past. Trainees worked out carrying shields made of twigs that were woven in such a way as to be double the normal weight of wicker-work and wooden swords that were double the weight of real swords. In the morning and afternoon they practised at the *palus*, which each recruit stuck in the ground so that it was 6 (Roman) feet high (5 feet 8 inches in modern measurements).[59] The recruit treated the *palus* as an imaginary opponent, which was approximately the size of a tall Roman. The moves described by Vegetius give us some sense of the nature of the *dictata*:

> *[The trainee] pretended he was now attacking his opponent's face, now threatening his sides, sometimes striving to cut his knees and legs. He would draw back, spring forward, and attack his imaginary opponent. He would apply every kind of attack, every technique of warfare. And in this practice, caution was observed so that the recruit tried to inflict a wound on his opponent in such a way that he in no way laid himself open to a blow from his opponent.*[60]

The teachers in the *ludus* were called *doctor* or *magister* and were usually ex-gladiators or, in some cases, active gladiators, who passed on their knowledge and experience to their students. Included in Martial's litany of the achievements of the great gladiator Hermes is the statement that he is 'both an (active) gladiator and a *magister*'. Martial also points out that he is skilled in all methods of fighting.[61] Normally, a *magister* or *doctor* would teach only one or two styles of fighting. We hear of *doctores* who taught styles of fighting employed by various types of gladiators: *thraex*, *hoplomachus, murmillo, provocator* and *secutor*.[62] Juvenal's female student-gladiator seems to be learning two different styles of fighting indicated by the two kinds of protective armour she possesses. For the first style of arma-ment, the poet lists a belt worn around a loincloth (*balteus*), an arm protec-tor consisting of thickly wrapped linen (*manica*), 'crests' (perhaps a crested helmet), and a greave (a metal protector) on the left leg. This last piece of equipment on the left leg suggests that the gladiatorial type here may be the *secutor* ('pursuer').[63] Her other armament (helmet and linen leg protectors on both legs) is enough to tell us a different kind of gladiator is indicated but is too vague for an exact identification.[64]

The *ludus* as living quarters

The *ludus*, which was not only a training institution but also served as living quarters for gladiatorial troupes, existed at Rome from at least the second century BC. Travelling troupes might not have their own *ludus*, but presum-ably they would stay at a *ludus* in the town or city where they were going to perform, either paying rent or receiving hospitality as a professional cour-tesy. Eppia, a senator's wife who fell in love with a gladiator named Sergius belonging to a travelling *familia*, followed him to Alexandria in Egypt.[65] It is likely that she and her lover stayed at the famous *ludus* in Alexandria. Although we hear of only a few specific gladiator schools in Republican times, there must have been a great number of gladiator troupes housed in small gladiatorial schools at Rome in the first century BC. This is indicated by the danger the Roman Senate saw in their presence at Rome during the imminent threat of the Catilinarian revolution in the 60s BC. It was the con-cern of the Senate that the revolutionaries might attempt to use gladiators as a military force. The Senate had learned the hard way what military suc-cess a gladiator-led army could achieve during Spartacus' revolt. Therefore, the Senate decreed that these *familiae* be transferred to Capua and neigh-bouring towns in southern Italy.[66]

In the late Republic, Capua surpassed Rome as a centre for gladiator training and lodging. The most famous schools were located in Capua, like those of Batiatus and Julius Caesar. The choice of Capua as a site for a gladiatorial school was not fortuitous. Capua, like Praeneste (modern Palestrina) and Ravenna in Italy, and Alexandria in Egypt, was thought to foster good health in gladiators because of their sea breezes.[67] Although climate was important for gladiators, diet was even more crucial for these athletic men. The food served at gladiator schools (known by the generic term *sagina*) may deservedly have had a reputation for being unappetizing. A fictional gladiator describes the *sagina* he was fed at a school as 'worse than any hunger'.[68] On the other hand, the typical gladiator diet, which Juvenal calls *miscellanea* ('hodge-podge' or 'potluck'), was no doubt nourishing and designed to produce strength.[69] We know that, from the earliest days, barley was the chief staple of gladiators' diet. In fact, gladiators were often called *hordearii* ('barley men').[70] The cheapness of this grain no doubt made it popular with *lanistae*. The portions, as the diet of men engaged in such a profession required, were generous, even larger than the rations given to Roman soldiers. Tacitus notes that Vitellius served gladiator-sized rations to his soldiers during the civil wars of AD 69.[71] Another indication of the large amount of food gladiators consumed is Augustus' banishment of *familiae gladiatoriae* in schools at Rome to a distance of 100 miles from the capital during a famine.[72] The large number of these *ludi* probably represented a considerable drain on the food supply.

The living conditions in a *ludus* were no doubt substandard. There were complaints about the 'filthy condition' of the cells in which gladiators were required to live.[73] The cells in the *ludus* at Pompeii were quite small, between 32 and 49 square feet, accommodating two or at most three men. In as much as there were no beds, the inmates probably used straw mattresses.[74] The *ludus* was not a prison as such. There were gladiators who were allowed to leave and return as they wished. Nonetheless, it was a prison for those gladiators who could not be trusted. They were usually kept in chains in a separate part of the *ludus*. Juvenal mentions a prison within the *ludus*.[75] A fictional inmate of a *ludus*, a freeman who had been sold to a *lanista* by pirates, was naturally desperate to escape and therefore could not be allowed the freedom to come and go. He compares his *ludus* unfavourably to a work-farm (*ergastulum*) where inmates worked in chain gangs and protests the 'disgraceful confinement' to which he was subjected.[76] As we have seen, Spartacus and his comrades were kept under lock and key because they were believed most likely to attempt escape – a belief that later proved to be well founded. But even the rebellious Spartacus was allowed to live with his wife in his cell.[77] A woman who lived with a gladiator in a *ludus* was called a *ludia*, that is, 'a woman of the *ludus*'.[78] The word often had a derogatory meaning. The Eppia mentioned earlier is referred to by Juvenal as a *ludia*, which in this case seems to mean something like 'a gladiator groupie', a woman who formed a temporary relationship with a gladiator.[79] The famous gladiator Hermes attracted the attention of the *ludiae*. Martial calls him 'the focus of the groupies' affections'.[80] It may be hard to think of gladiators as family men, but some gladiators had not only wives but children as well who were housed in the *ludus* or, sometimes even in a private house. In epitaphs, the wife is often mentioned as responsible for having set up the memorial for her dead husband. In one epitaph there is a reversal of the favour: a veteran *eques* ('horseman gladiator') named Albanus, stationed at the *Ludus Magnus* in Rome, had set up a memorial for his 'dearest wife' Publicia. In another, a certain Euche, who set up a memorial for her gladiator husband Faustus, is called a *contubernalis*. One could not contract a legal marriage with a slave, so a man and his slave partner who lived under the same roof were referred to as *contubernales* (literally, 'sharing the same tent'), something like our 'common law spouse'.[81] Suetonius tells the story of an *essedarius*, whose four sons' urgent request that he be discharged completely from service as a gladiator was granted by Claudius.[82] There is a moving epitaph of Urbicus, a *secutor*, who at age 22 was killed in his eighth fight, leaving behind his wife Lauricia and a 5-month-old daughter Fortunensis.[83] Some schools even allowed fans to visit on a regular basis to keep up with the latest gladiatorial news. Apuleius criticizes the uncle and guardian of his stepson for allowing the boy to waste so much time in a *ludus*, talking with the *lanista* about the names, fights and wounds of his gladiators.[84]

The criminal background of many of the men in the *ludus* probably made life as difficult as the living conditions. These were rough men, whose belligerent character was suited to their profession as a gladiator. Many of them had been judged guilty of the most heinous crimes: temple-robbing, arson and murder.[85] They probably made it especially tough on inexperienced newcomers in the *ludus* by subjecting them to verbal and physical abuse as a kind of initiation ritual.[86] From the point of view of the *lanista*, however, the crimes committed by these inmates before entry into the *ludus* were irrelevant as long they did not seriously harm other members of the *ludus*, and were not disobedient.

The social structure of the *ludus* reflected the Roman love of organization and hierarchy. Each category of gladiators was divided into four segments named after the post used for training exercises: first, second, third and fourth *palus*.[87] Gladiators of the same gladiatorial type were ranked in these hierarchical groups according to the number of times they had been victorious in the arena. For example, all the *thraeces* in the school were divided in these four ranks. Robert notes that, in inscriptions, gladiators very seldom mention their membership in the two lowest classes (*tertius* and *quartus palus*).[88] There was no glory in advertising membership in these lowest ranked groups. On the other hand, gladiators trumpeted their membership in the *primus* and *secundus palus*.[89] Record-keeping was an important function in the *ludus*. Slave functionaries called *tabularii* or *commentarienses* ('secretaries') kept careful records of winners and losers in the arena and other details in order to keep the status of each gladiator up to date within each category. These records were also useful in putting together programmes for spectators (*libelli*).[90] Knowing the records of paired gladiators added interest to the fight and was useful in placing bets, a favourite activity of the Romans at gladiator shows. The *primus palus* in each category of fighting style consisted of the most successful gladiators in the *ludus*, while the *quartus palus* contained those with the smallest number of victories. The gladiator in training, called a *tiro* ('apprentice'), could become a part of this ranking system only when he was promoted to the status of 'veteran' after his first bout, if he survived. In fact, many *tirones* never received that promotion because they were killed in their first bout. A *tiro* could be quite young. A funerary inscription honours a gladiator who entered the *ludus* at age 17.[91]

The leader of a group of gladiators of the same type (*thraeces, murmillones*, etc.) in a school received a title derived from name of the highest-ranked group in that category. He was called the *primus palus*. For example, the emperor Commodus, whose fantasy of gladiatorial glory was nourished by his unbalanced mind, considered himself the leading *secutor* ('pursuer') in that category in Rome and thus was given (or took) the title of *primus palus*, which entitled him to a special cell in what was probably the largest gladiatorial school in the empire, the *Ludus Magnus* in Rome. Commodus was extremely proud of his unearned top ranking among *secutores* in the *ludus.* In order to memorialize his imagined excellence as a gladiator, he had the following words inscribed on the base of the colossal statue of Nero adjacent to the Colosseum, the head of which he had replaced with his own likeness: '*primus palus* of the *secutores*, the only left-handed fighter to win . . . twelve thousand matches'.[92] This number of wins seems grossly exaggerated even for a narcissistic emperor like Commodus. Could the source (Cassius Dio) have got the number wrong? Possibly. Herodian gives the much more realistic number: one thousand.[93] No matter what the number of 'victories' Commodus may have won, his success was due to the fact that his opponents were smart enough to concede victory to him rather than lose their own lives, if they won.[94] In a further act of self-promotion, he made more changes to the statue. His extreme fascination with, and participation in, the events of the arena led him to identify closely with Hercules, the patron saint of gladiators and arena hunters. Therefore, he proclaimed himself a second Hercules by adding a club (Hercules' signature weapon) and a bronze lion (the Nemean lion, killed by Hercules as his first labour) at the feet of the statue.[95]

The *familia gladiatoria* in a *ludus* was multi-ethnic. Their native lands were widely scattered across the empire, from Spain to the near and middle east.[96] Eastern gladiators frequently made their way west, and occasionally gladiators from the west are found in the east.[97] Despite the cultural and language differences, emotional attachments among gladiators were quite common; there are numerous examples of surviving comrades paying for the burial of their cellmates.[98] Sometimes all the members of the troupe (*familia*) chipped in to pay for the burial.[99] Robert gives an example of a funeral monument set up by a certain Paitraeites (an alternative spelling of the common gladiator name Petraites) and other cellmates in the *ludus* for their beloved colleague Hermes (not the Hermes celebrated by Martial).[100] An extraordinary example of loyalty among gladiators is an epitaph telling of members of troupe of *paegniarii* ('play gladiators', who did not use lethal weapons) in the *Ludus Magnus*, who paid for the burial of one of their fellow *paegniarii*.[101] What is unusual about this act is that the deceased, Secundus, had died at age 98, five or even six decades after the end of his gladiatorial career. Strong friendships were also formed in the *ludus* between teacher and student. A trainer (*doctor*) in a *ludus* in Brixia (modern Brescia) paid for the burial of a *provocator* ('challenger') named Antigonus, while at Rome a *doctor* named Marcion did the same for another *provocator* by the name of Anicetus.[102] Generosity in this area could also come from other sources. Non-gladiatorial friends took care of the burial of a *thraex* called Volusenus; fans of a gladiator named Glauco in Verona helped his wife finance his burial.[103] On one occasion, a *munerarius* honoured three gladiators whose deaths contributed significantly to the success of his *munus* by building a tomb for them.[104]

It was not unusual for friendships to be formed not just among gladiators of the same type but also across types. Thus, since members of the same *familia* fought each other in the arena, it was not uncommon for friends to be matched against each other.[105] Seneca writes of men in the *ludus* 'living with each other and fighting each other'.[106] Cicero notes that a *murmillo* killed a thraex, who was his friend.[107] No doubt the pairings in some cases even involved two cellmates. An inscription from Rome mentions a *retiarius* and a *murmillo* as cellmates, a possible pairing in the arena.[108] Helmets with visors that covered the face made it easier to wound and kill an opponent who, in some cases, was a close friend.[109]

There was some segregation in the *ludus*. Juvenal tells us that light-armed gladiators were kept separate from the heavy-armed.[110] The poet criticizes a *retiarius* for having rejected the heavy armature of a *murmillo*, *secutor* or *thraex*, expressing a strong condemnation: 'You have earned the scorn of the city.'[111] One could argue that a light-armed gladiator in combat with a heavy-armed opponent is owed greater respect for his courage, but in the Roman mind, the heavy armour (helmet, shield and so forth) bestowed a much greater aura of virility. The vulnerability of the *retiarius*, whose defensive armour consisted only of minimal protection for the left shoulder and arm and both shins, seems to have suggested effeminacy.[112] This attitude is best illustrated in Homer's *Iliad*, when the Trojan Hector considers removing his armour and approaching Achilles, with a proposition to end the war by giving back Helen:

> *I am afraid that if I go up to him, he will not pity me*
> *Nor will he respect me, but he will kill me naked as I am*
> *Just as if I were a woman.[113]*

There was even some separation within the same gladiatorial type. Volunteer *retiarii*, probably because they were inept amateurs, were kept separate from the regular professional *retiarii*, as Juvenal tells us, in a remote part of the school.[114] The difference between these two types of *retiarii* may have been signified outwardly by the wearing of a tunic by the volunteers and the naked torso of the professional.[115] Then there were the effeminate homosexuals among the gladiators whom Seneca says were banished to 'the repulsive' (*obscoenam*) part of the school where they practised their 'disease'.[116]

The *ludus* was a common feature of large towns and cities throughout the empire. Extant inscriptions often tell us how the construction of a *ludus* was financed. For example, in the town of Este in northern Italy, a *ludus* was built at public expense and, at Praeneste, a private citizen (his name has been obliterated by damage to the stone) paid for the *ludus* out of his own pocket. He also built a brand new *spoliarium*.[117]

Although there were many gladiatorial schools throughout the empire, archaeology can provide us with significant evidence of material remains in only one town outside Rome: Pompeii, where the preservation of buildings has been good because of their burial under tons of volcanic ash during the famous eruption of Mount Vesuvius in AD 79. The first *ludus* in Pompeii was a residential house dating from the first century BC which was used as quarters for what must have been a limited number of gladiators.[118] This house continued to serve as a *ludus* during the first half of the first century AD. Its use as a *ludus* is revealed by the great number of graffiti found on the columns of the house's peristyle, which were no doubt written by the gladiators themselves.

Sometime in the middle of the first century AD, Pompeiian gladiators were given a larger space for living quarters and training. A *quadriporticus*, a central courtyard surrounded on all four sides by a portico containing cells and larger rooms was converted into a *ludus* (Figure 1). This structure had originally been used by theatregoers during intermissions at the theatre to stretch their legs out of the sun (without artificial lighting, plays were presented during the day) or to avoid cold winds. Its identification as a *ludus* is also confirmed by the discovery of gladiatorial armour (helmets, greaves, shields and one belt) in the cells as well as some interesting gladiatorial graffiti. The inscription of a certain Samus is typical of these graffiti. He speaks of himself in the third person: 'Samus, [the winner] of one victory, one [laurel] crown, a *murmillo* and an *eques*, lived here'.[119] He is especially proud of his crown, which was a gladiator's reward for an outstanding performance in victory. Samus also notes his versatility in being able to perform in the arena as either a *murmillo* or as an horseman gladiator. A gladiator

Figure 1 *Ludus* at Pompeii. Tarina Peterson, with permission

named Mansuetus inscribed his vow to Venus, the patron divinity of Pompeii, to dedicate his shield to her if he should win.[120] Also included among these graffiti are the much-quoted boasts of two gladiators, proud of their success with the opposite sex: Celadus, a *thraex* and Crescens, a *retiarius*. Celadus calls himself 'the one whom girls sigh for' and 'the one whom girls honor'.[121] Crescens refers to himself as 'the lord of girls' and, as 'the netter [*retiarius*] of girls at night'.[122] He is a typical example of Tertullian's description of gladiators as 'the most enthralling objects of love to whom women surrender their bodies'.[123] In Crescens' case, however, there is another consideration with regard to his sex appeal: the fact that he was a *retiarius*. Since the *retiarius* did not use a shield, his body was more exposed to the spectators than any other gladiator, making this type of gladiator a sexually charged figure. Although some took the *retiarius*'s near-nakedness as a sign of effeminacy, the *retiarius* also could embody heterosexual attraction. This seems to be the case in Artemidorus' interpretation of a dream in which the dreamer fights a *retiarius*: the dreamer will marry a sexually promiscuous woman.[124] It should also be noted that there was another important reason for female fascination with gladiators in addition to physical attraction. Hopkins and Beard write of a *nostalgie de boue* ('longing for the

gutter', literally 'mud') among upper-class Roman women who were attracted by the degraded social status of gladiators.[125] A female slave in
Petronius' *Satyricon* criticizes the sexual tastes of her mistress, who shows a
predilection for slumming. She says that sexual arousal is only possible for
her mistress with men who are socially far beneath her: servants with
hitched-up tunics, gladiators, who fought with a minimum of body cover,
muleteers and actors.[126] A common slur against unpopular Romans of
note was that they were fathered by gladiators. Upper-class women were
commonly accused of affairs with gladiators, like Faustina, the wife of the
emperor Marcus Aurelius and the mother of the 'gladiator' emperor Commodus.[127] Another prominent example is Juvenal's story about the senator's wife named Eppia who ran away to Egypt with a gladiator named
Sergius mentioned earlier in this chapter. The poet points out that Sergius'
actual looks did not seem to justify her obsession with him:

> *What did Eppia see in him that she allowed herself to be called a*
> *gladiator groupie? For her dear Sergius had been shaving for a*
> *long time already and with a wound in his arm was looking*
> *forward to retirement. Moreover, there were many disfigurements*
> *evident on his face, for example where it had been chafed by his*
> *helmet and then there was the wart on his nose and the unpleasant*
> *disorder of a continually dripping eye. But he was a gladiator.*
> *This profession makes them all Adonises. She preferred a*
> *gladiator to her children and homeland and to her sister and her*
> *husband. It is the sword that they love.*[128]

After the conversion of the *quadriporticus* to a *ludus*, the open courtyard
became a training ground. A sundial found in the courtyard was probably
used as a timing device for the gladiators' exercises. The two stories of space
behind the four porticoes were converted into living quarters for the gladiators, and on these two levels there were approximately seventy cells that
housed at least two gladiators each. The capacity of approximately 140 gladiators at one time permitted the presentation of a good-sized *munus* outside
of Rome.[129] There were larger rooms that must have served as the kitchen,
dining room and storerooms, and a meeting room (*exedra*) with images of
gladiatorial armour on its walls. Another room may have served as a stable
because the skeletons of a horse and a man were found there. Perhaps the
horse was used by horseman gladiators. The prison is identifiable because of

the shackles attached to the walls which made it impossible for a fettered man to stand. Four skeletons were found in the prison but they were unchained. Also found in one of the cells was a female skeleton wearing jewels, suggesting that this *ludus* was accessible to the public.[130] What this woman was doing in a gladiator cell is open to all sorts of speculation. She could have been having an affair with gladiator or merely had sought the gladiator school as a last refuge during the final destruction of the city. The discovery of a skeleton of an infant in the *ludus* might be further evidence that some gladiators lived with their families in the *ludus*.[131]

Imperial gladiators

Julius Caesar set the direction of the gladiatorial system that was to characterize the imperial era with the ownership of his own *ludus* and enormous *familia gladiatoria* in Capua. Just before the beginning of the civil war with Pompey, Caesar was planning another *ludus* in Ravenna, which was not built until after his death, probably by his adopted son Octavian, who was later known as Augustus. Caesar had recognized that the possession of a large number of gladiators was not only a sign of his ability and willingness to entertain the people but also a symbol of his political power supported by the favour of the people. Caesar's gladiators became known as *Iuliani* ('Julius' gladiators'). (Note that Julius is a surname. His first name was Gaius.) After his assassination, they retained this name when they were inherited by his adopted son Octavian, who became a member of the Julian family.[132] These gladiators became the nucleus of what eventually was known as the imperial *familia gladiatoria*. Under the Julio-Claudian dynasty, *Iuliani* was the generic name for gladiators owned by the emperor. Imperial gladiators were not just stationed in Rome, but were found throughout Italy and the rest of the empire. These gladiators represented the best sword fighters available throughout the empire and could usually be relied upon on to give the best show. Nero formed another group of imperial gladiators named after himself, the *Neroniani* ('Nero's gladiators') which coexisted with the *Iuliani*. No other Julio-Claudian emperor named a *familia* after himself. Nero's fervent devotion to his gladiators was indicated by his extravagant gift of a magnificent house and a large amount of cash to one of his *Neroniani*, a *murmillo* named Spiculus. Suetonius comments that the value of these gifts was equal to the wealth of a Roman

general who had enjoyed a triumph.[133] This observation is meant to highlight the inappropriateness of Nero's act, which gave a mere gladiator
financial equality with a Roman aristocratic hero. With the end of the Julio-
Claudian dynasty in AD 69, the names *Iuliani* and *Neroniani* were no
longer relevant and ceased to be used. Imperial gladiators began to be
known merely as the gladiators of the *princeps* ('first citizen'), or of Augustus, or of Caesar, all three of these words having acquired the meaning of
'emperor'.

We have some information about the imperial schools of Caligula and
Claudius, but it amounts only to odds and ends. (Tiberius had little interest
in gladiators.) Pliny the Elder says that Caligula had twenty pairs of gladiators in his school and that two of his gladiators, as noted in Chapter 1, were
famous for their unblinking stare.[134] A gladiator named Studiosus from
Caligula's school was well known for having a right arm longer than his left,
no doubt because of his constant practice with the sword.[135] Caligula took
a close personal interest in his school, as shown by the story of his habit of
practising with a gladiator (*murmillo*) from his school. Both used wooden
weapons. When the gladiator threw himself prostrate on the ground in admission of defeat (a wise act for any opponent of this unstable emperor),
Caligula treacherously stabbed him with a real dagger and then ran around
the practice area with a palm branch, as winners in real gladiatorial duels did
in the arena.[136] Of Claudius' school we only hear of the name of the
procurator: Sulpicius Rufus.[137] The first evidence of a *procurator* as administrator of an imperial school is from the time of Augustus in reference to
the famous imperial school in Egyptian Alexandria.[138] The *procurator*, generally of equestrian rank, was an agent of the emperor in various capacities.
Many procurators had significant administrative experience outside the
gladiatorial system, even governing imperial provinces as a representative
of the emperor. P. Bassilius Crescens served as procurator of the *Ludus
Matutinus* ('Morning School'), an imperial school for the training of animal
fighters, in addition to his supervision of the grain supply at Ostia.[139]
P. Cominius Clemens, who had been prefect of the praetorian fleets at
Misenum and Ravenna and procurator of the imperial province of Dacia
Apolensis (modern Romania) served as procurator of an imperial gladia-
torial school in northern Italy.[140] In the late second century AD, T. Flavius
Germanus at different times was procurator of the *Ludus Matutinus* and
the *Ludus Magnus* at Rome. He was also the supervisor (*curator*) of

Commodus' grand triumph in 180 AD.[141] The appointment of able, experienced men like these as *curatores* of gladiator schools was no doubt a big step forward in the professionalization of the gladiatorial system. Procurators not only administered individual schools, but sometimes were in charge of all the schools in a given area that cut across the boundaries of provinces.[142] For example, in the west one procurator administered the imperial schools in northern Italy, Pannonia and Dalmatia, the last two provinces encompassing the area of modern Austria, Hungary and the former Yugoslavia. Another procurator named L. Didius Marinus had experience in supervising imperial schools in both the west and the east: (in the west) the Gauls, Britain, Spain, Germany and Raetia (modern Switzerland and Bavaria); (in the east) Asia, Bithynia, Galatia, Cappadocia, Lycia, Pamphylia, Cilicia, Pontus, Paphlagonia (all nine provinces covering most of the area of modern Turkey) and Cyprus.[143] These procurators were not former gladiators like many *lanistae* but astute businessmen who, on behalf of the emperor, supervised the acquisition, training, maintenance and rental of imperial gladiators.

Imperial gladiators naturally were featured in the *munera* given by the emperor, but they could be also rented out to an *editor* who was willing to pay a higher price for the sake of a quality show. Procurators of imperial schools regularly rented out gladiators to *editores* throughout Italy and in the provinces. These rentals made the imperial schools a money-making proposition for the emperor. In Pompeii, the aedile A. Suettius Certus presented *Neroniani*, while an *editor* named M. Mesonius was able to present both *Iuliani* and *Neroniani* at his *munus*.[144] Also in Pompeii, N. Festus Ampliatus gave a *munus*, the significance of which is indicated by a monumental tomb that memorialized it.[145] An inscription on the wall gives the results of the gladiatorial duels on the last day of Ampliatus' *munus*.[146] All the gladiators mentioned in this inscription are *Iuliani*. It is notable that these gladiators are called by their individual names; usually inscriptions when referring to imperial gladiators just call them *Iuliani* or *Neroniani*. Therefore, we can be certain that these gladiators were among the best of imperial gladiators, well known by name.

Since imperial gladiators belonged to the emperor, technically he could sell them, but this was not normal practice. Emperors usually did not want citizens to have access to a resource that could win them significant public favour. It would also have diminished the emperor's stock of top-notch gladiators. The supply of imperial gladiators was already subject to loss in the normal course of events as they appeared in *munera*. Although imperial gladiators most often fought ordinary opponents, they were sometimes matched against each other, ensuring that at least some would be killed.[147] The only emperor who sold imperial gladiators was Caligula, and that was under circumstances better described as the theatre of the absurd. Caligula, having found that the imperial treasury was almost empty (due to his financial irresponsibility), resorted to a desperate measure to replenish it. He auctioned off gladiators from his imperial school. Aponius Saturninus, a distinguished man who had held the office of praetor, made the mistake of nodding off to sleep as he attended this auction. Caligula, immediately sensing an opportunity, told the auctioneer to watch the frequent nods of Aponius as he slept. The auctioneer realized that Caligula wanted him to interpret the nods as signs of bidding. Before Aponius awoke, he had bought thirteen gladiators for 9 million sesterces, an enormous sum of money.[148]

Medical care

Imperial gladiators generally enjoyed excellent physical care. Tired and aching muscles were worked back into shape by skilled masseurs (*unctores*). Under Commodus, there was a noted masseur at the *Ludus Magnus* nick-named Pirata ('Pirate').[149] Most important of all, physicians (*medici*) looked after the gladiators' general health and cared for their wounds. Medical care was also available in lesser gladiator schools, but probably of much lower quality. In such schools, even if there was a trained medical doctor in resi-dence, his care was usually inferior. In some cases, *lanistae*, having gained some practical medical knowledge by experience, administered medical treatment themselves.[150] On the other hand, some imperial schools had at their disposal a whole staff of doctors who were of the highest quality.[151] The most famous doctor of a *ludus* was a Greek named Galen, the greatest physician and medical writer of the ancient world, who early in his career was appointed gladiatorial doctor by the high priest in charge of the imperial cult of the province of Asia (AD 157–161).[152] The *ludus* where Galen worked was in Pergamum (modern Bergama), the greatest city of the province and one of the first provincial cities to have an imperial cult. The *ludus* in this city was one of the most prestigious gladiatorial schools in the Greek east.

On assuming his position at Pergamum, Galen's first concern was the diet of his gladiators. He complained that their current diet, barley gruel mixed with beans, produced an undesirable flabbiness in their body, and substituted more nutritious food.[153] Galen, however, was not just a nutritionist. His expertise in treating wounds, especially those of the thigh, was quite effective in keeping his gladiators alive and in condition to fight again. During his tenure at this school (almost four years), only two gladiators died from injury. To appreciate this achievement fully, one must consider that sixty gladiators had died during the term of Galen's predecessor as *medicus*.[154]

Other imperial schools probably could not approach the excellence in medical care that Galen provided, but no doubt still provided the best care available in the area. Arena hunters in Corinth showed their gratitude for the excellent medical care provided by their doctor by setting up a statue of him in the arena near where the animals came out of their cages.[155] We also hear of the name of a medical doctor in the *Ludus Matutinus* at Rome, Eutychus, recorded in an inscription on a family tomb which he had constructed.[156] Whether owned by the emperor or a *lanista*, gladiators and *venatores* represented a large investment. The prudent owner kept them in the best physical shape possible.

The character of imperial gladiators

Imperial gladiators enjoyed the best training, armament and accommodation. Thus it is not surprising that the gladiators' morale was high in the imperial schools. It would be rare for an imperial gladiator to be less than eager to fight and prove his worth. Although most imperial gladiators were slaves, there probably would have been virtually no need in imperial schools to apply force to get them to fight. Imperial gladiators were made of stronger stuff and were imbued with an abundance of competitive spirit. During the reign of Tiberius, the great gladiator Triumphus chafed under the infrequency of *munera*. His comment has become famous: 'How our beautiful age perishes!'[157] The philosopher Epictetus gives more details about how imperial gladiators reacted to infrequent appearances in the arena:

> . . . *among the imperial gladiators, there are some who are annoyed because no one leads them forth [from the* ludus*], or pairs them in fights and they pray to the god and they approach their procurators with requests to fight in the arena.*[158]

This was the reputation of the imperial gladiators, which led Roman spectators to look forward to their appearance in the arena. Perhaps we get the
best sense of how imperial gladiators were viewed by Roman spectators
from Suetonius' mention of a standing promise that the emperor Domitian
had made to spectators at the annual quaestorian games in December: to
present two pairs of his imperial gladiators, if requested by the crowd.[159]
This favour of Domitian was in accordance with a custom of allowing
the crowd to request gladiators in addition to those who had been advertised before the *munus*. The added gladiators were called *postulaticii*
('requested') in contrast to the scheduled combatants, who were known as
ordinarii. It might be interesting to speculate on Domitian's motivations
for this promise. First, Domitian had a strong interest in spectacles,
especially gladiatorial games, which he spruced up with novelties, such as
presenting gladiatorial games at night with female and dwarf gladiators.[160]
Moreover, Domitian had revived the annual quaestorian games in December, which had not been given for about a decade, so he must have felt some
responsibility for their success.[161] The board of quaestors, who were legally
required to finance the December *munus*, were relatively young magistrates
(in their early thirties) on the lowest rung of the Roman political ladder.
The quaestors may not always have had the financial resources to rent the
best gladiators, so their shows may have gained the reputation of falling
below the standard set by the *munera* of the emperor. Suetonius records
one occasion when the quaestors' *munus* may not have pleased the spectators, because they took Domitian up on his promise. In response, the emperor ordered two pairs of gladiators from his imperial school to appear last
in the arena, probably to give the *munus* a grand finale and make the crowd
forget what had gone before. Suetonius' description of their appearance is
brief but significant: they appeared 'in imperial splendor', a phrase that must
refer to the impressive armour they were wearing, which no doubt gleamed
in the bright sunlight.[162] We can imagine the rest. They were most likely
carrying their helmets as they entered the arena, as gladiators usually did
when they marched into the arena in procession, and in all probability were
better-looking than the ordinary gladiator.[163] Beauty of face and body was
much valued, especially in imperial gladiators, and was reflected in their
monetary value.[164] There must have been great excitement among the
crowd at the appearance of these four gladiators. This initial thrill of their
appearance was no doubt soon replaced by the anticipation of two great

fights as one would expect of gladiators with superior fighting skills and great professional pride. Although Suetonius does not record anything about the duels themselves, we may presume that the crowd enjoyed the fights immensely, especially if the preceding part of the show had been disappointing. Given the pride that Domitian no doubt took in his *familia gladiatoria*, it is somewhat ironic that gladiators from his school took part in his assassination.[165]

The imperial *ludus*

Early in the first century AD, imperial gladiators were housed in pre-existing schools in Ravenna and Capua, but more imperial schools were needed, especially in Rome. Around the middle of the first century AD, two schools had been built in Rome that had no specific name besides *ludus*, one for gladiators and one for beast fighters. After the building of the Colosseum (dedicated in AD 80) in the heart of the city, there was a need to centralize the housing and training of gladiators near their place of performance. It made sense to build a school immediately adjacent to the Colosseum rather than having to transport gladiators a long distance from imperial schools in Praeneste and Capua. Late in his reign, Domitian (AD 81–96) may have begun to restore the existing gladiator school, but more likely he began to build a completely new structure. Its name was the *Ludus Magnus*, but before it was completed, he was assassinated. Trajan started the building all over again and it was finally finished under his successor, Hadrian. Domitian built two other gladiatorial schools in roughly the same area: the *Ludus Gallus* and the *Ludus Dacicus* (their exact location is not known). There is hardly any evidence available beyond the mere mention of these schools, but the former was probably for training Gallic prisoners of war and the latter for training Dacians, who must have been plentiful at Rome after the two military expeditions Domitian had sent against Dacia. There were even more Dacian prisoners after Trajan's two successful campaigns there in the early second century. Included in this complex was an *armamentarium* (a gladiatorial armoury), a *sanitarium* (hospital), a *spoliarium* and a *choragium*, a warehouse for stage properties used in the arena.

The *Ludus Magnus* was built adjacent to the Colosseum to which it was connected by an underground passageway to allow gladiators to make their way to the arena without being seen and to transport animals to the arena without having to take them through the streets. As its name indicates, it was a huge structure, undoubtedly the largest in the empire, which housed hundreds of gladiators, a large staff of trainers, referees, medical doctors, masseurs, armourers, maintenance personnel, administrative officials and their staff, and other functionaries. We know the names of two low-level managers of the *Ludus Magnus*, Nymphodotus and Hyacinthus. A man named Tigris served as a courier. A certain Demosthenes was a maker of the *manica* (perhaps also at the *Ludus Magnus*), a protective sleeve worn by gladiators. One of the most respected positions in the *ludus* were the trainer/ referees, former gladiators who had distinguished themselves in the arena and had been granted release from fighting and their freedom (more in Chapter 3). Trophimus was the name of a *secunda rudis* (instructor/referee second class) in the *Ludus Magnus* as probably was Q. Titius Lathricus. Cornelius Eugenianus and Flavius Sigerus, each a *summa rudis* (instructors/ referees first class), the former in Rome and the latter in Mauretanian Caesarea (North Africa). Another important functionary was the herald, whose job it was to communicate with the crowd in the arena. We do not have the name of a herald at the *Ludus Magnus*, but we meet a herald in an epitaph, T. Claudius Celer, who had served in that position in Ancona (central Italy) and whose burial was taken care of by a *secunda rudis* named Beryllus and all the officials of the *ludus*.[166]

Except for its monumental size, the plan of the *Ludus Magnus* is very much like that of the gladiatorial barracks of Pompeii, a structure with a central exercise area surrounded by living quarters (cells) for the gladiators attached to the inside of the outer walls (Figure 2). The one difference is that the exercise ground of the *Ludus Magnus* is surrounded by seating arranged in the oval shape of an amphitheatre. As one might expect, the arena of the *Ludus* is significantly smaller than that of the Colosseum, but still about the size of arenas outside of Rome. The seating could accom- modate as many as three thousand spectators, who could indulge their fascination with gladiators on a daily basis, watching them practise.[167] This is a good indication that fan interest was generated not just by bloodshed and death but also by an appreciation of the art of fencing, since gladia- tors practised with wooden swords or blunted metal swords. Imperial glad- iators at last had a home worthy of their talents in the greatest city of the empire.

Figure 2   A model of the *Ludus Magnus* showing the three tiers of gladiator quarters and the practice arena with seating Rome, Museo della Civiltà Romana. © Jona Lendering; from www.Livius.org, with permission

The high costs of gladiators

The steady rise in prices of gladiators during the late Republic and the early empire was fuelled by a mounting demand for them. One only has to compare the 4,000 sesterces required as a minimum expenditure for a *munus* given by the authorities in the Roman colony of Urso (modern Osuna) in Spain (middle 40s BC) with the cheapest category of *munus* offered free to the public (30,000–60,000 sesterces), as stipulated by imperial legislation late in the reign of Marcus Aurelius (AD 161–80).[168] Of course, allowance has to be made for inflation over a more than two-century period, but it should be noted that the figures given in the legislation were price controls establishing prices lower than they had been in the past.

As we shall see, almost every *editor* wanted to surpass his predecessors in the quantity and quality of his *munera*. Fortunes were lost in pursuit of bigger and better *munera*. During the early imperial period, there were attempts to prevent prodigal spending on *munera*. When Augustus gave the board of praetors control of *munera*, he tried to minimize the financial problems they might face by assigning them an appropriation from the imperial treasury to help defray their costs. He also forbade any one of the praetors to spend more than his colleagues and limited them to two *munera* a year with no more than sixty pairs of gladiators.[169] Augustus wanted to ensure that there would be no more ruinous competition among aristocrats with each trying to outdo his rivals at any cost. Tiberius, followed his adoptive father's policy in this matter. He decreed a reduction in the expenses of gladiatorial shows by strictly limiting the number gladiators in a *munus*.[170]

Competition among wealthy elites in the provinces, however, continued unabated and uncontrolled. By the end of the second century AD, the situation had reached a crisis. High priests of the imperial cult in various cities of the provinces were being bankrupted by their sponsorship of *munera* associated with the worship of the emperor.[171] We hear from one aristocrat in Gaul, who considered his fortune lost when he was appointed high priest and appealed to the emperors to be released from this onerous financial burden.[172] This complaint is contained in a famous inscription engraved in bronze called the *Aes Italicense* ('the bronze from Italica'), which was found in an amphitheatre near the Roman town of Italica in Spain (near Seville).[173] This inscription contains a record of a Senate discussion of a proposed decree of the co-emperors Marcus Aurelius and his son Commodus limiting the size of *munera* and the prices of gladiators in the provinces and outlines in detail how this is to be accomplished.[174] Imperial policy had contributed to the problem when Aurelius drafted gladiators into his armies fighting barbarian invasions from the north, creating a shortage in gladiators and a steep rise in their value.[175] The government also had imposed a 25–33 per cent tax on money made by *lanistae* on the rental of gladiators, who in turn passed this business expense on to their customers by increasing their prices for gladiators.[176] This tax brought an estimated 60–120 million sesterces annually into the imperial treasury, which *munerarii* throughout the empire were paying on top of the already inflated cost of the gladiators. David Bomgardner estimates the modern value of the tax at approximately £375 million–£750 million, or roughly $690 million–$1.5 billion.[177] This meant that *munerarii* throughout the empire were spending an enormous amount of money just on gladiators, not including the other major expense of a *munus*: the importation of animals for the *venationes* along with other necessary expenses. Thus, the emperors decided to repeal this tax and place controls on the prices of gladiators to protect *munerarii* from financial ruin.[178]

The emperors' proposal involved the creation of categories of *munera* and gladiators according to cost. The categories are differentiated according to the amount of money the *editor* was willing to spend, with subdivisions consisting of prices permitted for gladiators of various levels of quality, from high to low (except for the highest category in which the prices of gladiators are listed from low to high). The legislation does not take into account different types of gladiators (*retiarii, secutores*, etc.) and mentions only briefly *munera assiforana*, which were small gladiatorial shows given for profit, perhaps with the *lanista* as *editor*.[179] These shows were to retain their old limit in cost of 30,000 sesterces.[180]

Below, categories 1–4 refer to the range of the total cost of a show, while items a–e refer to classes of gladiators according to cost per gladiator. The first two categories of *munera* allow the *editor* to choose among three classes of gladiators, while the last two categories have five. (HS is the Roman abbreviation for sesterces.) As Michael Carter argues persuasively, the reason for this discrepancy is that the relative costs of gladiators in the legislation is based on the four *palus* ranks in the *ludus*, discussed earlier with the addition of the *tiro* class, the gladiator in training with no experience in the arena.[181] For example, in 1 and 2 below, c would be the cost of the *tiro*, b of the fourth *palus* and a of the third *palus*. The reason for the absence of the second and first *palus* in 1 and 2 is that it would be financially foolish to risk upper-level gladiators in these low-priced shows. As one would expect, all four categories of the *palus* ranking system (along with the *tiro* class) are accounted for in the five price levels of the two most expensive shows.

1) *31,000 to 60,000 HS*
   a. *5,000 HS*
   b. *4,000 HS*
   c. *3,000 HS*
2) *60,000 to 100,000 HS*
   a. *8,000 HS*
   b. *6,000 HS*
   c. *5,000 HS*

3) *100,000 to 150,000 HS*
   a. *12,000 HS*
   b. *10,000 HS*
   c. *8,000 HS*
   d. *6,000 HS*
   e. *5,000 HS*
4) *150,000 to 200,000 HS*
   a. *6,000 HS*
   b. *7,000 HS*
   c. *9,000 HS*
   d. *12,000 HS*
   e. *15,000 HS*[182]

The key provision to limiting spending is the requirement that the *editor* choose an equal number of gladiators from each class from high to low to counteract the tendency of *editores* to select only the most expensive gladiators to produce the best quality show. There is one other provision: in addition to the gladiators who fight in duels, the *munerarius* must rent an equal number of fighters called *gregarii* ('fighters in a group') who fight in small infantry skirmishes. These gladiators naturally were inferior in quality to the duellers. This difference is reflected in their price: 2,000 sesterces for a team leader and not less than 1,000 sesterces apiece for the rest. This provision of the legislation seems to be an attempt to 'beef up' the *munus* without significantly greater expense to compensate for the smaller number of duelling gladiators the *munerarius* would be able to hire. One illustrative example should be sufficient to explain how this system works. Suppose that the *munerarius* was willing to spend between 150,000 and 200,000 sesterces on gladiators who fought in pairs, the most expensive of the four categories of show (category 4 above). First, one needs a sense of perspective to appreciate how much the new imperial legislation benefited an *editor* of a high quality *munus*. In the middle of the first century AD, a character in Petronius speaks of a local patron in an unnamed Italian town being able to spend 400,000 sesterces on a *munus*.[183] Compare this outlay (which would have been significantly higher over a century later) to the cap of 200,000 sesterces allowed by law for the most costly *munus*. In order to keep within the prescribed range for expenditures on gladiators, he could choose three gladiators from each of the five classes, which would come to a total of 147,000 sesterces for fifteen gladiators, seven pairs with one gladiator to serve as a replacement. In addition, he would have to choose fifteen *gregarii* at a minimum of 1,000 sesterces apiece, except for the team leader, who would get 2,000 sesterces, for a total of 16,000 sesterces. The grand total would be 163,000 sesterces.[184] Besides the benefit of lower expenditure for a *munus*, another effect of these stipulations was to forestall accusations of stinginess against the *editor* for giving a bare bones show. After all, he was just following the law.

The problem with the model of the ratio of price to number of gladiators suggested above is that seven matches seems arguably much too low a number for the highest quality *munus* of the high priest at Pergamum, the most prominent provincial centre of the imperial cult in the Greek east, if not in the whole empire. There is, however, another possibility. Michael Carter maintains that these prices were not for the lease of the gladiators, but in fact represented their purchase value. He points out that the prices given in the legislation are comparable to the purchase prices of other kinds of slave performers. Thus, the lease price would be a percentage of the overall value of the gladiator. The lease rate for each gladiator would not be fixed, but determined by negotiation between the *lanista* and the representative of the high priest, anywhere from as low as 2 per cent to as high as 20 per cent or more. (Carter argues that the *editor* would not have wanted to have direct contact with the lowly *lanista*, who, like his charges, was contaminated with *infamia*.)[185] Some gladiators in the same price level would command a higher lease rate, while others would be leased at a lower rate.[186] It would all depend on the results of the bargaining. For the sake of argument, suppose that these two bargainers were negotiating in the context of the most expensive *munus* (category 4 above) and decided on an average lease rate of 10 per cent for the trained gladiators. This rate would allow the *editor* to hire twenty trained gladiators in each price class, a total of one hundred gladiators. The cost would be 98,000 sesterces for the trained gladiators and 101,000 sesterces for an equal number of *gregarii*, amounting to a total of 199,000 sesterces. Raise the average lease rate to 15 per cent and the total number of gladiators and *gregarii* would fall to eighty, while a 20 per cent lease rate would buy the services of sixty-five from both groups. These numbers of combatants would have been more in keeping with the quality of show expected of the high priests in provincial centres. There is, however, an unknown factor here. Did the 200,000 sesterces cap include just the combatants or all the expenses of the *munus* like those outlined by Carter?

> . . . *officials to oversee the combats, animals for a* venatio, *and perhaps convicts* (damnati*) to be publicly executed . . ., not mention the costs of advertisement, gifts to be distributed to the people and preparing the amphitheatre . . . for the show.*[187]

If the cap included all expenses for the *munus*, the *editor* would have had to scale back dramatically the numbers of leased gladiators mentioned above to keep within the cap. Another expense of the *editor* cited by Carter (which likely did not count under the cap) is the huge sum that the *editor* would have had to put on deposit upfront to reimburse the *lanista* with the full purchase price for any gladiators seriously injured or killed in the *munus*. The *editor* could control this post-*munus* expense to some degree by ignoring the request of spectators to kill losing gladiators, but this practice came with the serious risk of losing the favour of the people, which he was seeking to win with the *munus*. On the other hand, however, the lower expenditures thanks to the legislation might have encouraged some *editores* to make more crowd-pleasing decisions.

Given the fact that the financial tables had been turned on the *lanistae* and they were feeling the crunch of lower prices for their product, it is likely that they would have held out for higher lease rates, especially in the case of *editores* willing to spend the highest amount of money allowed by the new law. The new limits on spending for *munera* represented a steep decline in cash flow for the *lanista* in comparison with the *munera* of the past. Moreover, some *lanistae* still owed back taxes on gladiator sales to the amount of more than 5 million sesterces, a debt that Marcus Aurelius and his son Commodus had proposed to forgive, at least in part, to relieve the financial pressure that their new decree put on the *lanistae*.[188]

Another cost-saving measure of this legislation applied only to Roman Gaul. There was an ancient and eagerly anticipated sacrificial ritual involving the death of victims called *trinqui* at spectacles given during the celebration of the imperial cult at Lyons, where the council of the three Gauls (Lucdunum, Belgica and Aquitania) convened. The measure put controls on the price that provincial procurators could charge *lanistae* for *damnati* to serve as *trinqui* (six gold coins or 600 sesterces per man) and on the price that *lanistae* could charge the high priests of the imperial cult who served as *munerarii* (2,000 sesterces per man).[189] This price control was very beneficial to the Gallic *munerarii*, who undoubtedly did not want to disappoint spectators by reducing the size of, or even omitting, this traditional part of the festivities. In 1955, Oliver and Palmer proposed a theory that the cheaper prices for *damnati* explains the famous persecution of Christians at Lyons in AD 177, who, instead of expensive gladiators, were used as *trinqui*.[190] This theory enjoyed general acceptance for a time, but in 1972 Musurillo pointed out that there is no support for this thesis in the ancient sources and other scholars proposed other more compelling reasons for the executions of Christians at Lyons.[191]

There was one other measure in this legislation that dealt with the financial plight of the provincial high priests. The decree sanctioned an informal practice of high priests in various provinces, which effectively passed over the *lanista* in the process of obtaining gladiators. In order to cut the costs of hiring gladiators, priests in some provinces, upon entering office, bought gladiators who had been purchased and trained by their predecessors. At the end of his term, he then would sell the gladiators to his successor at a higher price. The only stipulation that the decree adds is that the sale prices must follow its dictates, which were primarily designed to restrain the greed of *lanistae*.[192] Another benefit of the new legislation was the replacements for injured and dead gladiators for priestly *familiae* could be purchased from *lanistae* at more reasonable prices.

We do not know how effective this legislation was in solving the economic crisis. One would guess that it must have had at least temporary success, but more economic problems were coming. Inflation was creating a major economic problem during the third century as evidenced by Diocletian's edict in AD 301, which set maximum prices, in all probability including outlay for gladiators.[193] The cost of a *munus* was still a major problem in the late fourth century. A letter from the city prefect of Rome, Symmachus, to the emperors Theodosius and Arcadius in the late fourth century speaks of a need to limit expenses for shows including *munera* and warns of the possibility of wealthy men leaving the city to avoid the expense of a *munus*.[194]

Chapter 3

Gladiator Games in Action

Preliminaries

The *munus*, whether large or small, required elaborate preparation. The *editor* had to allow sufficient time for procuring a worthy gladiator troupe and all the apparatus necessary for putting on a show. Machinery and stage properties were part of the tradition of *munera*, especially in amphitheatres with an underground area. Procrastination by the *editor* could only result in a cancelled show. The architect Vitruvius stresses promptness as an essential quality of the sponsor of a *munus*:

> This fault [of the patron not being able to finish the task] exists not only in the case of constructing buildings but also in shows that are given by magistrates in the forum, whether of gladiators or of stage plays. To these magistrates neither delay nor postponement is allowed, but necessity compels them to complete the different aspects of the project in a limited amount of time, such as seats for the spectators, the putting in place of the awnings, and whatever, in accordance with the practices of show business, is provided for the people by means of machinery for their viewing pleasure.[1]

Advertisement

After obtaining gladiators by rent or purchase, one of the *editor*'s first concerns was the advertisement of his upcoming show. This involved having professional painters paint announcements called *edicta munerum* ('announcements of gladiator shows') on the walls of houses and public buildings. We know a good deal about these *edicta* from inscriptions in and around Pompeii. These announcements regularly contain the following information: the name of the *editor*, his credentials, the reason for the show, the contents of the show, the town or city in which show will be given, date(s), and any special features that might make the *munus* more appealing to potential spectators.[2] Sometimes the *editor* adds a condition to the date. An *editor* in his advertisement of a *munus* that was going to take place in late February or early March (the damaged text of the inscription is unclear on this matter) indicates to prospective spectators that the *munus* will be held on these dates only 'if the weather allows'.[3] This was a prudent warning for a *munus* given in these late winter months. On the other hand, another *editor*, advertising a *munus* to take place in July when he could be more confident of good weather, announces that his show will be held on the assigned date 'come rain or shine'.[4] The price of a seat never appears because, as noted earlier, almost all *munera*, whether in Rome or in the rest of the empire, were given as gifts to the citizens by prominent members of the community. The information given by these *edicta* is presented in hierarchical form from more to less important. The gladiatorial combat as the main feature of the *munus* is always mentioned first after the name of the *editor*, but no individual names of the gladiators are given unless their fame made them an extraordinary attraction.[5] Even imperial gladiators, except on rare occasions, are only referred to by their title: *Iulianus* or *Neronianus*. The beast hunt (*venatio*), a morning prelude to the afternoon gladiator show, is usually mentioned next, and with gladiatorial combat forms the nucleus of the *munus legitimum* ('a proper *munus*').[6] The most common added feature of *munera* is the presence of awnings, which were most desirable in the spring and summer, when spectators needed to be shaded from the hot Mediterranean sun.[7] Most *munera* were held in the spring, but awnings were not guaranteed by every *editor*, even at warmer times of the year.[8] As one would expect, awnings were not usually provided in the late autumn or winter, but there are even exceptions to this rule.[9] A less common added feature

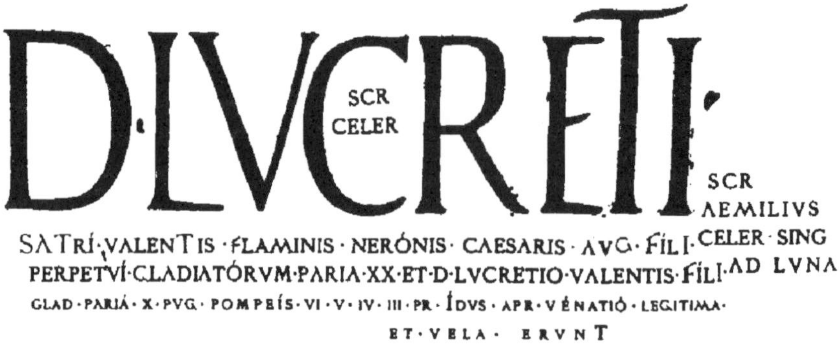

DLVCRETI·

SCR
CELER

SCR
AEMILIVS

SATRí·VALENTIS ·FLAMINIS· NERÓNIS· CAESARIS · AVG· FíLI· CELER· SING
PERPETVí·CLADIATÓRVM·PARIA·XX·ET·D·LVCRETIO·VALENTIS·FíLI·AD LVNA
GLAD · PARIÁ · X · PVG · POMPEíS · VI · V · IV · III · PR · íDVS · APR · V ÉNATIÓ · LEGITIMA ·
ET·VELA· ERVNT

Figure 3   *Edictum* of D. Lucretius Satrius Valens. Inscription painted in red in Region IX, insula 8 in Pompeii. Upon authorization of the Italian Ministry for Cultural Heritage and Environment

is the *sparsio* (literally, 'scattering' or 'sprinkling') which entails the distribution of gifts and/or the sprinkling of perfumed (with saffron) water on the crowd.[10] The introductory parade (*pompa*) of gladiators led by the *editor*, was not often included in advertisement. Perhaps it was such a regular feature of the *munus* that it seemed unnecessary to advertise it. One inscription does mention the *pompa*, but the show advertised lacks a gladiator show and consists only of secondary features such as a *venatio*, Greek sports, and *sparsiones*.[11] Thus the mention of the *pompa* is probably included because the *editor* wanted to inform his prospective spectators that, despite the absence of gladiators, the *pompa* would still be included in his show, but on this occasion consisting only of arena hunters and the other participants.[12]

An interesting example of an *edictum muneris* is the one advertising a *munus* given at Pompeii by a certain D. Lucretius Satrius Valens (Figure 3).[13] A translation of the inscription reads as follows:

> *Twenty pairs of gladiators of D. Lucretius Satrius Valens, priest for life* [flamen perpetuus] *of Nero Caesar, [adopted] son of Augustus [the Emperor Claudius], and ten pairs of gladiators of his son D. Lucretius Valens will fight at Pompeii from April 8 to 12.*[14] *There will also be a proper* [legitima] *beast hunt and awnings.*

Note that Lucretius specifies the number of pairs he and his son will present. Lucretius undoubtedly gives this information because thirty pairs of gladiators was a large number for a *munus* outside of Rome, and the quantity of gladiators was an important feature of a *munus*. If these matches were spread out evenly, there would be six matches a day for the five-day period.

Often no specific numbers are given in these *edicta*, which no doubt indicates that the number of pairs involved was not terribly impressive, otherwise the exact number would have been proudly proclaimed. The usual formula when specific numbers are not given is that 'a gladiatorial troupe (*familia gladiatoria*) of so and so will fight at Pompeii . . .'.[15] The mention of Lucretius' office as *flamen* of the emperor Nero reveals that he, as chief priest of the imperial cult, belongs to the most elite level of Pompeian society. The *venatio* is called *legitima* for the same reason as the number of pairs of gladiators is mentioned: to set off this *munus* from other lesser shows. A *venatio legitima* was one that included all the animals that a spectator could expect: large cats, bulls, bears, deer and boar.[16] It is clear that Lucretius had opened up his deep pockets and had spent very generously for this *munus*. In the inscription, his abbreviated *praenomen* (like our first name) and his surname appear in large capital letters, an indication of the pride that Lucretius took in his presentation. These large letters are also meant to catch the eye of the passer-by. Note that the awnings are provided even in the middle of April. This inscription is also notable because of the information that the painter included within and to the right of the *edictum*: *SCR CELER* ('Celer painted this') surrounded by the curve of the C of Lucretius and *SCR AEMILIUS CELER SING AD LUNA* ('Aemilius Celer painted this all by himself by the light of the moon').[17] The painting of this announcement in the middle of the night no doubt was intended to give Pompeians a pleasant surprise as they noticed the *edictum* early the next morning. Celer, indicating twice that he was the painter of this *edictum* in addition to mentioning the difficulty of the task, manages to give this advertisement for a *munus* the additional function of billboard for his own services.

An *edictum* of Nigidius Maius, another outstanding citizen of Pompeii, announces a *munus* with an *editor*'s proudest boast: that all expenses for the show will come from his own pocket with no contribution from the town treasury:

> *Twenty pairs of gladiators and substitutes* [suppositicii], *presented by the* quinquennalis, *Cn. Alleius Nigidius Maius without any cost to the citizenry, will fight at Pompeii.*[18]

It is odd that this inscription does not mention the date(s) of its presentation. I have no satisfactory explanation for this omission. Perhaps this inscription was an early general announcement which was followed up by a later and more specific one. The reference to 'substitutes' (*suppositicii*) has been interpreted in various ways. Some take it to mean that the winner of each of the twenty matches presented by Nigidius would have to fight another gladiator. The problem is that this arrangement would double the number of matches and the *editor* would have to rent sixty gladiators instead of just forty. It would in all probability have doubled the length of the spectacle.[19] More likely, these *suppositicii* were replacements that the *editor* employed under certain circumstances to maintain the goodwill of the spectators. For example, a *suppositicius* might replace a gladiator who had fought badly and lost very quickly or perhaps had been incapacitated in some way before the match. A *suppositicius* might even be called upon to test the endurance and ability of a winning gladiator who had revealed extraordinary strength and skill in the previous match. There might even be a less worthy motive. On one occasion, the emperor Caracalla forced a gladiator named Bato to fight two *suppositicii* after winning his first match. Not surprisingly, Bato was killed in the third match and in recognition of his performance was honoured by the emperor with a splendid funeral. Cassius Dio attributes Caraclla's use of substitutes in this case to his desire to see as much blood as possible in the arena.[20]

Nigidius most likely provided an unstated number of back-ups but probably not one for every match. This promise of substitutes reassured spectators that they were likely to see twenty good matches. He employed this back-up policy in at least one other *munus*.[21] Martial uses the term *suppositicius* in his praise of the great gladiator Hermes: 'Hermes is alone a substitute for himself'.[22] What Martial means is that there is no one who can replace Hermes and thus a *suppositicius* is unnecessary when he fights.[23] There is another term, *tertiarius* (literally, 'third'), which at first might seem synonymous with *suppositicius*, but is not. *Tertiarius* appears in a passage in Petronius' *Satyricon* in which the speaker criticizes an *editor* for his parsimonious ways:

> *He presented horsemen* [equites] *as small as those who appear in lamp decorations, you would think them farmyard roosters, one as thin as a rail, the other, bow-legged, another gladiator, a* tertiarius, *was a dead man who replaced a dead man, who had torn tendons. Another was a* thraex *of some quality, but he fought mechanically.*[24]

A *tertiarius* ('third man') would seem to be different from a *suppositicius*, who only fought when needed. The *tertiarius* was probably scheduled from the beginning to fight the winner of a given match. It is significant that the *tertiarius* appears in this passage complaining about a stingy *editor*. The device of the *tertiarius* allowed the *editor* to present more matches at lower cost, in essence two matches for the price of three, rather than four, gladiators. In the Petronius passage above, the *tertiarius*, like the other gladiators in the show, was worthless, virtually a dead man like the corpse he replaced. On the other hand, it would make sense that the *tertiarius* would usually have the advantage, since most winners of the first match were likely to be in no condition to give the fresher *tertiarius* a good fight.[25] In either case, the participation of a *tertiarius* virtually assured a match of diluted quality, but significant savings for the *editor*. An *editor* named Nonius Bassus provides another example of parsimony. An honorific commemoration of a *munus* he presented calls the forty scheduled pairs of gladiators he presented *ordinarii*, a term that means only the gladiators scheduled to appear fought.[26] He did not follow the generous custom that allowed the crowd to request the *editor* to add unscheduled matches at the end of the *munus*. As we have seen in the previous chapter, gladiators who fought in these extra duels were called *postulaticii* ('request gladiators').[27]

There is an additional comment to right of the text of the Nigidius Maius *edictum* (not included in the translation above) that is difficult to make complete sense of, but it is clearly an encomium to a certain Telephus, identified as a *summa rudis* (often written as one word: *summarudis*). He is complimented as an 'ornament of the *munus*'. The *rudis* was a wooden rod awarded by a *munerarius* to a gladiator, which symbolized his permanent release from service as a gladiator. Modern texts sometimes mistakenly call the *rudis* a wooden sword. The confusion stems from the use of the word *rudis* for both instruments, but the wooden sword used as a training device is always in the plural in Latin (*rudes*) with a singular meaning whereas the rod is always in the singular (*rudis*).[28]

The recipient of the *rudis* was known as a *rudiarius*. This reward was generally proclaimed by an *editor* urged on by the crowd during the *munus*.[29] The title of *summarudis* ('retired gladiator first class') was given only to the most distinguished of these *rudiarii*. They served as instructors in gladiatorial schools and/or referees of gladiator combats.[30] (The word is commonly used with the latter meaning.) As is evident from this inscription, these retired gladiators were greatly revered in the west and in the Greek east. There is an epitaph of a *summarudis* named Aelius inscribed on an altar in Ancyra (modern Ankara), whom the epitaph describes as 'an illustrious citizen of Pergamum' and 'belonging to an association of retired gladiators first class in Rome'.[31] The inscription goes on to list other important Greek cities that had honored him with citizenship, such as Thessalonika, Nicomedia, Larisa, Philippopolis, Apros, Berge, Thasos and Byza. To be awarded citizenship in a city not of one's birth was one of the highest honours in the ancient world. It is interesting to see what a difference a distinguished retirement made in the life of gladiator, who would never have been honoured in this way during his active career.[32] Removed from the *infamia* of a career as a gladiator, the *summarudis* became eligible for public honours. *Rudiarii* also enjoyed significant prestige. There was a strong demand for their appearance in the arena as gladiators. In the 20s BC, Tiberius paid 100,000 sesterces each to *rudiarii* to fight in funeral *munera* for his father and grandfather.[33] Appearance fees for *rudiarii* could go as high as 240,000 sesterces.[34]

Anticipation of the *munus*

A *munus* at Rome or anywhere else in the empire was a much anticipated event and this expectation was at least in part due the sporadic presentations of *munera*. It is sometimes wrongly assumed that gladiator games were almost a daily event in Rome, but this is far from the truth. In the Republic and the imperial period, gladiator games were a relative rarity, even under emperors who were active givers of spectacles, and that rarity was an important factor in the popularity of the games.[35] When Augustus gave control over the presentation of state-sponsored *munera* to the board of praetors, he forbade them to give a *munus* more than twice a year. Later in the first century AD, when the organization of these regularly scheduled gladiator games was transferred to the board of quaestors, the quaestors gave one *munus* annually in December. But even these regularly scheduled *munera* were suspended occasionally, depending on the whim of the emperor. All other *munera* were one-time events produced on special occasions by the emperor or sponsors favoured and approved by him, although, by the end of the first century AD, the giving of *munera* was virtually the province of the emperor alone. Even imperially sponsored *munera* might be suspended for long periods if an emperor, like Tiberius, was not particularly fond of gladiatorial games or a bloodless version substituted, as in the case of Marcus Aurelius. In towns of Italy, grass-roots pressure from the people was frequently a factor in inducing local elite, especially those whom they had entrusted with public office, to give a *munus* along with other entertainments. The formulaic phrase 'at the request of the people' (*postulante populo* or its equivalent) is often found in inscriptions praising these patrons for obliging their fellow citizens.[36] These inscriptions sometimes stress how quickly the patron responded favourably to the will of the people.[37] This is not to say, however, that there were not elites who were more than willing to take the initiative in return for the gratitude and favour of their fellow citizens. One sponsor in the town of Circeii (modern San Felice Circeo), apparently without any pressure from the people, built an amphitheatre at his own expense, and dedicated it with gladiatorial combat and a *venatio*.[38] When L. Flavius Silva Nonius Bassus, one of Vespasian's generals (and himself a Flavian), built an amphitheatre for his fellow citizens in Urbs Salvia (modern Urbisaglia) and dedicated it with a *munus*, he was no doubt inspired by Vespasian's building of the Colosseum and Titus' dedicatory *munus* rather by than any demands of the people.[39]

The emotional involvement of the people with a *munus* began when the show was first advertised, and grew to a fever pitch until the *munus* took place. The anticipation might be compared to a child's impatient wait for Christmas to come. Seneca uses the example of an approaching *munus* to illustrate the psychological condition of someone anticipating a future pleasure: 'Just as when the day of a gladiatorial *munus* is announced . . . they wish that the intervening days fly by. Every delay of an anticipated event is impossibly long'.[40] The excitement aroused by an upcoming *munus* can also be seen, and even felt, in this passage from Apuleius' *Metamorphoses* about an imminent *munus* in Greece:

> *There [in Plataea, a city in Greece] we heard frequent rumour about a certain Demochares, who was about to give a gladiatorial* munus. *He was a man from the noblest of families and extremely wealthy and outstanding in his generosity; he was going to provide pleasures for the people with a splendour worthy of his wealth. Who has a sufficient gift of eloquence to be able to describe in suitable words each and every aspect of the varied magnificence [of his show]?*[41]

A passage in Petronius' *Satryicon* describes in detail what excites the average man about an upcoming *munus*. It would appear that the speaker has seen an advertisement of the *munus* and cannot contain his enthusiasm. Besides the guarantee of significant bloodshed and death, the central attraction, the *editor* had promised the appearance of dwarf gladiators and a female chariot fighter (*essedaria*) as exotic sideshows. Perhaps even more tantalizing is the scheduled execution of a slave steward for having had sex with his master's wife. As a feature of the *venatio*, he will be thrown to the wild animals (*ad bestias*), but what is even better, his execution will provoke a dispute between two factions in the crowd. One faction consists of jealous husbands expressing satisfaction at the death of a slave caught in adultery with his master's wife; the other, characterized as 'lovers', will support the slave, excusing him because the master's wife is a slut and had probably forced him to have sex with her. No doubt, many public executions were routine and not terribly interesting to the crowd, but here, the acquaintance of the spectators with the details of the slave's offence and their different opinions about the execution would make this event even more interesting and exciting.[42] Enthusiastic anticipation was notably evident when Julius Caesar was about to present his grand triumphal games in 46 BC. No inconvenience was enough to discourage attendance at these games, especially the *munus*. Fans from the towns of Italy, who came to Rome for the show, had to stay in tents set up in the streets and along roads. The crowd was so great that some people, including two senators, were crushed to death.[43]

Cena libera

Another component of the preparation for the *munus* was the so-called 'free dinner', which was given by the *editor* and took place on the eve of the spectacle. The word 'free' as applied to *cena* suggests to us a dinner you do not have to pay for. *Liber*, however, is not used in this sense in Latin, but means something like 'limitless' or 'free from restriction'. As applied to *cena*, it probably had a double connation: a dinner unlimited in quantity at which one can indulge one's appetite to the fullest. The invitees were all the participants in the next day's *munus*: gladiators, beast fighters and condemned criminals (*damnati*) who were to be put to death in the arena the next day. This custom seems to be in the tradition of the condemned man's last meal, but this was only true of the *damnati*.[44] Gladiators and beast fighters probably enjoyed this meal more, since their death was by no means certain. The menu was an enticing one, consisting of costly foods with an invitation to indulge one's appetite to the limit. Plutarch writes of the food 'pleasing the stomach'.[45] One of the purposes of this dinner was the expression by the *editor* of his gratitude to the participants in the show, whose suffering and death would bring him great public favour.[46] A North African mosaic from El Djem (modern Tunisia) may show a boisterous drinking party in the amphitheatre following a *cena libera*. It depicts five partygoers reclining at table, probably professional *venatores* who the next day will fight the sleeping bulls depicted at the bottom of the picture. The five revellers have presumably been partaking of the wine contained in a large mixing bowl and two jugs in front of the table, offered to them by an attendant on the right. Above the head of each reveller is a short inscription: 'We will take our clothes off! We have come to drink! You all are talking too much! Let's have fun!' The fifth inscription ('We are holding three!') is quite cryptic and there is no satisfactory explanation of this comment. The revellers must have been getting quite boisterous, because another attendant on the left warns them: 'Silence! Let the bulls sleep!'[47]

The *cena libera* was often held in a public place such as the town forum, with tables set out in the open air.[48] The meal would have taken place in the late afternoon. The public was invited to observe the participants in this dinner and even talk to them. The location and the involvement of the public suggest another purpose of the *cena*: advertisement. The *munus* would take place, or at least begin, on the next day and the anticipation of the show was pushed to a peak by this dinner. If the public had any doubt about attending, the *cena* might change their minds.

The evidence suggests that more went on at the *cena libera* than overindulgent eating. A passage in Plutarch speaks of Greek gladiators ignoring the food and making provision for their wives by entrusting them to their friends and freeing their slaves in the event of their death in the arena.[49] In essence, these gladiators were making their wills, showing consideration for those whom they would leave behind if they were killed in the arena. The anonymous account of the martyrdom of Perpetua and her friends has preserved for us some interesting information about the behaviour of Christian *damnati* at a *cena libera*. The author of this account describes the dinner as an expression of spiritual love (*agape*) among Christians rather than as a typical *cena libera*. That love, however, did not extend to pagan observers at the *cena*, whose curiosity obviously annoyed the Christians. They were quick to respond harshly to the inquisitiveness of visitors to the dinner. Citing the happiness that they will find in the next day's suffering, they threaten observers with the judgement of god.[50] Apparently, these Christian *damnati* were more tolerant of pain and suffering than of attempts to humiliate them; on the other hand, they had much to be bitter about.

The *munus*: events preceding gladiatorial combat

Pompa

The *pompa* ('procession') was a regular feature of the *munus*. It got the *munus* off to a dignified start and offered an excellent opportunity for the spectators to express with applause and shouts (*acclamatio*) their gratitude to the sponsor, who led off the procession. Figure 4 is the top panel of three of a bas-relief depiction of a *pompa* from Pompeii. The other panels present the two main events of the *munus*: gladiatorial combat and the *venatio*.[51] The procession, which is to be viewed from right to left, begins at the far right of the top segment. The first person in the procession is about to enter the arena, which is indicated by the triangular object in the upper right hand corner, probably a representation of the awnings (*vela*), a frequently advertised feature of the *munus*.[52] The first two figures wearing togas at the head of the procession are lictors, usually attendants of magistrates with executive

Figure 4 Pompeian bas-relief: *pompa*. Necropolis at the Stabian Gate. (The panel has been divided into two segments, one above the other.) Naples, Museo Archeologico Nazionale

powers.[53] Lictors, however, may been provided as an honorary escort to all *editores*, even those who were not magistrates. Behind the lictors are three trumpeters, who provided musical accompaniment for the procession.[54] Then come two armourers working on gladiatorial armament carried on a platform by four slaves.[55] The sculptor's inclusion of armourers in the procession is probably a reference to the examination of arms (*probatio armorum*) by the *editor*, which took place in the arena after the procession was finished. In this ceremony, the *editor* would check all gladiatorial armament, especially the swords and daggers to see if they were sharp enough to do real damage. We hear of the emperor Titus allowing two aristocrats, who were plotting against him, to perform this task as he sat close by them in order to assure them that he did not intend to do them any harm.[56] The next two figures are arena attendants (*ministri*), one carrying a tablet, which could be used to transmit information to the spectators, and the other a palm branch, a symbolic award given to victorious gladiators. The figure in the toga behind the attendants is no doubt the *editor* himself dressed in a toga, the star of the *pompa*, who is looking back at six *ministri* (two on the far left of the top segment and four on the far right of the bottom) carrying shields and helmets of the gladiators who will fight later. Undoubtedly the gladiators themselves would have also taken part in the actual procession but were probably omitted from the bas-relief to save space.[57] In any case, they are depicted in action in a lower panel not included here.[58] We have no information about the identity of this *editor*. He could have been a *duovir* of Pompeii, one of the two executive officers of the town, or a priest of the local imperial cult (like D. Lucretius Satrius Valens above) or even a wealthy private citizen. Although the *editor* of a *munus* was normally a man of great social and political stature in the community, wealthy freedmen occasionally gave *munera* in their home towns. Not surprisingly, the poet Martial expresses contempt for these low-born *editores*: 'A shoemaker gave you a *munus*, cultured Bononia [modern Bologna]; a fuller gave one for you Mutina [modern Modena]: what's next, an innkeeper?'[59] After the attendants carrying shields and helmets comes another attendant carrying an unidentifiable object in his left hand. Behind him is a musician playing a short curved trumpet (*lituus*). The procession ends with two *ministri* leading horses which will be ridden into combat by gladiators known as 'horsemen' (*equites*), who traditionally appeared in the opening event of the *munus*.

In Lucian's *Toxaris*, we hear of another kind of parade of gladiators, called a *propompē* ('a procession in advance [of the event]'), which takes place three days before a *munus* presented in the city of Amastris (southern shore of the Black Sea). This parade consists of young men hired to fight in the *munus*, who march through the town's forum beginning early in the morning to advertise the *munus*.[60] There is no unequivocal evidence that processions of gladiators took place before the day of the *munus* in Italy for the purpose of advertisement. It has been suggested, however, that gladiators belonging to one of Julius Caesar's assassins (D. Brutus) might have gathered at Pompey's theatre on the day of the assassination under the pretext of advertising an upcoming *munus*.[61] If this were the case, their real purpose would have been to protect the assassins after Caesar's murder.

Venatio

Up until the early empire, gladiatorial combat and the *venatio* were, for the most part, stand-alone events, but a kind of natural attraction gradually brought them together so that eventually the *venatio* joined with the gladiator show in the same day-long event.[62] The *venatio* had much in common with gladiatorial combat. Both involved violent fights that could end in death for either opponent. The lives of gladiators, beast fighters and even their animal opponents could be spared by the *munerarius* because of courageous fighting. All these arena performers could win fame and glory by outstanding performances in the arena. The primary meaning of the word *venatio* was 'hunt in the wild', but applied to a spectacle, it meant 'a staged hunt in the arena'.[63] As a spectacle, the *venatio* featured human hunters attempting to kill animals of all kinds and sizes, but especially large and dangerous predators such as lions, tigers, leopards, bears and even elephants. There were two kinds of beast fighter, a *venator* ('hunter') and a *bestiarius*, literally 'a beast man', i.e. 'one who fought wild animals'. The difference has been interpreted variously, but I believe that, at least during the Republic, it was mostly a matter of equipment and dress. The *venator* wore no armour and his weapons were the *venabulum* ('thrusting spear') and the *lancea* ('a light throwing spear'), whereas the *bestiarius* resembled a gladiator with helmet, shield and sword.

The arena *venator* wore a tunic like his real-life counterpart who pursued prey in the wild running after his dogs (Figure 5).[64] Speed was an essential

Figure 5 Venator spears leopard. Galleria Borghese, Rome, Italy/Alinari/Bridgeman Art Library Ltd

attribute of the hunter both in the arena and in the wild.[65] Although Italian hunters hunted small prey and even larger prey such as boar in Italy, they did not have the experience of dealing with the kinds of large and dangerous predators that were imported from North Africa and other parts of the empire. Thus, it is not surprising that during the first century or so of the *venatio*, native hunters were imported along with their prey. These foreign hunters were familiar with the hunting of large prey such as lions, leopards and elephants. For example, in 93 BC, Sulla gave a *venatio* in which one hundred lions, a gift of King Bocchus in Mauretania (modern Morocco), were for the first time allowed to range freely in the arena.[66] The king also sent native Mauretanian spear throwers no doubt because of their expertise in hunting these animals back home. There were probably no hunters available in Italy who could have served as worthy opponents to these powerful animals. Lucius Domitius Ahenobarbus in 61 BC imported a hundred Ethiopian hunters to fight the same number of Numidian bears.[67] When Pompey staged a *venatio* that involved a group of twenty elephants, he brought in skilled Gaetulian hunters (modern southern Algeria).[68] When crocodiles were first exhibited in Rome sometime in the late first century BC or early first century AD, they were escorted by crocodile hunters from the Egyptian town of Tentyra (modern Dendera) who supervised their display in the arena.[69] Imported hunters with long familiarity with their prey probably served another purpose: the feeding and care of the animals before the show. By the first century AD, foreign hunters whose skills were honed in real hunts in the wild became less necessary. A class of professional hunters had begun to be developed in Italy, who were recruited from the same sources as gladiators and trained in a school for arena hunters to kill large predators.[70]

The *bestiarius*, on the other hand, was entirely a creature of the arena. In fact, *bestiarii* may originally have been gladiators transferred to the *venatio*, using the same armour and wielding a sword (Figure 6). Gladiators and *bestiarii* were linked in the Roman mind. On one occasion a politician, accused of illegally giving a gladiatorial *munus*, defended himself by claiming that the participants in his spectacle were not gladiators but *bestiarii*.[71] Although this transparently false claim was weakened by the obvious difference between gladiator games and a *venatio*, this rationalization would have been completely nonsensical if it had not been for the similarity of these two types

Figure 6 Bestiarius and *venator* in the Circus Maximus. Museo Nazionale Terme Rome/Gianni Dagli Orti/The Art Archive

of fighters. Cicero refers to gladiators and *bestiarii* in the same breath as armed guards of his friend Milo.[72] A speaker in Petronius' *Satyricon* criticizing inept gladiators he had seen in a recent show compares them unfavourably to *bestiarii*, who apparently were considered inferior sword fighters.[73] The *bestiarius* and the *venator* could appear together in the same *venatio*, as can be seen in Figure 6.

It should be noted that Junkelmann sees the gladiator-like fighters who appear in artistic representations of *venationes* as only a different type of *venator* and points out that the heavy-armed hunter disappeared from artistic representations, leaving the light-armed *venator* as the main human actor in the *venatio*. Like most other scholars, he identifies the *bestiarius* as an assistant to the *venator* who served as animal keepers and provoked the animals to fight in the arena.[74] This indeed may have been true of the later imperial period, but I believe that the evidence shows that the *bestiarius*, at least until the mid-first century AD, had been a heavy-armed fighter of wild animals. The incorporation of the *venatio* into the *munus* may have been a critical factor in the demotion of the *bestiarius* as a heavy-armed beast fighter to a subordinate of the *venator*. Perhaps the givers of this new form of *munus* wanted the variety created by limiting the fighter with shield and other armour to gladiatorial combat as a contrast to the light-armed *venator* who fought without any body armour at all. Seneca twice refers to a *ludus bestiarius* ('beast fighter school'), which seems to indicate that *bestiarii* were still being trained as professional beast fighters in the mid-first century, but I suspect that this was just a popular name preserving an old usage that was popularly applied to the official name of the school: *Ludus Matutinus*.[75] The name used in Justinian's *Digest* may reflect more accurately the character of the animal fighters school in the imperial period: *ludus venatorius* ('the school for *venatores*').[76] In this period, the word *bestiarius* seems to have referred primarily to someone condemned to be thrown to the beasts (*ad bestias*).[77] The term is appropriate to those who incurred this penalty because they were sometimes given weapons (but no defensive armour) to use against the beasts or were expected to fight unarmed. We know that Julius Caesar, in 65 BC, gave silver-plated weapons to convicts who were thrown to the beasts.[78] Although silver-plating may have enhanced the look of these weapons, it certainly would not have improved their effectiveness. Even regular weapons given to *noxii* were purposely not of sufficient quality to be effective fighting tools. The object of this penalty was to make the execution as entertaining as possible without interfering with its desired result: death for the *noxius*.

In discussing Claudius' interest in arena events, Suetonius links *bestiarii* closely with the *meridiani*, literally 'the noon people', suggesting that *bestiarii* were victims thrown to the beasts during the *venatio* whereas the *meridiani* were *noxii* who incurred other forms of execution at the noonday spectacle, which immediately followed the *venatio*.[79] A Senecan anecdote reveals even more clearly the *bestiarius* as a man who is thrown to the beasts. In the arena, a lion recognizes his former trainer among the *bestiarii* and rescues him from the other lions.[80] The *bestiarii* here seem more to be virtually helpless victims rather than professional beast fighters. A late piece of evidence from Tertullian refers to the *bestiarius* 'as an evil man', that is, a *noxius* condemned to death in the arena.[81]

Although the word *venatio* refers primarily to the battle between men and wild animals, it is also an umbrella term that includes a number of other events: animals fighting other animals, exhibition of exotic animals seen at Rome for the first time, executions of *noxii* by being thrown 'to the beasts', and presentation of performing animals. Images from the famous Zliten mosaic provide us with important evidence about these various events of the *venatio*. Sometimes those condemned to face the beasts were bound to a stationary post in the ground or on a platform, or in a little cart (Figure 7) or were just restrained from behind by an attendant (Figure 8). Another way of forcing *damnati* to face the animals was to whip them from behind (Figure 8), a technique sometimes used on reluctant gladiators.[82]

Large beasts fighting each other was a favourite attraction of the *venatio*. Seneca reports that bulls and bears were often tied together and when one animal was victorious, the other, if not dead, was then killed by a *confector* (literally, 'a finisher'), whose job it was to kill animals that had been seriously wounded but not killed by their opponent.[83] The winning animal might even fight another day (depending on its condition).

Figure 9 shows us a bear and bull linked together with a wounded wild ass in the lower left-hand corner. In this case, two chains attached to a metal ring connect them, rousing both animals to a fury because of their inability to detach themselves. A *noxius* is forced to perform the unenviable task of unlinking with a curved stick these two ferocious beasts in the frenzy of battle. In all likelihood, one or both of these animals eventually would be provoked enough by his proximity to turn on him. The fear that the *noxius*

Figure 7   Zliten mosaic: *noxius* in cart attacked by leopard. Villa at Dar Buc Amméra, Tripolitania. Archaeological Museum, Tripoli. Roger Wood/Corbis

Figure 8   Zliten mosaic: *noxius* forced by man to confront a leopard. Gilles Mermet/akg-images Ltd

Figure 9 Zliten mosaic: bear, bull and *noxius*. Villa at Dar Buc Amméra, Tripolitania. Archaeological Museum, Tripoli. Roger Wood/Corbis

feels in attempting to accomplish this task is shown by his tentative approach. He steps widely to keep himself at the greatest possible distance from the animals as he tries to detach them.[84]

Indeed, wild animals in the arena often had to be provoked to fight each other or human opponents. Many beasts were rendered passive when they were released from a dark underground area into a bright sunlit arena surrounded by thousands of noisy spectators. One method of spurring these animals to action was to throw a stuffed dummy (*pila*) at them. There were, however, some animals that needed little or no incentive to attack. The poet Martial tells us of a bad-tempered rhinoceros that used a bull as a *pila*, a tame tigress that tore a lion to pieces, an elephant that gored a bull, and another rhinoceros that tossed a bull in the air.[85]

Another animal versus animal event of the *venatio* was the pursuit and killing of deer or boar by a pack of hunting dogs (Figure 10). Ovid refers to it in a simile as if it were a common feature of the *venatio*: '. . . just as the deer, about to perish in the morning sand, is the prey of dogs'.[86] The 'morning sand' is a reference to the *venatio*, which took place in the morning. The dogs worked in concert with a human hunter as they would in the wild. Some of these hunting dogs achieved fame by their prowess in the arena. In the fourth century AD, seven Scottish hounds that participated in a *venatio* given by the son of Symmachus, the prefect of Rome, won

Figure 10 Zliten mosaic: *venator*, deer, wild goats, dogs and boar with trainer. Villa at Dar Buc Amméra, Tripolitania. Archaeological Museum, Tripoli. Roger Wood/Corbis

the esteem of Rome.[87] In an epitaph for an arena bitch, Martial makes the dog speak of her training administered by master trainers of the amphitheatre and her noble death in a fight with a huge boar.[88] Figure 10 also contains an example of a performing animal: a boar, which sits up on his haunches as his trainer (perhaps a dwarf) prepares to throw an apple (?) to him. (The trainer appears to be holding a similar fruit in his right hand with others in reserve in a fold of his tunic.) Salvatore Aurigemma sees the clumsy movements of this beast as a note of comedy amidst the bloody tragedy of the amphitheatre.[89]

Besides the bloody violence, there was also a strong element of intellectual curiosity in the Roman fascination with the *venatio*. This can be seen in the pages of Pliny the Elder's *Natural History*, which has considerable space devoted to the animals of the *venatio*. Until the coming of the *venatio*, the urban population of Rome had little chance to observe the wild animals even in the rest of Italy, much less distant provinces. There were no public menageries in Rome like our modern zoos. During the late Republic, wealthy aristocrats like the famous scholar M. Terentius Varro and the great orator Q. Hortensius Hortalus did keep private menageries (*vivaria*), which consisted of animals such as hares, deer, wild sheep, boar, wild goats and other quadrupeds. These animals were kept to amuse guests and to provide meat for the table.[90] Nero's *vivarium* on the grounds of his Golden House (*Domus Aurea*) seems to have been a much larger-scale version of the late Republican private *vivarium*. Suetonius tells us, without giving much detail, that it consisted of 'a large number of every kind of herd animal and wild beast'.[91] The only menagerie that approached the modern zoo in size and variety was maintained by the emperor Gordian III (AD 238–244). The animals in this menagerie were meant to amuse the public, but not in a zoo. Gordian had intended to present these animals in the arena in a celebration of a triumph over Persia. He died before he could achieve this victory and his *vivarium* fell into the hands of his successor, Philip the Arab, who used them in a *venatio* in the celebration of Rome's millennium in AD 248. Some of the animals Philip merely presented to the public in the arena and all the rest were killed in various animal hunts.[92]

As noted in Chapter 1, the *venatio* brought awareness to Romans of their far-flung empire from which the great beasts of the arena had come and gave them a sense of their domination of nature.[93] The latter theme can be found in the geographer Strabo's comment on the gratitude of North African nomads to Roman hunters collecting wild animals in the region for *venationes*. These hunts allowed the nomads to gain control of the area and devote themselves to the settled life of agriculturalists.[94] The hunters were so effective at their work that certain species of animals became extinct in over-hunted regions. A fourth century AD orator expresses regret that elephants had vanished from Libya, lions from Thessaly, and hippopotami from the area of the Nile.[95]

Once wild animals were captured and transported to Italy, some Romans could not resist the attempt to improve on nature, applying artificial enhancements to wild animals. Seneca deplores the appearance of a lion tamed to tolerate a gilded mane, preferring an unadorned lion with an unbroken spirit.[96] In a *venatio* given by Gordian I in his aedileship, there were three hundred Moorish ostriches dyed a vermillion colour.[97]

Roman spectators were also fascinated by the behaviour of wild animals, whether in the heat of battle or in performing tricks. Some animals demonstrated an intelligence that struck Romans as close to human.[98] The *venatio* points up a paradox of the Roman character: their appreciation of the beauty, strength and intelligence of wild animals in contrast to their assumption that it is normal and even admirable to slaughter them for pleasure.[99]

The givers of *venationes* were proud of the large numbers of animals slain at their own shows to entertain the people. Augustus in his *Res Gestae* boasts that in the twenty-six *venationes* he had given during his rule, approximately 3,500 animals were killed. He takes pains to point out that these were African animals, that is, he had gone to the great expense of obtaining exotic large predators such as lions and leopards and not local animals such as boar, hares and deer.[100] This impressive number, however, was far surpassed by Titus during the dedications of the Colosseum and his Baths when 9,000 animals were killed, and later in the early second century AD during the celebration of Trajan's victory over the Dacians, when, in shows over a period of 123 days, 11,000 animals were slaughtered.[101]

A detailed account of a typical *venatio* survives from the late empire contained in a letter from the ostrogothic ruler of Italy, Theodoric (AD 493–526) to the consul Maximus, composed by his secretary Cassiodorus.[102] In the absence of any earlier such accounts, the description is valuable as a representation of the state of the *venatio* in the last stage of its history. The account of a *venatio* does not describe the killing of any animals. An earlier part of the letter, however, does mention the awful fate that arena-hunters could suffer when confronted by wild beasts:

> *And if [the hunter] is not good enough to escape from a wild animal, he will not be able to have a proper burial: with the man still alive, his body perishes and before the body can be be properly disposed of, it is savagely eaten. Captive, he becomes food for his own enemy and he satiates the one whom he desires to be able to kill. . . . The spectacle . . . in its action is horrible to an unimaginable degree.[103]*

Apparently the *venatio* of the late empire emphasized acrobatics. The letter focuses on the dangerous stunts performed by *venatores* in the arena. The emphasis is on the hunters deceiving and evading the animals in an acrobatic manner, thus rousing them to a fury. Lethargic beasts made for a dull *venatio*. Here is Cassiodorus' account:

> *First, trusting in a fragile wooden pole, [a hunter] runs to confront the beasts and that which he really desires to escape, he seems to seek with a great rush and both the predator and prey proceed at an equal pace, nor otherwise can [the* venator*] be safe, unless he rushes upon what he desires to avoid. Then with a high jump into the air, his bent supine limbs are thrown high*

into the air just like the lightest cloth and the animal passes quickly beneath, before [the hunter's] body can descend. Thus it happens that the animal which is tricked can seem more tame. Another hunter, taking advantage of four panels that rotate around a central pole and keeping close to his opponent, escapes, not by running away, nor does he put himself at a distance, but follows his pursuer, placing himself near to his pursuer at a run, so that he may avoid the mouths of bears.

Another man stretched out on his stomach on a low bar, teases a deadly beast and unless he took risks, he would not survive. Another man opposing a very savage animal protects himself with a portable wall of reeds, in the manner of a hedgehog, which, suddenly going on to its back and gathering itself together, hides and although it has not really gone away, its little body is not seen. For just as [the hedgehog], when danger approaches, having rolled itself into a ball is defended by natural spines, thus the man, protected by stitched-together wicker, is rendered more fortified by frail reeds. In the arena, other men from behind, so to speak, an array of three small doors dare to provoke the savage animals waiting for them, hiding themselves by means of these latticed gates, now showing their faces, now showing their backs, so that it is almost a miracle that they, whom you thus see running speedily through the claws and teeth of lions, can escape. Another man is brought close to the wild beasts on a rolling wheel: another is placed on top [of the wheel] so that he may be removed from danger. Thus this wheel resembling the treacherous world refreshes one with hope, while it tortures the other with fear: nevertheless [this wheel] smiles on all but only so that it can deceive them.[104]

Some of the devices employed in this account need further comment. The four panels on a pivot is reminiscent of a device called the *cochlea* (also spelled *coclia, coclea*), which the first century BC scholar Varro says was used in the arena when bulls fought men or other large animals.[105] It has been described as a circular cage, open on one side, which delivered beasts into the arena. It rotated on a pivot so that as it revolved it sent only one animal at a time into the arena.[106] In Theodoric's time, however, the *cochlea* was used by arena-hunters for a different purpose: to tease the animals while keeping themselves protected from attack. The apparatus was like modern revolving doors with four panels attached to a central pole, but unenclosed. The hunter could baffle pursuing animals by placing himself between two

panels and pushing the panel in front of him at a run to keep the device rotating, thus explaining the oxymoronic trope above of the hunter following
his pursuer. Cassiodorus says that the device was used with bears, but it
could also be used with other large predators like lions, as is depicted on the
lower section of the dyptych of Anastasius, consul in AD 517.[107] The pole
vaulting needs no further explanation, except to add that this technique was
also popular in Greece and the Greek east as the following poem from the
Greek Anthology shows:

> *A man stuck a pole in the ground and throwing his body into the air was
> bent head first. Having provoked the animal underneath his jump, he
> landed with nimble feet. [The animal] did not catch him. The crowd gave
> a great shout and the man escaped.*[108]

The 'hedgehog' device would seem to be a wicker sphere large enough to
hold a man, which had projecting spines to discourage an animal from tear-
ing it apart and getting at the man. The crowd no doubt enjoyed seeing
large animals pushing this 'ball' around the arena.[109] The description of the
two men and the rolling wheel might be a see-saw-like device that exposed
the man closer to the ground to the animals as it put the other out of
reach.[110] The man supine on the low bar no doubt would have been acro-
batically expert at keeping himself just out of reach of the animals. As
Cassiodorus' description suggests, the three latticed doors, when men stood
in open doorways, served to tease the animals and, when closed behind the
men as they ran from the pursuing beasts, provided safe haven. The latticed
doors are said to be 'in an open area', which may mean that they were set in
the arena wall or in a free-standing wooden wall just in front of the arena
wall.[111] Men in a doorway either holding cloths or gesticulating with a hand
to catch the attention of the beasts and tease them can be seen in amphitheatre scenes on North African mosaics.[112] It has been argued that these
stunts were merely simulated combat, perhaps to avoid harming expensive
animals, while at the same time putting the human participants at risk.[113]
The ivory diptych of Areobindus (AD 506), however, indicates that the
killing of wild animals was still the main feature of the *venatio* in the early
sixth century.[114] While the *venatio* served as a prelude to gladiatorial combat throughout most of its history, it was destined to outlast its featured
partner in the *munus* by over three quarters of a century.

The noonday spectacle (*meridianum spectaculum*)

For the first century and a half of gladiatorial combat, the show began early in the morning and continued throughout the day with no intermission. In 61 BC, a lunch break was instituted, during which spectators left the amphitheatre, a custom that continued at least into the third century AD.[115] After all, sitting for seven or eight hours without intermission must have strained the limits of human endurance, no matter how popular the entertainment. There were some spectators, however, who were willing to stay in their seats during the break for various reasons (perhaps for fear of losing their seats while they were out). Sometime in the reign of Caligula or of Claudius, a diversion, inspired by the popularity of the *ad bestias* executions in the morning *venatio* that had begun sometime in the early empire, was presented to fill the void between the *venatio* and the afternoon gladiator show. This was the event that became known as the 'noonday spectacle' (*meridianum spectaculum*), which featured the execution of convicted criminals (purchased by the *editor* from the authorities).[116] Like the executions during the *venatio*, the number of executions at noon depended on the quantity of convicts available at any given time. Thus, there were no doubt some *munera* which did not feature this event because of the unavailability of victims or the inadequate budget of the *editor*.[117] Obviously, expense would not be a crucial consideration when the *editor* was the emperor and thus, the number of executions, depending on availability, was usually large, but in the rest of Italy where *munera* were smaller in scale in comparison with Rome, the number of executions was much more limited. For example, the epitaph of an *editor* from the town of Peltuinum (central Italy) lists four *noxii* executed in a three-day *munus* he had given, while another *editor*'s epitaph from Beneventum (southern Italy) mentions four *noxii* who were executed during a four-day *munus*.[118]

Before the introduction of noonday executions, the noon interval in the *munus* apparently had been used for light entertainment, perhaps provided by 'play gladiators' (*paegniarii*), who entertained the crowd by fighting with wooden weapons and whips mimicking the deadly serious fighting of real gladiators. One day the philosopher Seneca remained in his seat, expecting a change of pace from the violence of the morning's *venatio* like the diversion described above. What he probably saw first was nearly naked men chained to each other marched into the arena as a prelude to their execution.[119]

Their punishment required that they fight one another to the death. Seneca strongly objects to the way the *damnati* were forced to fight. They were armed with swords, but without helmet and shield, with the result that their whole body was exposed to their opponent's thrusts, which very often found their mark. There was no need for the fencing skills of the professional gladiator in these fights. Seneca calls them 'pure homicides'. A man who had killed his opponent was forced immediately to fight a survivor of another fight and so on. In the end, all were killed, having carried out mutually their sentence of death.[120] It should be noted, however, that Seneca is not protesting the death penalty for the *damnati*, but the savagery of the spectacle, which is far removed from the sport of gladiatorial combat, and its negative effect on the spectators. The fans of the noonday event preferred quick bloodshed and death in great quantity. They preferred inartistic killings to the contests of trained gladiators. Seneca, repulsed by the bloodthirsty behaviour of this crowd, quotes the shouts of the crowd to attendants in the arena given the responsibility forcing reluctant combatants to fight:

> 'Kill him, whip him, burn him!' 'Why does he face his opponent's sword so timidly?' 'Why is he so tentative in killing his opponent?' 'Why is he so reluctant to die?' 'Force him with blows to risk being wounded!' 'Make them exchange blows with their unprotected chests!'[121]

No doubt what Seneca misses the most in these free-for-all bloodbaths is the lack of moral meaning. In contrast to gladiatorial combat, there was no opportunity to admire the courage of the fighters since they usually had to be forced to fight, making a noble death impossible.[122]

Claudius was a great fan of these murderous combats among the *damnati*. While most other spectators left the arena for lunch, Claudius stayed to view the spectacle and even sought to add to the number of the *damnati*. If he was angered by a mistake made by members of the arena staff, he condemned them to fight in the arena on the spot.[123] Claudius must have been somewhat uneasy about the pleasure he took from these public executions, because he dealt with this shame in an odd way. He had a statue of Augustus removed from the arena so that it would be spared the sight of wholesale slaughter, an act which aroused much laughter behind his back.[124]

It should be noted that this method of executing prisoners based on the gladiatorial model was not the only punishment carried out at the *meridianum spectaculum*. There were other even more hideous tortures: hanging, the *eculeus* (a wooden horse on which the victim was mounted and then tortured by the application of pulleys and weights), a stake driven through the back of the head emerging through the mouth, the *tunica molesta* ('the grievous tunic'), made of flax and smeared with combustible substances like pitch, in which the victim was burned to death, 'the frying pan' or 'iron seat', on which victims sat until their flesh roasted), and dis-memberment by means of horse-drawn chariots sent in different direc-tions.[125] As horrible as these punishments were, they were in fact not motivated by sadism, but to promote the maintenance of good order in Rome, which like other pre-industrial states, lacked a real police force or a prison system. These harsh public executions sent a message to law-abiding citizens that the state was acting aggressively to protect them. There was also a psychological dimension to these drastic physical penalties. Public punish-ment was, by its very nature, humiliating because it allowed the community to be entertained by the victim's suffering. The humiliation was exacerbated by a spirit of mockery that permeated the whole process of the execution. Here are three examples that encapsulate the derisive tone of Roman execu-tions. The first one is the execution of the deposed emperor Vitellius, and although it does not take place in the arena, it has much in common with practices there:

> . . . *with his hands tied behind his back and a rope around his neck, half naked in torn clothes he was dragged into the Forum, suffering mockery consisting of words and deeds all along the Via Sacra. His head was held back by his hair, just as happens to condemned criminals [in the arena] and the point of a sword was held under his chin, to force him to hold his face up to be viewed and not let it hang down. Some pelted him with excre-ment and mud and others called him an 'arsonist' and a 'glutton', while other members of the crowd criticized the defects of his bodily appearance: his extraordinary height, his red face from excessive wine drinking, his fat belly, and one weak thigh because of a chariot accident. . . . Finally at the Gemonian Stairs, he was tortured and put to death slowly and then dragged by a hook into the Tiber.*[126]

Informers, although they did not suffer the death penalty, were similarly forced to face the crowd in the arena with their heads forcibly bent back-wards in order accept the derision of the crowd.[127] An inscription from the town of Grumentum (southern Italy) perhaps provides more evidence in this regard, reporting that, at a *munus*, each of the *noxii* to be executed was 'elegantly dressed'. This might have been an attempt to mock the convicts for some perceived pretension of theirs that involved fancy clothing.[128] Humiliation was also prominent in the passion of Jesus. He was mocked for his claim to be king of the Jews by dressing him in a royal cloak and placing a crown of thorns on his head. In addition, a placard identifying him as 'king of the Jews' was attached to his cross.[129]

At the end of the noonday event when the arena was strewn with bodies, there appeared two arena attendants (*ministri*), one representing Dis, the god of the underworld, and the other, Mercury, the escort of the dead to the underworld. According to Tertullian, Dis, carrying a hammer, removed the bodies of the dead with the help of other attendants, dragging them by means of a hook out of the arena.[130] Mercury was easily recognizable because of his winged cap and his staff, which was partially made out of metal so that it could be heated to test whether there were any *damnati* feigning death. The role of these 'gods' in the noonday event was clearly characterized by comic parody.[131] Tertullian mentions how he and his companions 'amidst the light-hearted cruelties of the noonday event laughed at "Mercury" testing with a branding-iron to see if those who are apparently dead are really dead'.[132] In the case of Dis, the laughter might have been evoked by the incongruity of the divine king of the dead performing the menial task of cleaning up the arena.[133]

These comments of Tertullian have spawned dubious claims that hammer-wielding attendants impersonating the Etruscan death spirit Charun or Dis dispatched gladiators who were feigning death.[134] The reason for these dubious assertions is the fact that Tertullian refers to the *damnati* in the passage discussed above as 'gladiators'.[135] He is, however, using the word loosely as a blanket term, because it is clear that he is talking about the *meridianum spectaculum* and not gladiatorial combat. One can understand this confusion because, as we have seen, the *damnati* often fought each other with swords. Another source of confusion is the depiction of Charun holding a hammer in a fresco from the François tomb at Vulci (fourth century BC), which has led to its identification with Tertullian's hammer-wielding Dis. The wide gap in time between these two infernal deities, however, makes this identification unlikely.[136] The function of the hammer is another problem. The attendant impersonating Dis could have employed it to finish off dying *damnati*, but not gladiators, as is sometimes claimed.[137] Junkelmann says that the hammer brings to mind an execution, which is entirely appropriate to the *meridianum spectaculum*, but I would have to add, not in any practical way.[138] Since Tertullian explains the function of Mercury's rod, but not that of the Dis' hammer, it is more likely that the hammer was merely symbolic. Ville tentatively suggests that Dis or Charun may have escorted stretchers carrying the corpses of gladiators out of the arena, but only at certain times and places throughout the empire. He, however, argues against a significant role for Mercury (such as giving the signal to start the combat) and, in accordance with myth, proposes the function of 'divine herald' in the arena.[139]

The afternoon combat

Gods of the arena

Although the gods Hercules and Mars had a place in the hearts of gladiators, there is no doubt that Nemesis was the reigning divinity of the arena.[140] Not surprisingly, she was also popular among soldiers.[141] Both the soldier and the gladiator, whose careers entailed a high risk of death, trusted their fate to her. The awe that her great power evoked in her devotees is evidenced in an inscription found in Rome, in which she is addressed in both Greek and Latin as 'the great Nemesis, queen of the universe [and] great avenging queen of the city'.[142] Despite her great power, she was viewed as goddess who would listen to human prayers. An inscription from Apuli in Dacia labels her with the epithet 'most receptive to prayers'.[143] Her cult was popular throughout the empire. For example, an inscription from a shrine of Nemesis (*Nemeseion*) in Halicarnassus (modern Bodrum in southwest Turkey) records the sacrifice of a pig to the goddess by a *retiarius* named Stephanos, either to accompany a prayer for victory or as an act of thanksgiving for a victory.[144] The cult of Nemesis was also prominent in the western provinces. A room was found in an amphitheatre in Chester in the north of England which contained an altar to Nemesis.[145] When things did not turn out well in the arena, the goddess might be blamed. In an epitaph found in Verona, a deceased gladiator in his epitaph is made to advise other gladiators not to trust Nemesis because the goddess deceived him (by not preventing his death).[146] There were also cults of Nemesis attached to amphitheatres in Aquincum (Budapest) in the province of

Pannonia, in Carnuntum in the province of Noricum (southern Austria) and in Carthage.[147] Nemesis was closely associated with three other goddesses connected with the amphitheatre: Fortuna, Victoria ('Victory', the counterpart of the Greek *Nike*) and Diana, the patron divinity of *venatores*. M. Velleius Zosimos, a priest of 'the unconquerable Nemesis' commissioned a bas-relief depicting Nemesis, Victoria and Ares (Greek counterpart of Mars). Nemesis is shown holding scales in her right hand with a wheel of fortune at her feet, revealing her virtual identification with Fortuna. This bas-relief is located in a theatre in Philippi (Macedonia), which had been converted for the presentation of *venationes* and gladiatorial combat.[148] The inscriptions above from Aquincum and Carnuntum give further evidence of syncretism (Diana/Nemesis and Juno/Nemesis). Futrell's excellent analysis of the cult of Nemesis reveals the goddess as 'the power of changing fortune' and 'a distributor of good and bad. . . . The amphitheater, like the empire itself, was an instrument of fate, who, personified as Nemesis, personally supervises the spectacles of Rome'.[149]

Prolusio

Before the gladiator fights began in earnest, there was a warm-up period (*prolusio*), just as in any modern sport.[150] As a preliminary exercise, gladiators engaged in shadow fencing with wooden swords.[151] In an analogy, Seneca contrasts the *prolusio* with a real gladiatorial fight:

> *How stupid it is to wave your sword in the air when you have heard the signal for battle. Get rid of those practice weapons of yours. Now is the time for real weapons.*[152]

Cicero points out that some exercises were more for show than anything else.[153] For example, Samnite gladiators brandished spears although they never used such weapons in battle in the arena.[154] The *prolusio* was accompanied by music provided by horns accompanied by a water organ (*hydraulis*), which continued through each match until it ended with the release of the loser or his death, no doubt greatly enhancing the dramatic mood of these events in the arena, like a musical score for a film (Figure 11).[155]

We hear of another preparatory exercise that was more psychological than physical. Cicero refers to this exercise as 'that gladiatorial routine', the arousal of anger as an emotional spur to courage.[156] It calls to mind the

Figure 11 Zliten mosaic: horn players (standing figure plays the *tuba* and seated figures the *cornu*) and organist with the couch of Libitina for dead or dying in background. A *summarudis* restrains the sword hand of a victorious *eques* while an *editor* makes a decision on *missio* requested by the defeated *eques* on the ground. Note the backwards gaze of the referee, probably towards the unseen *editor*. Villa at Dar Buc Amméra, Tripolitania. Archaeological Museum, Tripoli. Roger Wood/Corbis

'trash talk' employed by modern athletes. Cicero quotes the speech of a great gladiator Pacideianus referring to his opponent:

> *If you are interested, I will defeat and kill him, he said. This is the way it will happen: I myself before I receive his sword in my face, will thrust mine in that wretch's stomach and lungs. I hate the man; I will fight him in a rage, nor will it take longer than for both of us to grasp our swords in our right hand. This is how much I am filled with fervour and hatred of him.*[157]

The listing of events

The pairings of the gladiators in a *munus* were made ahead of time by the *editor* in the days before the show. During the Republic and early empire these decisions would have been made in consultation with the *lanista* from whom the *editor* had rented the gladiators.[158] Later, when the imperial schools had been established, the emperor, who was most frequently the *editor* at Rome, no doubt consulted with the *procurator* and instructors of the school. As early as the first century BC, the pairings of gladiators were published ahead of time in pamphlet form and sold in the streets.[159] Cicero calls this pamphlet 'the pairings of gladiators' (*gladiatorum compositiones*).[160] In the imperial period, the pamphlet was called a *libellus munerarius*, literally, 'a little book of the *munus*', or more simply a *libellus*.[161] Ovid shows us how common these pamphlets were at gladiatorial games, when he recommends as a way to meet girls at a *munus* asking a girl to borrow her *libellus*.[162] Seduction of women may have been easier at a gladiatorial show, given Roman women's notorious sexual fascination with gladiators. While watching almost naked muscular men fighting in the arena, a woman might have found herself ready to settle for a more available man in the crowd. This pamphlet, sold a day or so before the *munus*, gave the number of pairs, the names of gladiators paired together, the order of their appearance and their previous record in the arena.[163] The *libellus* was useful to the spectator because the public notices of the *munus* (*edicta munerum*) usually gave only the number of pairs without specific names of gladiators, unless famous gladiators were scheduled to appear. Another publication was available to fans who were not able to attend the *munus* so that they could find out the winner of each match. The results of matches were published regularly in a kind of newspaper called *acta diurna*, 'daily journal'.[164] We can get a sense of what these reports were like from an inscription on a wall in Pompeii. It is a long inscription, but two examples will suffice. Only the most crucial information is presented for each match: the style of fighting of each fighter, the names of the two opponents and, if applicable, their special status as imperial gladiators, the result of the match, and how many fights each gladiator has had:

> *Hoplomachus vs Thracian: Cycnus, a* Julianus, *won. Nine fights. Atticus, a* Julianus, *was released. Fourteen fights.*[165]

In the Latin original, this information, except for the names of the gladiators, was conveyed concisely by abbreviations in order to save space. Here is the Latin for the first selection:

O T
V Cycnus Iul
VIIII
M Atticus Iul XIV

O = *hoplomachus* (the 'h' was silent and spelling often followed pronunciation) and T = *thraex*; V = *vicit* ('won'); Iul = Julianus; with the Roman numerals VIIII and XIV the word *pugnarum* ['of fights'] is understood, indicating how many fights each opponent has had ('[a gladiator] of nine fights . . . of fourteen fights'), and M = *missus* ('released') in reference to the loser whose life was spared.

The gladiators

Types of gladiator

Gladiators were not an undifferentiated group of sword fighters; they were divided up into categories based different styles of armour, weapons and fighting. Sometimes it is hard to determine with certainty the type a gladiator depicted in surviving ancient representations. We must accept the possibility that occasionally variety in armour and weapons was allowed within a given gladiator category.[166] For the most part, however, gladiators conformed generally to type. During the Republic, there were five known gladiator types: *samnis* (Samnite), *gallus* (Gaul), *thraex* (Thracian), *provocator* ('challenger') and *eques* ('horseman'). The first three types are ethnic in origin, that is, their armour, weapons and style of fighting were derived from peoples who had engaged in war with the Romans: the Samnites, Gauls and Thracians. As noted earlier, these gladiator types must have developed from the practice of forcing prisoners of war from the same region to fight each other wearing their characteristic armour and employing their distinctive fighting styles. In time, the names of these three ethnic gladiatorial types no longer indicated warriors native to these regions, but merely a gladiatorial style. These ethnic gladiatorial types throughout the Republic kept the memory of Rome's past military successes alive by re-enacting them in the arena. The Samnite and the Gaul, the earliest gladiator types we know of, did not survive much beyond the Republic; only the *thraex* survived into the imperial period and remained popular into late antiquity. The Samnite and the Gaul, however, may have produced descendants under different names. Luciana Jacobelli argues convincingly that the Samnite gladiator disappeared during Augustus' reign because the Romans wanted to avoid insult to a people who had become their loyal allies.[167] In fact, this may have also been the reason for the disappearance of the *gallus*. By the early empire, the Gallic provinces had become thoroughly romanized. In the ancient world, it was believed that the *murmillo* was descended from the Gaul, while it has been recently claimed by Junkelmann that the *murmillo* and the *secutor* are actually survivals of the Samnite.[168] We know nothing about the Gaul and very little about the Samnite. Horace says that Samnites fought slow, protracted duels. This perhaps indicates that they were weighed down by heavy armour.[169] The poet also implies that Samnites only fought other Samnites. Like the later *secutor*, the Samnite wore a greave on the left leg only.[170] In addition to the *thraex* and the *essedarius*, a British import of the early empire, ethnically neutral gladiator types like the *murmillo, secutor, retiarius, hoplomachus, veles, provocator* and *eques* were the staples of gladiatorial shows during the imperial period.

The best way of differentiating the different categories of gladiators is by means of variations in the standard armour: helmet, shield, an arm guard (*manica*), loincloth (*subligaculum*) held in place by a metal belt (*balteus*), and metal greaves (*ocreae*), often backed by wrappings of quilted linen, which were sometimes used independent of greaves. Of these pieces of armour, the shape of the helmet and of the shield (rectangular or round, small or large) are most useful in assigning a gladiator to a specific category.

Eques

One type of gladiator easy to identify is the *eques* ('horseman'), a lightly armed fighter who fought both on horseback and on the ground. It is clear that the *equites* were real horsemen. Cicero reports that the crowd's hissing of an unpopular politician startled 'the gladiators and their horses'.[171] These gladiators with horses could only be the *equites*. An *eques* always fought an opponent of the same category.[172] The only detailed description we have of the *equites* in a *munus* comes from a medieval author Isidore of Seville (seventh century AD), but his overall knowledge of gladiators accords well with the ancient sources, thus giving credence to the evidence he provides:

> *Of the several types of gladiators, the first contest involves the equestrians. Two* equites, *preceded by military standards, entered the arena, one from the west, the other from the east, riding on white horses, wearing smallish golden helmets and carrying light weapons.*[173]

Note that the *equites* had the honour of being the opening act of gladiator shows.[174] Isidore's description makes it easy to understand why the *equites* were first in the programme. The *equites* riding white horses and golden helmets provided an impressive prelude to what was to follow. The *eques* wore a tunic and brimmed helmet with visor and two feathers, a tunic (in contrast with most gladiators, who are naked to the waist), a medium-sized round shield, a *manica*, and linen leggings.[175] Isidore notes the *equites*' 'fierce determination in accordance with their courage' as they entered battle. The battle must have begun on horseback with lances. Isidore speaks of

Figure 12 Madrid mosaic: Two *equites* and two referees. Bottom panel: beginning of fight; top panel: end of fight. Madrid, Museo Arqueológico Nacional. The Art Archive/Corbis

one *eques* jumping off his horse and the other falling, no doubt unseated by a blow of his opponent's lance. The fight continued on the ground with swords, if necessary. Despite their equestrian character, surviving artistic depictions concentrate on the *equites* fighting on foot as in Figures 11 and 12.[176] There are two inscriptions on the mosaic in Figure 12: *Quibus pugnantibus Symmachius ferra misit. Maternus* [vs] *Habilis* [names of the two gladiators] and *Haec videmus* and *Symmachi, homo felix. Habilis* [vs] *Maternus.* They are translated thus: 'Symmachius [the *editor*] provided weapons and armour for these fighters. Maternus vs Habilis.' 'These are the things that we saw. O Symmachius, you are a fortunate man [to be able to give such a good show]! Habilis [vs] Maternus.' The direct address to the Symmachus represents an *acclamatio* ('shouts') of the crowd, honouring him for his show. The symbol that looks like a zero (after the name Maternus) with a diagonal line through it is actually the Greek letter *theta*, the first letter of the noun *thanatos* (death), which indicates the fate of Maternus (see also Figure 25).[177]

Provocator

The *provocator* ('challenger') was another gladiatorial type that originated in the Republic and survived into imperial times. Cicero mentions the *provocator* in the same speech along with the *equites* and the Samnites.[178] The *provocator* looked much more like a standard gladiator than did the *eques*. His visored helmet was not brimmed and had a neck guard in the back. He wore a loincloth (*subligaculum*), standard attire for all gladiators except for the *eques*, and a greave on his left leg. The shield of the *provocator* was concave and rectangular. Perhaps his most identifiable feature was the breastplate he wore, held on the body by straps that met at the back, which protected the upper chest.[179] No other type of gladiator wore any protective armour on the chest.

Thraex

The *thraex* was the sole survivor into the imperial period of the ethnic-based gladiators of the Republic. It is uncertain when the *thraex* became a gladiatorial type at Rome. There are two possibilities: (1) when Rome took Thracian mercenaries captive in the war against Perseus (171–167 BC), or (2) when many Thracians were taken as prisoners in the Mithridatic wars in the 80s BC (as mentioned in Chapter 1). The fact that Cicero (106–43 BC) was first to mention the *thraex* seems to argue for the latter.[180] Indeed, Spartacus was an ethnic Thracian, but we do not know whether he was trained as a *thraex* in Batiatus' school. The *thraex* was traditionally paired with the *hoplomachus* and the *murmillo*. In fact, the *thraex* was among the first gladiators to be paired with a different gladiatorial type. The purpose behind pairing different types of gladiators was to produce matches that were more interesting. The armour, weapons and style of fighting of each gladiator represented both advantages and disadvantages when matched with another gladiatorial type. If the advantages and disadvantages balanced well, then it was more likely that a good fight would result. For example, the main weapon of the *hoplomachus* was a thrusting spear, which gave him an advantage when he was paired with the *thraex*, who wielded a short, curved sword (*sica*). On the other hand, the *hoplomachus* had only a very small circular shield to defend against his opponent's sword attacks, while the *thraex* had a larger rectangular shield to protect himself from his opponent's spear. This principle of compensation and balance was frequently applied to pairings in the imperial period.

There was a factor, however, that could upset the ideal of balance in pairing gladiators. A speaker in a practice oratorical exercise puts the difference between fighting a *hoplomachus* and a *thraex* on the same level with the difference between fighting a right-handed or left-handed gladiator, a dissimilarity that was considered to be significant because of the rarity of left-handers.[181] The normal matching of right-handed opponents presented a balance of defence and offence with the sword hand of both gladiators immediately opposite the shield-bearing hand of his opponent. Conversely, when a left-handed gladiator faced a right-hander, his sword hand was immediately opposite the sword arm of his opponent. K. M. Coleman argues that this situation gave a decided advantage to the left-hander, who could directly attack the unshielded side of his opponent, while the right-hander had been trained to attack with his right arm moving across his body to get to his right-handed opponent's unshielded side. Wiedemann goes so far as to suggest that some right-handed gladiators chose to learn how to fight left-handed to inspire fear in their right-handed opponents.[182] Baudoin Caron rightly casts doubt on Wiedemann's use of Seneca the Elder and Cassius Dio as sources for his claim and questions Coleman's argument, claiming that in a match involving a right-hander and a left-hander, both had the same advantage of being able to attack each other's unshielded flank directly.[183] It is clear, however, that the Romans believed left-handedness in gladiators to be a significant advantage. Junkelmann points out that left-handedness was important enough to be recorded along with the type of gladiator in inscriptions.[184] It seems more likely, however, that the advantage of the left-hander was more psychological than physical. Even today, left-handers in tennis, boxing and baseball are thought to have an advantage over their right-handed opponents.

The armament of the *thraex* was similar to that of other gladiators such as the *hoplomachus* and the *murmillo*, but there were significant differences. The *thraex* carried a fairly small, oblong shield (*parma* or its diminutive *parmula*) that was significantly lighter than that of the *murmillo*. Junkelmann estimates the weight of the *thraex*'s shield at 6.5 pounds in comparison with the murmillo's shield, which he considers the heaviest item among the *murmillo*'s armament, weighing between 35 and 39 pounds.[185] The brimmed helmet of the *thraex* had a high crest topped by the image of a griffin, a mythological monster with the head and wings of an eagle and the body of a lion (Figures 13 and 14), the companion of Nemesis, as we have

Figure 13 Helmet of the *thraex* with griffin finial and visor. Museo Archeologico Nazionale, Naples, Italy/The Bridgeman Art Library Ltd

Figure 14 Funerary monument for *thraex* M. Antonius Exochus. Note the curved *sica* (to the left of his right arm), his helmet (over his left shoulder) between the front legs of a griffin (instead of a griffin finial) and his two metal greaves. He holds the palm of victory in his left hand and there is a half-visible crown (indicating an outstanding performance) behind him to his right. Drawing of 16th century of lost original: Codex Coburgensis. Coburg, Kunstsammlungen de Veste Coburg, Germany

seen, a divinity closely associated with gladiators.[186] The weapon of the *thraex* was also distinctive: a short, curved sword (*sica*) in comparison with the more usual medium length straight sword (*gladius*) (Figure 14). There is evidence that the *sica* could give the *thraex* an advantage in certain situations. A duel depicted on the Zliten mosaic shows a *thraex* employing a *sica* effectively at a point in the action when the *gladius* would have been virtually useless.[187] His opponent's attack on the back of his neck puts the *thraex* in an awkward position, requiring him to raise his shield to counter the blow. The elbow-shaped *sica*, however, allows the *thraex* to take the offensive by delivering with an upward movement a serious puncture wound just below his opponent's right buttock (in the mosaic blood streams profusely from the wound to the ground) that would not have been possible with the straight *gladius*.

Since the *thraex* had a relatively small shield, he needed greater protection for his legs, so he wore quilted linen leggings that served as a backing for metal greaves on his shins and continued all the way up his thighs to his hips under his loincloth.

Hoplomachus

The *hoplomachus* ('heavy-armed in battle'), a gladiatorial type modelled to a degree on the Greek hoplite, as its name suggests, was a traditional opponent of the *thraex* and the *murmillo*. The *hoplomachus* was somewhat similar to the *thraex*. They both wore a *manica* on their right arm and, because of their smaller shields, wore the extra-long quilted linen leggings. Their weapons, however, were quite different: the *hoplomachus* used a thrusting spear as a primary weapon and a dagger as a back-up. On the other hand, the difference in shields was significant. The shield of the *hoplomachus* was circular and concave, but quite small, whereas the *thraex*'s shield was larger and rectangular, but only capable of protecting his torso. Since both shields were fairly small, they were both included in the category of *parma*, whereas the *murmillo*'s shield (*scutum*) was significantly larger, covering almost his whole body from neck to feet.

Murmillo

The *murmillo* was one of the most heavily armed gladiators, whose helmet was notable for its prominent angular crest (Figure 15). His large shield

Figure 15   Murmillo helmet with prominent crest and visor. Bettmann/Corbis

(*scutum*) was oblong and concave in shape, providing protective coverage of just about his whole body, on a par with the shields of the *provocator* and the *secutor*. It has been suggested that the word *murmillo* is derived from *mormulos*, Greek for a kind of fish.[188] This assumption is based on a passage from Festus, which quotes a humorous song sung (or recited) by a *retiarius* to a Gaul (the gladiator type): 'I do not attack you, I attack a fish. Why do you flee me, Gaul?' Festus explains that the *murmillo* was an offshoot of the Gaul, whose helmet was decorated with the image of a fish.[189] In the song, the *retiarius*, who employed the tools of a fisherman (net and trident) in the arena, uses the *murmillo*'s origin to mock him. Since the *murmillo* was an early opponent of the *retiarius*, Festus' claim is perfectly plausible, but not confirmed by other sources and there is no other evidence of any gladiator wearing a helmet with the image of a fish, unless one is willing to see the angular crest of the murmillo's helmet as a stylized dorsal fin.[190] On the other hand, in the ancient mind, the *retiarius* was closely connected with the sea. Arnobius compares Neptune, who carries a trident, to a *retiarius*.[191] At least one *retiarius* had the stage name *Aequoreus* ('of the sea'), an epithet of

Neptune. The discovery of a *galerus* decorated with images of a dolphin, anchor and crab would seem to strengthen the connection of the *retiarius* with the sea, but Junkelmann points out that sea motifs have been found on the armour of other gladiator types.[192]

The *murmillo* and the *thraex* were at the centre of a conflict of fan partisanship based on the size of their shields: the *scutarii*, rooters for the *murmillo*, who carried the *scutum*, and the *parmularii*, supporters of the *thraex*, who carried the comparatively small *parma*. Although this rivalry focused on the *murmillo/thraex* pairing, it also included the less common *hoplomachus/murmillo* pairing, another example of the *parma* versus the *scutum*.[193] In comparison with the virtually body-covering *scutum* of the *murmillo*, the *parma* or *parmula* (diminutive) of the *thraex* was approximately half the size. Thus the *thraex* was at a significant disadvantage, and, as we hear from Martial, rarely won matches with the *murmillo*.[194] Martial notes the great uproar of the *parmularii* when the *thraex* did win.[195] Therefore, it would seem that the contention between the *parmularii* and the *scutarii* was in essence between fans who favoured the underdog and fans who liked to back a winner. This rivalry reached the highest levels of Roman society. Caligula was a *parmularius*. Suetonius tells us that Caligula placed some *thraeces* in charge of his German bodyguard, and that 'he reduced the armament of the *murmillones*'.[196] What this vague statement probably means is that Caligula reduced the size of their shields. Caligula's devotion to the *parma* even led him to fight as a *thraex* with a real weapons (but not in arena).[197] On the other hand, Nero was a *scutarius*, as his fabulous gifts to the *murmillo* Spiculus (mentioned earlier) indicate. His devotion to this *murmillo* lasted until the end of this life. When it became clear that Nero would lose his throne, he wanted this same gladiator to kill him.[198] The emperor Titus sided with the *parmularii*, joining the common folk in public demonstrations and using insulting words and gestures against the *scutarii*.[199] Domitian, one of Rome's most tyrannical emperors, was in this matter consistent with his political philosophy, supporting the dominant *scutarii* and wreaking cruel vengeance on the *parmularii*, who were vociferous in their support of the *thraex*. Domitian, who identified very closely with his gladiators, considered any verbal assault on the *scutarii* an attack upon himself. Any offence given to him was made more heinous by his claim of divinity, since he considered any affront an act of impiety deserving the most serious punishment.[200] Thus, he condemned numerous *parmularii* to death by fire in the arena. Pliny the Younger writes of Domitian's victims in this case as paying for 'his wretched pleasures by becoming part of the spectacle and being subject to the hook and fire'. This is a reference to the penalty of *crematio*, after which the body was dragged out of the arena by means of a hook.[201] On another occasion, a man of some distinction, a *paterfamilias* (the head of an extended family) in the Colosseum shouted loud enough for Domitian to hear: 'A *thraex* could hold his own against a *murmillo*, but not against the *editor* [i.e., Domitian himself].' Domitian's immediate reaction was to have this man dragged from his seat into the arena and thrown to the dogs, while wearing a placard reading: 'I am a *parmularius* who spoke impiously'.[202]

As mentioned earlier, occasionally the two carriers of the *parma* fought each other: the *thraex* and the *hoplomachus*.[203] One example of this pairing is the famous match between Verus and Priscus during the inauguration of the Colosseum described by Martial in his *Book of Spectacles*.[204] The emperor Titus, the *editor*, after a long fight in which neither gladiator could gain an advantage ordered both opponents to continue the fight without their shields (*posita . . . parma*, 'with the *parma* having been laid aside').[205] This pairing might help explain why Titus, an avid *parumularius*, was so generous in his grant of discharge to both gladiators.[206] The *parmularius/ scutarius* controversy lasted at least to the end of the second century AD (and probably further), as is clear from Marcus Aurelius' boast that he had been taught by his father not to take this trivial issue seriously.[207] The fanatical devotion to gladiators based on the size of their shield is analogous to the allegiance of Roman chariot racing fans to team colours rather than to individual drivers. The epitaph of an oil dealer named Crescens, proudly proclaims that he is a 'supporter of the blue faction of chariot drivers and of gladiators who use the *parma*'.[208]

Retiarius (*'net-man'*)

Of all gladiators, the light-armed *retiarius* (Figure 16, gladiator on left) is the easiest to identify for various reasons.[209] While all other gladiators resembled soldiers to a degree in their armament (helmet, shield, greaves and sword), the *retiarius* wore no helmet, was armed with a trident (*fuscina*), dagger and net, had no shield, and wore a metal protector on his left shoulder (*galerus*), a piece of equipment worn regularly by no other gladiator.[210] The *galerus* was necessary because, without a shield and a helmet, the

Figure 16 *Retiarius,* referee (*summarudis*) and *secutor.* Villa of Nennig, Germany. Bildarchiv Preussischer Kulturbesitz, Berlin/Hermann/Scala London

retiarius was exposed to attack on his left shoulder and the left side of his head. The lack of a shield also required that the *retiarius* wear a *manica* on his left arm, instead of his right, as did other gladiators who had a shield to protect their left side. He wore other standard equipment: the *subligaculum* (loincloth) with a *balteus* (metal belt), and greaves on both legs.[211]

As we have seen above, the earliest regular opponent of the *retiarius* was the *murmillo,* who, by the middle of the first century AD, began to be replaced by the heavily armed *secutor,* perhaps a variation on the *murmillo.*[212] The *retiarius* with his right hand threw the net at his opponent to entrap him (the net had lead weights, which facilitated throwing it with accuracy). The *retiarius* in Figure 16 has already thrown his net unsuccessfully and uses his trident. In Figure 17, the *retiarius,* having lost his trident, has no choice but to engage his opponent at close quarters with his dagger. The contest between the *retiarius* and the *secutor* was one between gladiators who were polar opposites. The *retiarius* was one of the most lightly armed gladiators, whereas the *secutor* ('pursuer') was one of the heaviest. Thus, the *retiarius* needed

Figure 17   Zliten mosaic: *retiarius* with dagger, bleeding from a leg wound. Villa at Dar Buc Amméra, Tripolitania. Archaeological Museum, Tripoli. Roger Wood/Corbis

all his weapons plus significant agility to even the odds in battle with his opponent. Using foot speed to tire out his heavily armed opponent was one of the strategies of the *retiarius*. In Juvenal, a *retiarius* named Gracchus flees his *secutor* opponent, although this particular example may illustrate cowardice as much as strategy.[213] An epitaph from Dalmatia (modern Croatia) identifies a deceased *retiarius* as Rapidus, an apt name for this type of gladiator, while another from Parma characterizes the departed *retiarius* as 'nimble' (*alacer*).[214] The net could turn the tide of battle in the *retiarius'* favor by hindering the movement of the *secutor* but was no guarantee of victory. In a mosaic from Madrid (Figure 18) there are two panels showing two different stages of a fight between a *secutor* named Astyanax and a *retiarius* called Kalendio. In the lower panel, Kalendio has ensnared Astyanax in his net and is trying to inflict a wound with his trident on Astyanax's knee. In the upper panel, Kalendio has lost his trident and is trying to defend himself with a dagger. Although we are not shown the end of the fight, the Greek *theta* following Kalendio's name in both panels reveals the result of the match.

Figure 18 Madrid mosaic: Astyanax (*secutor*), Kalendio (*retiarius*) and referees. Madrid, Museo Arqueológico Nacional. The Art Archive/Corbis

Although the regular dress of the *retiarius* consisted only of the *subligaculum*, some *retiarii* wore a tunic. The sources refer to this type of *retiarius* as the *retiarius tunicatus*.[215] For example, the *retiarius* Kalendio in Figure 18 wears a tunic that partially covers his left arm and from the middle of his torso to just above his knees. (The regular tunic extended further upwards to the neck, covering the shoulders and the upper arms.) The question is, what was the significance of the *tunic* for the *retiarius*? Since it served no practical purpose, it surely must have had some kind of symbolic significance. Some have taken the tunic worn by a *retiarius* as a sign of his homosexual effeminacy and associate it with that part of the gladiatorial school that housed gladiators with this tendency, as mentioned in Chapter 2.[216] This interpretation is based on Juvenal's reference to 'the shameful tunic'. This, however, is probably a misunderstanding of the poet's meaning.[217] Why the tunic should be associated with sexual disgrace is unclear. The horsemen gladiators (*equites*) wore tunics and were not accused of sexual deviancy. Suetonius mentions the *retiarius tunicatus* in a passage that hints at not even a subtext of homosexual effeminacy. The biographer reports a group fight (*gregatim*) arranged during the reign of Caligula between five *retiarii tunicati* and five *secutores* that took a strange turn even before the match could begin.[218] Although the prime attraction of any *munus* was its individual duels between two gladiators, we hear occasionally of group fighting among gladiators, which was probably popular among less discerning fans. The special skills of the gladiator could not be fully appreciated in a gang fight. The *tunicati* laid down their tridents, surrendering to the *secutores*, an act that apparently implied a request that their life be spared. The *editor* (unnamed, perhaps Caligula) rejected their appeal and ordered their deaths. Before they could be dispatched by the *secutores*, one of their number, ignoring the command of the *editor* (from which there was no appeal), picked up his trident and killed all five of the *secutores*. This flagrant violation of normal procedure in the arena so angered Caligula that he issued an edict calling it 'most cruel murder', cursing those who had watched it.[219] This evidence seems to require another meaning for the tunic worn by some *retiarii*. Early in the twentieth century, S. G. Owen argued persuasively that when Juvenal called the *retiarius'* tunic 'shameful', the epithet actually applied to the wearer of the garment and not to the tunic itself, suggesting that the tunic was worn by *auctorati* to differentiate themselves from slave *retiarii*.[220] Juvenal mentions another *retiarius tunicatus* named Gracchus, a noble guilty of homosexual effeminacy, who became the bride of another man, but his tunic has nothing to do with his sexual preference.[221] Gracchus' performance in the arena is unprofessional in its ineptitude. He throws his net but misses badly. Having failed to entangle his *secutor* opponent, he flees but not without looking up at the spectators to make sure he is recognized.[222] Juvenal adds that Gracchus' *secutor* opponent 'endured a dishonour worse than any wound when he was ordered to fight with [the inept] Gracchus'.[223] No doubt like many an upper-class *auctoratus*, Gracchus was an unskilled amateur who would have been scorned by professional *retiarii* and forced to live with other *retiarii tunicati* in isolation from authentic *retiarii* in the *ludus*.[224] If Gracchus' unprofessional behaviour could be taken as typical of *retiarii tunicati*, it would go a long way towards explaining the peculiar behaviour of the *tunicati* in Suetonius who surrendered without fighting and perhaps even the treachery of the one *tunicatus* that enabled him to kill five *secutores*.

Secutor

From at least the middle of the first century AD , the *secutor* ('pursuer') became the traditional opponent of the *retiarius*. In fact, the *secutor* seems to
have been created with the *retiarius* in mind as an opponent as is indicated
by the alternative name *contraretiarius* ('anti-*retiarius*'), as if the only
reason for the existence of the *secutor* was to provide an interesting opponent for the *retiarius*.[225] The *secutor* and *murmillo* are almost identical in
their armament, wearing a *manica* on the right arm, greaves, and a long
concave shield on the left. Like all other gladiator types (except for
provocator), the *secutor* had a completely unprotected torso, although there
is one example from Tomis (Constanta in modern Romania) of a *secutor*
wearing a what looks like a coat of mail, leaving only his neck vulnerable to
a deathblow.[226] The most important difference between the two gladiators
is the helmet. In contrast with the *murmillo*'s visored helmet with a brim
and feathers, and high, extended crest, the *secutor*'s helmet had no brim or
visor but reminds one of an inverted fish bowl with its virtually round and
smooth surface, covering the whole head down to the chin, with a small
crest and two tiny eyeholes (Figure 19). The small eyeholes are meant to

Figure 19   Secutor helmet. Arles, Musée départemental de l'Arles antique

protect the *secutor* from the three prongs of the *retiarius'* trident. Wider eyeholes would increase the risk of being blinded, at least in one eye. A larger crest would have made it easier for the *retiarius* to entangle the *secutor* in his net or fend him off with the trident. These protective measures were designed to prevent a short match in which the *retiarius* could achieve an easy victory. On the other hand, these advantages were counterbalanced by an attenuated field of vision for the *secutor*, which would have made it difficult for its wearer to keep track of both the *retiarius'* net and trident, and a reduced air supply, which could quickly tire out the *secutor* in any pursuit of his mobile, light-armed opponent.[227] The *secutor*'s helmet gave the gladiator a rather menacing, inhuman appearance, which created a dramatic contrast with the very human-looking and vulnerable *retiarius*. It is not surprising that the *retiarius/secutor* pairing became the most popular combination in gladiatorial shows.

Veles

The *veles* was a lightly armed gladiator about whom we know little. As Isidore of Seville informs us, the *velites* fought each other with spears, which they threw at both close and more distant range. They were apparently quite popular with spectators, perhaps because their style of fighting represented a change from the usual close sword fighting of most other gladiators.[228] There is no evidence regarding their armour, but in as much as they are lightly armed, we might guess that they wore either a tunic or just a *subligaculum* and carried a small shield. The head covering was probably a leather cap instead of a heavy metal helmet. One interesting point is that, unlike all other gladiators, the *veles* had a counterpart with the same name in the Roman army.

Lesser known gladiator types

Some or all of the gladiator types discussed in this section may indeed have been popular, but the sources both literary and graphic do not provide much information about them.

Essedarius

The name of this type of gladiator comes from a Gallic word, *essedum*, 'a two-wheeled war chariot' and means 'one who fights from a chariot'. The *essedarius* as a gladiatorial type was no doubt inspired by the chariot fighters that Roman soldiers under the command of Julius Caesar had seen in Britain. Thus, the *essedarius* is another example of a foreign soldier assimilated as a gladiator into the arena. Julius Caesar mentions them quite frequently and describes their manner of fighting in real warfare:

> *[The chariot fighters] ride about everywhere throwing spears and create much panic in [our] ranks because of their horses and the sound made by the wheels, and when they have made their way among the troops of [Roman] cavalry, they jump down from their chariots and fight on foot.*[229]

The *essedarius* fought other *essedarii*, beginning the match from their chariot and then finishing the battle on foot, a sequence of fighting similar to that of the *equites*, who began the contest on horseback.[230]

The following gladiators may have been sideshow entertainers, who performed in between the regular gladiator matches.

Laquearius

The word *laquearius* means 'lasso man'. The only evidence we have of their style of fighting comes from Isidore of Seville. The fighting style of *laquearii* is somewhat similar to that of the rodeo cowboy who lassoes a calf from horseback and wrestles him down. The *laquearius*, however, works on foot and his job to ensnare men with his lasso and throw them to the ground. Lafaye claims that the *laquearius* used his lasso to strangle his opponents.[231] Isidore says that his opponents both flee from him and run after him.[232] This cryptic statement might make sense if, as is most likely, the *laquearii* fought each other. Then the pursuer, when he misses ensnaring his opponent with his lasso, needs to collect his rope and as a result becomes the pursued.

Andabata

The *andabata* fought blindfolded or perhaps with a helmet that covered his eyes. Naturally, this gladiator only fought other *andabatae*. Since we hear nothing of this gladiator from imperial writers, most likely the *andabata* had disappeared from the arena by the end of the Republic. With its similarity to a 'pin the tail on the donkey' game, the performance of the *andabatae* must have aimed at a comic effect, but sometimes with deadly results.

Junkelmann calls the fight between two *andabatae* 'a battle of macabre grotesqueness'.[233] Cicero's mention of the *andabatae* seems to imply that they were not a significant attraction in the arena.[234] It is not known whether the *andabata* had his own special armament or other gladiatorial types took turns playing the *andabata*.

Paegniarius

The word *paegniarius* means something like 'play gladiator'. Whatever that is supposed to mean, it is clear that the *paegniarius* did not employ deadly weapons. Whatever weapons he used probably produced at most bruises and minor cuts. The purpose of the *paegniarii* was probably to provide a respite for spectators from the bloody violence of gladiatorial combat. They could have performed during the interval between gladiator duels, or, as was suggested earlier in this chapter, they may have provided the light entertainment that Seneca was looking forward to during the lunch break in the middle of a *munus*, only to be outraged by the bloody *meridianum spectaculum*.[235] There is, however, no evidence linking them to any specific portion of the *munus*. Although their 'playful' style set them off from their gladiatorial colleagues, they were nonetheless considered real gladiators and were housed in the *Ludus Magnus*.[236] In the only literary reference we have to this gladiatorial type, Caligula, in one of his psychopathic moods, forced distinguished heads of families with notable physical disabilities to perform in place of the *paegniarii*.[237] No doubt Caligula believed that the sight of disabled older men of some note engaging in mock fights would serve as acceptable substitutes for the *paegniarii*. Their ineptness caused by inexperience, age and disabilities probably achieved the same result as the professional skills of the *paegniarii*. We do not hear of what reception the crowd gave to Caligula's mean-spirited mockery of upstanding Roman citizens. Although there may have some who were shocked by this behaviour on the part of their emperor, there were probably many spectators who enjoyed the display. The average Roman spectator had high tolerance for witnessing acts that we would condemn as gratuitous cruelty.

A third century AD mosaic from Nennig, Germany (Figure 20) is generally taken to depict *paegniarii*, although the fighters go beyond what we would today consider 'play'. We see two fighters attacking each other, one with a whip and the other with what seems to be a stick. They are clothed

Figure 20 Paegniarii. Villa of Nennig, Germany. Gianni Dagli Orti/The Art Archive

from neck to knee, perhaps to protect them from serious injury, and wear what appear to be metallic leggings on their calves. Attached to their left arm is a small concave shield, from the top of which project slightly curved (metal?) rods. These rods may have served to fend off blows.

Sagittarius

As the name indicates, this gladiator is an archer (*sagitta* = 'arrow'), but the evidence for this gladiatorial type is very slight. An inscription from Venusia (modern Venosa) announces the presence in a tomb of twenty gladiators, one of whom is a *sagittarius*.[238] A bas-relief in Florence depicts two armoured archers fighting each other, framed by two other gladiator pairs similarly engaged.[239] Was it simply a matter of two archers shooting at each other? An analogy used by the poet Persius seems to support this interpretation: 'We strike and in turn expose our legs'.[240] If this line really does refer to arena archers, then we might think of fighters protected by armour from head to waist, but without any linen leggings or greaves, shooting at each other and suffering arrow wounds on their bare legs.[241] The *sagittarii* posed a security problem with their ability to make lethal shots from a distance. They were likely watched closely in the arena by well-armoured soldiers.

Scissor, hastarius, dimachaerus *and* pontarius

These four gladiator types are known only by name. *Scissor* means 'carver', *hastarius*, 'spear man', *dimachaerus*, 'a fighter with a dagger in each hand', and, *pontarius*, 'a platform fighter'.[242] The name *scissor* ('carver') provides no hint of this gladiator's performance in the arena. *Hastarius* could easily be another name for a *hoplomachus* who carried a spear. *Pontarius* seems to be a general term for any gladiator who fought on a platform. There is pictorial evidence that the *retiarius* was occasionally pitted against one or two *secutores*, whom he fought while standing on a platform, accessed by steps on one or both sides (Figure 21). Note that the more lightly armed *retiarius* was given the more advantageous position against the heavily armed *secutor*, no doubt in order to give the *retiarius* a chance of victory.[243] When he had to deal with two *secutores*, he was given piles of stones stacked in pyramid shape on the platform to help him fend off his two opponents as they tried to reach him. If the *retiarius* were able to kill or seriously wound one of them before the other reached the platform, then he had a

Figure 21   Pontiarii. Trieste Museum

much better chance of defeating the other *secutor*.[244] This form of fighting must have been popular with spectators because, in an inscription from Pompeii in which the components of two *munera* are listed, the *pontarii* are the only specific category of gladiator mentioned.[245] Like the *pontarius*, the *dimachaerus* may not be a separate category of gladiator, but, as Robert points out, could be a *retiarius* or even a heavy-armed gladiator of various categories who wielded a dagger or short sword in each hand: a 'specialization', as Junkelmann calls this form of fighting.[246]

A provincial gladiator: cruppellarius

The various provinces into which Gaul was divided took up gladiatorial combat with enthusiasm as part of their romanization. We know that the *gallus* became a popular gladiator type at Rome early in the history of gladiatorial combat, but it is doubtful that the *gallus* would have ever been accepted in Gaul, since he was created as a reminder of Gallic defeat. There seems, however, to have been at least one native gladiatorial type that was created in Gaul and did not appear in arenas outside that area: the *cruppellarius*. We hear of this Gallic gladiator type only once, when a group of *cruppellarius* were recruited by a Gallic rebel named Sacrovir in the early first century AD to fight against the Romans. On the evidence that we have, these gladiators were virtually useless in war and perhaps boring in the arena. They were covered from head to toe in virtually impenetrable metal plating of some kind (mail?), but were so hindered by the heavy armour that they could not inflict significant damage on their opponents. In battle against the Romans, their protective covering was an effective defence against spears and swords, but the Roman soldiers eventually got the best of them by chopping at their armour with axes, pickaxes, pikes and forked poles to expose their bodies to attack.[247]

Female gladiators

The Romans were fond of novelty in their entertainment, and there was no greater novelty than the spectacle of women appearing as gladiators in the arena, particularly aristocratic women. Female gladiators represented the contradiction of one of Rome's most cherished traditional values, the association of women with the household and various domestic tasks. When a woman fought in the arena, she was abandoning her female role and invading an exclusively masculine area of martial virtue and, when she fought as a professional gladiator, she, like a freeborn man, incurred the dishonour of *infamia* by taking up a disgraced profession. The scandal created by this act was probably even greater in the case of a woman. But as is the case even today, scandal fascinated the Romans despite societal disapproval, leading them to flock to see such performances and fuelling the desire of performers to attain notoriety by fulfilling this demand.

We hear of no female gladiators during the Republic, when women were less free to pursue their own desires. The legal and moral control that the *paterfamilias* wielded over his family, especially female members, was not to be questioned. The power of the family patriarch seems to have been a sufficient deterrent to female members of the family from putting themselves on display in the theatre or in the amphitheatre. Women, however, began to acquire greater freedom in the late Republic and early empire, so it is not surprising that we first hear of women wanting to perform as gladiators. The threat of *infamia* was apparently no longer enough to discourage individual women from volunteering themselves. By the early first century AD, the number of women fighting in the arena was sufficient to spur the Senate into action. In AD 11, a *Senatus Consultum* ('Decree of the Senate') was issued imposing an age restriction on both freeborn men (25 years old) and women (20 years old) before they could sign themselves up as gladiators or act on the stage.[248] This decree appears to be designed to stem the tide of impressionable young aristocrats, swept away by the romance of the arena and the stage, from volunteering their services in these venues. Eight years later, a second decree was issued to deal specifically with the problem of women from senatorial and equestrian families serving as gladiators. It would seem that, during this eight-year period, women from these two upper classes had begun to appear on the stage and to fight as gladiators in the arena in even greater numbers. The *Senatus Consultum* of AD 19 took a stricter approach. It forbade women of these classes to appear on the stage or become gladiators and prohibited *lanistae* from hiring them. The reason for these prohibitions given in this decree was that the *infamia* that these aristocrats incurred diminished the dignity of their respective classes.[249] Another penalty was added: those who disobeyed this decree were to be deprived of a proper burial with a funeral.[250] The existence of both these decrees indicates the active interest of women of all classes in fighting as a gladiator and the desire of Roman spectators to watch them perform.

Apparently, the decree of AD 19 was either forgotten or ignored during the reign of Nero, because more and more freeborn women were becoming performers in the theatre and the arena. Tacitus calls attention to the large numbers of upper-class women and senators who suffered disgrace because of their appearances in the arena.[251] Another historian who expressed chagrin at such behaviour was Cassius Dio, who was himself a member of the senatorial class. He points out that their service as gladiators and as arena hunters was in some cases voluntary and, in others, forced by the emperor. These aristocratic men and women, encouraged by Nero's appearances on-stage, engaged in other activities in public equally productive of *infamia* such as singing and dancing, playing musical instruments, acting in plays, and driving horses in the Circus Maximus.[252] Nero presented an ethnic variation on the female gladiator when he gave a *munus* in Puteoli hon-ouring Tiridates, the king of Armenia, in which Ethiopian women (along with Ethiopian men and children) fought as gladiators.[253] A character in Petronius' *Satyricon* mentions an *essedaria*, a female gladiator who rode in a British war chariot, as a featured attraction in a *munus* in southern Italy.[254] Female gladiators continued to appear in the arena throughout the rest of the first century AD and during the second. Aristocratic women who per-formed in the arena, both in gladiatorial combat and in the *venatio*, were a special target of Juvenal's satire. He complains of a certain Mevia who par-ticipated in the *venatio* as a *venator*, dressed up like an Amazon with one breast exposed and carrying hunting spears.[255] He also rails against women who disgrace their famous ancestors by training as gladiators in the *ludus*, wearing the typical gladiatorial armour from helmet to greaves.[256] The ulti-mate disgrace would be if this training were for real gladiatorial combat. Cassius Dio seeks to put the best face possible on a *venatio* given during the dedication of the Colosseum, when he expresses relief that the women who participated in this event were not of the two upper classes.[257]

Suetonius credits Domitian with being the first emperor to incorporate female gladiators and arena hunters into a nocturnal *munus* in the amphithe-atre by torchlight.[258] The female gladiators do not seem to have been taken seriously in Domitian's shows. The poet Statius speaks of these feminine fighters as 'untrained and ignorant of weaponry'. Moreover, they were pre-sented in conjunction with dwarf gladiators, who appeared immediately after them. Since the Romans were less than sympathetic to physical deformity,

Figure 22 Two female gladiators. British Museum, London, © The Trustees of The British Museum

combat involving dwarfs was for laughs. Statius depicts Mars and the person-ification 'Bloody Courage' (*Cruenta virtus*) laughing at the dwarfs in close combat, wounding and threatening death to each other in a comic parody of real gladiatorial combat.[259] The same comic effect would have been achieved when, on occasion, female fighters were matched against dwarfs, truly a bizarre combination, but probably much enjoyed by the spectators.[260]

In a bas-relief found in the Greek east at Halicarnassus two female glad-iators are depicted in combat (Figure 22). There is no way of telling their social rank; they could be aristocrats or ordinary women, but they appear to be real gladiators. They are heavy-armed fighters, but it is not clear to what specific category of gladiator they belong. They are not wearing their helmets, which are on the ground on either side of what seems to be a plat-form on which they are standing. Otherwise they sport the usual equipment of the heavy-armed gladiator: shield, *manica, balteus, subligaculum* and greaves. The reason for the helmets on the ground will be dealt with later in this chapter in 'Gladiatorial combat'. The medium size of their concave rectangular shields offers the possibility that both are *thraeces*, but there are some problems with that interpretation. The *thraex* did not usually fight another *thraex*, and their weapon appears to be a straight short sword or dagger rather than the Thracian's curved weapon (*sica*).[261] It has been suggested that they are *provocatores*, who did fight each other, but there is no evidence of the breast plate protecting the upper torso, characteristic of that type of gladiator. If the helmets on the ground were represented more clearly, we might be able to be more exact about their gladiator type. Both gladiators have one naked breast exposed that is not covered by the shield, which may mean that they fought with naked torsos just like most male gladiators. Completely naked torsos would suggest that these female gladiators sought equality with male gladiators, who (except for the *provocator*) wore no protective armour on their upper body as a badge of courage.

The inscription below them gives their names: Amazonia and Achillia, appropriate pseudonyms for female gladiators. The name Amazonia refers to the mythical female warriors who fought with one breast exposed. Achillia is the feminine form of Achilles, the greatest of all Greek legendary fighters. In fact, ancient spectators would have recognized in these names a reference to the legend according to which Achilles killed the Amazon Queen Penthesilea, ally of the Trojans at Troy, without realizing that she was woman until he stripped her armour.[262] The Greek word *apeluthēsan* ('they were released') indicates that they both fought well enough to impress the *editor* and the spectators, so that the former called it a draw and allowed both to retire from the arena to fight another day. This suggests that these female gladiators were not aristocratic women on a lark, but lower-class women who were fighting for their lives.[263] The fact that this match was thought deserving of durable commemoration in sculpted marble indicates how seriously these gladiators were taken. This slab may have been commissioned and put on public display in Halicarnassus by the *editor* to remind his fellow citizens of the great show he had put on, but this is not how *editores* usually memorialized their shows. An *editor* typically celebrated his *munus* with paintings displayed in locations frequented by the public, and privately with mosaic floors depicting various events in his *munus* in a reception area for all his guests to see.[264] Thus it has been argued that this relief could have been set up in the *ludus* in which these women were trained as an example of their achievement.[265]

In the late second century or early third century AD, Septimius Severus proclaimed a ban on upper-class female gladiators, citing essentially the same reason as the senatorial decree of AD 19.

> *The women in this contest fought so energetically and savagely, that they were the cause of other elite women becoming the object of jokes and as a result, it was decreed that no woman should ever again fight in a gladiatorial duel.*[266]

We only hear of female gladiators once more, in an inscription from the Roman port of Ostia in which a local magistrate named Hostilianus credits himself with being the first to present female gladiators in that city.[267] M. Cebeillac-Gervasoni and F. Zevi date the inscription to the second half of the second century AD, most likely before the ban.[268] In the inscription, Hostilianus is called 'the administrator of the young people's games' (*curator lusus iuvenalis*) in Ostia. The participants in these youth games were members of a paramilitary youth organization called a *collegium iuvenum* ('an association of young people'), consisting of aristocratic youth.[269] These organizations existed in towns and cities throughout the empire. They trained young men and, on occasion, young women, in martial arts, including swordsmanship. An inscription from Carsulae (north of Rome, near modern San Gemini) mentions a gladiator who was a trainer of youths (*pinnrapus iuvenum*).[270] Cebeillac-Gervasoni and Zevi have suggested that the female gladiators in Hostilianus' show could have been trained in the *collegium iuvenum* at Ostia (Rome's seaport), perhaps under his supervision. They also have proposed that Hostilianus' female gladiators may have been presented in the context of the games (*iuvenalia*) that were required of the young men and women as demonstration of their acquired skills rather than at the normal *munus*.[271] These women no doubt fought with wooden weapons or, at worst, with dulled swords. Coleman, however, interprets this evidence differently. She dates this inscription to a period after Septimius Severus' ban on aristocratic female gladiators and argues that the use of the word *mulieres* ('women') rather than *feminae* ('ladies') means that no aristocratic women were involved in this show, and thus would not have violated Severus' ban. She also points out that it is likely that other shows involving female gladiators had been presented in various towns, of which no record has survived.[272]

Gladiator names

The names of gladiators were an important aspect of their mystique. Most gladiators chose stage names that projected an attractive gladiatorial image of themselves to the spectators. On the other hand, many gladiators used their real names. Most of those who did so were undoubtedly *auctorati* and used the three names, typical of Roman citizens, as an attempt to differentiate themselves from the slave gladiators, their social inferiors. An example of one of these three-part names is one that a graffiti artist painted on the side of a tomb in Pompeii above his depiction of a gladiator, L. Raecius Felix.[273] Sometimes *auctorati*, following usage in everyday Roman life, used only their *praenomen* ('first name') and their *nomen* (surname) like M. Attilius, who defeated Raecius. Another possibility for a freeborn *auctoratus* was to be known just by his *nomen* or by his *cognomen* (third name).[274] Nonetheless, despite the dignity and status that these three names brought to numerous gladiators, they lacked the imaginative aura of stage names.[275] In adopting pseudonyms, gladiators drew heavily on Greco-Roman myth and legend, which was familiar to most spectators. Obviously, the sobriquet 'Achilles' excited the imagination much more than L. Raecius Felix. Greek and Roman epic provided a rich resource for appropriate gladiatorial names, especially since the heroes in these works fought duels with swords. The pseudonyms that follow are a selection from the numerous surviving pseudonyms: Patroclus (best friend of Achilles), Diomedes (one of the leading Greek warriors), Aias/Ajax (second greatest Greek warrior), Hector (leading Trojan warrior) and Turnus (Aeneas' chief opponent in the *Aeneid*). Other heroic legends such as the story of the Argonauts and the Seven against Thebes were also favoured sources, for example: Polydeuces (Latin Pollux), the famous boxer and immortal brother of the mortal Castor (also a gladiatorial name), and Bebryx (Argonauts); Eteocles, Polyneices, Tydeus, Hippomedon, Amphiaraus and Parthenopaeus (from Theban legend). The names Eteocles and Polyneices are particularly fitting because of the fratricidal sword duel they fought for the kingship of Thebes. We know that two brothers in Smyrna (modern Izmir on the western coast of Turkey) took the names of the quarrelling Theban brothers, but in real life their feelings for each other were quite different as Polyneices' epitaph reveals: 'Eteocles [set up this monument] in memory of his brother Polyneices, an *essedarius*'.[276] Two names, Bebryx and Tydeus, add a frisson of ruthless savagery to a gladiator's image. Bebryx ('the Bebrycian') undoubtedly refers to a character in the *Argonautica*, Amycus, the arrogant king of the barbarian Bebrycians, who ignored the laws of hospitality by immediately challenging any stranger arriving on his shore to a boxing match and then killing him. His last opponent was the Argonaut Polydeuces, whose training in the techniques of boxing enabled him to defeat and kill Amycus, a victory of civilized skills over brute force.[277] Tydeus alienated his patron divinity, Athena, by eating the brains of his Theban opponent, Melanippus.[278] The adjectival names Ferox ('arrogantly savage') and Pugnax ('combative') carry the same meaning, but without the specific savagery in the stories of Amycus and Tydeus. There were other legendary heroes whose names gladiators favoured, such as Perseus, who beheaded the Medusa, Bellerophon, who rode the flying horse Pegasus, and Meleager, who killed the monstrous Calydonian boar (also a good name for a *venator*). Another category of adjectives and nouns (both Latin and Greek) stress victory and superiority in general: Victor ('winner') and in its passive form, Invictus ('invincible'), the Greek equivalent of which was Anicetus, Neikophoros ('victorious'), Exochus ('mightiest'), Amaranthus ('unperishable'), Triumphus ('triumph') and Tyrannus ('tyrant'). Stephanos ('crown') is a very popular gladiatorial name because it signifies the pursuit of excellence. A crown was awarded not just to any winner of a gladiatorial contest, but to one who has performed outstandingly.

Not all gladiator names were suggestive of martial virtue and force. There are some names that suggest trickery and/or skill. Hermes and Autolycos, for example, were both mythical tricksters. The pseudonyms Argutus ('keen-minded') and Pardos ('leopard', a wily predator) have the same connotation, while Capreolus ('wild goat') suggests light-footedness. Another group of gladiator names from Greco-Roman myth emphasize beauty and sexual attractiveness and no doubt were a further stimulus to women who were vulnerable to the sexual appeal of gladiators: Hippolytus (a handsome youth who rejected all women and died for this offence against Aphrodite), Hyacinthus (a beautiful young man loved by Apollo) and Eros/Cupid, the god of love himself.[279] Sometimes adjectives were used as names with the same intent: Kallimorphos, ('of beautiful form'), Euprepes ('good looking'), Euchrous ('having a good complexion') and Decoratus ('handsome').

Gladiators were also fond of using stage names to associate themselves with precious jewels and with gold. Perhaps gladiators named Amethystus ('amethyst'), Beryllus ('beryl') and Smaragdus ('emerald') had these gems set into their armour and weapons as decorations. Aureolus ('golden') was a favourite name of leading gladiators.[280] The Greek stem '*chryso-*', meaning 'golden', appears frequently in gladiatorial names: Chrysanthus ('golden flower'), Chrysopetasus ('golden hat', probably a reference to Hermes' broad-brimmed hat) and Chrysomallos ('golden fleece'), a reference to the story of Argonauts. Two other golden names suggest an association with Eros: Chrysopteros ('of golden wing', an epithet of Eros) and Chryseros ('golden love'). Finally, the popular sobriquets Columbus and Palumbus ('dove' and 'ring dove') seem odd for gladiators, emphasizing gentleness over violence. These names may be intended to be ironic as seems to be the case with the names Trupheros ('dainty') and Hilarus ('cheerful').[281]

Great performers in the arena

We know that certain gladiators attained great fame and popularity, but it might seem surprising, given the honours heaped on athletes today, that there seems to be so little praise of star gladiators in Roman literary sources. There is also no record of statues of gladiators in comparison with the hundreds of statues of great Greek athletes we read about in Greek sources such as Pausanias. The reason for this neglect is the disgrace associated with the profession of gladiator. There was one writer, however, whose enthusiasm for gladiators led him to dedicate a poem of praise to a contemporary star of the arena. The name of the gladiator was Hermes, whom the poet Martial lavishly praises for his skills, competitive character, and his overwhelming superiority among gladiators. Each line of the poem begins with the name Hermes:

1 *Hermes, the martial pleasure of the age;*
Hermes, trained in the use of all weapons;
Hermes, both gladiator and teacher;
Hermes, the stormy terror of his gladiator school;
5 *Hermes, whom alone Helius fears;*
Hermes, before whom alone Advolans falls;
Hermes, trained to win without killing;
Hermes, the only gladiator who can substitute for himself;
Hermes, the enricher of ticket scalpers;
10 *Hermes, the care and despair of gladiator groupies;*

Hermes, proud user of the warlike spear;
Hermes, threatening with his marine trident;
Hermes, the object of fear in his soft cap;
Hermes, the glory of universal Mars;
15 *Hermes, singular in all ways and three times unique.*[282]

Martial's emphasis is on Hermes' unusual versatility, to which he refers in lines 2 and 11–15. Apparently, Hermes, although familiar with all styles of fighting (2), had mastered the fighting styles of three different types of gladiators; usually, a gladiator specialized in only one. The three types here are the *hoplomachus* ('spear', 11), *retiarius* ('trident', 12) and *veles* ('soft cap', 13). Hermes' choice of these three gladiatorial types suggests that he was not much of a sword fighter, since none of these three types used that weapon. The *hoplomachus* used a lance and dagger, the *retiarius*, a trident and a dagger, and the *veles*, a throwing spear. Hermes seems not to have been the strongest of gladiators because both the *retiarius* and the *veles* were light-armed gladiators and the *hoplomachus*, while not exactly light-armed, was somewhere in between in this regard, carrying a small, round shield weighing only about 4 pounds. It is not surprising that Hermes was already a teacher in the gladiator school, while he was still an active gladiator (3). His versatility made him particularly valuable as an instructor. Helius ('sun god') and Advolans ('the flying gladiator', a reference to his speed) are apparently outstanding gladiators who have been defeated by Hermes. Especially notable is Hermes' ability to win without killing (7), which suggests that not all gladiators were out to kill their opponents unless it was necessary. His mastery of weapons was such that he could employ them with just enough force to inflict non-lethal wounds that would cause his opponent to submit. Hermes also possessed the *sine qua non* of a great gladiator: women found him sexually attractive (10).

Martial also praises an animal fighter named Carpophorus in two poems. The praise, however, although effusive, is much less specific and somewhat formulaic. In both poems from his *Book of Spectacles*, Martial associates Carpophorus with the achievements of mythical heroes such as Hercules, Jason, Theseus and Meleager, who killed or subdued monstrous animals.[283] Martial's three poems (one for Hermes and two for Carpophorus) represent the only extant paeans to specific fighters in the arena. Other gladiators had to settle for the ephemeral applause of the crowd and whatever monetary awards the *editor* deemed appropriate as recognition of their victories in the arena. The gladiator and the animal fighter were men of the moment (sometimes a very brief moment) and not for the ages.

It should be noted, however, that human performers were not the only ones to achieve fame in the arena. There were large predators whose success in killing hunters or performing tricks in the arena brought them such fame that they were given names and their images were artistically represented. For example, a North African mosaic from Rades celebrates famous trained bears with impressive names: Braciatus, Gloriosus, Simplicius, Alecsandria, Fedra (the tragic heroine Phaedra) and Nilus ('the Nile'), while a mosaic from Curubis (modern Kourba in Tunisia) honours two bears who were obviously effective killers named Crudelis ('cruel') and Omicida ('man-killer').[284] The Magerius mosaic from Smirat in Tunisia honours four courageous leopards which were killed by equally famous hunters. The leopards were named Victor ('winner'), Crispinus ('Curly', a common Roman cognomen), Luxurius ('pleasure-loving') and Romanus ('Roman'). While the average person had to be satisfied with watching these beloved animals in the arena, an emperor could indulge his enthusiasm more immediately. Valentinian I (AD 364–375) kept two female bears, *Mica* ('Gold Flake') and *Innocentia* ('Innocence'), renowned as 'devourers of men' in cages just outside his bedroom. Innocence, because of her great success in killing human opponents in the arena, won the equivalent of a gladiator's *rudis*, when Valentinian released her into the woods. Ammianus Marcellinus, who tells this story, carries the parallel with a gladiator even further when he calls Innocence 'well deserving' (*bene meritam*), a phrase commonly used in the epitaphs of gladiators to sum up their careers.[285]

The main event: gladiators in the afternoon

The mood

The atmosphere of the combat was serious and even sombre. The menace of violence and death pervaded the arena. A passage in a rhetorical exercise presents a fictional recruit's reaction to his first appearance in the arena. His words vividly present the terrors of the arena for participants and even for the crowd. After all, the excitement of vicarious fear that was aroused in spectators by identifying themselves with the gladiators was part of the fun.[286] Romans, who were not jaded by the overload of violent entertainment that we moderns are regularly subject to in films and on television, would have been especially vulnerable to the brutal sights and sounds they experienced in the arena.

> *Now the day was here and the people had now gathered for the spectacle of our [i.e., the recruit and his fellow gladiators] suffering and now those about to perish, having been put on display in the arena, had led a procession of their own death. The* munerarius *took his seat, about to gain public favour at the cost of our blood . . . one thing . . . made me miserable, that I seemed inadequately prepared; to be sure I was destined to become a victim of the arena; no gladiator had cost the* munerarius *less. The whole arena resounded with the apparatus of death. One man was sharpening a sword, another one was heating plates with fire, some gladiators were being struck by rods, others, by whips [all these devices were used to force reluctant gladiators to fight].[287] You would have thought these men were pirates.[288] Trumpets blared with their funereal sound [trumpet music was associated with funerals]; after the couches of Libitina [= 'stretchers'] were brought in, there was a funeral procession before those carried out [of the arena] were even dead. Everywhere there were wounds, moans, gore; every possible danger was evident.[289]*

Gladiatorial combat

At a large-scale *munus*, the spectators could expect to see twelve or thirteen matches in an afternoon, which would take at least three hours to complete.[290] This estimate is based on the presumed average length of a gladiatorial contest being between ten and fifteen minutes. One would also have to allow some extra time for those matches that required the *editor* to make a life or death decision and for normal breaks between matches. This time would have been used by arena attendants called *harenarii* ('sand men') who cleaned up the bloody sand with rakes and sprinkled it with water.[291]

What was a gladiatorial match like? Surviving ancient art such as paintings and mosaics give us still-life depictions, but modern re-creations in films often provide a better representation of these fights. There is one literary description of gladiatorial combat in Lucian's *Toxaris*, although the account is very brief. It is fictional, but no doubt Lucian had seen real matches. The fight takes place in the Greek city of Amastris on the southern shore of the Black Sea. Two friends, Toxaris and Sisennes, both Scythians, who have lost all their possessions to thieves, find out about a *munus* to be held in three days' time. Apparently, the show was organized in a rather impromptu way, without the careful preparation typical of most *munera*.[292] The *editor* of this show was recruiting gladiators with an offer of 10,000 drachmas to anyone willing to take part in the gladiatorial show. Sisennes enthusiastically decides to take up the offer and, on the day of the *munus*, leaves his seat in the theatre and enters the fighting area. With characteristic bravado, he decides to fight without a helmet. The match then begins:

> *Taking his position [Sisennes] fought helmetless and right away he himself is wounded, having been cut behind the knee by a curved sword [His opponent was a* thraex.*] with the result that much blood flowed. I [Toxaris] was already dying with fear, but [Sisennes] alertly pierced with his sword the chest of his opponent as he was boldly rushing in for the kill. As a result, his opponent fell before his feet and he, in bad shape himself, sat on the corpse and came close to dying himself, but I ran to him, helped him up and comforted him. And when he was dismissed as the winner, I picked him up and carried him back to our quarters.*[293]

This fight is really quite a simple one with a quick decisive result. One must remember that the gladiators described here are amateurs, attracted by the offer of cash for their participation. It is not surprising that these two young men seem to be ignorant of defensive techniques, leading to a short, bloody fight. Moreover, the quick death of Sisennes' opponent eliminates the need for a dramatic life or death decision by the *editor*. The crowd does not have the opportunity to recommend discharge or death for the losing gladiator. If Sisennes had not been able to continue after initially being seriously wounded by his opponent, he would have had two choices: to fight on in his weakened condition until he was killed by his opponent (or by some miracle won the match), or to ask the *editor* for release (*missio*), which, if granted, would have allowed him to walk (or be helped) out of the arena.[294] If he chose the first option and was killed, his result would have been reported as *stans periit* (literally, 'he died standing'), an honourable death. If he chose the latter option, he would have given a clear signal to the *summarudis* and to the *editor* by lifting his left arm and raising the index finger of his left hand (Figure 23). Often this gesture would be accompanied

Figure 23 Zliten mosaic: a *hoplomachus* waits while his opponent, a *murmillo*, having discarded his shield as a sign of submission, asks for *missio* (*stans missus*) with an upraised index finger of his left hand. Villa at Dar Buc Amméra, Tripolitania. Archaeological Museum, Tripoli. Roger Wood/Corbis

by the discarding of an important piece of equipment such as a helmet, shield or sword. Sometimes the gladiator conceding defeat would merely lower his weapon.[295] In a Pompeian graffito, the gladiator L. Raecius Felix has thrown his helmet to the ground, while the gladiator seeking *missio* in Figure 23 has thrown off his shield from his left forearm and hand so that he can signal submission with his finger. These are signs of an admission of defeat, but it still mattered whether the gladiator made them while standing or from various lower positions (sitting, leaning, squatting or kneeling) on the ground. An epitaph of a gladiator named *Flamma* ('Flame') shows that this was an important difference.[296] The inscription records that Flamma died at age 30, having had thirty-four matches, of which he won twenty-one and then mentions two kinds of *missio*: *stans* [*missus*] ('released while standing') and *mis*[*sus*] ('released not standing').[297] These releases account for twelve of his losses (*stans* eight times and *missus* four). The missing loss was of course his final bout in which he was killed. Flamma was undoubtedly proud that the number of releases standing is twice those requested from the ground. In only four of his losses had he been beaten so badly that he could not get up to request *missio* from a standing position. The fact he requested and had been granted *missio* from a standing position mitigated the shame of his losses on eight occasions.

There is one other category of release, *stantes missi*, which is the plural of *stans missus*, but has a different meaning: a draw rather than a defeat. The opportunity for the release of both gladiators was infrequent, since both opponents had to request *missio* simultaneously. The poet Martial recorded a celebrated instance of this result during the inauguration of the Colosseum (mentioned earlier).[298] The gladiators in this match, Priscus and Verus, had been fighting intensely for an extended period of time with no decisive outcome. Titus stopped the match and imposed a new condition (*lex*, 'rule'): that both gladiators lay down their shields (*parma . . . posita*, with their shields laid aside') and fight until one raised a finger in surrender (*ad digitum*).[299] Titus' *lex* was designed to bring the match to an end more quickly. Both gladiators would have lost their main defence against serious wounds to the torso. When this solution did not achieve its intended result, the crowd, impressed by the efforts of these evenly matched gladiators, began to demand *missio* for both of them. Things came to head when both gladiators eventually asked for *missio* at the same time.[300] The obvious intent of his *lex* had been to determine a winner, but the simultaneity of their requests for *missio* now allowed him to make a decision fair to both gladiators in recognition of their epic match. Titus pronounced the match a tie, declaring both gladiators winners with the presentation of palms, symbolic of victory. In addition, Titus granted *missio* in its ultimate form, a complete discharge from their service as gladiators, symbolized by the presentation of the *rudis*.[301] Another example of *stantes missi* can be seen on the bas-relief from Halicarnassus discussed earlier, in which two female gladiators appear in full armour except for their helmets (Figure 22). The legend in Greek, *apeluthēsan* ('they were released'), appears above the two fighters. Coleman has compellingly argued that their heads are bare because they have performed a gesture of surrender, placing their helmets on the ground on either side of the platform on which they are standing. Thus, *apeluthēsan* is a Greek translation of the Latin *stantes missi*. Just as the match of Priscus and Verus received a poetic monument to commemorate its rare outcome, the discharge of Achillia and Amazon was memorialized with a stone monument for the same reason.[302]

If, however, *missio* were not granted to the losing gladiator, it would mean that the petitioner would be killed by the victorious gladiator in a ritual that would bring a dramatically powerful end to the contest. First the referee (*summarudis*), stepped in with his rod to keep the two fighters separate (Figure 23), or just restrained the sword hand of the victorious gladiator while the *editor* made his decision (Figure 11). The task of preventing the winning gladiator from attacking a gladiator who had requested *missio* was the primary responsibility of the *summarudis*.[303]

The *editor* had the final word on the matter of life or death of a gladiator, no matter how vociferous the crowd was in support of or against, a gladiator.[304] The failure to comply with his decision was not tolerated. During the reign of Commodus, a number of victorious gladiators apparently showed reluctance to kill their defeated opponents when the emperor denied *missio*. Commodus' punishment was swift and severe. He had the disobedient gladiators chained together and forced them to fight each other in a group. They were bound so close to each other that some gladiators accidentally killed those who were not their immediate opponents.[305]

It should be noted, however, that some *editores* seem to have been willing on occasion to leave the decision to grant release or not up to the winning gladiator. The emperor Caracalla told a defeated gladiator to direct his request for *missio* to his opponent. This pronouncement could put the winning gladiator in a difficult situation. The losing gladiator could have been a comrade or even a cellmate in their *ludus*. If, however, he followed his first inclination and spared his opponent, he might offend the emperor in appearing to be more merciful than his ruler. Thus, he regretfully chose the safer option for himself and refused *missio*.[306] An epitaph of a gladiator named Urbicus seems to presume that an *editor* had granted him the power to decide whether his opponent would live or die. In the epitaph, he speaks to those gladiators who read this inscription on his tomb: 'My advice is that you condemn to death a gladiator whom you have defeated.' Apparently, Urbicus had granted *missio* to his opponent, who on a later occasion had killed him.[307] (Note that it is the custom in epitaphs for the deceased to speak to passers-by.) In their own epitaphs, some gladiators speak of their own compassion towards their rivals in the arena, who were probably fellow members of the *familia*. For example, Olympus says that he spared the lives of many opponents.[308]

The *editor*'s life-and-death decision was not made in a vacuum. There were a number of factors that could come into play. First, the *editor* invited the spectators to give their opinions. Spectators who had been won over by a display of courage and skill by the petitioner would shout *missum* ('[I want him] released') or *missos* ('[I want] both gladiators released'). An inscription records what was probably the chant of two competing factions among the spectators in reaction to both opponents' request for *missio*: *missos missos, iugula iugula* ('Release them, release them; cut their throats, cut their throats!'[309] The shouts in favour of *missio* were often accompanied by gestures such as shaking the flaps of the toga or waving handkerchiefs.[310] If the *editor* decided to spare the losing gladiator, he used a hand signal, which consisted of turning the thumb, pressed to the fist, down towards the ground, a sign of approval among the Romans.[311] Those spectators who disagreed or merely wanted to see a man put to death shouted *iugula* ('cut his throat') and turned their thumb upwards pressed against the closed fist in a gesture called 'the hostile thumb' (*pollice infesto*).[312] A poem in the *Anthologia Latina* confirms the tie between the 'the hostile thumb' and the fate of a defeated gladiator: 'even the defeated gladiator is hopeful in the cruel arena although the crowd threatens him with the hostile thumb'.[313] The 'thumbs down' gesture given by the Vestal Virgins in Jean-Léon Gérôme's famous painting *Pollice Verso* (1872) (Figure 24) is a commonly understood gesture of disapproval in modern times, but had just the opposite meaning in the ancient world. Anthony Corbeill argues that, in the Roman mind, the thumb was symbolic of the penis and thus this gesture would be the ancient equivalent of giving the losing gladiator 'the finger'. He also argues that the modern 'thumbs up' sign did not have a positive meaning until the twentieth century. (Clearly, however, the modern thumbs-down sign had already acquired a negative meaning by the time of *Pollice Verso*.) Corbeill describes the development of this gesture: 'In parallel to the representation of the phallus in Roman antiquity, the originally apotropaic significations of the thumb came to be perceived as hostile and threatening.'[314] Thus, Juvenal's famously ambiguous phrase 'turned thumb' (*pollice verso*) as a sign of condemnation from the spectators means specifically 'with upturned thumb'.[315] Of course, Juvenal did not need to explain that to his readers, who were quite familiar with the gesture.

Figure 24 *Pollice Verso* (Jean-Léon Gérôme). Note the Vestal Virgins in the upper right-hand corner giving the anachronistic 'thumbs down' signal. Phoenix Art Museum, Arizona, USA/ The Bridgeman Art Library Ltd

If there were a clear consensus among the crowd for either discharge or death, there would be pressure on the *editor* to please them. We know that spectators usually liked to see the request for *missio* answered negatively by the *editor* so that they could see what amounts to an execution of the losing gladiator by his victorious opponent. *Editores* seeking public favour would often grant their wish. Juvenal, in his rant against men who had been lowly musicians and arena attendants but were now wealthy enough to give *munera*, notes that they, in their desire to ingratiate themselves with the spectators, went along with crowd's desire to deny *missio*: 'they kill to please the spectators'.[316] Another important consideration was economic. When an *editor* decided not to grant *missio*, he was obliged to compensate the *lanista* from whom he had rented the gladiator, and the more valuable the gladiator was, the more the *editor* had to consider whether he wanted to add a considerable payment to the significant amount of money he had already spent on his *munus*. Thus, it is unlikely that a valuable commodity like a 'star' gladiator would be denied *missio*. Moreover, because he was freeborn, an *auctoratus* would be given more consideration with regard to *missio* than a slave gladiator. Veteran gladiators were also more likely to be spared when they lost. An inscription records a *munus*, given by a certain M. Mesonius, in which the veterans lost and were released: a *dimachaerus* in his twenty-first fight lost to a *hoplomachus* in just his third and was released; an *essedarius* in his fifty-second match lost to another *essedarius* in his twenty-seventh and was spared.[317] Sometimes, personal motives came into play, affecting the *editor*'s decision, as when Claudius wanted to order the death of the gladiator Sabinus, the prefect of the German bodyguard under Caligula, but was persuaded by his wife Messalina, who had been Sabinus' lover, to spare him.[318] Of course, the desire to avoid outlandish expenditure was not always the primary motivation of an *editor* who wanted to please and impress the crowd. If he adopted a policy of no release in his *munus*, he was likely to produce a permanent record of his generosity (to the spectators), as did the *editor* in a third century AD inscription from Minturnae, which credited him with presenting eleven matches over a four-day period and denying *missio* to eleven gladiators.[319]

If the *editor* was not the emperor and the ruler was present at the *munus*, the *editor* could be intimidated by the imperial presence when he was deciding the issue of *missio* and thus would follow what he knew to be the emperor's usual policy in this matter. Ovid points out that when Augustus entered the amphitheatre as a spectator at someone else's *munus*, a defeated gladiator was sure to be granted *missio*, although the preference of the *editor* and the crowd might have been just the opposite.[320] By the middle of the first century AD, however, spectators increasingly preferred a more lethal result. A character in Petronius' *Satyricon* talks enthusiastically about an upcoming *munus* in which the gladiators will fight to the death.[321] It is during the reign of Augustus that we first hear of a new condition or *lex* laid down for combat by some *editores: sine missione* ('without release'). This meant that surrender with a request for *missio* would not be allowed. The fight will be to the death. Augustus reacted negatively to this new policy and established a ban on fights *sine missione*.[322] Augustus' preference for *missio* seems to have been a desire to preserve what had been the custom in gladiatorial fights up to his day: virtually automatic release for the petitioning gladiator. His ban may have been occasioned by a *munus* given by Lucius Domitius Ahenobarbus, the grandfather of the emperor Nero. Suetonius gives only a very general reason for Ahenobarbus' offence: 'he [Domitius] gave a *munus* that was of such savagery that Augustus was forced to restrain him with an edict after a private reprimand had failed'.[323] One possibility is that the practice which Suetonius characterizes as 'savagery' (*saevitia*) was Domitius' *lex* of *sine missione* for all the matches in his *munus*. Another possibility is that Domitius, without officially proclaiming a policy of *sine missione*, merely refused *missio* to all gladiators requesting it, thus producing the same results as a declaration of *sine missione*, as probably was the case with the *editor* at Minturnae mentioned above. A fictional *munus* in southern Italy in Petroniius' *Satyricon* was apparently advertised as requiring fights to the death. The phrase used is 'without escape' (*sine fuga*), most likely synonymous with *sine missione*.[324] This perhaps suggests that Augustus' ban was occasionally ignored outside of Rome. Drusus, a son of the emperor Tiberius, was the *editor* of a *munus* along with his brother Germanicus (AD 15), in which he was censured both by shocked spectators and his father for 'rejoicing excessively in blood however cheap'.[325] Although the Romans normally saw nothing wrong with gladiators being killed, there was too much 'cheap' blood shed in this *munus*, even for jaded Roman spectators. Now, the question is what specifically made this *munus* so bloody? It is unlikely that Augustus' ban on *sine missione* matches would have been flouted openly during the reign of his adopted son, Tiberius. In all probability, it was the extra-sharp swords that Drusus supplied to his gladiators, which became known as 'Drusian' swords and no doubt produced significantly worse wounds in comparison with ordinary swords.[326] The policy of the emperor Marcus Aurelius, who was averse to the bloodshed of gladiatorial combat, was never to give sharp swords to his gladiators when he was *editor*, but to supply them with blunted weapons.[327] David Potter argues that gladiators rarely fought in matches in which the death of one opponent was a condition. He also points out that while the emperor was free to impose a *sine missione* condition on his *munus*, *munerarii* in the provinces had to get his permission.[328]

The emperor Claudius followed in the footsteps of his two ancestors Domitius Ahenobarbus and Drusus (both members of the Claudian clan) in the matter of gladiators. Suetonius characterizes his behavior as an *editor* as 'cruel and bloodthirsty' because of his policy that even an accidental fall of a gladiator would result in his death. Apparently, Claudius justified this principle by counting the position of the fallen gladiator on the ground as an admission of defeat and an appeal for *missio*. Once a gladiator fell, Claudius automatically denied *missio*. He imposed this policy not only when he was *editor*, but also on other *editores*.[329] On the other hand, Claudius sometimes could act generously as an *editor*. On one occasion, he released an *essedarius* when he was supplicated by the gladiator's four sons, an incident discussed earlier in a different context. Claudius was then moved to send an attendant around the amphitheatre carrying a placard advising the people to beget children in light of how valuable his four sons had been to the *essedarius*.[330]

Once the editor had made his decision, a fanfare from the arena orchestra signalled his readiness and all attention would be turned towards him as he gave either a positive or negative hand signal. This moment can be seen in Figure 11. A *summarudis* restrains the right arm of a victorious *eques* as a horn player, accompanied by the other musicians, signals the moment of decision.[331]

There were specific expectations of how a defeated gladiator should behave after he was refused *missio*. Just like soldiers, gladiators were trained to give unquestioning obedience to their superiors. The most important aspect of this obedience was their complete submission to the decision of the *munerarius* and an unflinching reception of the deathblow (Figure 25).[332] Of course, the ideal was not always attained in practice. Some gladiators, facing imminent death, did not behave so courageously, a behaviour that annoyed the crowd which had come to expect higher standards.[333] Nonetheless, Cicero believed that gladiators generally provided an example of what behavioural miracles 'practice, preparation [and] habit' could create. What amazed Roman intellectuals about gladiators, who were in large part slaves, was the admirable courage they commonly exhibited, a moral quality which was thought to be characteristic only of freeborn men. Seneca gives the example of a gladiator who had not shown any courage throughout the whole match, but when denied *missio*, 'offered his throat to his opponent and guided the wavering sword to its destination'.[334] He also notes that losing gladiators would rather display their courage to the crowd by being dispatched by their opponent in the arena than having their throat ignobly cut in the *spoliarium*.[335]

There is one other possible outcome of a gladiatorial duel: both gladiators kill each other. This was not a common occurrence in the arena, and because of its rarity, was considered a significant event. When two gladiators

Figure 25 Borghese mosaic: Astacius, ordered by the *munerarius*, delivers deathblow to his opponent. Note 'theta' symbol over dead gladiator in lower right-hand corner. Torrenova, Borghese Gallery. Alinari Archives/Corbis

killed each other, Claudius had a set of small knives made out of their swords as a memento of the occasion.[336] The scholiast Porphyrion, in an explanatory note on one of Horace's *Satires*, mentions that an epic match between Bythus and Bacchius, two of the most famous gladiators of the late first century BC, resulted in the death of both fighters.[337]

Even *damnati* could be released, although it happened rarely. Such a release occurred in Claudius' famous *naumachia* ('staged naval battle') on the Fucine Lake, when all the *damnati* who survived the fighting were released because of their bravery. The most unusual case of a released *damnatus* is that of Androclus (to be discussed in Chapter 5), who won the hearts of the crowd and the emperor when he told the story about his earlier kindness to a lion that did not attack him in the arena. A good part of this story is fictional, but the details of its conclusion in the amphitheatre are almost certainly authentic. At Rome, the release of a *damnatus* was an *ad hoc* decision of the *editor* (usually the emperor), but in the provinces, this kind of release was eventually incorporated into the law with specified conditions. A statute in Justinian's *Digest* orders that the presiding official at a *venatio* in the provinces should not release someone condemned *ad bestias* just 'because of the favour of the crowd', but only if the *damnatus* has the kind of 'strength and skill' appropriate to a performer in the arena at Rome. Even in this case, the provincial *editor* should first consult the emperor.[338] An animal in a *venatio* might even win *missio* if, like a gladiator, it won the favour of the crowd and the *editor*. Martial tells a story of the emperor's release of a doe, which, having outwitted pursuing hounds with her twists and turns, stopped in front of the emperor's box and seemed to adopt a suppliant stance. The emperor granted the request and the dogs did not harm the doe. According to Martial, this was the result of the emperor's divine power: one of the poet's servile flatteries of the emperor.[339]

Survival odds and life expectancy

The life and death decisions of the *munerarius* bring to mind certain questions. What were the chances of survival for a gladiator in a given match? How long were their careers, on average? In order to calculate the survival odds of gladiators, Ville has used inscriptions that record deaths and survivals in matches and give the age of gladiators at death. The statistics that Ville, or any scholar, presents cannot pretend to scientific precision because of the haphazard survival of inscriptions.[340] The inscriptions involving gladiators obviously represent only an infinitesimal percentage of all the gladiators who fought in ancient times. Epitaphs of gladiators, which are an important source of our knowledge of gladiatorial careers, exist only for those gladiators whose surviving friends and/or family had the resolve and the financial resources to commemorate his professional life with a tomb and an inscription. Given this limitation, however, statistical averages based on minimal evidence are still valuable for the approximations that they provide us. Ville says that the odds of a gladiator surviving a match in the first century AD were nine to one in his favour.[341] Hopkins and Beard, using a different set of inscriptions as evidence (which they honestly call 'a ridiculously small sample'), do not differ substantially from Ville. They calculate the survival rate of the first century AD as slightly over eight in ten.[342] During this period, *missio* seems to have been the norm. Only the incompetent or the cowardly were refused release. In the second and third centuries AD, however, Ville states that survival rate decreased by half, so that a gladiator had only slightly less than five chances out of ten to leave the arena alive.[343] An extreme example is a *munus* that was given in AD 249 in Minturnae discussed earlier. The editor denied *missio* to the losers of all 11 matches.[344] Ville sees the reason for this as the increasing competition among *editores* to win favour among the spectators, who wanted to witness a death in every match. By the second century, the denial of *missio* had become the rule rather than the exception.[345] *Missio* was awarded only when the loser had impressed the *editor* and the crowd with his bravery.

In reality, the odds of survival were different for each gladiator in accordance with his level of skill and experience. Not surprisingly, a majority of inexperienced gladiators were killed in their first or second fights. Highly skilled fighters naturally had a much better chance of survival, but there were other factors involved in their greater probability of survival. First, gladiators of the highest level, such as imperial gladiators, were only matched with gladiators of similar proficiency on special occasions (to lessen the risk of serious injury or death of very expensive gladiators); for the most part, they fought inferior combatants. Thus, these proficient gladiators piled up very impressive records of victories during their long careers. Ville cites gladiators who won from 30 to 150 career victories.[346] As we have seen earlier, star gladiators were too valuable to be denied *missio*. This was also true to a lesser degree of merely good gladiators. Ville also ventures an average age of gladiators who died in combat based on sixteen epitaphs that give age of the deceased. His calculation is 27 years of age, but he rightly does not propose this average with any great confidence.[347] Hopkins and Beard suggest a significantly lower number for the average: 22.5 years.[348] While there is no doubt that becoming a gladiator increased the risk of an early death, one should not exaggerate the statistical significance of the early deaths of gladiators. Wiedemann notes that one has to judge the lifespan of gladiators in the context of life expectancy among their non-gladiatorial contemporaries.[349] In ancient Rome, there was a considerable risk of an early death even for non-gladiators. Three out of five persons died before the age of 20.[350] On the other hand, there were some gladiators whose careers were relatively long. For example, the gladiator Flamma died at age 30 having fought thirty-three times.[351] We cannot be sure how many years it took him to compile thirty-three fights, but approximately a decade might be a reasonable guess. M. Antonius Niger, a *thraex*, died at age 38, but he had fought only eighteen times.[352] Since his three names indicate that he was a freeman, he was no doubt an *auctoratus*, who probably signed up later in life for a limited period and perhaps died a natural death.

There were also the lucky few who were successful enough to survive until they were granted a complete release from their service as gladiators (*rudiarii*). It seems that there were different periods of service as a gladiator before a criminal condemned to a gladiator school (*damnatus ad ludum gladiatorium*) became eligible for the *rudis* according to the nature of the crime. An edict of Hadrian states that a man convicted for cattle rustling had to fight in the arena for at least three years before he could receive the *rudis*. A *munerarius* could make a special grant of freedom along with the *rudis*, but normally the receipt of the *rudis* did not mean that the convict was automatically a freeman.[353] Although the convicted cattle rustler had escaped the dangers of the arena, he still could not become a freeman until after the fifth year.[354] One presumes that during the two-year period he was still confined to the *ludus*, assisting in the training of other gladiators or even doing odd jobs. We have no evidence of how long the waiting period was for those guilty of other crimes. One thing, however, is certain; this release did not come quickly.[355] The sources speak of 'old' and 'decrepit' gladiators, probably in their mid to late thirties.[356] Ville mentions four *rudiarii* who had participated in various numbers of matches over the course of their careers: one in perhaps as many as eighteen, two others, eleven each, and one as few as seven.[357] How long a career does each of these numbers represent? It impossible to tell since we have no idea how often, on average, they fought in a given year. Hopkins and Beard suggest that gladiators fought an average of just under two times a year, whereas Coleman proposes an average of two or three fights a year. Both estimates represent a low frequency of fighting, which probably was true only of the best gladiators.[358] It would seem logical that star gladiators, worth more alive than dead to their *lanista* or *procurator*, fought a smaller number of duels annually than did their lesser colleagues. Ville gives an example of an imperial gladiator who he calculates had fought in less than six *munera* annually, and of another who had only five combats in four years.[359] On the opposite end of the spectrum, we hear of gladiators fighting more than once in a *munus*. A *thraex* named M. Antonius Exochus (Figure 14) fought twice in a *munus* celebrating a posthumous triumph of Trajan.[360] In the first match on the second day of the *munus*, Exochus, a *tiro* ('apprentice gladiator'), fought another *tiro* named Araxes to a draw. (It was normal practice for a *tiro* to fight another *tiro*.[361]) In the second match on the ninth day, Exochus defeated a more experienced gladiator named Fimbria in his ninth fight.[362] Perhaps Exochus had impressed the crowd so much in his first fight that the *editor* brought him back for an encore, but at least allowed him six days to recover from his first match.[363] The participation of *suppositicii* or *tertiarii* in a *munus* required that their opponents had to fight twice in the same day. There are recorded examples of one gladiator fighting two opponents, and of another who faced three opponents, in the same day.[364]

Rewards of the gladiator

After the match, the *editor* presented the winning gladiator with various rewards for his victory. The winner received a palm branch, symbolic of victory, which he carried as he circled the amphitheatre to the enthusiastic applause of the crowd.[365] There was another symbolic prize, a laurel crown, which was at first given to gladiators for an extraordinary victory. In time, however, *editores* began to behave like college professors who contribute to grade inflation. They awarded the laurel crown automatically so that it was devalued and was no more prestigious than the palm branch. Thus, when career records were compiled and memorialized in inscriptions, the absence of the laurel crown became more meaningful than its presence. If the number of crowns did not match the number of victories, then the number of victories left over was obviously not terribly impressive.[366]

Victory in a gladiatorial contest, however, brought more than just symbolic compensation. After the match was over, the *editor* handed a cash prize directly to the winning gladiator. Suetonius provides us with a description of an award ceremony in which a good-natured Claudius counted aloud in unison with the crowd and on the fingers of his left hand as he doled out gold coins to the winner with his right.[367] The valuable metal plate on which these coins were piled was also part of the prize.[368] The gladiator, however, could not keep all his prize money. It had always been the custom for the lion's share of a gladiator's cash reward to go to his *lanista*. Legislation of Marcus Aurelius and his son Commodus (AD 177–180) set the division of prize money at 1:3 for a free gladiator and 1:4 for a slave.[369] Although gladiators were no doubt overjoyed to be rewarded with money, this kind of prize was not a matter of great pride. When the accomplishments of gladiators were recorded on their epitaphs, there is only mention of the symbolic prizes they have won (palms and crowns). As Valerie Hope points out: 'No gladiator is described in terms of his monetary worth or the extent of his winnings'.[370]

Various pleasures of the *munus*

The violence of the *venatio* and gladiatorial combat naturally provided the primary pleasures of a *munus*, but the spectacle had other features that gave great pleasure to the crowd. Spectators would certainly be disappointed if the *editor* omitted too many of these extra features. An inscription from the Greek city of Mylasa (modern Milas in south-western Turkey) consists of a decree honouring a high priest of the imperial cult (his name is not found in the surviving part of this inscription) for a *munus* he gave.[371] The decree lists specifically what the crowd enjoyed about the *munus*.

The inscription stresses the incredulous wonder, amazement and shouts of the crowd at the sight of the gladiators' beauty and strength in the *pompa*.[372] The spectators' positive reaction is also evoked by the generosity of the *editor*, who spent a great amount of money on the gladiators' armament with its gold ornamentation.[373] Although only gold is mentioned in the surviving portion of this inscription, Robert believes that silver was probably also used in this *munus*.[374] Silver was a common enhancement of gladiator armour. Pliny the Elder writes that, when Julius Caesar gave funeral games in honour of his father in 65 BC, 'the whole apparatus of the arena was silver', including the silver ornamentation of the gladiators' armament. Even *damnati* who were condemned to fight wild animals in the *venatio* of this *munus* were given weapons adorned with silver. Pliny adds that this practice was much imitated in the towns of Italy.[375]

The Mylasian *editor* generously added a scattering of roses and gifts among the spectators.[376] Roses may also have been strewn on the arena floor as can be seen from amphitheatre scenes on two North African mosaics.[377] As for the main show, the high priest supplied gladiators of every type.[378] The variety provided by these different styles of fighting was important to the success of a *munus*. The interest of the crowd, however, was not completely technical. There is mention early in the inscription of the gladiators competing for their lives.[379] This could merely be a reference to the general risk of death that was present in every gladiatorial duel, but more likely it meant that the bouts were fights to the death. (The *muner-arius* may have received permission from the emperor.) All these features of this *munus* illustrate the *editor*'s willingness to go the extra mile in pleasing the people, thereby creating mutual goodwill between the *editor* and the spectators.[380] At the end of the inscription, the high priest is praised for sur-passing all expectation with his generosity.[381] This, no doubt, is a reference to the end of the *munus* when the high priest, like a modern stage per-former at the end of the show, received shouts of approval and thanks from the crowd (*acclamatio*). This inscription from which we have obtained so much evidence about the *munus* at Mylasa, was publicly displayed in the city and was itself a commemoration of the great event and a tangible expression of the people's gratitude.[382]

The public banquet (*epulum*) was another popular 'extra' of the *munus*. Probably the most famous *epulum* was given by Domitian in the Colosse-um. The poet Statius saw this banquet as especially notable because of the 'liberty' it exemplified: 'every order ate at one table: children, women, men of the lower orders, equestrians and senators'. Moreover, Domitian dined with his subjects, no doubt a poetic hyperbole merely referring to Domit-ian's presence in the amphitheatre when the *epulum* took place.[383] Statius describes this huge banquet.

> *Behold, there a group of good-looking people elegantly dressed enter the seating area, not smaller in number than those seated. Some carry bread-baskets and snow white napkins and splendid foods; others distribute mel-lowing wine.*[384]

The public banquet mentioned in Petronius in a southern Italian town would have been on a very modest scale in comparison with Domitian's grand feast.[385]

Another popular feature of the *munus* was a *sparsio* (literally 'a sprin-kling'), a word which had two different meanings in association with the *munus*. One kind of *sparsio* involved gifts or tokens for gifts that were thrown to the crowd (*missilia*, literally, 'things thrown'), like the gifts scat-tered at the *munus* in Mylasa above. At a show sponsored by Nero the following were thrown to the crowd, creating a mad scramble among the spectators: 'various kinds of birds, a variety of foods, tokens [to be ex-changed] for wheat, clothes, gold, silver, gems, pearls, paintings, slaves, beasts of burden, tamed wild beasts and finally, boats, apartment buildings and farms'.[386] At the inauguration of the Colosseum in AD 80, the emperor Titus threw round wooden tokens into the crowd from the upper part of the auditorium, which could be redeemed for food, clothing, silver and gold vessels, horses, beasts of burden, cattle and slaves (no boats, apartment buildings and farms this time!). Those who were lucky enough to catch one of these tokens with the gift inscribed on it could exchange it for the prize at a distribution centre.[387] The *sparsio*, however, could cause disturbances among the crowd. Seneca notes the chaos and the ill will that arose among the greedy crowd in the rush to grab the gifts or the tokens.[388] Another kind of *sparsio* involved spraying the crowd with perfume, usually the essence of saffron mixed with water. Seneca mentions an impressive spray that reached from the bottom of the amphitheatre to its highest point accomplished by water pressure.[389] With the heat in the spring and summer and the unpleasant smells generated by the *venatio* and the carnage of gladiatorial combat, this spray came as welcome refreshment that cooled and deodorized.[390]

In imperial times, there were occasionally unscheduled events which, although they no doubt made the crowd nervous, added an unexpected thrill to the *munus*, at least for those spectators who were lucky enough not to be directly involved. Normally the anonymity of a large crowd protected individual spectators, but sometimes a spectator caught the attention of the emperor at the wrong time and gave offence. Roman spectators were not beyond hurling verbal abuse at the emperor.[391] The crowd had to be prepared for almost anything, especially when the *editor* was an unstable and tyrannical emperor like Caligula or Domitian. An offending spectator might suddenly find himself part of the show. For example, a certain Esius Proculus, who was nicknamed *Colosseros* ('colossal love-god') because of his beauty and large, muscular body, was suddenly ordered into the arena by Caligula to fight first against a *thraex* and then a second time against a *hoplomachus*, both of whom Esius defeated. Apparently, Caligula, who was envious of his handsome face and popularity with women, was determined to punish him. He then ordered Esius to be dressed in rags and to be led in chains throughout the city. After displaying him to a group of women, he had his throat cut.[392] Then there was the man, mentioned earlier in this chapter, who taunted Domitian about his partiality to gladiators with large shields. The crowd was immediately treated to his execution when he was thrown to hunting dogs in the arena.[393]

Crowd behaviour

Crowd participation, whether with shouts or with gestures, was constant throughout the *munus*. They unabashedly volunteered their comments on the action, gave advice to the gladiators, or even expressed their opinions on matters external to the show such as politics. As one would expect, significant moments in combat elicited the most powerful crowd reactions. When a gladiator was felled by his opponent, the crowd exploded. Shouts of '*hoc habet!*' ('He's had it!') or '*peractum est!*' ('It's all over!') could be heard all over the amphitheatre.[394] If something happened to upset them, the spectators could act, as Seneca suggests, like a child throwing a tantrum, especially if a gladiator did not live up to their expectations:

> *Why does the crowd become angry with gladiators and unjustly think that they have been done an injustice because [the gladiators] are unwilling to accept their fate [after* missio *has been refused]? They believe that they have been treated with contempt and transform themselves in expression, gesture and passion from a spectator into an enemy.*[395]

One reaction when spectators were upset, was to throw objects. In the late Republic, the crowd threw stones at Vatinius, an unpopular politician, when he entered the amphitheatre. Later, when Vatinius was about to give a *munus*, he got the aediles to issue an edict that spectators could throw only fruit into the arena. A waggish jurisconsult named Cascellius, when asked whether a pine cone was a fruit answered: 'If you are going to throw it at Vatinius, it's a fruit!'[396]

The passions stirred up in the crowd were powerful. Seneca reports that whenever he was a part of a large throng at a spectacle, he returned 'more greedy, more ambitious, and more pleasure-seeking. No, I should say rather crueler and more inhumane, because I was among human beings.'[397] The philosopher is talking about the noonday spectacle in which convicts were executed, but it is also relevant to the reaction of Augustine's young friend, Alypius, to his first experience of gladiatorial combat. Previously, Alypius had expressed only hostility and contempt for this spectacle, but was dragged into the amphitheatre by his friends. Here is Augustine's complete account of Alypius' first experience of the amphitheatre, which gives a vivid impression of the noise and sights of the arena. Augustine locates the amphitheatre at Rome, no doubt the Colosseum with as many as 50,000 spectators at full capacity. It is no wonder that the attention of the young provincial Alypius was usurped by the overwhelming noise of the crowd.[398]

> *When they arrived there and occupied whatever seats they could, the whole amphitheatre was seething with monstrous delights. Alypius closed his eyes so that the awful goings-on might not enter his consciousness, but if only he had stopped up his ears! For when one of the gladiators fell in combat, and a huge shout of all the spectators had powerfully resounded in his ears, he was overcome by curiosity, and as it were prepared to see whatever had happened and once it had been seen to disdain it. He opened his eyes and was struck with a greater wound in his soul than the gladiator whom he desired to see had received in his body. He fell more wretchedly than that gladiator whose fall had provoked the shout that entered through his ears and opened up his eyes with the result that his mind, still bold rather than brave and much weaker due to its greater reliance on itself than on you [i.e., Christ], was struck and thrown down. As soon as he saw blood, he drank in the savagery; and not turning away, kept his gaze fixed and absorbed the madness and delighted in the criminal combat, and was made drunk with bloody delight. Now he was not the same person that he was when he had first arrived, but one of the crowd which he had joined and a true companion of his friends who brought him there. Need I say more? He watched, shouted, became excited, and took away from the amphitheatre a madness, which would bring him back not only with those friends who dragged him there in the first place, but also without them as he dragged others to the spectacle.*[399]

Tertullian also warns his Christian readers of the powerful emotional influence that the crowd in the amphitheatre can wield over the individual: 'What will you do once you are caught in that floodtide of wicked applause?' Tertullian's recommendation is that Christians stay away from the amphitheatre.[400] Many Christians, however, did not heed Tertullian's advice. Some even attended the executions of their fellow-believers.[401] The allure of gladiator shows for Christians is evident in Jerome's *Life of St Hilarion*.[402] The saint was tormented by regularly recurring temptations that appeared to him in visions: a naked woman, a sumptuous feast, and a gladiator show, including a recently killed gladiator, who begged Hilarion for burial.

Like modern young men who are attracted to violence in films and on the television, ancient youths like Alypius were particularly vulnerable to the violent attractions of the gladiator games. A young man in a declamation describes his own behaviour as he watches his friend fighting in his stead in the arena. As he watches, he 'fights' the match along with his friend, mimicking the movements of his friend by ducking the attacks of an imaginary opponent and standing up straight when his friend went on the offensive.[403] This kind of behaviour also took place at the chariot races. Silius Italicus in his *Punica*, no doubt inspired by his first-hand observation of crowd behaviour in the Circus Maximus, presents his spectators imitating the prone position of the charioteers leaning over the reins as they drive their horses, and shouting the same commands to the horses as the drivers.[404] It should be also noted that women could be similarly affected by action in the arena. The Christian poet Prudentius writes of a rather overenthusiastic Vestal Virgin who jumps out of her seat when a blow is delivered by one of the gladiators, and votes with her '[up]turned thumb' for the death of the loser. In addition to this passion for bloody violence, she proclaims her lust for the victorious gladiator, whom she calls her 'darling' every time he stabs his opponent in the throat.[405] Not all female spectators, however, were as fiercely involved in the matches as this Vestal Virgin. Consider the woman named Martha who sat at the feet of the wife of the famous general Marius and correctly predicted the winner of each match.[406] Spectators were capable of gentler emotions. They sometimes formed an emotional bond with certain arena performers, which was evident when they mourned their deaths, as in the case of a favourite gladiator or even a wild animal.[407] This emotional engagement could also consist of fierce hatred, as is demonstrated by curse tablets (*tabellae defixionum*), on which they inscribed prayers to various deities to take action against a performer they disliked. The prayers on these tablets were most commonly directed at chariot drivers, but were also used to wish harm to gladiators and animal fighters. Here follows a *defixio* wishing injury and failure to a *venator* named Gallicus inscribed on a lead tablet and found in the amphitheatre at Carthage.[408] The repetitions in the Gallicus curse are indications of the intense hatred that the writer feels for the *venator* and, moreover, are an attempt to persuade the divinity addressed to grant the wishes expressed in the *defixio*. Depicted on the tablet is an image of a god with the head of a serpent, holding a spear in his right hand and a lightning bolt in his left.[409]

> *Kill, destroy, wound Gallicus, the son of Prima, at this hour in the ring of the amphitheatre . . . bind [with a spell] his feet, his limbs, his mind, the*

very marrow of his bones. Bind Gallicus, the son of Prima, so that he cannot kill a bear or a bull with one or two blows, or kill a bull [and] a bear with three blows. In the name of the living omnipotent [god] bring this about now; now, quickly, quickly; let a bear crush and wound him.[410]

Despite the emotional involvement of the crowd in the violent action of gladiatorial combat and the *venationes,* crowd control was never a major problem in the amphitheatre at Rome. Although we do hear of factionalism among fans of gladiator games (*parmularii* versus *scutarii*), this partisanship lacked the emotional power of the circus factions designated by colours (Reds, Blues, Greens and Whites) and never resulted in more than verbal abuse among fans. At least, at Rome, rioting did not occur in the amphitheatre, as it did in the theatre and the circus. We do not hear of any disturbance comparable to the catastrophic Nika riot (AD 532) involving fans of the Blue and the Green chariot racing factions at Constantinople, which began in the hippodrome and spread to the streets, resulting in the destruction of a large part of the city and 30,000 deaths (probably somewhat exaggerated by the sources).[411] A cohort of soldiers (*milites stationarii*) was stationed in the amphitheatre, circus and theatre, but there is no record of their having to deal with serious disorder at gladiator games.[412] As Alex Scobie explains:

> It seems, then, that spectator violence at the three main forms of public entertainment in the Roman world [gladiator shows, circus games, and dramatic presentations] . . . was inversely proportionate to the degree of violence inherent in each of the three types of spectacle.[413]

It is not clear in the sources who these *milites stationarii* were: members of the Praetorian Guard or soldiers from the urban cohorts led by the city prefect.[414] Sandra Bingham argues persuasively that, at least through the Julio-Claudians, the soldiers providing security at spectacles were members of the Praetorian Guard. She traces the development from a personal bodyguard of the emperor at the games to 'a regularized security detail of guard members . . . as an extension of this bodyguard'. The urban cohorts, having half as many men as the Praetorian Guard, would have had enough to do to perform their primary task: keeping order in the streets.[415] In AD 56, Nero briefly removed this military guard from the various entertainment sites on the pretext that watching over spectators was not a proper military duty.

Cassius Dio tells us that Nero, who loved the violent disturbances that took place occasionally at theatres and racetracks, hoped that the absence of soldiers would encourage more riots, but even the lack of guards does not seem to have promoted rioting in the amphitheatre.[416]

Outside of Rome, the story was rather different. At a *munus* in Pompeii (AD 59). Pompeians clashed with spectators from the neighbouring town of Nuceria. Tacitus, our only source for this riot, does not say how many people were killed and wounded in this melée, but the number must have been significant, with the Nucerians getting the worst of it. In all likelihood, there was no military guard stationed in the Pompeian amphitheatre, but even soldiers might not have been able to quell this disturbance.[417] Tacitus never explains clearly the specific reason for the riot, but it obviously was rooted in a pre-existing animosity between the citizens of the two towns. For hostility among the spectators to percolate to this degree, the two groups cannot have been sitting intermingled with each other, as they would have been at Rome where seating was assigned according to class. Solidarity of cause could only have developed if each side in the conflict was sitting with their own partisans. The violence was prefaced with verbal abuse between citizens of both towns and quickly escalated to the throwing of stones and the wielding of weapons and even spread outside the amphitheatre. This incident was serious enough to require the attention of the Roman Senate. Its decision was, first, to ban *munera* at Pompeii for a ten-year period; second, to dissolve illegal social clubs called *collegia*; and, third, to exile the *munerarius* Livienus Regulus, for his role in inciting the riot.[418]

As in modern sports, ancient arena sports had fan clubs, which proclaimed their enthusiasm for gladiator games and the *venatio* and rooted for specific arena performers. These fan clubs were no doubt offshoots of youth organizations (*collegia iuvenum*) mentioned earlier, which were dedicated to sports. We hear of these fan clubs both in the Greek east and in the west. In Termessus, Miletus and Ephesus, the clubs have the name *Philoploi* ('Lovers of Arms'). There were also fan clubs devoted to the *venatio*, for example, *Philokunēgoi* ('Lovers of the Hunt'). In Verona, the fan club of a *retiarius* named Glaucus, in conjunction with his wife Aurelia, paid for a funerary inscription honouring him. The name of the club was *Amatores* ('Lovers', i.e., 'fans' [of Glaucus]). An honourable burial was a real concern of gladiators, many of whom did not have a family or fans (like Glaucus) financially able to pay. The fate of many gladiators was an anonymous mass grave. We hear of a *collegium* ('club') devoted to the god Silvanus, consisting of a gladiatorial troupe belonging to the emperor Commodus and various arena functionaries, one purpose of which was no doubt to provide proper burial for its members. The *collegium* consisted of twenty-three gladiators, one *manica* maker, one masseur and seven men designated as *pagani* (meaning uncertain). The administrators of the club were a freedman of the emperor and a *cryptiarius*, a custodian of the crypt, where, according to Hermann Dessau, gladiators often practised.[419]

Fan enthusiasm for gladiatorial combat was also evident outside the amphitheatre. When there was no live action to enjoy in person, Romans liked being reminded of the action of the arena by pictorial representations in various artistic media, both public and private. Gladiators in action were a favourite subject for paintings, which were displayed by *munerarii* in public places in commemoration of *munera* they had sponsored. These paintings attracted the attention of the public, reminding them of the *munerarius'* generosity to them. This practice had been begun in 132 BC by a certain C. Terentius Lucanus, who commissioned paintings of gladiators in action in commemoration of a funeral *munus* he had given in the Roman Forum in honour of his grandfather. He exhibited these paintings in the Grove of Diana, an important centre of the worship of that goddess in central Italy.[420] A freedman of Nero who had given a gladiator show in the town of Antium (modern Anzio) had paintings of gladiators displayed in public porticos there.[421] Petronius' Trimalchio expresses the desire to have his tomb decorated with paintings of the great gladiator Petraites. Domestic art, such as decorated cups, lamps and mosaics, commonly featured gladiators. Trimalchio had silver cups adorned with a combat scene involving Hermeros and Petraites.[422] Although Horace in one of his *Satires* has a slave confess his addiction to paintings of gladiators, it is likely that many a master felt the same thrill in viewing them.

> . . . *I gaze at the fights of [the famous gladiators] Fulvius, Rutuba and Pacideianus with their straining leg muscles. Painted with red chalk or with charcoal, they appear to be really fighting: brandishing their weapons, they attack and parry . . .*[423]

Modern fans are clearly not alone in indulging their fascination with their favourite sport through the medium of pictorial representations.

Chapter 4

A Brief History
of Gladiator Games

The Republic

After the first *munus* in honour of Junius Pera in 264 BC, the next *munus* mentioned in the historical record took place in 215 BC. This *munus* was given in connection with the funeral of M. Aemilius Lepidus, who had twice been elected consul and held the prestigious office of augur.[1] Could forty-nine years actually have passed between the first and second *munus* at Rome? Perhaps the custom of giving a gladiator show at a funeral did not catch on immediately after its first occurrence in 264 BC and Lepidus' family revived it. Indeed, one could argue that there might have been initial resistance to the bloody violence of gladiatorial combat, but it is doubtful that a martial people like the Romans would have had such tender sensibilities. After all, gladiator shows found acceptance rather quickly even among the Greeks, who were more culturally refined than the Romans. In 175 BC, when the Greek king Antiochus Epiphanes imported gladiator games from Rome and presented them at Antioch, his subjects were shocked at first but it did not take them long to change their minds. Soon gladiator games were all the rage.[2] Another possible explanation for this gap is that Rome was too busy with the first Punic War (against Carthage, 264–241 BC) and the beginning of the second Punic War (218–215 BC). This interpretation, however, does not take into consideration the twenty-three year gap between these two wars, nor the fact that the *munus* for Lepidus was in the year *following* perhaps the worst Roman military disaster in their history: Hannibal's overwhelming victory at Cannae in 216 BC. In fact, Donald Kyle argues compellingly that Cannae provided a strong impetus to the growth of gladiatorial combat by reassuring insecure Romans with demonstrations of brutal violence. This message was strengthened by the fact that slaves were recruited to fight as soldiers for Rome, men of the same status as gladiators.[3] Another possibility is that *munera* were given during this period, but none was of sufficient note to find its way into the historical record. The historian Livy tells us that for the year 174 BC many *munera* were given, but all of them were insignificant except for one, which he describes.[4] As a general principle, it should be remembered that the *munera* mentioned in literary sources and inscriptions are no doubt only a small percentage of those actually given in ancient Rome. Unless a *munus* was of significant size and given by a person of consequence, it was unlikely to attract the attention of ancient historians. No doubt there were countless *munera* given at Rome and throughout Italy by magistrates and private citizens that were almost immediately forgotten.[5]

Livy tells us that Lepidus' *munus* consisted of twenty-two pairs of gladiators, a significant leap from the three pairs of 264 BC. In addition, the length of the *munus* was extended to three days from the presumably one-day *munus* of Junius Pera. The matches were probably distributed more or less evenly over the three-day period. Perhaps the most significant change is that of location from the Cattle Market (*Forum Boarium*) to the Roman Forum (hereafter referred to simply as 'the Forum'), the social, political, juridical and religious centre of the city. This change seems to indicate a full acceptance of the idea that gladiatorial combat was a proper Roman way to honour a deceased relative. Another consideration would be the growth in popularity of gladiatorial combat. The planners of the *munus* obviously anticipated that twenty-two pairs of gladiators over a three-day period would attract a sizeable audience requiring the large open space of the Forum. It should be noted, however, that we cannot automatically assume that the heirs were always free to do what they pleased. The decision to give a *munus*, number of gladiator pairs, date and the place of the *munus*, all could have been dictated by the terms of the will of the deceased.[6] In one case, the requirement in a will that offspring give a *munus* was used as a threat. The poet Horace tells us of a miser named Staberius, who in his will ordered his heirs to inscribe on his tomb the amount of their inheritance, requiring them to give a *munus* consisting of one hundred pairs of gladiators (a large show for a private sponsor and extremely expensive) if they disobeyed his order.[7] Apparently, Staberius wanted his posthumous generosity to his descendants to be advertised publicly.[8] Other examples of testamentary *munera* will be discussed later in this chapter.

The dramatic increase in pairs of gladiators over the modest three in 264 BC suggests that by 215 BC the three sons of Lepidus saw the *munus* as an opportunity not just to venerate their father but also to enhance family reputation and honour (and specifically their own) by a public display of conspicuous consumption at the symbolic heart of Rome. Here we see an early example of the competition among aristocrats to give bigger and better spectacles. Roman nobles now had another outlet for their desire to distinguish themselves: the *munus*. It is apparent that to give a *munus* with the same or smaller number of gladiators might constitute an embarrassment for the giver of the spectacle. The growth in number of gladiators and overall magnificence would continue through the rest of the Republic and into the imperial period when emperors, with their unlimited resources, gave gargantuan *munera* that dwarfed any presented in the Republic.

Immediately following his brief account of the *munus* for Lepidus, Livy reports the celebration of the *Ludi Romani* of 215 BC:

> *The curule aediles, C. Laetorius and Ti. Sempronius Gracchus, consul designate . . . gave the* ludi Romani, *which were repeated over a three-day period.*[9]

Ludi were religious festivals that offered entertainment in honour of the gods, such as chariot racing, often referred to as 'circus games' (*ludi circenses*, because they took place at racetracks (*circi*) such as the Circus Maximus), and dramatic presentations (*ludi scaenici*), usually presented in the Forum. The reference to the three-day length of the *ludi Romani* is notable here. The extension of Lepidus' *munus* to a three-day show made it as long as the *ludi Romani* in honour of Jupiter, the most prestigious of annual *ludi*.[10] This is not to suggest, however, that mere length could give a privately sponsored *munus* the stature of the venerable *ludi Romani* or any other *ludi*. After all, the *munus* was in honour of a human being, albeit an important member of the Roman aristocracy, while the *ludi* were in honour of the gods. It does, however, suggest the growing importance of the *munus* in competition with the entertainments given in the *ludi*. It seems probable that Lepidus' sons were responding to a public demand for a kind of show that the Roman people had found especially entertaining.

The next recorded *munus* was given by the sons of M. Valerius Laevinus, a prominent general who had served as first commander in the Macedonian War against Philip V and had succeeded the great M. Claudius Marcellus (popularly called 'the sword of Rome') as general in Sicily. In the view of the Romans, however, Laevinus' greatest honour was probably his leadership of the embassy that brought the cult of the Magna Mater, otherwise known as Cybele, to Rome from Pessinus (now the town of Balhisar, in central Turkey) in 205 BC. The transfer of Cybele (represented by a simple stone) and her cult to Rome had been ordered by a Sybilline oracle as necessary for the expulsion of the Carthaginian general Hannibal from Italy. Two years later Hannibal was forced out of Italy back to Africa and Rome eventually won the war. The goddess had rewarded Roman hospitality with victory and Laevinus had played a significant role in achieving that result.

When Laevinus died in 200 BC, his two sons gave a *munus* in honour of their father consisting of twenty-five pairs of gladiators.[11] This represents only a small increase over the twenty-two pairs presented at Lepidus' funeral, which may have been due to limited funds. The next recorded *munus* was in honour of P. Licinius Crassus (183 BC), whose most notable achievement was his election to the position of *pontifex*, one of a college of *pontifices* which supervised the Roman state religion.[12] Livy does not give us the identity of the sponsor(s) of this *munus*, but undoubtedly it was given by his son(s) or some other close male relative. After a period of seventeen years, twenty-five pairs of gladiators were no longer thought an impressive number and the sponsor of Crassus' *munus* upped the ante to sixty pairs, more than doubling the size of Laevinus' show. Although Livy does not specify the duration of Crassus' *munus*, we can make an educated guess about its length. We know that at Lepidus' *munus*, twenty-two matches required three days to complete, an average of slightly more than seven contests a day, but this must have been a leisurely pace. A *munus* given for Flamininus (discussed below) presented thirty-seven matches in a three-day period, which (if distributed evenly) probably meant twelve on each of two days and thirteen on the third day. By this standard, the sixty matches of Crassus' *munus* would require about five, or at most six, days to complete, although we must consider the possibility of a more rushed schedule.[13] The sponsor of Crassus' *munus* added a three-day *ludi funebres* ('funeral games'), which, like the state *ludi* in honour of the gods, no doubt included chariot races and dramatic shows. These entertainments were enhanced further by the addition of a distribution of meat (*visceratio*) and a public banquet, which were to become frequent features of aristocratic funerals. What is most significant here is the prominence given to the gladiatorial games, which in their length overshadowed all other events associated with Crassus' *munus*.

The steady increase in numbers of gladiatorial pairs since 264 BC was suddenly interrupted by the *munus* (174 BC) for the famous general T. Quinctius Flamininus, conqueror of the Macedonian king Philip V and an important agent in the growth of Roman dominance in the Greek east.[14] Livy notes that there were several *munera* given in this year of no special importance. Flamininus' *munus* stood out among them, but the thirty-seven pairs of gladiators presented represented a significant decrease of twenty-three pairs in comparison with the grand show for Crassus. The relatively small number of combats in Flamininus' *munus* can be better appreciated by comparing it with a *munus* consisting of thirty pairs given in 132 BC by a certain C. Terentius Lucanus for his grandfather, a person of little note as indicated by the fact that his full name has not even been recorded.[15] The decrease is especially surprising because of the stature of Flamininus. The sources give no reason for this comparatively small show. Perhaps it was purely a matter of the personal preference of Flamininius' son, who decided to cut the budget for gladiators in order to spend more lavishly on other popular enhancements such as a *visceratio*, a public banquet (*epulum*) and stage plays.[16] On the other hand, the rising costs of a *munus* in this period may have been a factor in the son's decision. After all, Livy points out other contemporary *munera* were even smaller.

There is evidence that by the middle of the second century the cost of a *munus* spectacular enough to honour the memory of a great Roman was soaring into the stratosphere. A good indication of the spiralling costs of the *munus* is the funeral of L. Aemilius Paullus, who defeated Perseus, the son of Philip V, at Pydna in 168 BC and died in 160 BC. Since the books of

Livy that deal with this period are not extant, we must rely on the Greek historian Polybius, who shows no interest at all in the number of gladiator pairs that are an important detail in Roman accounts, but does give us evidence of the cost of a large-scale gladiator show in this era. Polybius reports that when Fabius, one of Paullus' sons, found that the cost of financing a *munus* prevented him from honouring his father in this way, his brother Scipio (who had been adopted into the Scipionic family), and later was commander of the Roman army that defeated Carthage in the third Punic War, contributed half the expenses.[17] The Greek historian adds that a magnificent *munus* that would befit a great conqueror cost a minimum of 30 talents.[18] It is impossible to estimate with any confidence the modern value of a sum of money in the ancient world. Polybius, however, gives us a general idea of the value of 30 talents when he describes the amount as a 'great sum of money' (*plēthos*). Paul Veyne estimates that this sum would suffice for the pay of 1,500 soldiers for one year.[19] In Roman terms, this amount would be around 720,000 sesterces. An even more specific indication of the value of 30 talents is the fact that Paullus' whole estate was worth a little over 60 talents.[20] Paullus was not a hugely wealthy man, but still very well off.[21] Thus, the cost of the *munus* would have been half the total worth of the estate of an at least moderately wealthy man. And this for a one-time event, lasting for, at most, six days. No doubt the cost of *munera* had been driven up by the burgeoning popularity of gladiatorial combat, which is illustrated by the following incident during Paullus' *munus*. The playwright Terence had first presented his play *Hecyra* ('The Mother-in-law') at the *Ludi Megalenses* in 165 BC but the play was brought to a complete halt by noisy people drawn to other events such as rope dancing (tightrope walking) and boxing. Undeterred by this fiasco, Terence presented the play at the *munus* in honour of Paullus in 160 BC. There was trouble again. During the second act, a rumour circulated outside the theatre (a temporary wooden structure in the Forum) that there was going to be a gladiator show in the theatre.[22] In later times, gladiator combat was advertised publicly well before the show, but in these early days, scheduling and advertisement were doubtless somewhat haphazard. The reaction of the crowd outside the theatre was to rush in and fight with the audience of the play for seats for the gladiator show.[23] There is no better evidence of the Roman people's feeling regarding gladiator combat. No other entertainment could compete with the *munus* in attracting an audience.

The *munus* and late Republican politics

The trend of spending greater and greater sums of money on the *munus* and associated events continued unabated into the first century BC. Cicero disliked this expenditure. He criticizes those who lavish money on public banquets, distributions of meat, *munera*, *ludi* and wild-beast fights as 'wasteful' and urges that money would be better spent on ransoming captives from kidnappers and helping friends in various ways, such as paying off their debts, giving them dowries for their daughters, and assisting them in the acquisition of assets. He claims that people remembered spectacles for only a short time or soon forgot them.[24] Cicero's claim, however, is exaggerated and true only of unexceptionable gladiator shows. Grand *munera* were well remembered and, as we will see, not only honoured the deceased and his family but redounded greatly to the political profit of a giver of a *munus*. Cicero disagrees with the Greek philosopher Theophrastus' (370 – *c.* 285 BC) who had a positive view of such spectacles:

> [Theophrastus] goes too far in praising the magnificent outfitting of popular spectacles and believes that ability to spend money in this way is the reward of wealth.[25]

Cicero, however, was fighting a losing battle here; the ancient world in general agreed with Theophrastus. The wealthy in both Greece and Rome were under great social pressure to spend their money on spectacles to entertain their fellow citizens, and in Rome this was especially true of gladiator shows. The pressure was difficult to resist. The benefits of such a spectacle, however, did not flow down a one-way street. The *editor* received the gratitude and goodwill of his fellow citizens. The rewards for an *editor* are specified in the letter written by Pliny the Younger to Maximus quoted earlier: a reputation for generosity and general magnanimity.[26] A speaker in a rhetorical exercise, who has been condemned to fight as a gladiator, bitterly complains that the *editor* gains popular favour at the cost of his, the speaker's, blood.[27] A reputation for generosity of spirit could greatly benefit an *editor* on election day. Julius Caesar is a prime example of the influence that spectacles in general and a lavish *munus* in particular could have on the Roman people's political decisions. As Plutarch writes:

> While he was aedile, [Caesar] presented three hundred and twenty pairs of gladiators and with other expenditures and extravagances such as plays

*and processions and public banquets, he made the people forget the am-
bitious presentations of those before him. Thus he disposed the people to seek
new offices and new honours with which to repay him.*[28]

Cicero characteristically downplays the importance of the *munus* to a political career. In a letter to C. Scribonius Curio, quaestor in the province of
Asia, Cicero tried to convince the young man not to lock himself into an
enormously expensive gladiatorial show. Cicero urges that a candidate seeking political office should rely on his own 'nature, study and fortune' rather
than gladiatorial contests.[29] No doubt a political candidate should ideally
be judged by these criteria, and not according to his ability to finance extremely expensive spectacles, but to say, as Cicero does, that everyone is 'fed
up' with these entertainments is simply not true. Cicero is speaking here
more as a philosopher than a politician. Curio was caught up in the political
competition involved in the offering of a *munus* and other spectacles. He
had already sent an agent to Rome to announce a *munus* in honour of his
father, an important first step in the giving of a *munus*. Once the announcement of the *munus* had been made, there was no turning back, without a
backlash of resentment from the people. It would have been political suicide, after having announced the spectacle, not to carry through with the
show. Unfortunately, we do not know how many pairs of gladiators took
part in Curio's *munus*; presumably, it was a decent number, neither excessively large nor embarrassingly small. In either case, the number would likely
have been recorded. He did introduce, however, an innovation that seems
never to have been repeated. On the last day of the *munus*, Curio presented
combats between gladiators who were victorious in the first day of the
munus (as noted earlier, it was unusual for a gladiator to fight more than
once in a *munus*).[30] Apparently, Curio's *munus* bankrupted him, with the
result that Caesar was later able buy his political support.[31] Bankruptcy was
not an unusual consequence of giving a *munus* in the late Republic. Indeed,
Caesar had also experienced insolvency as a result of his lavish *munus* in
65 BC. As we shall see in Chapter 6, Curio's *munus* was one of Rome's most
memorable, but not for the number or quality of gladiators involved.

It was the duty of the magistrates called curule aediles to organize the
annually celebrated *ludi* with financial help from the state treasury, but by
the late Republic it was expected that these magistrates should contribute
any expenses for further enhancements of the *ludi* from their own pocket.

Although this financial responsibility was extremely burdensome, for the most part Roman nobles accepted this duty because it was essential to their political careers.[32] If an aedile impressed the Roman people with his *ludi*, he greatly increased his chances of being elected to the next higher magistracy, the praetorship, which was the gateway to the consulship, the crowning achievement of a politician's career.[33] An even better strategy was to sponsor a private *munus* in addition to the public *ludi*. It is due to the overwhelming popularity of gladiatorial combat in comparison with the public *ludi* that ambitious aediles put enormous sums of money into their *munera*. The popularity of the *munus* extended beyond the city of Rome throughout the towns of Italy where pressure was often applied by citizens to force the presentation of a *munus*. For example, the behaviour of the citizens of Pollentia (modern Pollenzo) shows the lengths to which the people, desperate for the opportunity to enjoy a *munus*, were prepared to go. When a centurion died in the town of Pollentia, the citizens, with the assent of some magistrates, refused to allow the body to be removed from the forum (where the funeral took place) until his heirs agreed to contribute money for a *munus*. The emperor Tiberius reacted quickly with military force and a large number of citizens and magistrates were imprisoned for life, a rare punishment among the Romans.[34] As W. Nippel has pointed out, a disturbance like this was rare at Rome because of the great number of gladiator games given there.[35] This was not the case in towns of relatively meagre means outside Rome. There were, however, limits to the people's desire to enjoy a *munus*. Nicolaus of Damascus reports a will that stipulated that the deceased's boy lovers fight each other as gladiators. The reaction of the people (location unknown) was so negative that the man's will was annulled.[36]

It is often assumed that the *munera* at Rome were popular primarily among the common people and less loved by the elites, but this is a misperception. The wealthy upper classes were an even more important target group for aspiring politicians giving *munera*. The Roman poor were not the only audience for gladiator shows. The two upper classes, the senators and knights, were equally enthusiastic spectators, who enjoyed preferred seating with the best view of the arena. In fact, a much larger percentage of the elite classes attended *munera* than of the much more populous lower classes. Their political support was much more valuable for political candidates.[37] The reason for this was the manner in which elections to the two highest magistracies were conducted. In elections to the praetorship and consulship, the wealthier you were, the more your vote influenced the outcome. The elections were held in the centuriate assembly, in which the Roman people were divided into voting units called 'centuries' because they (nominally) contained one hundred voters. In practice, these units sometimes contained fewer voters and often more. Each century had one vote determined by the will of the majority within that century. The order of voting was determined by property census, that is, the richer you were the earlier you voted. The wealthiest citizens, a small minority in the state, were spread out among the greatest number of centuries, which voted before those of lesser wealth. For example, the poorest citizens greatly outnumbered the wealthier classes, but were placed in one century, which voted last. In the Roman mind, this arrangement was justified by the principle that the two magistracies that held the power of life and death over their fellow citizens should be elected by those with the greatest financial stake in the administration of the state. Thus, if the centuries containing the wealthiest citizens were unanimous in their choice, winners in the races for the praetorship and the consulship could be declared after only 197 of the 373 centuries had voted. The poorest citizens might not even have the opportunity to cast a vote. There was one other safeguard in place to increase the influence of the rich in this voting assembly. One century from among the wealthiest citizens was chosen by lot to vote first to give a signal to the other centuries as to how they should vote (*centuria praerogativa*, literally, 'the century that was asked first [for their vote]'). Since the selection of the century by lot was deemed the will of the gods, this practice was believed to give the state a better chance of electing magistrates who enjoyed divine approval.[38] It should be noted, however, that the wealthiest Romans were not always unanimous in their choice of candidates, and on those occasions, poorer citizens got an opportunity to influence the election. Nonetheless, even in this case, the goodwill of the elites was still important to a candidate, because their dependants (*clientes*) would routinely vote for the candidates their wealthy patrons endorsed. Although the *editor* no doubt wanted to please all who attended his *munus*, it is clear that the satisfaction of the upper classes was even more politically important than that of the lower.

To be sure, successful spectacles given in one's aedileship by no means guaranteed high political office.[39] For example, M. Aemilius Scaurus during his aedileship (58 BC) used up all his personal financial resources and also incurred great debt, won the praetorship, but failed in his bid for the consulship. In contrast, Cicero as aedile avoided excessive expense for spectacles and did not give a *munus*, but was still able to attain the praetorship and consulship.[40] Ignoring the Romans' enthusiasm for shows, however, could be politically disastrous. Sulla, later dictator of Rome, lost his run for the praetorship because he had chosen not to stand for the aedileship and therefore had not given any games. His friendship with the king of Mauretania in North Africa had created the expectation in the Roman people that, as aedile, he would present outstanding *venationes* with large North African cats, which were immensely popular at Rome. In revenge, the voters rejected his bid for the praetorship.[41]

More than any other politician, Julius Caesar embraced the strategy of using entertainments to advance his political career. In 65 BC, he, along with his colleague in the aedileship, Marcus Bibulus, presented both the *ludi Romani* and the *ludi Megalenses* on a lavish scale, but Caesar in the same year chose to sponsor an optional *munus* in honour of his father, in which he presented 320 pairs of gladiators, a *munus* of unparalleled numbers and length.[42] Ville suggests 15–20 days.[43] Plutarch believes that Caesar's *munus* along with other spectacles such as plays, processions and banquets was the most costly set of shows that had ever been presented up to that time.[44] Caesar's grand *munus* of 65 BC must have accounted for a large part of the enormous debt that he had accumulated when he was about to set out to govern the province of Spain in the year after his praetorship (ex-consuls and ex-praetors usually governed provinces in the year after their magistracy).[45] Caesar had borrowed heavily to finance his various spectacles and his creditors prevented him from leaving until he paid his debt. Crassus, one of the richest men in Rome at the time, co-signed the debt to allow Caesar to set out to his province.[46]

We find out from Suetonius that Caesar in 65 BC had planned to present more than the 320 pairs he actually presented.[47] The biographer does not say what the number originally was, but it was enough to frighten his political enemies, who suspected that Caesar had marked these gladiators for revolutionary activities in addition to the *munus*.[48] After all, it had been only six years since the defeat of Spartacus and his fellow gladiators, who had moulded an army of 120,000 slaves and peasant farmers into an effective fighting machine, imposing a number of surprising defeats on Roman armies. In the 60s BC, Caesar was viewed as a revolutionary, a possible supporter of Catiline, whose conspiracy would be revealed by Cicero and defeated in 63 BC. Caesar's political enemies believed that he might use this large group of gladiators to silence them with a show of force or even to overthrow the government. In any case, in the face of the outcry and a prohibition by the authorities limiting the number of gladiators that could be kept in Rome at one time, Caesar backed down and agreed to the smaller (but still imposing) number of 320 pairs. Two years later, there was still concern in the Senate not only with the large number of gladiators in Caesar's school in Capua, but also with the large concentration of gladiators in Rome with its various schools. A senatorial decree ordered that the gladiator troupes in Rome should be distributed among Capua and neighbouring towns.[49] Cicero, who was consul at the time (63 BC), sent an army to Capua under the command of a quaestor, his friend Sestius, who drove out of the city a certain C. Marcellus for having paid frequent visits to a very large troupe of gladiators, probably those belonging to Caesar.[50] Caesar's gladiators were still perceived as a possible threat to peace fourteen years later, on the eve of the civil war between Caesar and Pompey, when the consul Lentulus, a Pompeian, gathered together gladiators from Caesar's school into Capua's forum and gave them horses with the intention of using them as a cavalry force against Caesar. Lentulus' fellow Pompeians, however, warned him against this plan, so instead he used them as a garrison elsewhere in Campania.[51] During the Republic, gladiators, because of the *infamia* of their profession, were not thought worthy to fight in the Roman army but in the imperial period were allowed to serve as soldiers in times of emergency.[52] The rest of Caesar's gladiators, who seemed to be on the point of making an escape from their barracks, were billeted by Pompey with local families, two to each house, thus diffusing the heavy concentration of gladiators in one school.[53] Caesar's gladiators were a hot issue at the time. Cicero had discussed this matter with Caesar in an exchange of letters and had given him some friendly advice, probably to disband them.[54]

Gladiators and political violence

The fears aroused by Caesar's gladiators were not unfounded. In the chaos of the last years of the Republic, politicians used gladiators both to advance their political designs and to protect themselves against their political enemies.

Politician-owners found it convenient and cost effective to purchase gladiators rather than just rent them from *lanistae*. Thus, after the show, politicians could use their gladiators as bodyguards and/or as fighters in their small private armies. How prevalent this political use of gladiators was is indicated by Varro's mention of five gladiatorial troupes: Cascelliani, Caeciliani, Aquiliani, Faustiani, Scipionarii, each of which was named after a prominent politician of the first half of the first century BC: A. Cascellius, M. Caecilius Metellus or Q. Caecilius Metellus Nepos, Aquilius Gallus, Faustus Sulla, and Metellus Scipio.[55] Although there is no specific evidence that Cascellius and Gallus used gladiators for political purposes, in all probability just the fact of their ownership indicates that they did. The *Caeciliani* could have belonged to either of two politicians, both of whom were associated with gladiators: M. Caecilius Metellus or Q. Caecilius Metellus Nepos. The former gave a *munus* in 60 BC.[56] The latter in 62 BC used a gang consisting of gladiators and other ruffians in his attempt to force passage of a law that would have made Pompey commander against the Catilinarian conspirators, which, according to Plutarch, would have given him supreme power at Rome. Metellus brought his gang of gladiators into the Forum and stationed them on the steps of the temple of Castor and Pollux to intimidate his political enemies.[57] Faustus Sulla had an armed bodyguard consisting of three hundred gladiators (*faustiani*), which he was ready to use if necessary, and Asconius notes that Q. Metellus Scipio surrounded himself with 'armed men', most likely the *scipionarii*.[58] Even Cicero, who consistently denounced gang violence, had a group of young men from Reate armed with swords, whom he used during the Catilinarian conspiracy. It is unlikely, however, that any of them were professional gladiators.[59]

Gladiators played a significant role in the gang warfare in Rome during the 50s BC.[60] These gangs were used by both sides in the political conflict of the last days of the Republic between the optimates ('the best people') and the *populares* ('champions of the people'), the revolutionary party. In 57 BC, the infamous *popularis* enemy of Cicero, P. Clodius, used gladiators to break up an assembly that was going to vote on the recall of Cicero from exile (which Clodius himself had engineered), by wounding and killing some of the participants.[61] He had obtained these gladiators from his older brother, Ap. Claudius, who had purchased them in anticipation of a *munus* for their deceased father.[62] Cicero gives a second-hand report of this event in his *Defence of Sestius*, describing this gladiatorial attack in somewhat exaggerated, but generally accurate, terms:

> *You remember then, jurors, that the Tiber was filled with the bodies of citizens, the Forum was cleansed of blood by sponges, with the result that all thought that such a great number and display [of gladiators] was not sponsored by a private citizen or plebeian [i.e., Clodius], but by a praetor of patrician rank [i.e., Ap. Claudius].*[63]

Cicero casts this event in the image of a *munus* with Ap. Claudius as the *editor* and the man behind this attack carried out by his brother. Later in the same speech, Cicero, says that these gladiators were apprentices that Clodius was trying to pass off as veterans (much more desirable for a successful gladiatorial show) to use for his father's *munus* during his aedileship.[64] Cicero was recalled from exile by the passage of a law soon thereafter.[65] After his return, Cicero tells how he had thwarted a violent incident planned by Clodius, aided by gladiators:

> *I stayed home as long as things were in chaos when it became known that your slaves, who had long been prepared by you to kill good men, along with your gang of wicked and incorrigible men had come to the Capitolium [area on Capitoline Hill where the temple of Jupiter Optimus Maximus was located]. When this was reported to me, he informed that I stayed at home and had not given you and your gladiators the opportunity to renew the slaughter. After I received the news that the Roman people had gathered on the Capitolium . . . and that some of your henchman having thrown away their swords and others having them snatched from them had fled in terror, I came not only unsupported by the force of any troops, but with just a few friends.*[66]

T. Annius Milo, a friend of Cicero, who employed gang violence in support of Cicero's return from exile, was not loath to use gladiators. Milo was very much man of the arena, who, Cicero said, 'had squandered [the equivalent of] three patrimonies' on spectacles, including a gladiatorial *munus*, in his successful pursuit of the praetorship.[67] Thus, it is not surprising that he began to incorporate gladiators into his political gang, including two of the best-known gladiators of the day, Eudamus and Birria.[68] He also purchased a troupe of gladiators and wild-beast fighters (*bestiarii*), which in the late Republic were virtually indistinguishable from gladiators, to use as a private army against Clodius and his followers.[69] The purchase had to be arranged through a third party because the owner of the troupe was a political enemy. The ruse worked much to the embarrassment of the seller when he found out the real identity of the buyer.

Gladiators had a minor role to play in the circumstances surrounding the assassination of Julius Caesar. Cassius Dio writes that the assassins of Julius Caesar had placed gladiators in Pompey's theatre, where the fateful meeting of the Senate took place at which Caesar was murdered. The pretext was that the gladiators were going to participate in a show in the theatre, but the real purpose of their presence was to back up the assassins.[70] These gladiators belonged to D. Junius Brutus Albinus, who was anticipating his sponsorship of a *munus*.[71] Plutarch says that one of the reasons that D. Brutus was invited to join the conspiracy was because he owned a gladiator troupe.[72] These gladiators played no role in the assassination, but Velleius Paterculus tells us that they afterwards accompanied the conspirators when they occupied the Capitoline Hill, giving them an aura of power.[73]

Scheduling the funeral *munus*

In the last years of the Republic, the sole reason for giving a *munus* ostensibly remained the same as it had been since its inception at Rome: to pay tribute to a dead male relative, but the reality was that most *editores* were as much concerned with winning votes as with honouring the dead. For example, Julius Caesar gave his famous *munus* for his father twenty years after his father's death. This delay was not entirely unreasonable since Caesar was only 14 or 15 when his father died. Something similar occurred in the case of Faustus Sulla, the son of the dictator Sulla. Faustus was only 8 years old when his father died, so it is not surprising that he waited eighteen years to honour his father with a *munus*. Also like Caesar, there was suspicion by his political enemies that the gladiatorial troupe Sulla had purchased was really to be used for 'murder and political disturbance' because he had acquired it such long a time before giving the *munus*.[74] But there was a difference between the two cases. Caesar, like many other politicians, offered his delayed *munus* during his aedileship, when it could be combined with the *ludi* that the aediles were legally bound to give and thus have the maximum positive effect on his political career. Faustus, on the other hand, gave his *munus* before he was of an age to hold a major political office.

Since his father had ordered in his will that Faustus give a *munus* in his honour, it may have been that a date had been fixed by the will, which Faustus was duty-bound to honour.[75] It is clear that the motivating force behind Faustus' *munus* was *pietas*: devotion to his father. Conversely, Caesar's motive was obviously his desire for political advancement. He was 35 years old when he gave his *munus* in 65 BC and he could have easily done it ten years earlier at an age similar to that of Faustus. The *munus*, which had started out as a gift to the deceased, had now become primarily a gift to the people to influence their votes.

The *munus* as bribery

In the final years of the Republic, bribery of voters and jurors became more and more common and the aedile's use of the *munus* began to be considered just a more subtle form of corruption. There were two laws that sought to lessen the powerful effect of the *munus* on the electorate: the *Lex Calpurnia*, and the later *Lex Tullia*, sponsored by Cicero.[76] We do not know much about the *Lex Calpurnia* except that one of its provisions forbade a candidate to distribute seats at a *munus* by tribes.[77] The 'tribes' referred to here were thirty-five political divisions of the Roman people forming the basis of the centuriate assembly that elected consuls and praetors.[78] The *Lex Calpurnia* recognized the profound influence that gladiator shows had on the elections of the most powerful magistrates, but banning the distribution of seats was only a superficial cure for the problem. The real issue was the giving of these shows by politicians who intended to become candidates for the highest magistracies. The *Lex Tullia* was more ambitious. We get a sense of the wording of the law from a reference that Cicero makes to it in his *Defence of Sestius*: '[my law] expressly forbids anyone to give a gladiatorial show within a two-year period in which he has stood or is about to stand for office'.[79] (Elections took place in July of the year before the successful candidate took office in January.) In his *Against Vatinius*, Cicero describes the law in almost exactly in the same words, but adds: 'unless the day [for a *munus*] has been prescribed in a will'.[80] This exception takes care of the situation in which a son (or some other male relative) is required by the deceased's will to give a *munus* within this two-year period. For the Romans, filial devotion to one's paternal ancestors took precedence over political matters. An example of the testamentary exception in the

Lex Tullia is the *munus* that C. Scribonius Curio gave in 52 BC for his father who died in 53 BC, leaving a will that ordered his son to give a *munus* in his honour. The *munus* could not be given as a part of Curio the elder's funeral because his son was away in the province of Asia serving as quaestor and could not legally return to Rome until 52 BC. The testamentary exception of the *lex Tullia*, however, allowed him to give the *munus* in 52 BC and run in 51 BC for the aedileship he hoped to hold in 50 BC.[81] It would seem that the elder Curio's will had specified that his *munus* must be given within twelve months of his death, because Curio, like most other politicians, must have preferred to delay the *munus* until he was curule aedile, when he could get the greatest political benefit.

Here is how Georges Ville interprets the terms of the *Lex Tullia*.[82] The two-year period begins on January 1 of the year preceding the year in which the election takes place and ends once the election has taken place.[83] How does this work in practice? In effect, the terms of the *Lex Tullia* made it legally impossible for a politically ambitious aedile to give a *munus*. Before the *Lex Tullia*, an aedile would have given his *munus* during his year of service and declared his intention to stand for the praetorship early in the year after his aedileship with the memory of his *munus* still fresh in the mind of the voters. (A candidate could not run for office while holding another office.) The election would have taken place in July of that year, and, if successful, he would have assumed the praetorship in the second year after his aedileship. In order to observe the 'two-year rule' of the *Lex Tullia*, however, if an aedile of the year 60 BC gave a *munus* in that year, he would not be able to run for the praetorship in 59 BC. He would have to wait until 58 BC to declare himself a candidate for the praetorship of 57 BC. Note that the *Lex Tullia* presumes that the positive effect of giving a *munus* in one's aedileship would be greatly diminished by waiting an extra year before running for the praetorship.

We hear of one case in which the *Lex Tullia* was ignored, apparently with impunity. Cicero accused P. Vatinius of breaking the *lex Tullia* by giving a gladiator show while running for the praetorship of 55 BC in the previous year.[84] In his own defence, Vatinius claimed that he had presented not gladiators, but *bestiarii* in a *venatio*, taking advantage of the fact that both *bestiarii* and gladiators used swords and wore similar armour. Vatinius somehow escaped prosecution on this charge and his campaign for the praetorship, aided by significant bribery, was ultimately successful.[85]

Caesar's last *munus*

Julius Caesar gave another *munus* on a lavish scale in 46 BC, a forerunner of the grandiose imperial *munera*, as part of his triumphal celebrations. He had announced in 52 BC that he would give a *munus* in honour of his daughter Julia, who had died in 54 BC, the first known *munus* in honour of a woman. This show must have aroused incredible excitement, especially among those who remembered the great *munus* of his aedileship in 65 BC. In 46 BC, Caesar celebrated four triumphs on four separate days for his victories in Gaul, Egypt, Pontus (north central Turkey) and North Africa. Caesar promised a *munus* and a banquet (*epulum*) in memory of Julia such as had never been seen before.[86] It would seem that Caesar was acting like a candidate for office, but he was now in effect the ruler of Rome, having been appointed *dictator* for life in the same year. His *munus*, however, still had a political purpose. Despite his overwhelming power, he still needed the support of the people to counter the ill will that he had stirred up among aristocratic defenders of the Republic. After all, he had come to power through his opposition to conservative elements among the senatorial aristocracy of which he himself was a member.[87] He also had to overcome the fear that his recent victories over Pompey and other political rivals in the civil wars had inspired in the people. Many Romans remembered what had happened when Sulla achieved his dictatorship after numerous military victories. Sulla published proscription lists of political enemies, which led to the deaths of thousands of Romans. The people's fears were exacerbated during the triumphal procession honouring his victory over Egypt, when they saw Arsinoe, a member of the Egyptian royal family and sister of Cleopatra. The sight of a famous woman like Arsinoe, who had once even been proclaimed queen, now a slave, aroused their pity and, despite their admiration of Caesar, made them think they too might become slaves of Caesar. Although the Roman people admired Caesar for his achievements, his demonstration of his personal power in these triumphal celebrations was alarming, as in the case of the unprecedented number of his official bodyguards (*lictores*).[88] On the other hand, the effect of the lavish entertainments was overall more comforting than alarming to the people. At the height of his political power, he had decided to spend vast amounts of money on the people rather than on himself. As Nero did a century later, Caesar could have used this money to build a vast palace that proclaimed his despotic power over his subjects. Instead, he tried to win (and in good part succeeded in winning) the hearts and minds of the people, setting an example followed by future good emperors, who preferred to be considered patrons of the people, rather than an autocratic ruler.[89] Caesar understood well the principle later formulated by Fronto: 'the Roman people are preoccupied by two things especially, grain and spectacles; rule is judged not less by trivial things than by serious things'.[90]

The number of pairs of gladiators presented in Caesar's *munus* was not recorded, but undoubtedly it was significantly large. After his grand show of 65 BC in which 640 gladiators took part, Caesar would not have presented a smaller number in a *munus* for his daughter given in connection with his triumphal games. Cassius Dio, the only source to bring up the topic of number, begs off giving a figure because of the difficulty of finding the truth among the grossly exaggerated estimates.[91] Caesar was determined to produce a gladiator show that satisfied the spectators. In pursuit of this objective, he ordered that the famous gladiators he planned to present in his *munus* be removed immediately from a match if the spectators were not pleased by their efforts and held in reserve for future contests.[92] Caesar proved a good psychologist in this matter. The prospect of suffering the humiliation of disqualification for a poor performance would encourage these proud veterans to give their all. It was not enough just to present gladiatorial combat; the crowd expected good matches and Caesar did not want his *munus* to be ruined by the inadequate effort of the combatants. Caesar also required that all apprentice gladiators (*tirones*) fighting their first match in his *munus* be instructed by members of the equestrian and senatorial classes skilled in the use of arms.[93] Caesar was apparently trying to give a more dignified aura to his *munus* by associating at least some of his gladiators with upper-class Romans who had gained their martial expertise as officers in the Roman army.[94]

Caesar's upcoming *munus* must have aroused enthusiasm among the aristocracy because a senator named Fulvius Sepinus wanted to fight in full armour. Caesar, however, did not indulge his desire. A senator fighting as a gladiator could only bring shame to himself and his class. Caesar rejected the request, but did allow a former senator named Q. Calpenus to fight.[95] The fact that Calpenus was no longer a senator, a position normally held for life, meant that he had been removed from the Senate, probably because of some scandal. Thus, there was no reason why he, already disgraced, should not take up a disgraced profession. Caesar, however, had no compunctions about allowing equestrians to fight, among whom was the son of a praetor.[96]

Caesar issued a ban on senators fighting in the arena, a decree that was formalized by a decree of the Senate in 38 BC, six years after his assassination.[97] Even so, less than ten years after this decree of the Senate, Octavian, Caesar's adopted son, although he was staunch supporter of senatorial dignity, allowed a senator named Q. Vitellius to fight in the arena.[98] There is no evidence that the ban was removed. Augustus probably just granted an exemption for the occasion, as seems to be implied by Augustus' later extension of Caesar's ban to include equestrians and descendants of senators (22 BC).[99] In AD 11, equestrians were allowed to fight as gladiators without incurring disgrace. Cassius Dio comments that the ban on equestrians fighting in the arena was useless since it could not prevent them from engaging in this activity.[100] Law enforcement was always a problem in Rome. The appearance of equestrians in the arena was overwhelmingly popular and attracted a great deal of interest.[101] Augustus went so far as to show his approval of this practice with his attendance at *munera* featuring equestrian gladiators.[102] His flexibility in these matters was no doubt influenced by his desire to please the crowd. In the imperial period, Roman spectators cared about the status of gladiators: they preferred a free gladiator to a slave, and an upper-class gladiator to a lower-class freeman.[103] This preference was based on the belief that the higher a volunteer gladiator was on the social scale, the more heart and desire he had for fighting, since he was doing it voluntarily. Perhaps Roman spectators had seen too many slave gladiators who were reluctant fighters. The prejudice against slave gladiators is evident in a passage from Petronius' *Satyricon*. Petronius has one of his plebeian characters tell his friends that

> We are about to enjoy an excellent munus *in three days on a holiday;* the gladiator troupe is not owned by a lanista, *but consists of numerous freedmen.*[104]

These freedmen had apparently taken up the career of a gladiator as an independent business enterprise and, as their own bosses, were willing to risk life and limb to entertain the crowd, thereby ensuring further employment.[105]

Despite Augustus' leniency in the matter of equestrians, the Senate again banned their participation in gladiatorial shows, probably in the last years of

Augustus' life.[106] Despite this ban, knights appeared occasionally in the arena during the reigns of Caligula and Claudius, because of special exemptions, but under Nero the appearance in the arena of not only knights but also senators became epidemic.[107] Nero himself, who, as emperor, had no worry about being tainted by *infamia*, had set an example for the senators and equestrians by appearing in Rome as a singer and musician and even acting in plays, professions, like that of gladiator, that would have disgraced any Roman citizen.[108] Thus, it is not surprising that the two upper orders in large numbers, in some cases to please their increasingly tyrannical emperor, were willing to fly in the face of social disapproval by fighting as gladiators in the arena.

The emperor Vitellius banned the participation of the two upper classes as combatants in *munera* in AD 69.[109] His decree, however, did not survive his brief reign (less than three months). Roman elites continued to fight in the arena at least until the late second century AD. When the emperor Marcus Aurelius (AD 161–180) was dubious about the candidacy for public office of a former gladiator, the candidate pointed out that he saw many praetors in the Senate who had fought in the arena during his career as a gladiator.[110]

The transition from Republic to empire

The revolution that ended with the replacement of Republican government with imperial rule had a profound effect on the giving of *munera*. The civil wars that took place after the assassination of Julius Caesar led to a final confrontation between Octavian, the adopted son and heir of Caesar, and Marc Antony, who had allied himself with the Egyptian queen Cleopatra. There was a naval battle off the coast of Actium (31 BC) on the western coast of mainland Greece, in which Octavian and his military adviser Agrippa were the victors over Antony and Cleopatra. As a result, Octavian was left as the sole ruler of the Roman world. He chose to cloak his absolute rule behind the appearance of Republican government and to pretend to be only a *princeps*, 'the leading man' of the state.[111] In 27 BC, the Senate honoured Octavian with the honorific title of 'Augustus'. He controlled the armies of Rome and the treasury, previously under the control of the Senate, whose power had been greatly diminished. Most of the old Republican magistracies still existed, but they were on their way to becoming honorary rather than a locus of power for their holders. No one was nominated for office or did anything significant once in office without the approval of Augustus.[112] Popular elections, undermined by Julius Caesar and Augustus, disappeared during the reign of Tiberius, Augustus' adopted son and successor. Elections now took place in the Senate, which was not eager to counteract the emperor's wishes. Thus, there was the appearance of constitutionality, but in reality Roman government had become a monarchy.

With these changes, the politics of the *munus* could not help but be transformed. During the Republic, the *munus* was entirely a private affair, at least nominally a duty performed by sons in honour of their fathers.[113] The only interest in gladiatorial combat that the Roman government demonstrated during the Republic was in 105 BC, when the Romans, at a time of military crisis (the terrible defeat by Germanic invaders at Arausio, modern Orange), sought the help of instructors from a gladiator school. The historian Valerius Maximus tells us that the consuls of that year, P. Rutilius and Cn. Mallius, hired teachers from the *ludus* of C. Aurelius Scaurus to train their soldiers in offensive and defensive manoeuvres, hoping to bolster their courage with better technique.[114] The consuls of 105 BC undoubtedly used state money to pay for this training, but there was no attempt to take control of the *munus*, as is sometimes claimed. No precedent had been established for governmental financing of *munera*.

Munera financed at least partially by public funds were known elsewhere in the empire before they existed at Rome. The charter of Urso (44 BC), a Caesarian colony in Spain, specifies that the *duoviri* were required to give a *munus* or theatrical entertainments for a four-day period during their magistracy. They had to pay a minimum of 2,000 sesterces out their own pocket and receive no more than the same amount from the public treasury.[115] By the first century AD, publicly financed *munera* were common throughout the towns of Italy. An inscription from Pompeii (AD 55) implies that public funds were used for *munera* when it praises an honoured magistrate for giving a *munus* 'without public expense'.[116] Later in the imperial period, we hear of the position of 'superintendent of the public *munus*' (*procurator muneris publici*) in the Italian town of Praeneste, where there was an important gladiator school.[117] In the same era, the term 'public *munus*' appears in two inscriptions from Fundi (modern Fondi).[118]

The first appearance of regularly scheduled state-sponsored *munera* at Rome was in the late first century BC. As we have seen, only in the last decades of the Republic did the government begin to appreciate fully the political dangers inherent in these shows and attempt to eliminate them through legislation (*lex Tullia*). Augustus' legislation of 22 BC effectively put the regulation of the *munus* into the hands of the emperor, to be used in whatever way he saw fit. Given the history of the *munus* during the last decades of the Republic, it is not surprising that Augustus early in his reign decided to establish more stringent controls over its offering. Perhaps Augustus was alarmed by the grand success of a *venatio*, given in 25 BC by a praetor named P. Servilius, in which three hundred bears and a like number of African beasts were slaughtered. As Cassius Dio notes, Servilius 'made his name' with this spectacle, just as many politically ambitious men had done during the Republic.[119] Just three years later, Augustus introduced legislation that made it difficult for anyone to use spectacles for political gain. He gave responsibility for all spectacles, including the *venatio* and gladiatorial combat, to the board of praetors.[120] Two praetors were chosen annually by lot from the whole college of praetors to undertake this task and were given a stipend from the public treasury for this purpose.[121] Any extra spending by one of the praetors on these spectacles from their own personal funds must not be greater than that of his colleague.[122] This spending limit no doubt was meant to stop any praetor from claiming greater credit for the show than the other praetor. There must have also been a restriction on the amount the praetors could spend out of their own pockets (perhaps the same amount as the governmental stipend?) because four years later Augustus permitted them to spend up to three times the amount they had received from the treasury, if they so wished.[123] Apparently, Augustus was feeling more secure in his position and saw less danger in the praetors' political ambitions than he had originally.

Like the *ludi* throughout the Republic and empire, the *munus* given by the praetors was an annual event, sponsored by the state. Remember that in the Republic, all *munera* and animal hunts were optional spectacles not legally required of the aediles (as were the *ludi*) but privately funded by them as an enhancement of the *ludi*. It is clear that in the matter of popularity, the relationship between the *ludi* and the *munus* was an example of the tail wagging the dog. Although the *ludi* were time-honoured ritual entertainments in honour of various gods, it is clear that they could not generate the same enthusiasm as gladiator shows, which became the primary instrument of the politically ambitious during the Republic.

Bad emperors like Caligula were especially suspicious of the private ambition that might lie behind the offering of a *munus*. As we have seen earlier, Caligula, desperate to refill an empty treasury, decided to sell gladiators from his imperial school at outrageous prices. He sold them not only to the two praetors who gave the annual *munus*, but even to private citizens, allowing them to ignore the law limiting the number of gladiators in a show. Some of the purchasers bought the gladiators willingly, while others did so out fear of offending the emperor. Caligula quickly had second thoughts about the sale and realized the threat the buyers might pose to his rule. Thus, he had the best gladiators of the group he had just sold poisoned.[124] A similar suspicion may have been behind Claudius' replacing the praetors with quaestors as managers of the anual *munus* and refusing to allow privately sponsored *munera* to be reported as given on behalf of his well-being.[125] By the time of Domitian, *munera* in Rome were given only by the emperor himself, a relative, or a magistrate as his representative.[126]

Despite the political changes at Rome, the changeover from Republican to imperial government had virtually no effect on the politics of towns in Italy. Politics in these towns was conducted as it had been in Rome under the Republic. Local aristocrats contended for offices with real power, to which they were elected by the people with no interference from the emperor. As in Republican Rome, the *munus* played an important role in getting candidates for public office elected. *Munera* continued to be given by candidates striving for political office. There is a passage in Petronius' *Satyricon* in which, Echion, a rag dealer, talks about an upcoming *munus* in a town in southern Italy. Echion is a fictional character but his comments no doubt accurately reflect the relationship between the *munus* and campaigning for public office. He expresses confidence that a *munus* to be given by a certain Titus, undoubtedly a candidate for public office, will be of excellent quality. On the other hand, Echion talks about a cheap *munus* given by one Norbanus and the harm that it will do to his campaign for an unspecified office. Echion imagines Norbanus' reply to his criticism: 'Nevertheless,' Norbanus said, 'I have given you a gladiator show.' Echion's responds: 'And I applaud you, but if you think about it, I gave more to you than I received. One hand washes the other'.[127] A disappointed spectator at a *munus* was a liability for a politically ambitious *munerarius*. Local political activity also persisted in the empire outside of Italy. The only interference in provincial affairs by the emperor we hear of concerns Roman provincial officials and not local politicians. For example, Nero issued a decree banning *munera* given by provincial magistrates and other officials, branding these shows as an attempt to distract the provincials from governmental abuses.[128] Wiedemann suggests that Nero's real motive for this decree was his fear that the popularity gained by giving *munera* might create rivals to his rule.[129] This ban does not seem to have survived Nero's death.

The annual state-sponsored *munus* stood as a guarantee that there would be at least one gladiatorial event a year to entertain the people. (Augustus had stated that he would allow two, if requested.) With strict governmental control of the *munus*, however, there must have been a steep decline in *munera* given by private individuals on their own initiative. Augustus had stipulated three requirements for the giver of an optional *munus*: permission from the Senate, the limit of two *munera* per year and a cap on the number of gladiators of sixty pairs.[130] No doubt the Roman people looked to the emperor to take up the slack. Some emperors responded more favourably than others in accordance with their personal like or dislike of gladiatorial combat. Augustus' record for sponsoring *munera* is instructive. Although fond of spectacle generally, and of gladiator games in particular, he was not a very active *editor* of *munera*. He tells us in his summary of his life's achievements (*Res Gestae*) that he gave gladiatorial *munera* three times in his own name and five times in the name of his sons and grandsons.[131] That amounts to only eight *munera* over a forty-five year reign, although it must be said that when he did sponsor a *munus*, it was of epic proportions. Augustus also mentions that he presented approximately 10,000 gladiators in these eight *munera*, an average of 1,250 gladiators per *munus*, almost twice the number of gladiators that Julius Caesar presented in 65 BC.[132]

The funeral *munus* was still in vogue in Rome of the early empire, but, like other *munera*, more and more limited to the emperor and imperial family. While Augustus was emperor, he gave two *munera* in memory of his chief general, Agrippa.[133] Funeral *munera* were also given during Augustus' reign by Tiberius for his biological father (Tiberius Nero) and grandfather (Drusus Claudius Nero) and by Augustus' step-grandchildren, Germanicus and Claudius (the future emperor), for their father Drusus (son of Livia, Augustus' wife, and brother of Tiberius).[134] Nero gave the last recorded *munus* of this type at Rome, for his mother Agrippina. The participants in this *munus*, however, were not trained professionals, but male and female members of the equestrian and senatorial orders.[135] There is no record at all of a funeral *munus* for a private citizen at Rome after the time of Augustus, although they continued to be given elsewhere in Italy, as Maximus' *munus* for his wife in Verona, discussed in Chapter 1.

Difficult times were coming for the *munus*. In AD 7, a budget squeeze led Augustus to discontinue the funding of the annual praetorian *munus*, which was not restored until thirty-two years later, under Caligula.[136] But why had the annual praetorian *munus* lain dormant so long? The responsibility for this dormancy can be laid at the feet of Tiberius, Augustus' adopted son and successor, who did not have the social skills needed for an *editor* of a *munus*. As Tacitus explains:

> *[Tiberius'] distaste for gladiatorial games is explained variously. Some say that crowds made him uncomfortable; others say that it was due to his melancholy personality and fear of comparison with Augustus' affable interaction with the crowd.[137]*

Perhaps it was during two funeral *munera*, one for his father and the other for his grandfather Tiberius (mentioned above), when he was for the first time the centre of attention as *editor*, that he learned to dislike the sponsorship of spectacles.[138] Moreover, in lines immediately preceding those quoted above, Tacitus gives a hint that Tiberius was troubled by gladiator games *per se*. In the first year of his reign, he rebuked his son Drusus, the *editor* of his own *munus*, for delighting too much in the spilling of blood.[139] In Cassius Dio, we read of Tiberius' dissatisfaction with another aspect of this same *munus*.[140] He refused to watch a gladiatorial duel between two knights, objecting no doubt to the degradation of their elite status by fighting as gladiators. Tiberius also banned the winner of this duel from fighting as a gladiator again.[141] After the *munus* given by Drusus mentioned above, there are no recorded *munera* given by the emperor or his family for the rest of Tiberius' reign.[142] There may have been *munera* given by private citizens, but they would have been too inconsequential to attract the attention of historians. This was a trying time for gladiators and their fans. As noted earlier, Seneca reports hearing a famous gladiator of that era named Triumphus complaining of the infrequency of *munera* under Tiberius: 'How our beautiful age perishes!'[143] Roman fans of the *munus* must have even been suffering as least as much. The combination of pent-up demand with the scarcity of gladiatorial combat at Rome at this time led to a terrible man-made disaster. A freedman named Atilius decided to take financial advantage of this situation by offering a gladiator show and charging admission (*munus assiforanum*). As a freedman, he probably had little chance of getting permission to give a *munus* in Rome, especially under Tiberius, so he constructed a temporary amphitheatre in the town of Fidenae, a little over two miles north of Rome. Unfortunately, his 'quick buck' philosophy led him to ignore proper building procedure. He built an amphitheatre that was not able to support the weight of a large crowd. Roman fans, consisting of men and women of all ages, came in large numbers, making the disaster even worse. The whole amphitheatre collapsed killing or seriously injuring 50,000 spectators. Atilius was exiled and the Roman Senate reacted with a decree that a property rating of 400,000 sesterces (the property qualification for membership in the equestrian class) was required for anyone giving a *munus*, along with an inspection of the foundation.[144] Tacitus ultimately blames Tiberius for the disaster, who 'had kept [the people] from their pleasures'.[145]

The *munus*, however, was an institution too deeply ingrained in Roman life and character to disappear completely. What Cicero (in a more positive mood about spectacles) wrote about games in the Republic was still just as true under the emperors:

> *The Roman people must not be deprived of the enjoyment of* ludi, *gladiatorial shows, and banquets . . . which signify generosity more than self-interested hand-outs.*[146]

The emperors were fully aware of the popularity of the *munus* among the people and its value to the political health of the state. Most emperors found the *munus* a valuable opportunity to display their 'wealth, power, and prestige' and even more importantly, to establish a firm bond between themselves and their subjects.[147] The *munus* was also a stabilizing force for the state by providing a 'safety-valve' for public discontent.[148] Public gatherings at Rome had long been opportunities for the Roman people to make their political opinions and complaints known. Cicero lists three kinds of gatherings where this was the case. The first two are specifically political meetings: the *comitia* (the centuriate and tribal assemblies) in which magistrates during the Republic were elected and legislation was voted upon, and the *contio*, a meeting in which magistrates gave information to voters and answered their questions before they cast their votes in the *comitia*.[149] Under Augustus, these political meetings were moribund. The *comitia*, having lost the function of electing magistrates early in the first century AD, passed their last bit of legislation at the end of the same century, and without them there was no need for the *contio*. The third public gathering mentioned by Cicero is the spectacle: the *munus* and the *ludi*.[150] In his speech *In Defence of Sestius*, Cicero provides an example of a *munus* used as a political forum. When Sestius, a tribune of the people and an advocate of Cicero's return from exile, made an entrance into the crowd attending a *munus* in the Forum, he was greeted with the applause of just about every person in attendance. Since the crowd at the *munus* consisted of men of all classes, from high to low, Cicero understood this greeting as a sign that the Roman people were unanimously in favour of his return from exile.[151] Another example of the people's support for Cicero was their hostility to Ap. Claudius, the brother of P. Clodius, who was behind Cicero's exile. On his arrival at a *munus*, Appius tried to avoid being seen by the crowd by crawling under the benches to reach his seat and was hissed by the spectators when he was finally sighted.[152] As noted earlier, the hissing was so loud that it startled both the horsemen gladiators (*equites*) and their horses.[153]

With the loss of formal opportunities for political expression, gladiator shows and other spectacles became even more important as an opportunity for the people to see and communicate with their emperor. Spectators could take the opportunity to make known to the emperor their desires with regard to certain issues. Josephus describes the ideal interaction between spectators and the emperor:

> . . . *with regard to things they need, [the Roman people], coming together in a large crowd ask their emperors, who, judging their requests legitimate, do not treat them with contempt.*[154]

Even Tiberius, despite his dislike of spectacles of any kind, at least early in his reign attended the *ludi* regularly 'for the sake of the good conduct of the crowd and of seeming to share their pleasure in the show'.[155] The populace liked an emperor who attended shows and shared their interest in what was going on. Julius Caesar was criticized for paying more attention to his business papers than the show when present at a spectacle. Augustus learned his lesson from the experience of his adoptive father and paid careful attention to the show, no doubt to the great delight of the crowd.[156]

Claudius was an expert at showing the spectators that he was having a good time at the games.[157]

The people responded well to the generosity of an emperor, when, as a *munerarius*, he gave a lavish show.[158] Having a good time, however, was not the only product of a *munus*. The people's sense of general well-being was boosted by the *munus*, which delivered a powerful message about the strict administration of justice and Rome's domination of their empire. The spectators could not help but be reassured when convicted criminals and prisoners of war served as gladiators or were thrown to wild beasts during the *venatio*, or executed at the noon event.[159]

The imperial *munus*

After the neglect of Tiberius, all that was needed for a restoration of the *munus* to its former glory was a more sympathetic emperor, and the next two emperors, Caligula and Claudius, filled that role well. Under these two emperors the *munus* was restored to former availability and underwent a change that gave it its now classic form. As we have seen, the imperial *munus* was a three-fold, all-day event, which began in the morning with a *venatio* followed by noontime executions and the afternoon gladiatorial combat, the main event of the day. It is impossible to pinpoint the exact time that this format came into being. It was probably a gradual process. The triumphal *munus* of Julius Caesar in 46 BC, however, must have been influential in this regard. This *munus* was transitional in at least two ways. Ostensibly, it was a traditional funeral *munus* in honour of his deceased daughter Julia, but at the same time it was part of a triumphal celebration, which set a precedent for future triumphing emperors such as Augustus and Trajan. Cassius Dio tells us that the temporary amphitheatre Caesar built for the *munus* was the site of both a gladiator show and a *venatio*, the first time we hear of these two entertainments being held in the same venue.[160]

The *venatio*, or staged animal hunt with other associated events, remained primarily a separate event in the early empire. Although Augustus, in the listing of entertainments that he gave during his reign in his *Res Gestae*, keeps his listing of his *munera* and *venationes* separate, there is evidence that in the last years of his rule the association between gladiatorial games and the *venatio* was becoming stronger and more popular.[161] In AD 6, the brothers Germanicus and Claudius, the future emperor, gave a funeral *munus* for their father Drusus. Part of this *munus* was a presentation of trained elephants. As we have seen, the performance of tricks by trained animals was a typical feature of the *venatio*.[162] There is no mention of a hunt, but that may be because the sources found it less interesting than the performances by the elephants. One wonders if one of the tricks performed by the elephants at this event, the imitation of the movements of gladiators, was designed to call attention to a new link between the *venatio* and gladiatorial games. Although the independent *venatio* continued to be given under Caligula and Claudius, at some point, perhaps in the latter's reign, a link between the *venatio* and gladiatorial combat had been forged. As Suetonius reports:

> [Claudius] gave numerous gladiator shows in different places:
> [for example] one in the Praetorian Camp to celebrate the anniversary
> of his accession **without a** venatio and the usual equipment and **a
> right and proper one** [iustum atque legitimum i.e., with a *venatio*] *in the
> Saepta ['Voting Enclosure'].*[163]

New functions of the *munus*

The *munus* had been acquiring new functions since the beginning of imperial period, some of which can be attributed to Augustus. During the Republic, the only acceptable reason for giving a *munus*, political considerations aside, was the commemoration of the dead. By the middle of the first century AD, however, the funeral *munus* was virtually obsolete, at least in the city of Rome. Augustus seems to have attempted to turn the *munus* into a religious rite. In 12 BC, Augustus presented gladiatorial combat as the primary feature of a festival called the *Quinquatrus* ('Five-day festival', 19–23 March). These games were in honour of Minerva, whose martial character was inherited from her Greek counterpart, Athena.[164] Ovid says that the last four days of the festival were devoted to gladiator games designed to please the 'war-like goddess'.[165] In the same year, Augustus sponsored a contest of armed warriors in Athens during the Panathenaic festival.[166] The source (Cassius Dio), however, does not refer to these warriors as *monomachoi* (Greek for 'gladiators') in reference to the event in Athens. He instead calls these competitions 'heavy armed contests' (*hoplomachias agonas*), which probably involved only blunted weapons. The most likely reason for this harmless substitution is that Augustus did not want to offend the Athenians. It is likely that Greeks in this period had not yet accepted gladiator games.[167] There had been an earlier attempt to connect the *munus* with a divinity. In 42 BC, the plebeian aediles, who were in charge of the games for Ceres (*Ludi Cereales*), substituted gladiatorial combat for the traditional chariot races (*circenses*).[168] Since the *munus* had never been associated with a divinity, the Roman public must have found this religious innovation too radical. It was not repeated. The *munus* in honour of Minerva seems to have suffered the same fate.

Augustus' creation of an annually recurring *munus* given by praetors represents a public admission of the real reason for gladiatorial combat: entertainment.[169] We do not know whether the praetorian *munus* was assigned to a specific time of the year under Augustus, but towards the middle of the first century AD, perhaps during the reign of Caligula, it was given in December. Under Claudius, the organization of the annual *munus* was transferred from the praetors to the quaestors.[170] The annual *munus* was still being given by the quaestors in December in the time of Domitian and continued on, with some interruptions, at least into the fourth century AD.[171] The calendar of Philocalus (AD 354) gives its specific dates in December: 2, 4, 5, 6, 8, 19, 20, 21, 23, 24.[172] Note that these gladiator games were interrupted for the celebration of the Saturnalia on December 17. As far as the Romans were concerned, the *munus* was not a proper way to worship the gods.[173]

There was, however, a popular innovation involving the *munus* that had a religious dimension involving prayer. This was the practice of giving a *munus* for the welfare (*pro salute*) of the emperor and his family. Ville notes that the offering of the *munus pro salute* presumes the striking of a bargain with a god or gods (although no gods are ever mentioned either individually or as a group) in which the lives of gladiators are exchanged for life of the dedicatee(s) of the *munus*.[174] One of the earliest recorded examples of this *munus* took place in the reign of Tiberius, when gladiator games were given in Pompeii for the welfare (*pro salute*) of Livia (Tiberius' mother and wife of Augustus) and the imperial family.[175] The *munus pro salute* was especially popular during the Neronian era. On at least one occasion, a stand-alone *venatio* was used for this purpose, which the future emperor Nero sponsored on behalf of his stepfather Claudius.[176] Nero as emperor was a recipient of *munera pro salute* given in Pompeii.[177] There were numerous *munera pro salute* given for Vespasian, no doubt during his final illness in AD 79.[178] At Pompeii, Nigidius Maius gave a *munus* for the dedication of an altar that was linked with the welfare of the emperor and his family.[179] The inscription that proclaims this dedication implies that sacrifices would be made on this altar for the welfare of Vespasian and his children. At Venafrum (modern Venafro) in Campania, a *munus* was given by certain Q. Vibius Rusticus 'for the well-being of the imperial household' sometime in the first century AD.[180]

Analogous to the *munus pro salute* was the vow made by individuals to fight in the arena as a sacrifice for the welfare of the emperor. When Caligula became seriously ill early in his reign, two men swore under oath to incur or risk death if the emperor should recover. A lower-class citizen named Afranius Potitus apparently promised to commit suicide, while an equestrian named Atanius Secundus, perhaps as an act of one-upmanship, announced that he would fight as a gladiator. When Caligula recovered, both men broke their promises, but the emperor forced them to keep their vows. Atanius died fighting in the arena.[181] Cassius Dio brands their behaviour as a servile attempt to win the goodwill of the emperor and a cash reward. The historian is probably right in not seeing any altruism in these vows. Atanius was not the only one to make such a vow. Suetonius describes a scene early in Caligula's reign on the Palatine Hill, where people, alarmed by the emperor's illness, kept a vigil. A number of these persons vowed that they would fight in the arena if he recovered.[182] The logic of this vow is perhaps rooted in an ancient religious practice in time of war, the *devotio* (discussed in Chapter 1), which was believed to be a means of saving the many by the voluntary death in battle of one man. A late biographer suggests that gladiatorial games (and the *venatio*) given by emperors going to war could be a kind of *devotio* in which the deaths of gladiators (and beast fighters) in the arena could satisfy the goddess Nemesis in exchange for the survival of citizens in battle. The biographer does not put much stock in this theory, but it provides an interesting parallel to similar thinking in Caligula's day.[183]

Munerarii found other occasions appropriate to be celebrated with a *munus*. Dedication of a building was often commemorated with a gladiator show. For example, Augustus gave *munera* to celebrate the dedications of the Shrine of Julius Caesar, the temple of Quirinus and the temple of Mars.[184] Nero inaugurated his famous wooden amphitheatre with a *munus*, as did Titus with the Flavian amphitheatre (Colosseum).[185] As we have seen above, *munerarii* in Italy followed their example. Another common occasion for a *munus* in the towns of Italy was to thank the electorate for election to a magistracy. The *munus* was also deemed an appropriate celebration for anniversaries. For example, Claudius gave a special *munus* in the Praetorian camp to celebrate the anniversary of his accession to the throne.[186] The consuls celebrated the birthday of the emperor Vitellius with a huge *munus* that took place at multiple sites throughout Rome.[187] Triumphs were another popular excuse for a *munus*. Before the Battle of Actium, Antony, confident of victory, gathered a group of gladiators for his post-victory *munus*. Of course, Antony never got a chance to use them in a show, and his conqueror, Octavian celebrated his victory at Actium with his own *munus*.[188] Victorious emperors in the imperial period who gave *munera* as triumphal celebrations include Domitian and Trajan, both for their victories over the Dacians.[189]

Notable imperial *munera*

Nero (AD 57)

Nero gave a *munus to* celebrate the dedication of his new wooden amphitheatre that was remembered for the high social status of its gladiators. His gladiators consisted of six hundred members of the senatorial order and four hundred equestrians who fought as gladiators and another group from the same two classes who served as beast fighters in a *venatio*. Members of these two elite classes even served as arena attendants.[190] As we have seen, by the mid first century AD it was not unusual to find aristocratic Romans fighting in the arena, some forced to make a living because they had lost their fortunes or were disgraced because of involvement in a scandal. Suetonius, however, notes that this was not true of all the participants in Nero's *munus*. At least some of the aristocratic gladiators in Nero's *munus* fought voluntarily, with both their fortunes and reputations intact.

No doubt in keeping with the status and dignity of his upper-class gladiators, Nero ordered that no deaths should take place at this *munus*.[191] These gladiators from the highest echelons of Roman society probably fought with wooden training swords or blunted metal swords.[192] Nero might have hoped to appeal to the spectators' better instincts by focusing their attention on the technical skills of the fighters rather than on the sight of fighters wounded and dying. Oddly, Nero's rule of no death also applied to a third component of this *munus*: the *meridianum spectaculum* in which convicts and prisoners of war were usually executed. Although their life was spared, the *damnati* of this *munus* were not given their freedom, but perhaps given some non-capital penalty such as working on public projects. We know that Nero later had a policy of not executing prisoners of war and *damnati* in the *munus* because he needed them to work on his Golden House and other large projects such as a canal in southern Italy.[193]

One is struck by the novelty of this *munus*, which must have appealed to Nero, whose interest in entertainment was second to no other emperor. There may have been, however, more to this *munus* that just its novelty. One could view this *munus* as a daring experiment on Nero's part, an attempt to reinvent the *munus*. Ville called this *munus* 'one of the most extraordinary in the history of gladiatorial combat'.[194] Nero seems to be attempting to remove the *munus*, at least temporarily, from its degrading association with professional gladiators and beast fighters and the bloody violence they practised in the arena. His *munus* is reminiscent of one given by Scipio Africanus in 206 BC at Nova Carthago (modern Cartagena) in Spain in honour of his father and uncle, who had been killed fighting the Carthaginians. Livy comments on the unusual nature of the show, in which aristocratic Spaniards participated in the combat voluntarily and out of noble motives:

> The gladiatorial spectacle did not consist of the kind of men whom lanistae were accustomed to purchase, slaves from the slave market and freemen who put up their blood for sale. All the services of the fighters were voluntary and free. For some were sent by their chieftains to display an example of innate martial virtue of their tribe, while others proclaimed that they would fight out of regard for their leader [Scipio] . . .[195]

Gunderson's explanation of the popularity of Scipio's *munus* could also be applied to Nero's show:

> Indeed the [gladiator] show is a better show because the better sort of men are participating; and the fighters' volition is likewise testimony to their true valor.[196]

The question might be asked, why were the members of Rome's two upper classes in Rome in good standing willing to participate in Nero's elitist *munus*? Gunderson suggests three plausible factors: (1) the avoidance of *infamia* for those upper-class gladiators who did not receive financial compensation, (2) participation in bloodless combat with social equals, and (3) the opportunity to display one's *virtus* in public.[197] We have to be careful, however, not to make too much of an idealist out of Nero. He might have had an additional motive: the humiliation of the upper classes, which was a particular attraction for the common people.[198] Some of these aristocrats in Nero's *munus* were no doubt happy to fight in the arena for the money and/or the glory, but there must have been an element of coercion in their decision to fight. After Tacitus reports that Nero bribed prominent equestrians to fight in the arena, he comments that 'pay from a man who has the power to command applies the force of compulsion'.[199]

Titus (AD 80)

Two memorable *munera* were given by the emperor Titus for the dedication of the Colosseum. Both *munera* were enhanced by a *naumachia* ('staged sea battle'), one in the Colosseum and another at the *stagnum Augusti* in the Grove of the Caesars (*Nemus Caesarum*). The celebration was spread out over a period of 100 days, but we only know a few details of this schedule.[200] The *munus* in the Colosseum was *iustum et legitimum* with the traditional sequence of events: *venatio*, which included *damnati* thrown to the beasts, and gladiatorial combat. There is just one detail that is out of the ordinary. Martial, in one of his poems from his *Book of Spectacles*, places the parading of political informers in the arena before the morning *venatio*, rather than at its usual noontime slot.[201] This schedule is suggested by the position of this poem before those on the *venatio*. (The sequence of the poems is thought more or less to depict the original succession of events.[202]) It is clear that Titus was making a political statement by putting these informers on display right at the opening of the inaugural games of the Colosseum, indicating that he is making a fresh start by rejecting the use of informers.[203] Under bad emperors like Nero, informers (*delatores*) were encouraged by pecuniary rewards (a substantial portion of the condemned person's property) to give information that led to the conviction of wrongdoers. These rewards, however, fostered greed and led to many false charges and wrongful convictions, a practice that Titus was trying to discourage with this public humiliation and the penalty of exile. The gladiatorial show included the usual duels, but also staged infantry battles in the tradition of Julius Caesar, Augustus and Claudius.[204] The only thing specific we know about the gladiator show is the epic fight between Priscus and Verus, discussed in the previous chapter.

Domitian (AD 89)

Domitian was a prolific giver of *munera* and restored the annual quaestorian *munus*, which had fallen into disuse since the reign of his father, Vespasian. We do not have evidence of any single outstanding *munus*, except perhaps for one given in celebration of his Dacian victory, which included traditional infantry and cavalry fights in the Circus Maximus. We do know, however, that Domitian, like Nero, was fond of novelty. He presented gladiatorial combat at night in which upper-class women and senators fought as gladiators. As we have seen in the previous chapter, another innovation consisted of dwarf gladiators who fought each other, female gladiators, and cranes.[205] The fight between dwarves and cranes apparently was an enactment of the legendary battle between pygmies and cranes.

Trajan (AD 106)

Trajan gave a memorable *munus* in celebration of his victory over the Dacians. It was a gargantuan event requiring 123 days (probably non-consecutive) for completion, and involving 10,000 gladiators and the slaughter of 11,000 wild and tame animals.[206] Unfortunately, the sources provide no further details of this *munus*.

Commodus (AD 192)

The last imperial *munus* to be treated in this chapter was chosen because of its bizarre nature and the pathological personality of its *editor* and participant, the emperor Commodus. This *munus* took place not long before his assassination in AD 192 and probably hastened it. Commodus was the son of the philosopher-emperor Marcus Aurelius, who perhaps overindulged his son because of his long absences from Rome (totalling eight years) while he was fighting Germanic tribes harassing Rome's northern frontier along the Danube. For example, Aurelius made Commodus co-ruler when the boy was only 16. Although Aurelius was one of the most militarily active emperors, his son did not follow his example, preferring to make peace or to entrust military operations to someone else. Despite this distaste for real warfare, Commodus from an early age was utterly fascinated with the arena, rejecting his father's intense aversion to gladiatorial combat. Commodus' adolescent fantasies led him to fight as a gladiator, mostly in private, but he did appear in this particular *munus* as both a *venator* and a gladiator. Commodus was the only emperor to appear before the public as a professional performer in the arena. A number of emperors enjoyed practising with gladiatorial weapons, but only in private.[207] Nero apparently intended to appear in the arena as a *venator* against a lion, but it is not clear whether he actually did. The 'contest' between the lion and a naked Nero was supposed to be an enactment of Hercules' fight with the Nemean lion in which, like Hercules, the emperor would wrestle and club the animal to death. Suetonius only says that a lion was 'prepared' (drugged?) to face Nero in the arena, but does not say whether or not Nero actually carried through on his intention.[208] It would have been for the best, if he had not.

We have an eyewitness account of the events of Commodus' *munus*, faithfully recorded by Cassius Dio, an historian and a Roman senator. The *munus* was fourteen days long and each day was structured like the typical imperial *munus iustum et legitimum* with a *venatio* in the morning and gladiatorial combat in the afternoon.[209] There is no mention of a noontime spectacle. Commodus' exploits as an animal hunter in this *munus* will be discussed in the next chapter on the *venatio*. In the afternoons, Commodus fought both professional gladiators and athletes whom he challenged or the crowd chose. These combats were 'safety first' duels. When he fought real gladiators in the arena, he wielded a wooden sword, while his opponents had what Dio calls a *narthex*, a word which can mean 'cane', or 'stick', suggesting something much less substantial than the emperor's weapon.[210] Naturally, Commodus won every match because his opponents realized that it was the smarter course of action to allow him to win. One opponent, however, apparently intended to give Commodus a real fight and paid for this decision with his life. A gladiator named Scaeva ('Lefty'), when offered a dagger with a dulled point, rejected it and told the emperor that he would fight him unarmed. Commodus, fearing that Scaeva would wrest away his dagger and kill him, had him put to death. After this incident, he continued to fight gladiators in the same safe manner as before, but satisfied his penchant for real violence and bloodshed by killing wild animals in the morning *venatio*.[211]

We know that Commodus fought as a *secutor* and, if he followed normal practice, his opponents would have been *retiarii*. Not surprisingly,

Commodus won all these duels (Cassius Dio scornfully calls then 'shadow matches') and awarded himself 1 million sesterces as a prize each day, a huge monetary prize much greater than professional gladiators received. In these duels, the emperor also enjoyed the moral support of his chamberlain and his praetorian prefect, giving each man a kiss in celebration of victory. In private, Commodus was a more daring fighter, no doubt encouraged by the meagre fighting ability of his chosen opponents, who were chamber servants. In these 'gladiatorial duels' with real swords, he cut off a nose or an ear here and there and even killed some.[212] After his part of the afternoon show was over, Commodus took on the role of a *munerarius*, sitting in his usual spot on the podium dressed as Mercury, and pairing all the gladiators on the first day. These gladiatorial duels were bloodbaths with many deaths. He seems to have required that all duels, unlike his own matches, be to the death. When some victors refused to slay their opponents, Commodus ordered all the remaining gladiators to be chained together and forced to fight in a group, as noted in the previous chapter.[213]

This *munus*, however, ended rather strangely. After having required the senators to dress as they customarily did when an emperor had died, his helmet was taken out of the arena by way of the *Porta Libitiensis* ('the Gateway of Death').[214] Perhaps Commodus, realizing the hatred that the senators had for him, was taunting them with the hope that their desire for his death might come true. In any case, the omen was fulfilled. Commodus had planned to kill the new consuls on the day they took office (January 1 AD 193) and to assume that office dressed as a *secutor*. He, however, was prevented from putting this plan into action. His praetorian prefect, a chamber servant and his mistress conspired against him. He was strangled to death in his bath by an athlete.[215] His gladiatorial fantasy had finally proved fatal.

Paragladiatorial events

Staged infantry battles

As part of his celebratory games in 46 BC, Julius Caesar, ever the astute impresario, introduced two notable innovations: staged infantry battles and the *naumachia* ('staged sea battle'). According to Suetonius, on the fifth and final day, the programme of events was completed with a large-scale battle involving two armies, each consisting of 500 foot soldiers, 30 horsemen and 20 elephants.[216] The display of small armies engaged in battle, as

K. M. Coleman has written, is 'a predictable extension' of gladiatorial com-bat.[217] The accounts of Cassius Dio and Pliny the Elder supply details that are omitted by Suetonius. Dio mentions four separate battles: cavalry versus cavalry, infantry, two companies consisting of both cavalry and infantrymen fighting each other, and a fight between men on elephants.[218] Pliny says there were two battles: 20 elephants versus 500 infantrymen, and 20 tur-reted elephants with 60 foot soldiers (?) versus 500 infantrymen and 500 cavalry.[219] Pliny's account is probably more selective, concentrating on specific details that caught his interest. Dio and Pliny seem to agree on the elephants carrying towers filled with soldiers. Dio does not specifically men-tion the towers, but only that 'men fought from elephants', which seems to refer to this typical form of military combat employing elephants, well known to the Romans.[220] Caesar had to alter the Circus Maximus to accom-modate these battles. The turning posts at either end of the infield of the racetrack were removed to clear space for the two camps of soldiers engaged in these battles.[221] This was an opportunity for most Romans to experience first hand such warfare as had made Rome the mistress of a far-flung empire. These battles were not like modern bloodless re-creations of famous battles in which the participants pretend to be wounded or dead. The participants in these ancient battles for entertainment were prisoners of war and con-victed criminals who inflicted real wounds and death on each other.

Octavian continued this tradition of mass engagement as spectacle begun by his adoptive father. In 29 BC at the dedication of the shrine of Julius Caesar, Octavian gave a two-part *munus*: one part consisting of the usual gladiator duels and the other, a battle involving a large number of men on each side. The two sides in this battle were prisoners of war from two dif-ferent tribes: the Suebi and the Dacians. This battle was not an historical en-actment; the wide geographical separation of these tribes made any engagement in one of their homelands unlikely. What united them in this *munus* was their involvement with Rome and, more specifically, with the Julian family. Julius Caesar had defeated the Suebi in 58 BC, who were de-feated again by a Roman army in 29 BC, the same year as this *munus*. The Dacians had sided with Antony against Octavian in the recent civil war and were brought to Rome as prisoners of war.[222] This staged battle vividly demonstrated to the Roman public the success of the Julian family against both external and internal enemies. It is also a good example of Roman con-querors forcing prisoners of war to fight for their entertainment, a practice which in earlier centuries had led to the development of ethnic gladiatorial types such as the Samnite, Gaul and Thracian.

Claudius, following in the footsteps of Caesar and Octavian, gave a display of a mass engagement in the Campus Martius in a triumphal celebration of his victory in Britain, which took place some time soon after Claudius' return from Britain in AD 44.[223] What makes this spectacle unusual is that it depicted a Roman army storming a town. Special care had to be taken to ensure that there was no embarrassing reversal of history, an outcome that would ruin the triumphal celebration. Neither the emperor nor the spectators would have been pleased by a staged battle that the Romans lost.[224] There is, however, an interesting question: who were these 'Roman soldiers' in this battle? Were they actual legionnaires or a combination of prisoners of war and convicts, the usual candidates for spectacles of this kind? I would opt for the former. The idea of dressing up prisoners of war or convicted criminals as Roman soldiers would have been distasteful to the Romans. Making sure that real Roman soldiers would end up victors in this display was not difficult; overwhelming numbers could help ensure success. Other measures like giving blunt weapons to the Britons could be taken to minimize any risk to life and limb for the Romans. The spectacle ended with a re-enactment of the surrender of British kings, brought to Rome for the occasion to play their roles again for the benefit of the Roman people. Claudius must have provided to his fellow Romans a vivid example of Roman military might under the leadership of their emperor.

Naumachia

The other paragladiatorial event that Caesar added to his triumphal celebration in 46 BC was a *naumachia* ('staged naval battle'), a popular innovation and a natural partner of the infantry engagements in the Circus Maximus. The difficulty of staging a *naumachia* meant that it would never become a frequently given spectacle; instead, it was reserved for truly special occasions and given at Rome (or environs) by the emperor. The only information we have about Caesar's *naumachia* was that it was given in an artificial lake, either in the Campus Martius or on the other side of the Tiber, and involved two fleets of ships representing a naval battle between 'Tyrians' (= Phoenicians) and 'Egyptians'.[225] Although Caesar tried to give this *naumachia* an historical context with these names, there is no recorded sea battle between these two peoples. Historical accuracy, however, was not the point here. What does matter is the historical fantasy that the names of these opponents from exotic lands evoke.[226] No matter who were the opponents, however, there was one important requirement of this or any *naumachia*. The spectators had to be able to distinguish between both sides in the battle. Coleman suggests two ways in which this might have been accomplished. Affiliation could be designated either by contrasting colours for ships and participants' dress, or, more expensively, with the fighters' gear and ships representing more or less accurately what these opponents would actually have used in battle.[227] The crowd could have been informed regarding how to identify each side in the battle by means of placards and heralds.

The warships, consisting of biremes, triremes and quadriremes (ships with two, three and four banks of oars, respectively), had large numbers of armed fighters aboard.[228] The *naumachia* was conducted like a real naval battle. Although the skill of the ship's captain and oarsmen played a role in attempts to ram an opposing ship, the battle consisted primarily of fights on board ship between men armed with swords, but no doubt, as in the later noonday spectacle, without defensive armour. The *naumachia* served the same practical purpose as staged infantry battles: the deaths of all condemned criminals and prisoners of war participating as marines and oarsmen in the spectacle.[229] The *naumachia* provided a sensationally dramatic setting for their deaths, as they killed each other or were drowned when their ships sank. As in staged infantry and cavalry engagements, professionally trained gladiators did not participate in spectacles like these, whether on land or water, because their expertise would have been lost in the chaos of these battles, not to mention the tremendous expense due to the large numbers required. The point of these battles was not the individual display of skill, but the scale of the fighting. There must have been a large number of men who participated in Caesar's *naumachia*, but unfortunately no extant source attempted an estimate of the figure. Whatever its size, Caesar's *naumachia* must have contributed significantly to the immense crowd that filled Rome to bursting for Caesar's gala spectacles of 46 BC.[230] It is clear that Caesar had set an example for later emperors giving shows in celebrations of important occasions. The *naumachia* continued to be offered into the third century AD.

Augustus gave a *naumachia* that was part of a *munus* he presented for the dedication of the temple of Mars Ultor ('Mars the Avenger') in 2 BC.

This temple had been vowed to Mars by Augustus at the battle of Philippi in 42 BC, in which he avenged the death of his adoptive father by defeating his chief assassins, Brutus and Cassius. There are no details available about the gladiatorial combat, except that it took place in the *Saepta*, a voting enclosure in the Campus Martius. The historian Velleius Paterculus, however, praises not only the gladiatorial *munus* but also the *naumachia* as 'most magnificent spectacles'.[231] The *naumachia* took place on an artificial lake built by Augustus (*stagnum Augusti*) across the Tiber covering approximately 47 acres, probably elliptical in shape.[232] Altogether, three thousand fighters participated in this battle on thirty biremes and triremes, along with a large number of smaller vessels.[233] Given the amount of space available in the *stagnum Augusti*, the larger vessels were no doubt full size. This *naumachia* represented an historical naval battle between the 'Athenians' and 'Persians', the famous Battle of Salamis.[234] The 'Athenians' won on this occasion as they did in 480 BC, and perhaps there was some kind of management of the battle to make sure that history was not contradicted.[235] On the other hand, perhaps the outcome did not matter so much after all, since Roman forces were not involved.[236] Paul Zanker makes an interesting suggestion about the 'hidden meaning' of this *naumachia*. Just as the victories of the Athenians over the Persians in the fifth century BC had been interpreted in the Greek world as a victory of the civilized west over the barbarian east, Augustus' victory at Actium over Antony and the Egyptian queen Cleopatra had been viewed by the Romans in the same light.[237] If Zanker is right, the outcome of the battle would have had to be carefully managed in favour of the Athenians. This *naumachia* probably served as a substitute for a triumph over Antony, which could not be celebrated because the defeated enemy was a Roman.[238]

The most memorable of all *naumachiae* was given by Claudius in AD 52 as a completely independent event, which carried on the tradition of placing the opponents in a pseudo-historical context.[239] The opponents were the 'Sicilians' and the 'Rhodians', most likely an unhistorical conflict. This *naumachia* was given in a natural setting on the Fucine Lake (about 50 miles east of Rome), with the spectators sitting on the shores of the lake and on the mountainside, which served as a natural theatre. Presiding over this military occasion was Claudius in a general's cloak. He had won the right to wear this attire because he had led Roman forces to victory in Britain, but the reason for this *naumachia* was not a victory celebration. The *naumachia* was intended to celebrate an anticipated technological achievement: the draining of the very lake on which the *naumachia* took place. The purpose of this drainage was to make the area less subject to floods and to increase the availability of arable land. The eventual draining of the lake failed to achieve either of these goals.[240]

There are a number of reasons for the fame of this *naumachia*. The battle was given a mythical dimension by a 'Triton' who, raised by a mechanical device, emerged from the middle of the lake blowing a curved war trumpet as a starting signal.[241] (Triton was a minor sea divinity, often portrayed blowing a conch shell.) Then there was the matter of its scale. As Tacitus notes, Claudius' spectacle outdid Augustus' *naumachia* with larger and more numerous ships.[242] The sources differ on the number of ships that took part in this spectacle. Suetonius' numbers make the least sense: twenty-four triremes in total compared with Augustus' thirty biremes and triremes.[243] Since Augustus' *naumachia* consisted of thirty large ships on an artificial lake of limited dimensions, it does not seem reasonable that Claudius, undoubtedly eager to give an epic *naumachia* that would outdo past staged sea battles, would use six fewer large vessels on a much bigger natural lake. Cassius Dio and Tacitus give different kinds of information about the *naumachia*, but taken together their numbers make more sense than Suetonius'. Tacitus says that the ships were triremes and quadriremes, but gives no number. He is, however, the only source to give the number of participants: nineteen thousand, which must have included marines and oarsmen.[244] Cassius Dio does not give the number of participants, but says that the number of ships in the battle totalled one hundred.[245] If Tacitus is right about the number of fighters, there would certainly have to be a number of vessels significantly larger than the twenty-four mentioned by Suetonius to accommodate this many sailors. Cassius Dio's one hundred ships makes sense. Triremes required one hundred and seventy rowers and could hold up to forty marines.[246] If all these ships were triremes, one hundred ships and nineteen thousand participants means an average of one hundred and ninety rowers and fighters per ship. Since the quadriremes would have required more rowers, this average would have to be raised somewhat, but still seems within the realm of possibility.

It was at this *naumachia* that the fighters on shipboard addressed Claudius with the words that have been made famous by gladiator films: 'Hail, emperor, we who are about to die salute you'.[247] When what must have been a representative group of the nineteen thousand *damnati* spoke these words, they were probably on shipboard close to the shore with Claudius sitting on a chair on the shore. Film scriptwriters have been assigning these words to gladiators for so long now that they have been ingrained in the minds of the public as the formulaic opening of a gladiator show. It is clear, however, that gladiators never spoke these words. There is no record in the sources of gladiators speaking these words to a *munerarius*, and more significantly, competitive professional gladiators would never have gone into battle with such a defeatist attitude. These words, however, are appropriate to the *damnati* before a *naumachia*. They were about to enter a battle in which the emperor and everyone else expected them to die in fulfilment of the death penalty that had been imposed upon them. Their words appear to be an appeal for pity. Claudius, who was a bit of a jokester, answered: 'Or not', seemingly holding out some hope to the *damnati* that they might be allowed to survive if they fought well, as in fact turned out to be the case. The *damnati*, however, took Claudius' answer as a pardon and thought that they no longer had to fight. Claudius' first thought was to have them all killed on the spot, but that would have ruined his spectacle and would have been a difficult task, given that the *damnati* were armed. Instead, he ran along the shore, shouting threats and promises to get them to fight. When the battle finally started, the *damnati* at first made only a half-hearted attempt at fighting, but were eventually forced to fight to the death.[248] The force was applied by units of praetorian infantry and cavalry stationed on rafts, who had been given the task of preventing this large number of the armed *damnati* from escaping.[249] The praetorians also had some kind of fortified wall in front of them, from behind which they could employ artillery, shooting arrows and stones, while ships filled with Roman marines patrolled the lake. Claudius was taking no chances. The escape of a large number of these men could result in a disaster reminiscent of Spartacus' revolt in the prior century. Once the battle had begun in earnest, the *damnati* fought magnificently beyond all expectations. Tacitus comments that 'the convicts fought with the spirit of brave of men . . .'. This is strong praise from an historian who is usually contemptuous of all forms of spectacles and considers them not worthy of a place in the historical record.[250] In the end, the surviving *damnati* won release from the emperor in recognition of their ferocious fighting, unexpectedly fulfilling his tentative prediction.[251]

Nero included a *naumachia* as part of his *munus* of AD 57 in his new wooden amphitheatre, following the example of Augustus with a battle between 'Athenians' and 'Persians'. We have no details about the sea battle, such as the number of ships and of fighters. The only notable feature of this *naumachia* was the technology used in the production of the *naumachia*. Cassius Dio writes of a *sudden* influx of water into the arena, which suggests that it was supposed to surprise the spectators.[252] We can imagine the unsuspecting spectators being astonished by the rush of water into the arena. The surprise was heightened by the fish and other large marine creatures that were seen swimming in it.[253] Once the *naumachia* was over, the water was quickly drained and men fought duels (Cassius Dio does not call them gladiators), and participated in a massed infantry skirmish.[254] Thus Nero, within the space of one afternoon, had presented a *naumachia* and land battles in the same location, a spectacular technological achievement for the times.[255] Coleman comments:

> *The emphasis on the speed and suddenness of these engineering feats contributes to the impression that the emperors who commissioned them possessed superhuman powers.*[256]

What was certainly less spectacular was the *naumachia* itself, especially in comparison with that of Claudius. The arena of Nero's amphitheatre, even if it were approximately the same size as the arena of the later Colosseum, at best could have accommodated only a pint-sized *naumachia* with a few downsized ships and small number of combatants and rowers. It is obvious that the main point of Nero's *naumachia* was not its overall realism but its adaptation to the amphitheatre. The success of this display of technology led to a more complicated reprise seven years later. Cassius Dio reports that it took place in a 'theatre' (by which he means amphitheatre), no doubt in the same wooden amphitheatre as his first *naumachia*.[257] This time the show started with a *venatio* instead of a *naumachia*. Perhaps Nero changed the order of events in order to make the *naumachia* a surprise again, as on the previous occasion. After the *naumachia* (for which no details are given), the water was drained and gladiatorial combat was presented at the same location. What must have been the biggest surprise of all, after the combat, the area was flooded again for a public banquet on the water, hosted by Tigellinus, Nero's prefect of the Praetorian Guard, with the diners on what amounted to a large raft. While Nero and his guests dined on the middle of the raft, along its edges were taverns for unlimited drinking and brothels where sex was available on demand from women from all levels of Roman society.[258] A floating orgy!

As a climax of the dedication ceremonies for the Colosseum in AD 80, Titus presented a *naumachia*, representing a battle between the 'Corcyreans' and the 'Corinthians', a naval conflict that actually took place just before the beginning of the Peloponnesian War and was won by Corcyra. The location of the spectacle was the arena of the Colosseum. The flooding of the Colosseum for *naumachiae* was the subject of acrimonious controversy among scholars in the early nineteenth century.[259] Modern scholarly opinion seems to be in favour of the possibility of this practice. Coleman points out that the Colosseum was built on the site of Nero's artificial lake on his storied estate in the middle of the city, which presumed the ability to deliver water in large quantity into this area. She also asks that we imagine a shallow basin under the arena floor, like the ones in the Julio-Claudian amphitheatres in Mérida (Spain) and Verona, since the subterranean area (two stories deep) that is now visible in the Colosseum was probably not installed until at least the reign of Domitian.[260] We do not know which side won, or the number of vessels. As noted earlier, it would not have been difficult to ensure that the 'Corcyreans' won. As in Nero's two *naumachiae*, the ships undoubtedly were downsized vessels with a capacity of only a few marines and oarsmen. The elliptical arena of the Colosseum could have accommodated only two full-sized triremes, but there was no way that ships of this size could have been brought into the amphitheater through the regular entrances.[261] As with Nero's *naumachia* in AD 57, the battle itself and its scale were not the main point of the spectacle. In fact, it seems clear that Titus wanted to outdo Nero. Cassius Dio tells us that, after the *venatio* and the gladiatorial combat, there was a sudden influx of water into the arena.[262] Terrestrial combat was abruptly changed into aquatic conflict. Martial's comment on this spectacle focuses precisely on this mechanical reversal of nature and predicts the ultimate undoing of this exchange:

> *If you are a spectator who has just arrived from faraway shores, who is seeing his first Roman spectacle, so that this naval battle with its ships and the water that resembles the sea may not deceive you, this area was recently dry ground. You don't believe it? Watch while the waters are tiring out Mars; it will happen so quickly that you will say: 'here recently there was a sea'.*[263]

This trick could have only been possible with the use of a wooden floor that was taken apart and removed for the *naumachia* and reassembled when it was over. This may also have been the case with Nero's *munera* in his wooden amphitheatre. Titus' spectacle, however, introduced a new reversal. Dio tells us, somewhat imprecisely, that trained horses, bulls and other animals conducted themselves in the flooded arena as if they were on land. Performances of trained animals were a standard part of the *venatio*, but Titus had the honour of being the first to present a *venatio* in water. Two more aquatic shows followed the *naumachia*: one an enactment of the Hero and Leander legend and the other a water ballet featuring the Nereids (sea goddesses).[264] Since Hero and Leander both died by drowning, they were likely impersonated by *damnati* who were drowned in the course of the performance.

The land/water exchange was also the theme of Titus' second *munus* that took place on Augustus' artificial lake across the Tiber (*stagnum Augusti*). This *munus* repeats the events of the previous one in the Colosseum. Again there was a *venatio*, gladiatorial combat and a *naumachia*. The main point of this repetition is revealed by Martial's comment that 'whatever is seen in the circus and in the amphitheatre, the rich water presents to you, Caesar [i.e. Titus]'.[265] What was difficult to do in the amphitheatre was even more difficult to do on the water of the *stagnum Augusti*. Just as the Colosseum had to be modified to accommodate a *naumachia*, the *stagnum Augusti* had to be adapted for terrestrial events. Augustus' lake was partially covered over with a wooden platform in front of temporary stands, on which there was presented on the first day gladiatorial combat and a *venatio* and on the second day a chariot race (note Martial's reference to a circus). On the third day, a *naumachia* between 'the Athenians' and 'the Syracusans', an historical incident in the Peloponnesian War, took place on the lake. Three thousand fighters (again *damnati*) participated. This *naumachia*, however, did not end as it had begun, on the water. Its climax was an infantry battle on a small island in the lake, in which the 'Athenians', contrary to history, defeated the 'Syracusans' by capturing a wall constructed around a monument.[266] Obviously, the Romans were not sticklers for historical accuracy, but then again, during the imperial period they were more likely to identify themselves with the Athenians.

It is clear that Titus had taken Nero's similar spectacles in AD 57 and 64 as a challenge. Titus' show in the Colosseum (*venatio* and gladiatorial combat, climaxed by a *naumachia* and other aquatic events) at best only shows that Titus' powers were at least equal to those of Nero. What sets Titus apart from Nero was his imaginative spectacle at the *stagnum Augusti*. Titus had attempted a more difficult task. He adapted a lake created for the presentation of a *naumachia* so that land events could be held with little or no interruption.[267] Titus used the wooden platform that covered a portion of the lake to great effect. Perhaps most impressive to the spectators was the chariot race, which may have been run with the platform slightly submerged to give the impression that the chariots were riding on top of the water just as Neptune's chariot was supposed to have done. This seems to be what Martial is suggesting when he wrote in regard to Titus' *munus*: 'Triton saw the speeding chariots in the sea-dust [i.e., the spray] and thought that the horse of his master [i.e., Neptune] had gone by'.[268] Titus also went one better than Nero by having his *naumachia* turn seamlessly and surprisingly into a land battle on the lake. Spectacles like these by Nero and Titus were designed not just as entertainments for the people but also as demonstrations of the god-like powers of the emperor. Martial reinforces this impression by stressing the amazed reaction of the gods to Titus' *venatio*. Thetis and Galataea, two sea divinities, were startled by the presence of terrestrial animals in the water (perhaps pushed off the platform by attacking *venatores*) and Triton's astonishment at chariots running on top of the water. Martial gives the highest praise to Titus' *naumachia* on Augustus' lake: 'Let the Fucine Lake and the basin of Nero be long forgotten: future generations will know only this one *naumachia*'.[269]

Domitian also gave a *naumachia* in the Colosseum but we know nothing more of this spectacle beyond Suetonius' bare notice.[270] The biographer is much more enthusiastic about the multiple *naumachiae* Domitian presented on an artificial lake surrounded by seats that he had constructed on the other side of the Tiber in the area of the modern Piazza di Spagna (Spanish Steps). He claims that it was large enough to accommodate the number of vessels that would take part in a real sea battle.[271] We have evidence regarding only one of these *naumachiae*. Almost all the combatants were killed, but the only other notable thing about this spectacle was that many spectators died. This was the work of Domitian, one of Rome's cruelest emperors. While the sea battle was going on, there was a torrential rainstorm with high winds. Domitian immediately wrapped himself up in a number of woollen cloaks, but he would not allow the spectators to put on warmer clothing, thus causing many spectators literally to catch their death of cold.

An unusual *naumachia* was given by Sextus Pompey, the son of Pompey, in a natural setting on the open sea in the Straits of Messina between the toe of Italy and Sicily. This spectacle was given not as entertainment but to deliver a direct insult to Octavian. The *naumachia* celebrated Sextus' two naval victories over Octavian in 37 and 36 BC. Sextus, who had taken control of Sicily, presented his *naumachia* in sight of Octavian at Rhegium on the Italian coast with the purpose of mocking his defeated enemy.[272] Obviously, the battle was 'fixed' in favour of Sextus' fleet. Another curious example of a *naumachia* was a bloodless exhibition representing the Battle of Actium given privately by a friend of the poet Horace, Lollius Maximus, on his own lake. Lollius played the role of Octavian while his brother was Antony. Horace describes the boats used in this exercise as rowboats manned by slaves.[273] Lollius' re-enactment, like modern re-enactments of battles, was undoubtedly only harmless fun, with only pretend violence.

The last recorded *naumachia* was given by the emperor known as Philip the Arab in the celebration of Rome's millennium (AD 248), perhaps on Augustus' artificial lake.[274]

The end of gladiatorial combat

It would seem natural that the Christianization of the Roman empire played a major role in the decline and disappearance of gladiator games. Church Fathers were unrelenting in their attacks on this time-honoured spectacle. Their criticism focused on two aspects of these games: their idolatry and their cruelty. As for their idolatry, Christian polemicists believed that the *munus*, like all other spectacles, were closely associated with the pagan gods. Tertullian specifically condemns the *munus* because he believed that its origin was as a religious ritual of human sacrifice dedicated to the dead.[275] By the time Tertullian expressed this condemnation, however, the *munus* was no longer associated with funerals. Christian writers also linked gladiator games with the worship of Jupiter Latiaris, in which the statue of the god was washed in blood from the arena, and the cult of Saturn, a god often connected with human sacrifice. The cult of Jupiter Latiaris, however, had disappeared before the polemicists had begun to complain about it. The connection of gladiatorial combat with Saturn was either non-existent or at best tenuous.[276] The Christian poet Prudentius does not even mention Saturn in his passionate plea to the emperor Honorius to abolish gladiator games.[277] The Calendar of Philocalus (AD 354), which is careful to identify the gods connected with the various *ludi* throughout the year, does not mention Saturn or any other god when it lists the annual quaestorian *munera* given in December. As we have seen, the series of *munera* given by the quaestors in December was interrupted for the celebration of the Saturnalia in honour of Saturn on December 17. The distinction between the religious *ludi* and the secular *munus* is perhaps most evident in the fact that, during the Republic, the state financed the former and not the latter. The *ludi* which annually honoured the gods who protected Rome were indispensable to the survival of the state, whereas the *munus* was in essence an adjunct of funeral ritual that honoured deceased Roman nobles and their family. Although the state eventually subsidized the annual *munus*, the main consideration was political and not religious. The Roman people's hunger for gladiator games had to be satisfied to maintain the equilibrium of the state. The average Christian must have viewed the denunciations of the *munus* by writers like Tertullian with some scepticism.

The Christian accusation of cruelty of gladiatorial combat seems to be on more solid ground, but even here one must be careful not to view it anachronistically. Our concern about any sport that involved armed violence and a serious risk of death would be based on humanitarian values and focus on the welfare of the participants.[278] This is not the case with Christian attacks on gladiatorial combat. The focus is on the bad effects on the spectators watching these games. Augustine says that 'demons delight . . . in the cruelty of the amphitheatre'.[279] Therefore, attendance at a *munus* degrades the spectator to the level of a demon. This is most apparent in the effect that gladiatorial combat had on Augustine's young friend Alypius' quoted in Chapter 3.[280] Alypius comes away from the amphitheatre insensitive to the suffering of the gladiators and with a fanatical desire to come back and view more of the same, a virtual accomplice to murder. What we miss in these Christian denunciations is an expression of concern for the gladiators. The reason for this omission is that Christians were not very different from the pagans in their view of gladiators: their lives counted for nothing.[281] Actually, there is little particularly Christian about Augustine's overheated account of Alypius' experience. It is clearly in the tradition of Seneca's claim that bloody spectacles made him 'crueler and more inhumane' without any concern for the participants in the show.[282] Moreover, Christians were just as inured as pagans to public cruelty, which Wiedemann describes as 'a time-honored way of upholding justice and public order'.[283]

Christian polemicists, notwithstanding their passion and eloquence, had little negative effect on gladiator games. The average Christian took very little (or no) notice of critics of the games. Christians attended the games and took pleasure in them despite admonitions not to attend.[284] Moreover, wealthy Christians sponsored gladiator games. Even Christian emperors, despite their misgivings, were, as a rule, tolerant of the *munus*. A notable example is the emperor Theodosius (AD 379–395), a pious Christian. He was a defender of Christian orthodoxy, and fervent enemy of paganism, yet did not attempt to abolish gladiator games.[285] Constantine's edict of AD 325 in which he forbade the practice of condemning convicts to gladiator schools, is often cited as evidence of his intention to do away with gladiatorial combat. Constantine bases his explanation of this edict on a humanitarian premise, his objection to convicts spilling their blood in the arena:

> *Bloody spectacles in time of civil peace and domestic quiet displease me . . . it is better that they slave in a mine, so that they may experience the punishment of their crimes bloodlessly.*[286]

Since convicts had always been a major source of professional gladiators, this decree was a serious blow to the recruitment of gladiators and threatened the continued existence of the *munus*.[287] If this decree, however, was designed to close all gladiatorial schools and end gladiatorial combat, it did not achieve its purpose. Gladiator schools were still in existence at least in the first few years of the fifth century and, naturally, gladiator shows continued to be given in Italy and the Greek east.[288] It should also be noted that if Constantine really was opposed to gladiatorial combat, his opposition in this edict was clearly not absolute. His decree seems to imply that he finds the *munus* appropriate in times of war.[289] He certainly was willing enough to grant permission to the people of Hispello (modern Spello in central Italy) to offer gladiatorial games in their town.[290]

If Constantine's policy with regard to gladiatorial combat seems inconsistent for a Christian emperor, it is paralleled closely by the conduct of an earlier pagan emperor, Marcus Aurelius. Like Constantine, Aurelius disliked the sight of bloodshed, but never even attempted to abolish gladiatorial combat. That would have been unthinkable, just as it was in the time of Constantine. An emperor, notwithstanding his own personal inclinations, could not ignore the pleasures of the people without risking the loss of their support. Aurelius, a man of philosophical temperament, from his youth took no interest in gladiator games, finding them tedious and trivial.[291] As noted earlier, when Aurelius attended gladiator games, the combatants were only allowed to fight with blunted swords.[292] He, however, realized the importance of *munera* to the Roman people. When he augmented his army by taking gladiators from Rome to fight the Germans and the Marcomanni, he calmed the fears of the people that there would be no *munera* during these wars by directing the wealthiest *editores* to give shows in his absence.[293]

If Ramsay MacMullen was right when he wrote that 'Christianity made no difference' in the demise of gladiatorial combat, what was the cause of its decline and disappearance from the Roman empire?[294] Although Ward-Perkins warns against overemphasis on economic crisis in explaining the disappearance of gladiatorial combat, it is clear that it was one of the contributing factors.[295] Michael Carter, pointing to the disappearance of the banker (*argentarius*) from the sources in the late third century AD, argues:

> *The relative inaccessibility of credit my have contributed more than any other single factor to the gradual disappearance of gladiatorial* munera *in the fourth and fifth centuries* A.D.[296]

In all probability, the combination of the high expense of putting on a *munus* with the unavailability of credit led to infrequent optional shows. The plan of emperor Alexander Severus (AD 222–235) to replace the annual quaestorian *munus* given in December, with a *munus* given once every month suggests that there were not very many optional *munera* during the rest of the year.[297] This plan never came to fruition, but Gordian I, during his aedileship under Alexander, presented *munera* according to this schedule.[298] Could it be, as some have claimed, that the annual quaestorian *munus*, which was still being given in the middle of the fourth century, was the only gladiator show given through the whole year?[299] It is significant that when the historian Ammianus Marcellinus in the late fourth century lists the primary participants in Roman spectacles, he does not mention gladiators.[300] Throughout the fourth century, Germanic invasions brought economic disaster to many provinces, which led to the cessation of gladiator games in these areas. Rome suffered its first Germanic invasion in AD 410, when Alaric sacked the city. This was the beginning of the end for gladiatorial combat in the city. We hear of an attempt to revive the *munus* in Rome after 410, but it was only a desperate endeavour to revitalize a dying institution ultimately doomed to failure.[301] It is sometimes claimed that the emperor Honorius published a ban on gladiator games in the first years of the fifth century because of the violent death of a monk named Telemachus in an amphitheatre, most likely the Colosseum. Theodoret says that Telemachus tried to stop a gladiator duel as thousands of spectators watched. The crowd, upset by the monk's interference, stoned him to death.[302] Ville, however, has cast some doubt on the authenticity of this story. He sees this story as a popular legendary version of the death of St Almachius, who was slain by gladiators at the order of the city prefect. The reason for his execution was his protest of pagan superstitions and idolatry and not his demand for the end of gladiator shows.[303] The only gladiatorial legislation with Honorius' name on it exiled gladiators who had passed from gladiator schools into the households of senators.[304] Some have assigned responsibility for the apparent cessation of gladiatorial combat *c.* 440 to a decree of Valentinian III.[305] There is, however, no record of such a decree. Ville argues that Valentinian's ban on gladiatorial combat was published at the same time as the Theodosian Code (AD 438) and thus it was not felt necessary to include it in the Code.[306] It would seem, however, that if such a momentous decree had been issued, a mention of it would certainly have been recorded somewhere.[307] It is most likely that gladiatorial combat did not need an official ban to bring about its demise. The increasingly sporadic presentations of *munera* in late antiquity must be at least in part an indication of a declining public interest in them, but what would have led to this decline? Official Christian hostility to the *munus* may not have brought the *munus* to an abrupt end, but it probably did contribute to a change of attitude in the people. As the wealthy elite were increasingly converted to Christianity, potential *munerarii* may have found a different purpose for their money, which they diverted from extravagantly expensive *munera* to acts of Christian charity. A patron was more likely give to the poor or other charitable causes than spend a fortune on a gladiator show and to build or restore a church rather than restore or build an amphitheatre.[308] Moreover, constant complaints from the pulpit about the pagan atmosphere of *munera* may have finally begun to strike a responsive chord in the hearts of Christians, resulting in falling attendance. Most significantly, gladiatorial combat, which was perhaps the most important public symbol of Roman paganism, might have seemed outdated, an anachronism in a burgeoning Christian era. Alan Cameron is certainly not too far off the mark when he writes of 'a genuine change of popular taste'.[309] This change was no doubt a slow process. Perhaps it is best to think of a gradual decline of the *munus* until this popular institution finally disappeared after a life of nearly seven centuries.

Chapter 5

A Brief History of the
Arena Hunt

The Republican *venatio*

The earliest recorded *venatio* was given in 186 BC by the general M. Fulvius Nobilior, who had vowed to the gods that he would give *ludi* in return for victory in the Aetolian war. The *ludi* consisted of dramatic presentations (by Greek actors, a special treat), an entertainment typical of *ludi*, and two innovations. The first was athletic contests in the Greek style (most likely the combat sports: boxing, wrestling and *pankration*) and the second, a *venatio*. Livy merely says: 'a *venatio* of lions and leopards was given'.[1] He does not elaborate on what exactly went on in this spectacle. Were they for display or slaughter? Most likely, they were for both. Lions and leopards were probably enough of a novelty in Rome in the early second century that just their appearance was something of a sensation. Although Livy does not include the number of animals involved in these games, the quantity of animals eventually became a crucial piece of information in the reporting of *venationes*, like the number of gladiators in a *munus*. This can be seen in Livy's report of *ludi* given by the aediles in 169 BC, in which sixty-three lions and leopards, forty bears and an unspecified number of elephants appeared.[2] Despite Livy's reference to 'the appearance' of these animals, the large number of the animals suggest that they were killed by *venatores* and *bestiarii*. Livy also points out that this *venatio* was presented 'with growing magnificence', that is, surpassing previous *venationes* in the variety and in number of exotic wild animals. Already in the first half of the second century BC, the *venatio* had achieved considerable popularity in Rome. When the Senate issued a ban in 170 BC on the importation of African wild animals, the Roman people led by a people's tribune quickly reacted with a plebiscite that counteracted the ban, but only in the case of *venationes*.[3]

In the first century BC, the *venatio* reached even more impressive heights. In 58 BC, M. Aemilius Scaurus during his aedileship gave *ludi* that were a tremendous success and were long remembered. Cicero, who was a hard man to impress, praised Scaurus for giving 'the most elaborate and magnificent *ludi*'.[4] Writing in the first century AD, Pliny the Elder raved about the splendour of Scaurus' temporary theatre that he had constructed for his theatrical presentations (*ludi scaenici*).[5] Three and a half centuries later, the historian Ammianus Marcellinus mentioned Scaurus' presentation of wild animals never before seen at Rome.[6] The *venatio*, like gladiator games, had become a regular enhancement of *ludi* as an optional but not required entertainment, financed by the curule aedile as *editor*. Since Scaurus did not present a gladiator show, it would seem that his *venatio* was the real highlight of his *ludi*, featuring African animals, which were an absolute requirement for a high quality *venatio*. After Rome's victory over Carthage in the third Punic War (149–146 BC), the city and the coastal area (modern Tunisia) surrounding it became the Roman province of Africa, giving Rome control of an area rich in wildlife to exploit as a source for the *venatio*.[7] In the same *venatio* Scaurus presented for the first time at Rome a hippopotamus and five crocodiles. To exhibit these water animals in their element, Scaurus built in the Circus Maximus a temporary moat called a *euripus*.[8] A first-time appearance of an animal was a feather in the cap of the *editor*, making his *venatio* a greater attraction. It is easy for us, to whom these animals are familiar, to forget how exciting a novelty they must have been to the Romans, who had never seen their like before. Another feature of Scaurus' *venatio* aroused archeological interest among the Romans. The bones of an extremely large animal were brought from Joppa (modern Jaffa) in Judaea. Pliny the Elder describes these bones as almost 40 feet in length and taller than an Indian elephant (a dinosaur?).[9]

The size of the bones, however, was not the only point of interest; they were purported to be the remains of the sea monster that threatened the life of the mythical princess Andromeda, whose mother had offended Poseidon when she claimed that her daughter was more beautiful than the Nereids (sea nymphs). The flying hero Perseus rescued the princess from the monster. The combination of what most Romans took as 'history' and archeology must have been quite fascinating for the spectators. Greek myth would later play an even more significant role in the imperial *venatio* of the first century AD, as we shall see later in this chapter.

Strabo describes in some detail the presentation of the crocodiles at Scaurus' show, providing a good example of how new animals were exhibited in Rome.[10] There is no mention of the *euripus*, but only of a 'tank' and a device called a *pegma*, a moveable platform supported by scaffolding that could be raised and lowered mechanically.[11] The Tentyritae, the Egyptian crocodile-hunters who came along as keepers, used nets to move the crocodiles from the water to the platform, which Strabo describes as 'a basking place' for the animals. Presumably, the hot Italian sun would quickly calm down the crocodiles that had been so roughly displaced from the water. Their display on the *pegma* gave the spectators in the Circus Maximus a good view of the creatures as the platform was moved up and down. When the display was finished, the Tentyritae brought them back to the tank.

One of the most notable *venationes* of the late Republic was that given by Pompey for the dedication of his magnificent theatre in 55 BC, Rome's first permanent stone theatre. To match the grandeur of the new theatre Pompey chose to feature in his *venatio* the two most popular species known to the Romans: lions and elephants. Pompey presented 600 lions, no doubt the largest number of lions to take part in a *venatio* up to that time.[12] Although there is no historical record of what happened to them, we must presume that, like the elephants, they were killed. The choice of elephants by Pompey, Rome's greatest general at that time, was predictable, not just because of their size but also because of what the animals symbolized. Elephants had historical significance for the Roman people, who associated these huge beasts with warfare. Elephants were first introduced into Italy by the Greek general Pyrrhus (281 BC) who used them in his invasion of the peninsula. Quite naturally they served as a symbol of Pyrrhus' defeat when M. Curius Dentatus presented them in his triumph after his victory over Pyrrhus (275 BC). Twenty-three years later, around 142 elephants which had been taken from the Carthaginians in Sicily in the first Punic War, were brought to Rome. Pliny says that, according to one of his sources, they were killed in the Circus Maximus in order to dispose of them, while another source reports that they were driven around the racetrack with blunt spears in order to help the Romans overcome their fear of these huge animals.[13] This latter claim seems more plausible, because this exercise, showing that the Romans could control these huge, fearsome beasts, would go a long way towards exorcising whatever demons had troubled the Romans since they had first encountered them. Of course, the possibility remains that they were killed after they had served their purpose. During the second Punic war (218–201 BC), Hannibal presided over what turned out to be a foreshadowing of the Roman *venatio*. After forcing Roman prisoners to fight each other, he compelled the sole survivor of this tournament to fight an elephant. If he should survive this contest, he would be given his freedom. The Roman succeeded in killing the elephant, but Hannibal, fearing that news of this outcome would spread contempt for the military capability of his elephants, had the man killed on his way home. Pliny the Elder, who records this story, also mentions that the Romans had earlier found it easy to cut off the trunks of elephants in their war with Pyrrhus.[14]

Pompey in his African triumph in 81 BC had already shown an interest in the use of elephants to promote his career. Pliny the Elder tells us that it was on this occasion that the first harnessed elephants were seen at Rome, which drew Pompey's chariot in the triumph. Pliny also reports the belief that this manner of transportation was inspired by the story of the triumph of the god Liber Pater (a Roman name for Bacchus) in his conquest of India.[15] Thus, when it came to celebrating the dedication of his lavish theatre, it is not surprising that Pompey turned again to elephants for a grand finale on the last day of a five-day *venatio*.[16] Twenty elephants fought against Gaetulian hunters from North Africa in the Circus Maximus, the usual location for *venationes* during the Republic and the early empire.[17] Seneca differs with Pliny on the identity of the human fighters, assuming that they were condemned criminals.[18] It is more likely that Pliny is correct. Pompey would have wanted expert hunters for the grandest show he had ever given. The battle featured bloody action that the Roman crowd found tremendously exciting. One elephant which had been disabled by spears piercing its feet was still able to move slowly on its knees and grab the shields of its opponents, tossing them high into the air, almost as if it was performing a skilful trick. One elephant was killed by a single spear, which fatally wounded the animal just below the eye. The crowd's excitement, however, became terror when the elephants tried in concert to break down an iron fence that protected the spectators from the animals. The plaintive trumpeting of these animals when they could not break through the railing (which Pliny the Elder anthropomorphizes as an appeal for pity from the crowd) greatly troubled the spectators and led them to turn against Pompey, tearfully cursing their benefactor.[19] Cassius Dio's account of this incident tells of an anthropomorphizing claim that the elephants' trumpeting was a protest against the violation of an oath that African drivers had made to them that they would suffer no harm if they boarded the ships that would take them to Rome.[20]

It is interesting that the Roman spectators on this occasion showed some sympathy for the fate of these elephants, but we must not forget that it was only because of the extraordinary behaviour of these animals, which, as Cicero, an eyewitness, points out, the crowd saw as almost human.[21] Cicero indicates that the pleasure the crowd normally would have experienced at viewing the battle between men and elephants was spoiled by the danger that the wounded elephants posed for them and the impulse of pity evoked by the elephants' behaviour. This feeling of sympathy for the elephants, however, was only temporary. As J. M. C. Toynbee has pointed out, the crowd reaction in Pompey's *venatio* was the only ancient objection to the cruelty of the *venationes*.[22] Without a twinge of conscience, the Roman audience expected to see all the animals die in the *venatio* and occasionally a *bestiarius* or *venator*. Their expectations were usually realized.[23]

Even Cicero and Seneca, men of refined sensibilities, showed little concern for the elephants in this *venatio*. Cicero only complains of the sameness of even Pompey's grandiose *venatio*:

> *What delight can there be for a refined gentleman when either a relatively weak man is torn to pieces by an incredibly powerful beast or a magnificent beast is pierced by a hunting spear? . . . we did not see anything new.*[24]

Cicero acknowledges that the purpose of the *venatio*, like any other spectacle, is 'delight', which in this case was ruined by the monotony of events: a man is killed by a beast and a beast is killed by a man. On the other hand, Seneca, over a century later, sees a novelty in Pompey's *venatio*, but an unappealing one. Typically, the emphasis is on the suffering of human beings rather than of animals:

> *Did a leading man of the state and among leading men of the past, as tra-dition has it, of outstanding goodness [i.e., Pompey] think it would be a memorable spectacle to cause the deaths of men in a new way? Do they fight? That's not enough. Are they mangled? That is not enough. Therefore, let them be crushed by the huge weight of animals.*[25]

Seneca ignores the suffering of the elephants and only criticizes Pompey's obeisance to the Roman desire for novelty: his introduction of a new way of killing men. Seneca goes on to express distress about the quantity of human blood spilled at Pompey's *venatio*, which he takes as an omen of the blood shed later by Roman citizens in the civil war between Pompey and Caesar and by Pompey himself, when he was assassinated in Egypt.[26]

The Romans admired the great wild beasts that had become an increasingly common sight in the arena, but for the most part were not sentimental about them. The elephant continued to have a featured role in the *munus* in imperial times. Pliny the Elder says that during the reigns of Claudius and Nero, combats between individual fighters and elephants took place at the 'climax' of the *munus*, which Ville understands to mean the morning of the last day of the spectacle.[27] The honour of appearing on the last day was appropriate for the elephant, which was considered an 'imperial' animal in the sense of belonging to the emperor alone. Juvenal refers to elephants as 'the herd unwilling to serve any private citizen'.[28] In fact, the *Historia Augusta* identifies Aurelian (before he became emperor in AD 270) as the only private citizen to own an elephant, which he had been given by the Persian king. Aurelian, realizing the impropriety of his owning an elephant, gave it to the emperor.[29]

The *venatio* that Caesar gave as part of his triumphal games in 46 BC was one of the most varied of this kind of event that had been given at Rome up to that time. The events of the first four days took place in Caesar's temporary amphitheatre in the *Forum*, but the large number of participants involved in final day of the *venatio* required the space available in the more roomy Circus Maximus. The main attraction of the *venatio* was combat between men and lions. During the first four days of the *venatio*, four hundred lions were killed.[30] This number of lions quadruples the number presented by Sulla as praetor in 92 BC, but surprisingly is less than the number presented by Pompey in 55 BC.[31] Caesar, who had defeated Pompey at Pharsalia in northern Greece in 48 BC, no doubt would have wanted to outdo his dead rival by presenting a much larger number of lions. Circumstances, however, may have worked against Caesar in this matter. In the years before Pharsalia, Caesar had been collecting beasts in anticipation of giving a spectacle at Rome, but they had been killed by Lucius Caesar, probably a distant relative but a supporter of Pompey. Lucius' slaughter of these beasts along with his killing of the dictator's slaves and freedmen was why Caesar, despite his famous clemency, later ordered Lucius' death.[32] Caesar's loss of these beasts may explain why he, during his campaign against Pompey in 48 BC, confiscated lions belonging to C. Cassius, which he had procured and deposited in the Greek city of Megara in anticipation of his aedileship. The loss of these lions to Caesar was one of the reasons behind Cassius' hatred of the dictator, which led him to join with M. Brutus and other conspirators in the assassination. These lions, however, did not remain long in the possession of Caesar. Soon after Megara was captured by one of Caesar's subordinates, the citizens released the lions in the hope that they would attack the invaders. Instead, they turned against the Megarians and killed many of them.[33] Presumably, the lions disappeared into the surrounding countryside.

The Roman fascination with the slaughter of lions is easy to understand. In the mind of the Romans, what better way to demonstrate the mastery of wild nature than by killing these majestic animals? In the *venatio*, the lion was one of the greatest attractions and inspired great awe in the spectators. This is evident in Aulus Gellius' comment on lions that appeared in the Circus Maximus:

> *There were many savage wild animals that appeared there, large beasts whose beauty and ferocity had never been seen before. The surpassing fierceness of lions was a source of wonder . . .*[34]

Ever cognizant of the Roman spectators' desire for novelty, Caesar presented an event and an animal that the Romans had never seen before. The event, Greek in origin (from Thessaly, specifically), was the *taurokathapsia* ('bullfight'). Pliny the Elder's description of this event reminds us of the modern rodeo, although the purpose of the ancient contest was to kill the bull: 'It was the Thessalians who discovered how to kill a bull [by jumping] from horseback [and] twisting its neck'.[35] The *taurokathapsia* turned out to be a big hit. The event was revived in the first century AD by both Claudius and Nero.[36] The other featured novelty was the exhibition of a strange African animal that in its first appearance at Rome must have amazed the Roman audience. Here is Cassius Dio's description of this animal, which he calls a 'camelopard':

> I will give an account of the so-called camelopard, because it was then introduced into Rome by Caesar for the first time and exhibited to all. This animal is like a camel in all respects except that its legs are not all of the same length, the hind legs being the shorter. Beginning from the rump it grows gradually higher, which gives it the appearance of mounting some elevation; and towering high aloft, it supports the rest of its body on its front legs and lifts its neck in turn to an unusual height. Its skin is spotted like a leopard, and for this reason it bears the joint name of both animals. Such is the appearance of this beast.[37]

If you have not guessed it yet, Cassius Dio is describing a giraffe.

Performing animals

There was a lighter side to the *venatio*: trained animals performing tricks. Elephants were also stars in this feature of the *venatio*. Martial, with his characteristic hyperbole, reports that an elephant without any training knelt before the emperor Titus before a fight with a bull.[38] Although we may doubt Martial's claim about a lack of training, there is no question about the intelligence of elephants as was amply demonstrated in a *venatio* given in AD 6 by Germanicus, the nephew and adopted son of the future emperor Tiberius. He presented elephants dancing in costume. The presentation of performing animals might at first seem out of place in the *venatio*, which otherwise comprises violence and bloodshed, but performing animals well suited the overarching theme of the *venatio*: the human mastery of wild nature.

The primary effect of this performance by such large animals must have been comic. Aelian in his *On the Characteristics of Animals* gives a detailed account of the elephants' training and of their routine in the *venatio*.[39] We will be concerned with the latter here. Twelve elephants entered the amphitheatre divided into two groups of six each, each group on opposite sides, consisting of six males and six females. Each elephant was dressed in a costume typical of dancers and appropriate to the elephant's gender. All were decorated with flowers and performed steps that Aelian describes as dainty and feminine.[40] At the command of their trainer, they formed a line and then a circle, dancing to music while they sprinkled flowers on the ground with their trunks. According to Aelian, the next part of the show drove the spectators into a frenzy of appreciation. As if for a banquet, couches with cushions and luxurious coverlets were placed on the sand of the arena with large gold and silver bowls containing water next to the couches. Next to them were tables made of citrus wood and ivory, on which there were large amounts of meat and bread. The elephants, separated into male–female pairs, reclined at each couch and ate the food with the greatest refinement and restraint. This part of the show ended with a comic surprise. After draining the water bowls with their trunks as daintily as they had eaten the food, they squirted the water from their trunks, presumably at the crowd. Pliny the Elder's account of the same *venatio* differs from that found in Aelian and may refer to another part of the performance.[41] The ballet performed by elephants in Pliny's account is a manly dance, not feminine like Aelian's. It began with the animals throwing arrows with their trunks. Then some of the elephants imitated the movements of gladiators while others did a pyrrhic dance ('war dance'). Next, elephants did some tightrope walking and four of them carried on a litter another elephant, which mimicked a woman in the throes of childbirth.[42] Finally, Pliny mentions the banquet scene discussed above, which must have been the climax of the performance. His description is general without Aelian's details. He only says that the elephants came to the banquet couches that already had some people reclining on them and were able to take their places without disturbing any of them.

Damnatio ad bestias

Another feature of the *venatio* was the use of wild animals for executing convicts and prisoners of war, a punishment which the Romans called *damnatio ad bestias* ('condemnation to wild beasts'). The *ad bestias* penalty was one of the harshest sentences handed out by Roman judges, and could only be carried out in the context of the *venatio*. This restriction is evident in an account of the martyrdom of the Christian bishop Polycarp. At the public trial of Polycarp (*c*. AD 155), the Christian bishop of the province of Asia, the crowd demanded that he be placed in the arena with a lion. Philip the Asiarch, the judge at Polycarp's trial, was able to deny their request by explaining that since the *venationes* were over, the law prevented him from imposing the *ad bestias* penalty.[43] The crowd had to settle for Polycarp being burned alive.[44] Roman punishments for the most serious crimes strike the modern reader as incredibly severe, but their harshness and attendant public humiliation were meant to provide the greatest possible deterrence to crime. The *damnatio ad bestias* was, the Romans believed, one of the strongest deterrents. Being thrown to wild beasts involved slow torture for the victims as the animals tore their bodies to pieces before death came. This mode of execution turned the victim into animal food, a death that was arguably the most ignominious of all forms of Roman capital punishment. Although the *ad bestias* punishment is often associated in the popular mind only with Roman persecutions of Christians, the latter were never singled out as a group for this penalty. The Roman authorities also meted out this punishment to countless non-Christians. The reason for the association with Christianity is that Christian writers produced a significant body of literature on martyrs, who, as serious offenders in the eyes of the Romans, were often subject to this harsh penalty. Christian readers were fascinated by martyrs' willingness to suffer for their faith and took guilty pleasure in the gruesome details of their horrible deaths. The experience of thousands of non-Christians who were also executed in this manner did not arouse the same interest among pagan authors and thus were not recorded. As far they were concerned, all *damnati*, no matter what their religion, richly deserved their punishment. There was no reason to write a detailed account of any one person's execution by wild animals.

We first hear of the *ad bestias* penalty as military discipline incorporated into triumphal celebrations. L. Aemilius Paullus, after his victory over Perseus, gave triumphal *ludi* at the Macedonian city of Amphipolis (168 BC) and executed deserters by having elephants trample them as they lay on the ground.[45] Livy tells us that Paullus' son Scipio Aemilianus, celebrating his victory over Carthage in 146 BC, 'followed his father's example, giving games and throwing deserters to the beasts'.[46] This penalty was eventually extended to prisoners of war and criminals, probably in the first century BC. Although wild animals were not always effective agents of execution, any survivors among the victims would be held over for another show or executed by other means. For example, in the first century AD, Mariccus, a Gallic rebel, fell into the hands of the Romans and was condemned *ad bestias*. He was thrown to the beasts but because they showed little interest in him, his claim of divinity gained further credence among his supporters. His claim was ultimately proved false when he was put to death by other means in the presence of the emperor Vitellius.[47]

The jurist Ulpian tells us that young men usually received the *ad bestias* penalty.[48] This was not just because young men in ancient Rome were, as a group, more often guilty of serious crimes than any other segment of society. There was another consideration: their performance against wild animals. Young men could be relied on to make a better fight of it, resisting the animals to the very end, thereby providing a better show.[49] In Smyrna, a young Christian named Germanicus, having rejected a provincial governor's request that he deny his faith, provoked a beast by pulling it on top of himself. The crowd was mightily impressed by his courage.[50] The silence of the source on his ultimate fate probably means that he was killed.

Crimes that were punished by the *ad bestias* penalty included counterfeiting, temple robbing, and homicide in the course of a robbery.[51] At first, even freeborn men guilty of counterfeiting received this penalty.[52] By late antiquity, however, the *ad bestias* penalty was not considered appropriate for freeborn criminals. The *Codex Theodosianus* includes a decree of the emperor Constantine that, for the crime of kidnapping a son, slaves and freedmen be thrown to the beasts, while a freeman should suffer decapitation in a gladiator school, a more dignified and less painful death.[53] The following passage ascribed to Ulpian gives us an idea of where the *ad bestias* penalty stood in the hierarchy of punishments.

> *The proconsul [provincial governor] will have to decide the penalty for temple-robbery in accordance with the quality of the person and with the circumstances of the affair and of the time and of the age and sex [of the offender] either more severely or more mercifully. I also know that many [proconsuls] have condemned temple-robbers to the beasts; some even have burned them alive, while others have hanged them. But the penalty must be moderated to* ad bestias *for those who as a member of a gang have broken into a temple and carried away the [valuable] gifts given to the god at night. But if anyone has stolen something of medium value during the day, the penalty must be labour in the mines . . .*[54]

Note that the *ad bestias* penalty is considered a mitigation of what the some Romans felt were the two harshest punishments: burning alive and hanging. Condemnation to the mines (*ad metalla*), a penalty assigned here to a thief whose culpability was shared by the other members of a gang, was deemed a lesser penalty than *ad bestias*. The reason for this is that it did not involve immediate death, although that was usually the eventual result because of the back-breaking labour and the unhealthy conditions. Exile, as the least harsh of all the penalties, was reserved for freeborn citizens.[55] Judges, however, had wide latitude in assigning penalties, and sometimes freeborn citizens of the lower classes received one of the harsher penalties generally reserved for slaves.

Justinian's *Digest* mentions that notorious bandits were often hanged in the locale where they had committed murder. The reason for this practice was twofold: to deter others from the same crime and to provide comfort to the relatives of the murder victim. The *Digest* goes on to say that the *ad bestias* penalty could achieve the same results.[56] It was carried out in an even more public area (amphitheatre) and was widely advertised. As we have seen, sometimes the penalty had to be postponed until the next *venatio*, which could involve a delay of months.[57] The condemned would have to wait in prison for what must have seemed an interminable period. The prospect of being torn apart by wild animals must have evoked in its victims fearful anticipation of the pain and humiliation of such a degrading death. This prospect seems to have caused the suicides of two *bestiarii* (here = *damnati ad bestias*) slated to be executed in a *venatio* given by Nero (briefly alluded to in Chapter 3). Both examples illustrate the lengths to which some were willing to go to avoid this horrible fate. In the first case, a German, who was probably a prisoner of war, took advantage of the one weak point in the Roman security for prisoners: a prisoner was allowed to be alone when relieving his bowels. The German, having been given permission to take care of a sudden need, used a stick with a sponge attached, a device that Roman used as we use toilet paper, to suffocate himself by stuffing it into his mouth. Seneca comments with admiration that with this suicide the German 'insulted death' rather than become a recipient of the insult of this punishment. As Seneca remarks: 'the basest death is to be preferred to the foulest slavery'.[58] Another *bestiarius*, perhaps in the same *venatio*, while he was being conveyed in a cart to the arena, pretended to fall asleep and let his head fall between the spokes of one of the cart's wheels.[59]

There is evidence that slaves frequently suffered the *ad bestias* penalty unjustly. In the reign of Tiberius, the *Lex petronia* was passed, which took away the power of a master to condemn his slaves *ad bestias* without sufficient reason and required that the master first submit his reason to a judge for approval.[60] Ville sees this approval as a mere formality, but at least some judges must have taken the time to assess the reasons given by masters.[61] The abuse that this law tried to stop was the attempt by masters to make money from the sale of unwanted slaves, who were often guilty of little or no wrong, to *lanistae* or directly to *editores* for execution during the *venatio*. An illustrative example is the case of a fictional steward (slave) from Petronius, condemned *ad bestias* for having slept with his mistress discussed in Chapter 3.[62] The speaker points out that Glyco's wife was really at fault here, having forced the steward to have sex with her. He goes so far as to suggest that she should suffer the same penalty in the *venatio*, except in a form that was thought appropriate for an adulterous woman: to be tossed by a bull. Tertullian saw a similar abuse in the 'recruitment' of gladiators: 'To be sure, innocent men are sold into gladiatorial schools so that they may become victims of public pleasure'.[63]

Some provincial officials were not above ignoring the law to provide *ad bestias* victims for spectacles. Roman provincial officials had virtually absolute power; distance from Rome probably made some of them feel they could ignore the law with impunity. In 43 BC, a quaestor named L. Cornelius Balbus, apparently in charge of giving games in the province of Baetica (southern Spain), threw Roman citizens to the wild beasts in Hispalis (modern Seville), one of whom seems to have been condemned to suffer this penalty only because he was deformed.[64] Cicero accuses L. Piso Caesoninus, governor of Macedonia, of sending six hundred innocent men (probably not Roman citizens) to Rome to be thrown to the beasts in a show given by Clodius.[65] Although the number is probably exaggerated, Piso no doubt had sent a considerable group of unfortunates. It should be noted, however, that there were provincial officials who obeyed the law, as in the case of Philip the Asiarch, mentioned above. At Rome, only the emperor could get away with ignoring the law protecting freeborn Roman citizens from this penalty. On one occasion, Caligula, lacking convicts for execution in the *venatio*, arbitrarily chose members of the crowd to expose to the wild animals in a *venatio*. He cut out their tongues to prevent them from protesting.[66] At a time between *venationes* when the price of meat was high, he fed convicts to the beasts. Suetonius reports that Caligula gave no thought to his choice of victims, capriciously selecting groups of them to be fed to the animals.[67]

The reason that the Romans so often applied *ad bestias* penalty to Christians was their belief that this religious group threatened the very foundations of the Roman state with their unwillingness to recognize the state gods. The Romans had very strong feelings about this religious group. For example, Tacitus condemns them with the strongest possible language, calling them 'the object of hatred because of their disgraceful behaviour' and describing their religion as 'a destructive superstition' and 'hideous and shameful'. On the other hand, the Romans also had a strong sense of justice. Tacitus, in the same passage in which he condemns Christianity, reports that Nero used the Christians as scapegoats to distract his people from the rumour that he was behind the great fire of AD 64. In a private spectacle in his gardens, Nero applied the *ad bestias* penalty and other extreme punishments (*crematio* and crucifixion) to a large group of Christians who were implicated in the arson by informers. Some Christians wearing the hides of wild animals were torn apart by dogs, while others were crucified or burned alive at a spectacular night show. The crowd normally enjoyed the punishment of wrongdoers, but was aroused to pity by these horrible punishments, which they believed only satisfied Nero's cruelty and did not promote the welfare of Rome.[68]

A detailed contemporary account of *ad bestias* executions can be found in the *Passion of Saints Perpetua and Felicitas*, discussed in Chapter 1. The *Passion* nowhere names the geographical location of these executions, but there is general agreement that it must have been Carthage in North Africa.[69] The *Passion* does mention that the executions took place in a military amphitheatre.[70] The presentation of this *venatio* in a military amphitheatre makes perfect sense in that it was given by the procurator of the province to celebrate the birthday of Geta, the younger son of the emperor Septimius Severus.[71] Severus was a great champion of the army, realizing that his position as emperor depended on the support of his soldiers. His deathbed advice to his sons is famous: 'Enrich the soldiers; forget about everyone else'.[72] The celebration of the birthday of the emperor's son no doubt had special meaning in Carthage because Severus' family was of Punic origin. The Christians were from Thuburbo, about 40 miles west of Carthage, but it was only natural that they were brought to the city to be tried by the procurator of the province (a deputy for the governor who had died). Their punishment was carried out on March 7 203.

The group of Christians consisted of Vibia Perpetua, a young matron of a good family in her early twenties who had recently given birth; four teenage catechumens: Revocatus and his fellow slave Felicitas, Saturninus and Secundulus; and Saturus, probably an adult.[73] Despite the title of the work, Perpetua is the central character, with Felicitas playing only a minor role.[74] After their arrest, Perpetua and her colleagues were baptized and a few days later taken to the military camp prison, no doubt near the amphitheatre.[75] Perpetua describes her reaction to the prison:

I was terrified, because I had never experienced such darkness. What a cruel day: overpowering heat because of the overcrowding and the extortions of the soldiers. Lastly, I was worried sick about my baby.[76]

Two Christian deacons, using bribery, arranged for Perpetua's group to be moved into a cooler area of the prison. There, Perpetua breastfed her baby, which was nearly starving, and was allowed to take the baby with her when she returned to her area of confinement.[77] Perpetua and her group also suffered at the hands of a military tribune who believed rumours that the Christians would escape from the prison by means of magic incantations. As a result, they were put on a very meagre diet. Perpetua, not one to be quiet in the face of injustice, complained to the tribune, asking:

Why at any rate do you not permit us, who are well-known convicts, the property of Caesar, and about to fight [wild animals] on his birthday, to be fed adequately? Would it not add to your glory if we are led forth on that day with more flesh on our bones?

The tribune, taken aback by her complaint, made sure that they were treated more humanely and given more food.[78]

One day during the morning meal, Perpetua and her group were suddenly rushed to the place of their trial in Carthage's forum. The news of the trial spread throughout the city and attracted a large crowd. These spectators were no doubt curiosity seekers out for a good time. The interrogation of the defendants took place on a platform, probably erected specifically for this trial. Perpetua's fellow defendants confessed their guilt immediately. Their desire was to be convicted and sentenced to death as quickly as possible. Perpetua was the last to be questioned. When it was her turn, her father, carrying her baby on the steps leading up to the platform, drew

Perpetua aside and begged her to pity her baby by rejecting Christianity.[79] Perpetua did not get a chance to answer because the deputy governor Hilarianus immediately made the same plea.[80] Like many a provincial governor, Hilarianus was not eager to sentence Christians to death, especially when one of them was young woman like Perpetua from a good family, married and with a baby.[81] He must have thought that his request would be effective. It was not unusual for Christians to recant when faced with trial that could lead to their death. Eusebius points out that there were Christians who were not strong enough in their faith to disobey a provincial governor and could be intimidated to the point of recanting their faith.[82] On the other hand, there were some Christians, who actively embraced martyrdom, aggressively forcing the authorities to condemn them to death. Execution by wild beasts was a favoured penalty, which in the minds of many Christians brought a certain flair to the act of martyrdom. In AD 305, when eight Christian men demanded of the governor of Caesarea that they be thrown to the beasts, he frustrated their desire by having them beheaded.[83]

Like most Romans, Hilarianus was tolerant of other religions, but as a polytheist did not understand the unwillingness of Christians to worship the gods of the state. The emperor Marcus Aurelius had criticized the behaviour of Christians as 'mere obstinate opposition' and more appropriate to the tragic stage.[84] For pagan Romans, however, there was another and more serious consideration. Since Roman paganism was a state religion, the Romans looked upon any refusal to worship the gods of the state as an act of treason, which threatened to destroy the harmonious relationship between men and gods (*pax deorum* or 'peace of the gods'). This concern is illustrated by the fourth century AD controversy about the presence of an altar bearing a statue of the goddess of victory in the Senate house, which had been first installed by Augustus to celebrate his victory over Antony. Christians wanted it removed, while pagans were afraid that removal of the statue would lead to disastrous defeats in battle.[85] Leonard Thompson identifies other catastrophes that the Romans believed could be caused by Christian refusal to worship the state gods: natural disasters, social conflict and plague.[86]

Hilarianus then proposed what amounted to a test of Perpetua's loyalty to the emperor: he ordered her to sacrifice for the welfare of the emperor Severus and his two sons.[87] Perpetua, however, was unwilling to practise a ritual that was in essence a prayer to the pagan gods. When the deputy governor asked if she was a Christian, she uttered the self-damning words: 'I am a Christian.' At these words, her father again attempted to make her change her mind, but it was too late. Perpetua had confessed. Hilarianus, no doubt enraged by Perpetua's rejection of what he considered a reasonable request, ordered her father thrown down and beaten with rods. David Potter comments that a trial of Christians could become a 'contest of power' between the defendants and the magistrate, given a strong commitment to martyrdom on the part of the former. If the Christians recanted, he won; if they remained steadfast, he lost.[88] In this case, Hilarianus lost. He condemned her and her friends *ad bestias*, exactly what they all wanted. The new Christians joyfully returned to the prison.[89] James Rives points out that Hilarianus acted with a greater severity than necessary, because he could have refused to hear the charge and, once it was heard, was not bound by any law or decree to impose this aggravated penalty. He was in fact free to impose a lighter penalty, especially since Perpetua was in all probability an upper-class woman. Hilarianus' frustration aside, Perpetua's social standing was likely the most important factor leading to the more serious sentence. A respectable woman rejecting the values of her class and joining a cult believed dangerous to the Roman state set a bad example for her fellow citizens.[90]

As the day for the *venatio* approached, Perpetua's young slave friend Felicitas found herself in a dilemma. She was pregnant (in the eighth month) and there was a law against the public punishment of pregnant women. She desperately wanted to experience martyrdom with her fellow Christians and not with a group of real criminals, as might happen later after the birth of her baby. Three days before the *munus*, her colleagues, agreeing with her fears, prayed that she might give birth right away. Their prayers were answered and Felicitas gave birth, but suffered a very painful delivery. Her expressions of discomfort at the pain caused some attendants at the prison to taunt her. They asked her how she would deal with the pain of being torn apart by the beasts if she could not tolerate the pain of childbirth. Her reply was: 'Now I suffer what I suffer; then, however, there will be another [Jesus] in me who will suffer for me, because I will also suffer for him'.[91]

On the night before the *venatio*, the customary *cena libera* was held, which, as we have seen, was a public dinner for the participants in the next day's *munus*. The annoyance caused by curiosity seekers led to these chiding words from Saturus:

> *Is tomorrow not enough for you? Why do you gladly see what you hate [i.e., condemned Christians]? Today you are friendly, tomorrow you will be hostile. Take careful note of our faces, so that you may recognize us on that day.*[92]

The next day, when the condemned reached the amphitheatre, they were ordered to put on pagan religious dress: the men, the clothing of priests of Saturn, and the women, of priestesses of Ceres.[93] Like other aspects of their punishment, the purpose of this order was humiliation. Perpetua protested this order vigorously, pointing out that the condemned had cooperated as much as they could to avoid being subjected to this degradation and refers to an agreement that had been made earlier. The tribune was convinced by her arguments and they were allowed to come into the arena in their own clothing. While Perpetua entered the arena singing psalms, the three men, Revocatus, Saturninus and Saturus, took a more aggressive stance. They uttered threats in response to the rude gaze of the crowd and, through gestures, let it be known to the *munerarius* (Hilarianus again) that God would avenge the injustice they were about to suffer. The spectators were aroused to fury by this behaviour and demanded that they be made to pass through a gauntlet of *venatores* using whips. The Christians were pleased to suffer the same punishment that Jesus did. By this time, Hilarianus was no doubt only too glad to oblige them.[94]

Then began the main show. The men and women were dealt with separately.[95] The men went first. Saturninus and Revocatus were exposed to a leopard and apparently were able to fend off the animal, even though they apparently had been given no weapons. They were next placed on a platform, perhaps tied to stakes, and set upon by a bear. The purpose of this platform was to frustrate the bear temporarily in its desire to get at his human prey, making him even more eager for the kill. The bear finally found its way up a ramp attached to the platform where it attacked and apparently killed them, since we hear no more of them in the narrative.[96]

Next came Saturus' turn. Apparently, before the *munus* Saturus had mentioned what animal he preferred to face. With good reason, his greatest fear was to be attacked by a bear, which usually dreadfully mangled its victims before they died. His preference was for a leopard because he believed that this animal could kill a man with one bite. If the authorities knew of this preference, they ignored it, because the animal he had to face first was a wild boar to which he was tied so that the boar would be certain to attack him. There were, however, always surprises in the arena when wild animals were involved. The boar turned on the *venator* who tied the animal to Saturus and gored him to death.[97] Next, Saturus' greatest fear was realized. He faced the same situation as Saturninus and Revocatus had faced earlier: he was put bound on a platform near a caged bear.[98] Again, Saturus had incredibly good fortune. The bear refused to come out of his cage when it was opened.[99] Wild beasts could be unreliable executioners.[100] The famous martyr Blandina (Lyons, AD 177), a Christian slave, was tied to a stake and exposed to wild animals, which showed no interest at all in her. As noted earlier, wild animals were often intimidated by the strangeness of their surroundings as they were released into the arena and did not display the ferocity that the crowd expected.[101] Later, she survived being tossed by a bull and had to be put to death by the sword.[102] Thus, Saturus enjoyed a second reprieve, but, like the first one, it was only temporary.

Then came the women's turn. The instrument of their punishment was a wild cow.[103] The choice of a cow was not haphazard. Women were often forced to confront animals of the same gender.[104] The text says rather enigmatically that the Devil (i.e., the Roman authorities) used the wild cow to punish the female victims to 'rival their gender with the beast'. Shaw plausibly suggests that the cow was intended to mock the victim's gender and might even imply sexual wrongdoing, possibly lesbianism.[105] Perpetua and Felicitas were stripped of their clothes, wrapped in nets, and presented to the crowd.[106] At this point the spectators revealed their unpredictability. They were shocked and dismayed by the sight of the two women, especially because Perpetua's breasts were dripping with milk after the recent birth of her baby. The crowd's reaction seems to have had little effect on Hilarianus. His only concession was to send them out again without the nets and dressed more modestly in tunics. Perpetua faced the cow first and was tossed into the air, landing on her back. Her first thought was her modesty; she pulled what was left of her torn tunic over her thighs. Felicitas then rejoined Perpetua and they faced the cow together.[107] The cow knocked Felicitas down and Perpetua helped her to her feet. At this point, the spectators seemed to have had enough of the suffering of the two women, who were allowed to exit the arena through the *Porta Sanavivaria* ('Gate of Life') as a symbol of their temporary survival.[108] As in the case of Saturus, failure of an animal to kill was not grounds for exempting the two women from their death penalty. All the *damnati* would be killed one way or the other and, if not in this *venatio*, then in the next one.

Saturus, who had survived confrontations with a leopard, bear and wild boar, was then ordered to face a leopard for a second time. Saturus went to meet his fate with confidence that he would die quickly. The leopard administered a bite, but all it did was produce a great amount of blood and not death. As Saturus left the arena for a second time, the crowd began to chant '*salvum, lotum*', a phrase hard to translate idiomatically, but which means literally 'healthy, washed'. This chant, which used the words of a formulaic greeting of those exiting the public baths, was a mockery of Saturus' bloody appearance. The author of the narrative, however, interprets this as reference to the salvation of Saturus by a baptism of blood (the Christian meaning of *salvus* is 'saved'). Then the almost lifeless body of Saturus was taken 'to the usual place', a reference to the *spoliarium*, either a room in the amphitheatre or a small separate building. There, *damnati* who had survived the ordeal in the arena were dispatched by a *confector*. Hilarianus must have felt that the Christians, having survived the attacks of the beasts, earned a more private death away from the hostile eyes of the mocking spectators. The crowd, however, felt cheated of the pleasure of seeing the faces of the dying at the moment of death.[109] The narrator explains their wish: 'the people demanded that they come into the middle of the arena, so that they might join their eyes to the sword penetrating their body as comrades of homicide'. As we saw in Chapter 1, Perpetua and her friends, more than glad to accommodate them, were killed in the middle of the arena by an apprentice gladiator (*tirunculus*).[110]

A more upbeat example of the *ad bestias* penalty is the story of Androclus (Latin form of Greek name Androcles) and the lion. The tale is an illustrative example not only of the *ad bestias* punishment but also of the Romans' occasionally sentimental attitude towards animals. The story of Androclus is a variation of a popular story pattern (or what today we might call an 'urban legend') that has a large cat (lion or a leopard) shedding its ferocity and, through its demeanour, begging a man for help with a problem. The man overcomes his fear, helps the animal and earns the beast's gratitude. Pliny the Elder gives three versions of this story as examples of the gentleness of these animals. In the first example, the Syracusan Mentor in Syria finds his way blocked by a lion rolling on the ground and licking his feet. Mentor observes a wound in one of the animal's paws and removes a splinter to the great relief of the lion. Next, the Samian Elpis, after disembarking from his ship on to the coast of North Africa sees a lion with a wide-open mouth, which he perceives as a threat. When he climbs a tree, the lion does not follow him but lies down at the foot of the tree, constantly looking at Elpis with his mouth still open. Eventually, Elpis realizes that the lion has a problem, climbs down and removes a bone stuck in the lion's mouth that was preventing him from eating. The story ends with Pliny's comment that as long as Elpis stayed in Africa, the lion shared his prey with him. The third example has a philosopher named Demetrius (in an unnamed location), whose way, like Mentor, was blocked by a female leopard rolling on the ground and displaying great anguish. The leopard then leads Demetrius to a pit into which her cubs had fallen. He rescues them and the leopard demonstrates her gratitude by her playful behaviour.[111] This story pattern has been called 'the grateful lion'.[112]

The most famous version of this story is found in Aulus Gellius' (second century AD) *Attic Nights*. Gellius attributes this version to the first century AD scholar Apion, who told the story in his book *The Wonders of Egypt* (no longer extant). Apion's story takes place in the Circus Maximus in Rome, where, as part of a *venatio*, Androclus, a slave of the powerful governor of North Africa, is about to be thrown to the lions as a punishment for having run away from his cruel master. When a ferocious lion comes towards him, Androclus suffers the panic of man about to be torn to pieces. The lion, however, recognizes Androclus as the man who had removed a painful splinter from his paw in Africa and, in return had enjoyed the hospitality of the lion in his cave for three days, sharing the prey that the lion brought back from his hunts.[113] Androclus and the lion have a joyful reunion in the middle of the arena. Aelian, a contemporary of Gellius, adds the detail that the lion saved Androclus from being attacked by a leopard in the arena.[114]

Androclus, summoned by the (unnamed) emperor, tells him of the meeting with the lion in Africa. At the order of the emperor, Androclus' story was written down and shared with the spectators through the medium of placards carried around the amphitheatre by arena attendants.[115] The crowd's reaction was to demand *missio* for both Androclus and the lion. The emperor grants their request and orders that Androclus be given the lion. The story ends happily with Androclus leading the lion on a leash through the shops of Rome, where he is given money and the lion is showered with flowers, as those present say: 'This is the lion who is the host of a man; this is the man who is the doctor of a lion'.[116]

The events in the arena described in Gellius are credible. Although the story of the removal of the splinter is the stuff of legend, we have seen that it was not be unusual for a wild animal to refuse to attack a *noxius* in the arena. It is not even impossible that it chase away other animals to protect him. Seneca, a reliable reporter of events in the arena, tells such a story, in which a lion in the arena recognizes his former trainer, now an intended victim of the *ad bestias* penalty, and saves him from the other animals.[117] The reason for the lion not attacking is much more plausible in Seneca's anecdote. Seneca's lion is a trained animal, which for some reason had been transferred to a new role in the *venatio*. The recognition of his former trainer and the saving of his life, although unusual, do not overly strain credulity. Wild animals are known to develop strong bonds with their train-ers and carers.[118] In fact, it is not impossible that Apion's story was based on the event described by Seneca, which Apion attached to the legend of the grateful lion. If this was the case, Apion created a satisfying and impress-ive conclusion to an already popular legend.[119] Almost two thousand years later, George Bernard Shaw turned the story into a play, *Androcles and the Lion* (1913).[120]

Dramatization of the *ad bestias* penalty

During the last years of the Republic, a variation in the *ad bestias* penalty was devised that made the process more entertaining to the Roman audi-ence while at the same time providing a greater deterrent to crime. This innovation was in the form of a dramatic scene in which the *damnatus* was forced to play the central role. The purpose of the scene was to mock the condemned man and set up his death. As Coleman explains: 'the deterrent factor was the assumption . . . that no one would want to suffer such physi-cal torture, nor to provoke such humiliating *Schadenfreude*'.[121] Although there is no direct evidence, these 'playlets' were probably the innovation of Augustus. Towards the end of the civil wars there were serious problems with the maintenance of public order in Rome and Italy. Octavian dealt with them aggressively. For example, he ordered that the large numbers of runaway slaves that had joined the armies of his enemy, Sextus Pompey, be returned to the masters or their heirs or, if unclaimed, be put to death.[122] An even worse threat to public order were bandits who were plying their trade in large numbers. Augustus quickly eliminated this problem by executing many of these highwaymen.[123] Thus, it is not hard to see his hand behind the unusual execution of a famous criminal named Selurus, leader of a small army of bandits which had been terrorizing the area around Mount Aetna in Sicily.[124] His fame earned him the nickname of 'son of Aetna'. After his capture, Selurus, rather than being executed in the area where he had committed his crimes, was brought to Rome to provide an example to the whole empire. His execution was designed to mock him and single him out as a memorable example of how Romans deal with hardened criminals. Here is my attempt to reconstruct what happened by filling in the gaps in Strabo's description.[125] First, Selurus was placed on a *pegma* and tied up to prevent his jumping off. Then the platform was raised in the air to its full height to represent Mount Aetna and, metaphorically, the heights of criminality that Selurus had reached in his heyday, which were the cause of his imminent fall.[126] Compare Juvenal's metaphorical comment on the fall of Sejanus, Tiberius' praetorian prefect:

> . . . the man [Sejanus] who hoped for excessive honours and strove for excessive wealth, was constructing a high building, whence his fall would be from a greater height . . .[127]

For Selurus, the metaphor became reality. The *pegma* began to collapse upon itself until it reached its lowest level. At the bottom of the *pegma* were placed cages containing wild animals, which were designed to break apart under the pressure of its contraction. Once released, the animals killed Selurus. Apuleius (second century AD) mentions what appears to be a similar device, which he describes it as a kind of 'house' of several stories containing the wild animals.[128] Apuleius does not explain how this device accomplished the execution of those condemned to the beasts, but perhaps it worked in somewhat the same way as the *pegma* did in the execution of Selurus.[129]

Figures from history and myth sometimes provided dramatic settings for the execution of *damnati ad bestias*. One of these little dramas was based on Laureolus, a notorious bandit who had terrorized Rome.[130] He was caught and put to death (probably by crucifixion). His story became the basis of a well-known mime during the reign of Caligula.[131] The play seems to have been a morality tale depicting the triumph of 'authority over lawlessness'.[132] The story of Laureolus eventually found its way into the arena, enacted by a *damnatus* during the dedication of the Colosseum in AD 80. The punishment was crucifixion, which, however, lacked the timing and dramatic intensity required for an arena show. It was a slow method of execution that could take hours or even days, depending on various factors. Spectators at these events expected to see criminals die before their eyes, not a slowly languishing victim who might not die before they left the amphitheatre. Therefore, a wild animal was introduced to this scene, which provided a quicker and more violent end to the *damnatus*. The animal in this case was a bear imported from Scotland, which shredded the condemned's body as he hung on the cross.[133] The combination of crucifixion and wild animal attack seems new but it is only a variation of the common practice of tying a man to a stake and exposing him to a wild animal.

As for enactments based upon myth, one involved a *noxius* playing the role of the great mythical musician Orpheus whose music had the power to move all nature. Martial describes a forest scene in the arena in which Orpheus' music causes trees and rocks to move and charms wild animals. All this required a great deal of artifice: a mechanical device to put the artificial trees and rocks in motion and different species of animals trained not to attack each other and to appear to be listening to music. The ending of the episode, however, abruptly departs from the myth. Instead of 'Orpheus' being dismembered by a group of Thracian women, as in the myth, a bear tears him to pieces.[134] There are other examples of surprise endings to these mythical enactments. A *noxius* impersonating Daedalus, the mythical inventor of flight, suffered a death that had no connection at all with Daedalus' story. Like the 'Orpheus' above, he was killed by a bear.[135] Martial mentions that when 'Daedalus' was torn apart by the bear, he wished that he still had his wings. This suggests that the *noxius* was somehow flying before he was killed. Here is a possible scenario: the *noxius* wearing wings made an entrance from the air by means of some device like a crane with a cable attached.[136] He was set down in the arena and, once his wings were removed, a bear was released to dispatch him. In an enactment of the story of Hercules and the Bull of Marathon there was another surprise ending. 'Hercules' did not kill the bull as in the legend, but instead was tossed high into the air by his opponent.[137] These 'revisions' of the original stories were obviously required in order to give the wild beasts a central role in the execution.

The enactment of another myth added bestiality to the usual violence: Pasiphae's love for a bull with which she had sexual intercourse.[138] This performance took place as part of the dedication celebration of the Colosseum in AD 80. Part of its attraction was the novelty of a female victim, a departure from the more usual male convict and of the punishment. In his poem on this performance, Martial assures the emperor Titus that what took place in the arena was a real coupling of 'Pasiphae' and a bull.[139] The question arises: how was this accomplished? Perhaps it was, as Coleman suggests, simply a matter of 'Pasiphae' being covered with cowhide and having discharge from a cow in heat rubbed on her sexual organs. If penetration by the bull did not kill her, she, like Perpetua, would have been dispatched by the sword.[140] Another example of a punishment involving bestiality is found in Apuleius' *Metamorphoses*. A woman convicted of murder by poison incurred the *ad bestias* penalty, which involved sexual intercourse with an ass.[141] Clement of Rome notes that Christian women were sometimes forced to play mythical roles in the execution of their punishment, for example as Dirce, a queen of Thebes, who was tied to the horns of a bull and gored to death.[142] The enactment of the Dirce story was suitable to a *venatio* setting, and it provided a spectacular and grisly ending. Clement also mentions the Danaids, but their punishment for killing their husbands, carrying leaky water vessels for eternity in the underworld, hardly suits the needs of the arena. In this case, it is likely that a more sensational punishment was found for the Danaids, since, as we have seen, there was no requirement that the enactment follow the myth closely.[143]

There were other enactments that did not involve animals but may have been included in the *venatio* anyway. This seems to have been the case on at least one occasion in the punishment of a convict playing the role of Mucius Scaevola, the sixth century BC Roman hero who defied the Etruscan king by holding his hand in fire.[144] Martial says that a punishment of 'Scaevola' took place 'on the morning sand', the normal time for the *venatio*.[145] Martial wrote two poems about this punishment. The first one praises the *noxius* for being brave enough to put his hand into the fire.[146] The poet seems to have written the second one after he found out what really lay behind this act. The poet now says that the *noxius* only *seemed* to be courageous.[147] The *noxius* apparently had been offered a choice between being burned alive wearing the *tunica molesta* and putting his hand in the fire, and cravenly chose the latter. Coleman calls the less severe alternative punishment 'a mitigated penalty'.[148] Another example of the mitigated penalty can be found in the enactments of the myth of Attis, who castrated himself.[149] The criminal who was forced to play this role must have been given the choice of self-castration or death, since he would not have castrated himself if he was going to die anyway. Naturally the *noxius* chose the former.[150]

The legend of Hercules perfectly suited a spectacular execution by fire in the arena. His wife Deianeira had unwittingly given him a toxic piece of clothing that had the effect of fire on Hercules' body, leading to his consequent suicide on a pyre on Mount Oeta. During the reign of Nero, a criminal named Meniscus was burned alive (no doubt wearing the *tunica molesta*), for having stolen three apples from the grounds of the emperor's Golden House. The execution of Meniscus joins two events that are unconnected in myth to fit Meniscus' crime and punishment: Hercules' theft of the golden apples of the Hesperides and his fiery death on Mount Oeta:

> *Like Hercules before him, Meniscus stole three golden apples from the garden of the Hesperides belonging to Zeus [= Nero]. What does this mean? When he was caught, he became a great spectacle for everyone. Like Hercules before him, he was burned alive.*[151]

Why did Meniscus receive so severe a punishment for stealing these apples? One suggestion is that trespassing on the grounds of Nero's famous Golden House may have been considered an act of treason, which warranted the penalty of being burned alive (*crematio*).[152]

On one occasion, Commodus took part in an enactment that ranks with the cruelest of all discussed so far. Believing himself to be a second Hercules, he enacted in the arena the myth of the battle between the gods and the giants, in which the club-bearing Hercules fought on the side of the gods. He collected all the men he could find who had lost their feet through disease or accident. He had their lower extremities covered in such a way that they appeared to be half-human and half-snake, thus resembling the depiction of giants in ancient art. Commodus clubbed them all to death.[153]

The *venatio* and politics

Like gladiatorial combat and other spectacles, the *venatio* had political implications. Perhaps the best illustration of the connection between the *venatio* and politics is the exchange of letters between Cicero, who at the time (51–50 BC) was governor of the province of Cilicia (south-west Turkey) and M. Caelius Rufus, his ambitious protégé in Rome. In 51 BC, Caelius had made up his mind to run for the curule aedileship, which would give him the responsibility of organizing the solemn games for the *Ludi Megalenses* (in honour of the goddess Cybele) and the *Ludi Romani*. As we have seen earlier, the curule aediles were allotted a sum of money to help defray expenses, but an ambitious aedile, looking forward to higher offices such as the praetorship and consulship, would want to make the greatest impression possible, which meant paying from his own funds for attractive extras such as a gladiatorial show or a *venatio* or perhaps even both. In June of 51 BC, just before Caelius' election to the aedileship, he reminds Cicero of an appeal for leopards that he had made earlier.[154] The request was not unusual. Roman politicians used networking with allies in the provinces to obtain animals. Cicero's presence as governor in Cilicia with a small army at his command put him in ideal position to help Caelius obtain leopards from a province that was a significant source of these animals. There was no expense on Cicero's part since he could use his soldiers to do the tracking and capturing.[155] If Cicero carried through on his promise, he would greatly reduce Caelius' expenses, leaving him to pay only the cost of shipment and feeding of the animals. In August of 51 BC, Caelius writes again, renewing his request with greater urgency, underlining its importance.[156]

By September, Caelius seems exasperated by Cicero's unwillingness or inability to provide him with leopards. He tries to shame Cicero by pointing out that a Roman businessman named Patiscus in Cilicia had come through for his friend C. Scribonius Curio by sending him ten leopards and that Cicero should have provided Caelius with many times more. Curio's success in acquiring leopards actually turned out later to be boon for Caelius. Curio had intended to run for the curule aedileship of 50 BC, but suddenly changed his mind and ran for the tribunate of the plebs, a magistracy that did not involve giving games, therefore eliminating his need for the animals. Thus, he gave Caelius these Asiatic leopards plus ten more leopards from Africa. Curio's thirteen leopards were a generous gift, although Caelius probably had in mind a more impressive number of leopards for his *venatio*. In another letter, he urges Cicero to have his men search for these animals in areas adjacent to Cilicia, especially Pamphylia, where leopards were most frequently captured.[157]

The last letter we have from Caelius to Cicero on this matter was written in February of 50 BC, after Caelius had assumed the curule aedileship. Caelius seems bitter and at the end of his tether. The only mention of the leopards is in the very last line of the letter: 'It will be a disgrace for you that I do not have any Greek leopards'.[158] In early April, Cicero responds to Caelius with assurance that hunters are under to his orders to capture leopards, but they are now scarce in Cilicia. Cicero ends with a weak joke that leopards have decided to leave Cilicia for Caria, because so many traps have been laid for them. This letter was written on the first day of the Megalensian games, one of the *ludi* that Caelius as curule aedile had to organize.[159] He could have given a *venatio* with the animals that Curio had given him, but there is no evidence that he did. Since Caelius was also required to organize the *Ludi Romani* in September, he had one more opportunity to present a *venatio*. Unfortunately, we do not know whether any leopards from Cicero ever arrived at Rome before the *Ludi Romani* and we hear nothing more of Caelius' *venatio*.

In this correspondence between Caelius and Cicero, we get a sense of the problems of getting animals from their native habitat to Rome. Caelius writes that a group of men whom he had sent to Cilicia on another matter can be trusted to supervise the feeding and transport of the animals to Rome. Caelius even volunteers to send more men from Rome if necessary.[160] The shipment of animals was a precarious process, because, having suffered the trauma of capture, the beasts were prone to sickness and even death while being transported long distances from the frontiers of the empire to various urban centres in Italy and the provinces. They had to be carefully watched lest they escape and threaten the lives of the inhabitants of the region. Delays had to be kept to a minimum to make sure that they arrived on time for the spectacle. Nothing could be more devastating for an *editor*, who, having advertised the *venatio*, had to cancel it at the last minute.[161] As late as the fifth century AD, a law found in the *Codex Theodosianus* stipulates that the animals be transported under the management of escorts and that there be no more than a seven-day stopover in any city along the way. The statute imposes a hefty fine for violators.[162] A good example of what could happen to animals intended for a *venatio* is the case of a well-to-do man in Apuleius' *Metamorphoses* who was planning an elaborate *venatio* in Plataea in Greece. He spent a great deal of money on wild animals of various types, but most of this money went on bears, after large cats the most popular killers in the arena. In addition, he caught some bears himself and was given some by friends. In anticipation of his *venatio*, he maintained these bears at great cost to himself, but almost none of these bears survived to participate in the *venatio*. There were various causes of their deaths: being tied up in the hot sun, inactivity, disease, etc. The starving population of Plataea took advantage of the prospective *editor's* misfortune to gorge themselves on bear meat.[163]

After the assassination of Julius Caesar in March, 44 BC, M. Junius Brutus, the leader of the conspiracy, tried to use a *venatio* to win the support of the people. He had discovered that the citizenry had not reacted favourably to the killing of Caesar. Brutus feared that he himself might be killed by Caesar's veterans, so, shortly after the assassination, he and his colleague Cassius left Rome for southern Italy. At the time, Brutus was urban praetor, an office that required him to be absent from the city for no more than ten days at a time. There was, however, one pressing duty as urban praetor that he did not ignore: the organization of the *Ludi Apollinares* in July, which might help him win back the favour of the Roman people and even cause him and his associate Cassius to be recalled to Rome.[164] Since Brutus believed it was too dangerous to re-enter Rome to organize these games in person, he got Cicero's friend Atticus and C. Antonius, Marc Antony's brother, to help him with this task.[165] Although we hear of dramatic presentations and Greek athletic contests, typical fare of the sacred *ludi*, the central feature of this festival was a *venatio*.[166] It would appear that Brutus had already purchased animals, all of which he intended to present in his *venatio*. He was willing to give up whatever profit he might have made by holding back some animals and selling them, a frequent practice among organizers of *venationes*.[167]

Brutus earnestly entreated Cicero to attend these games to show the spectators that he had the political support of the great orator. Cicero probably fulfilled Brutus' request because the orator's reports of the *ludi* seem to be first hand. Cicero, in his public statements about these games, had to make the best of a bad situation. First, he had to explain and defend the absence of Brutus, passing over the real reason for it, that is, the prevailing attitude in Rome that Brutus and his conspirators were murderers and not liberators.[168] The spectators showed by their applause that they were pleased by most of the *ludi*. In his public statements, Cicero, a supporter of Brutus, however, found it necessary to interpret all applause as not what it was, a positive response to the show, but a political statement of support for Brutus.[169] In private, however, he dismisses the political significance of this applause.[170] According to the historian Appian, hired agitators aroused a feeling of pity for Brutus and Cassius and started a groundswell movement in favour of their recall, but an anti-Brutus group was able quash this demonstration of support by stopping the games.[171] Although the *ludi* in general, and no doubt the *venatio* in particular, did have its effect on the crowd it was not impressive enough to erase from their minds the generosity of the man who had won their hearts through his lavish shows and to induce them to embrace his assassins. Brutus, having failed to achieve his purpose with his *venatio*, left Rome with Cassius for the Greek east.

Some notable imperial *venationes*

Nero's venatio *(AD 57)*

A *venatio* was part of the *munus* that Nero gave for the dedication of his new wooden amphitheatre. An impressive variety of exotic animals was presented: arctic hares, horned boar, bulls, seals, bears and hippopotami. The only reference to the action of the *venatio* in Calpurnius Siculus' account of the spectacle reports that seals and bears were matched against each other.[172] Most likely, this battle took place in a flooded arena to give the seals some chance of escape from the bears. Although the Latin word for bears (*ursi*) has no modifier to indicate the animals' region of origin, it is certainly possible that these bears could have been polar bears, since they are the natural enemies of seals.[173] In this *venatio*, we first hear of a device that caused a sensation among the crowd: trapdoors which allowed animals and scenery to appear suddenly on the floor of the arena. The crowd felt a frisson of terror when they saw wild beasts burst into the sunlight through the trapdoors and were awed by the appearance of artificial strawberry trees (*arbuta*) through the sand in a cloud of saffron spray.[174] This scenery was intended to provide a proper forest setting for the animals in this *venatio*. Martial describes a *venatio* mentioned earlier that required similar scenery: rocks that crawled and trees that moved in response to the song of Orpheus.[175] Two centuries later, the emperor Probus (AD 276–282) gave a *venatio* in the Circus Maximus, for which he turned a large part of the racing area into a forest by setting up uprooted trees on a wooden platform piled up with dirt.[176] The association of *venationes* with forests consisting of real or artificial trees was such that the Latin word for 'forest' (*silva*) could serve as a synonym for *venatio*.[177]

Titus (AD 80)

The most detailed evidence we have about the *venatio* in all its variety and colour comes from Martial's *Book of Spectacles* written to commemorate the shows given by the emperor Titus in AD 80 on the occasion of the dedication of the Colosseum. Of the thirty-seven brief poems of this book, twenty-one are concerned with *venationes* that were part of this celebration.[178] The poems comment upon events that caught the poet's attention over a period of one hundred days.[179] We should not assume that Martial's poems touch upon all the events of the various *venationes* that took place in the celebration. For example, Cassius Dio mentions two pairings: cranes fighting cranes and elephants fighting elephants, about which we hear nothing from Martial or any other source.[180] What one author found notable was not always interesting to another.

Listed below are episodes with my commentary from the assorted *venationes* memorialized in his *Book of Spectacles*. Seven of Martial's poems deal with enactments of history and myth discussed above.[181] Six of these were discussed earlier and will be listed with minimal further comment, except for poem 19, which is mentioned for the first time. All these episodes are presented in the order in which they appear in Martial, which may represent the chronological order in which they actually took place during the dedication. In these poems, we are able to catch the flavour of the Roman *venatio*.

1. Sexual intercourse of 'Pasiphae' with a bull. (6)[182]
2. Martial notes the achievements of women as *venatores*. Martial claims that their exploits in Titus' animal hunts (the killing of lions) have overshadowed Hercules' killing of the Nemean Lion (one of his twelve labours). (7,8)
3. The crimes of the man playing the role of Laureolus surpassed those of the bandit of old. Owing to these crimes, the play (the mime in which Laureolus is executed) has become a reality. (9)
4. 'Daedalus' is killed by a bear (10).
5. A rhinoceros treats a bull as if it were a straw dummy. (11)

6. A lion, apparently in the middle of a routine, bites his trainer and in turn is killed by order of the emperor Titus. An important theme of this book appears here: the power of the emperor over savage nature. The poem ends with the question: 'How should men behave under such an emperor, who orders wild beasts to have a gentler disposition?' (12)

7. Martial points out the irony of a bear being stopped not by weapons, but by getting stuck in bird lime, a sticky substance put on branches to catch birds. Although Martial does not mention what happened after this, the bear was no doubt killed. (13)

8. In three poems, Martial writes about a pregnant sow killed by a hunting spear. The sow gave birth through the wound to piglets which ran from their dead mother. Martial seems to have found the paradox of simultaneous birth and death fascinating, but why he wrote three poems on this incident is difficult for the modern reader to fathom. It is a stark example of how different the ancient attitude towards these matters was from the modern.[183] (14,15,16)

9. The great hunter Carpophorus kills a boar, a polar bear, a lion and a leopard. Carpophorus is one of the few famous arena hunters we hear of (for two others, see item 14 below.) He is favourably compared to the legendary Meleager, killer of the monstrous Calydonian boar, because he killed four great animals to Meleager's one. (17)

10. A victim of the *ad bestias* penalty plays the role of Alcides (Hercules) and is tossed by a bull. Martial says sardonically that the 'bull carried Alcides to the stars', usually a metaphor for making someone famous, but here to be taken more literally. The poet uses this as an excuse to compare Titus favourably to Jupiter, whose bull carried Europa not as high as Titus' bull carried Alcides (Hercules).[184] The theme here is the divinity of the emperor. (18,19)

11. An elephant, which had just fought a bull, without a command worships Titus. The voluntary worship of the emperor here is no doubt the product of Martial's tendency towards fawning hyperbole. Again, the power of the emperor over nature. (20)

12. A tiger kills a lion. Martial notes that the tiger would have never done so in her native habitat on the southern shores of the Caspian Sea, but has become more ferocious in captivity. It would be impossible today for a tiger and a lion to run across each other in the wild, but in ancient

times, lions and tigers did share the same habitat in what today would be northern Iran. (21)

13. A bull that had tossed the straw dummies into the air, found that he could not do the same with an elephant and was killed. (22)

14. Before one *venatio*, Titus proves his generosity to the crowd by his response to a disagreement among the spectators about which *venator* they wanted to see. One group requested Myrinus, another Triumphus. Titus gave them both. This favour of Titus to the crowd is reminiscent of the practice in a *munus* of allowing the crowd to request gladiators in addition to the regularly scheduled pairings, although these requests were usually made at the end of the event. (23)

15. Orpheus (played by a *noxius*) who was able to move cliffs and forests with his song (this scenery was made to move mechanically) and so mesmerized animals that the wild mixed with the tame, is torn to pieces by a bear. Orpheus' ultimate submission to nature in this episode highlights by contrast Titus' power over savage nature, and his ability to mimic nature with his marvellous mechanical devices. Note that Titus as *editor* gets all the credit rather than the actual inventor of these devices. (24,25)

16. A rhinoceros tosses a bear, resists the attack of a pair of young bulls, and puts to flight a buffalo, bison and a lion, which fled right into the spears of *venatores*. (26)

17. Carpophorus, the great *venator*, appears again. This time he is compared favourably to four mythical figures: Hercules, Medea, Theseus and Perseus, who either killed monstrous beasts or, in the case of Medea, helped Jason yoke fire-breathing bulls. The reason for this favourable comparison is that Carpophorus killed twenty beasts in one *venatio*. (32)

18. A wily doe, pursued by hounds, stops in front of the emperor, behaving like a suppliant. The emperor, displaying his clemency, grants her request and with his divine power turns the hounds away. (33)

Commodus (AD 192)

On the mornings of the fourteen-day *munus* discussed in the previous chapter, Commodus participated in a number of *venationes* that took place in the Colosseum. Unlike his play–acting as a gladiator, Commodus had the skills of a professional *venator*. Herodian tells us that Mauretanian spearmen and

Parthian archers, generally considered the finest in the world, trained him. Commodus was reputed to have surpassed his teachers in these skills.[185] His hunting skills, however, far surpassed his courage. In the morning of the first day, he did not go into the arena with his feral opponents, but instead took a 'shooting fish in a barrel' approach. The arena of the Colosseum was divided by two intersecting walls into four 'pens' which contained altogether one hundred bears and prevented them from getting out of range of Commodus' spears. He took his position on a narrow platform with a railing that was connected to the arena wall and went around the whole arena. Thus, he was easily able to spear all one hundred bears at close range.[186] When Commodus stopped in the midst of all this carnage to take a drink of wine, the people and the senators, cowed by his psychopathic cruelty, shouted 'may you live [a long time]', the very opposite of what they were thinking.[187] At other times, the senators and the equestrians frequently shouted on command this obsequious jingle: 'You are lord, and you are first and most successful of all. You are a winner, you will be a winner. You are a perpetual winner, Amazonian'. Commodus received this epithet because he had been so taken with a portrait of his mistress Marcia dressed as an Amazon that he too wanted to appear in the arena dressed as an Amazon.[188] By the time of this *venatio*, all Rome had become disgusted with Commodus' erratic behaviour, but the senators and the equestrians, unlike the anonymous common people, had no choice but to attend. All realized that Commodus could have them killed for their absence. The plebs, who at least enjoyed anonymity, mostly chose not to be present.[189]

During the rest of the fourteen-day *munus*, Commodus continued to perform in the *venatio*. There is almost a sneer in Cassius Dio's eyewitness account of Commodus going down into the arena and killing domestic animals, which the emperor-*venator* did not have to pursue. Some came up to him willingly or if unwilling, were either led to him or brought in nets. On other occasions, Commodus killed a tiger, a hippopotamus and an elephant.[190] Given his concern with safety, one wonders how much help the emperor had in performing these usually extremely dangerous tasks.

Herodian, another eyewitness, gives a vivid account of a more impressive performance by Commodus as an arena hunter.

Animals from all over the empire were collected for him and beasts unknown before, which we wondered at in pictures from India and Ethiopia, from the south and the north, [Commodus] displayed to the Romans and then killed. All were astounded by his hand's accuracy. Taking arrows, the tips of which were crescent-shaped and shooting them at Mauretanian ostriches, quick-moving birds, both because of the speed of their feet and the arching of their wings. He decapitated them at the top of their necks and headless because of the force of the arrows, they still kept running around as if nothing had happened to them. When a leopard running at full speed seized upon a man summoned [into the arena], [Commodus], spearing the animal just before it was about to sink his teeth into the man, killed it and rescued him, striking the leopard's teeth. On another occasion, when a hundred lions were released into the arena from the subterranean area, he killed all of them with an equal number of spears.[191]

Commodus used one of the decapitated ostrich heads to deliver an ominous wordless message to his senators. Grinning, he held up to the senators the head of an ostrich he had just killed and with his other hand lifted his bloody sword as a warning. Some senators were on the verge of laughter (perhaps, a nervous reaction). Cassius Dio, a senator, was one of this group. He tells us that he helped his fellow senators to avoid offending Commodus by telling them to chew laurel leaves from the garlands they were wearing on their heads to suppress their laughter.[192]

The *venatio* in late antiquity

The *venatio* continued to be popular in Rome and elsewhere for a long time, outlasting gladiatorial combat. Even in the politically chaotic third century AD with twenty-three changes of emperor, *venationes* were still being given regularly. Gordian I (AD 238), when he served as an aedile, gave one *munus* per month, in each of which he included a spectacular animal hunt. Although the *Historia Augusta*, our source for the following *venationes*, has a tendency to exaggerate, even discounted figures would be impressive. The *Historia* says that at one of Gordian's *venationes* one hundred 'Libyan wild beasts' (large cats) participated, while at another show, one thousand bears.[193] The emperor Probus (AD 276–82) at one show presented one hundred lions, whose 'roars sounded like thunder'. Despite the large number of lions, this show was almost a failure. Probus ran into a typical problem. The male lions, when released from their cages, did not rush forward to meet their human opponents. Many were killed by arrows near their cages, rather than by hunters at close range with spears, a disappointing show for the spectators. Fortunately for Probus, he had a large reserve of more aggressive predators: one hundred Libyan leopards, one hundred Syrian leopards, one hundred lionesses and three hundred bears.[194] More notable was the show that Philip the Arab (AD 244–249), presented for Rome's millennium celebration of its founding in AD 248. In addition to one thousand pairs of gladiators, Philip's animal show included thirty-two elephants, ten elk ten tigers, sixty tame leopards, ten hyenas, six hippopotami, one rhinoceros, ten lions, ten giraffes, twenty wild asses, forty wild horses and numberless assorted (and unnamed) animals. All were slain.[195]

During the third century, an unusual feature was added to the *venatio*, a sort of do-it-yourself event in which wild and tame animals were released into the arena and spectators were allowed to kill them in any way they could. The reward for these amateur 'hunters' was not the glory of a professional arena hunter, but the animal meat which they could take home and feast upon. Julius Capitolinus, the author of the biography of Gordian I in the *Historia Augusta*, describes a painting he saw in the emperor's house depicting a *venatio* given by Gordian. In the painting were depicted two hundred stags, some identified as *palmati* ('having antlers shaped like the palm of a hand') and others as 'British'. In addition, there were thirty wild horses, one hundred wild sheep, ten elk, one hundred Cyprian bulls, three hundred Mauretanian red ostriches, thirty wild asses, one hundred and fifty wild boar, two hundred chamois (a type of mountain goat) and two hundred fallow deer. Capitolinus says Gordian 'handed over all these animals to the people to be seized [and killed]'.[196] Given the large numbers of animals, this event could have only been managed by releasing each group of animals to the crowd in the arena consecutively. Probus presented a similar event but with many more animals: one thousand ostriches, one thousand stags, one thousand wild boar, and a large unspecified number of deer, ibexes, wild sheep and other herbivores. The people were admitted to the arena and 'each seized whatever he wanted'.[197] In a *venatio* given by Elagabalus (AD 218–222) spectators 'seized' fatted cattle, camels and asses.[198]

This new feature of the *venatio* was actually only a variation of a practice that went back at least to the first century AD, in which tokens were thrown to the crowd, with which they could redeem valuable gifts, including meat from animals slain in the *venatio* (*sparsio*, discussed in Chapter 3). When, in the late first century AD, Martial writes that 'the generous token gives [to the people] wild animals watched in the arena', he does not mean that live wild animals were given to holders of these tokens, but that the holders received butchered meat.[199] Live birds, however, could be redeemed by those who had the proper token and taken home to be eaten. The birds were awarded by token because the previous practice of throwing the birds themselves (with their wings clipped) to the crowd resulted in their being torn to pieces.[200] Whenever gifts or tokens for redeeming gifts were thrown into the crowd, there was also danger that the scramble this created could result in injury among the spectators.[201] One wonders what injuries and even deaths occurred among the crowd when they were attempting to seize and kill large wild animals in the arena, as in the *venationes* of Gordian I and Probus, especially when many spectators in the arena must have been armed.

Christianity had no serious objections to animal hunts, and in times of economic crisis they were perhaps conducted on a smaller scale.[202] The last *venationes* ever given may have been the shows presented by Eutaricus Cillica, in AD 519, and by Anicius Maximus, in AD 523, to celebrate their accession to the consulship. Cillica was the son-in-law of Theodoric, the Christian king of Italy, who must have granted permission to give these shows. When these *venationes* were presented, over three-quarters of century had passed since the last gladiator combat had been given. There is no doubt that Theodoric found the *venatio* objectionable. In a letter to the consul Maximus, he calls the spectacle 'an abominable performance', 'a wretched contest', 'the worst in its action', 'a cruel game' and 'a bloody pleasure', but even Theodoric recognized that the great popularity of this spectacle among the people made its presentation mandatory. He tells Maximus that it is his duty to present these shows and to reward the *venatores* for the risks they incur more generously than other entertainers such as wrestlers, singers and organ-players.[203] One can detect in Theodoric's ambivalent attitude towards the *venatio* a hint of the admiration that had long ago been expressed for the courage of gladiators.

Although the *venatio* as a regular popular entertainment seems to have ceased in the sixth century, it seems never to have been forgotten completely. Bomgardner points out that in the sixteenth century the Sultan of

Fez put on a show that can only be described as a *venatio*. The Sultan's spectacle included the slaughter of a lion by *venatores* and a fight between a lion and bull. The *venatores* used the same technique of provoking the lion that was discussed in Chapter 3: hunters standing in open doorways that tease the animal into a furious charge and are closed at the last minute. The tradition of the *venatio* is also evident in European circuses that featured bear-baiting and trained animal acts, and even in the modern bullfight.[204]

Chapter 6

The Roman Amphitheatre and the Colosseum

The amphitheatre

As an architectural form, the Roman amphitheatre is one of the most influential buildings from antiquity. With its seating in the form of an ellipse surrounding an arena, it is the inspiration (with variations) for European and American football stadia.

Perhaps the oldest surviving permanent stone structure for the presentation of gladiators is the amphitheatre at Pompeii (*c.* 70 BC) (Figure 26).[1] Other amphitheatres in Italy may be older but cannot be reliably dated. The following inscription reveals the details of its origin:

> *C. Quinctius Valgus, son of C. [and] M. Porcius, son of M., fifth-year dual magistrates* [duoviri quinquennales] *were responsible for the building of this structure for public entertainment* [spectacula] *at their own expense in honour of the colony [i.e., Pompeii, which was a Roman colony] and gave the place in perpetuity to the colonists.*[2]

Valgus and Porcius were no doubt following the custom of thanking their fellow citizens for electing them to high office by giving a spectacle such as

Figure 26 Amphitheatre at Pompeii. Vince Streano/Corbis

gladiatorial combat and/or a *venatio* or, as in this case, erecting a public building. The impetus for building a permanent amphitheatre is connected with the fact that P. Sulla directed the foundation of Pompeii as a colony for his uncle's veterans, who no doubt were enthusiastic about a site for the paramilitary violence of gladiatorial combat.[3] Note that the building is called a *spectacula* (literally, 'seats for viewing a spectacle'); the Greek-derived word *amphitheatrum* ('structure for viewing in the round') was not used until the Augustan period. It is not freestanding like later amphitheatres. The arena was created by excavating earth, which was then heaped up as a support for the upper seating. The façade wall, which serves as a retaining wall for the excavated earth, has a blind arcade and staircases leading to a walkway and access to the seating.[4]

The city of Rome did not have a permanent stone amphitheatre until 29 BC, 235 years after the first appearance of gladiatorial combat in the city. Why this delay? Rome before 29 BC certainly did not lack generous patrons like the ones at Pompeii, who would have been glad to provide a permanent amphitheatre to their fellow citizens. The reason lies in the conservatism of the Roman authorities, who objected to permanent buildings dedicated to entertainment.[5] A permanent stone theatre was begun in 155 BC, but was met with opposition by the consul, Scipio Nasica.[6] The reasons for this resistance given by ancient authors (long after the fact) arose from various moral and political concerns. Tacitus mentions the danger of corruption of the Roman people, who might be tempted by the existence of a permanent theatre to waste day after day in idleness.[7] Valerius Maximus cites the diminution of Roman manhood that would be the result of sitting (like the Greeks) instead of standing at the *ludi*.[8] At the order of Nasica, the construction of the theatre was halted and the incipient structure demolished. In explaining his action, Nasica expressed two concerns: that the Roman people might be infected with Greek hedonism and that large gatherings of people in a compact area might lead to seditious rioting.[9] At the same time, there was a decree of the Senate forbidding the building of a theatre within a mile of the city.[10] By the middle of the first century BC, objections to a permanent stone theatre seem to have softened because Pompey built such a theatre, which was dedicated in 55 BC, but apparently even the great Pompey felt obliged to make obeisance to Roman scruples. In order to forestall objections, he employed the transparent charade of putting a small temple of Venus Victrix ('Venus the Conqueror') at the top of the seating area.[11] Thus, the seating area of the theatre could be said to be nothing but stairs ascending to Venus' temple. All the considerations that postponed the construction of a permanent stone theatre at Rome also delayed the building of a permanent amphitheatre.

Without a permanent structure, gladiator shows were given in available open areas. As we saw in Chapter 4, the first gladiator combat at Rome in 264 BC took place in the Cattle Market and later *munera* were moved to Forum, where there was a large open area, trapezoidal in shape. This area was approximately 320 feet long and 164 feet wide.[12] In the beginning, most spectators most probably stood around the action in accordance with Roman custom. There were, however, special places available that had been first used to view *ludi*.[13] These places were balconies projecting from the roofs of the buildings surrounding the Forum plaza and were no doubt reserved for upper-class Romans. The balconies were called *maeniana*, the name being derived from that of the censor C. Maenius, who first installed them in 318 BC. The term was later applied to the different levels of seating in the amphitheatre.[14] There would not have been an opportunity to view gladiators from these vantage points until the *munus* in honour of M. Aemilius Lepidus (216 BC), the first recorded gladiator show in the Forum. In the fourth and third centuries BC, the balconies must have been attached to the upper façade of houses that lined the Forum. Welch suggests that owners of the houses could have used the balconies themselves along with friends and clients or even rented them out to *editores*. In the early second century, shops and monumental basilicas replaced the houses, but this was not the end of the *maeniana*.[15] Balconies were attached to the second storey of the shops and were extended over the second-storey columns of the basilicas.[16] In accordance with the objection of Roman authorities to sitting while viewing entertainments, spectators stood on these balconies.[17]

At least by the middle of the second century BC (but probably much earlier), the objection of moralists to sitting at entertainment seems to have been overcome and it became the practice to erect temporary wooden seating for *ludi* and gladiatorial events in the Forum. The fight over seats between theatregoers and gladiator fans at the funeral games for L. Aemilius Paullus in 160 BC (described in Chapter 4) presumes the existence of temporary seating. It also reveals that the Romans presented gladiatorial combat in the theatre, as the Greeks did later.[18] The first we hear of seating in the elliptical form of an amphitheatre is from Plutarch in his report of an incident in 122 BC. Magistrates built seating 'in a circular form' (*en kulōi*) for a *munus* in the Forum, which they planned to sell to spectators.[19] We know that Plutarch does not mean a real circle but an oval because Cassius Dio uses the same word (*kuklos*) to describe the oval arena of the Colosseum.[20] The elliptical shape of these stands was designed to take advantage of the irregular space available in the Forum in order to accommodate as many spectators as possible and provide them with the best possible vantage points for viewing the action.[21] C. Gracchus, a tribune of the people, strongly objected to the lower classes having to pay for their seats, which went against the tradition of free seating at spectacles. Gracchus therefore ordered the seating to be taken down 'so that the poor could watch the spectacle for free'. There is no mention of the possibility of the poor watching the spectacle while standing, so the oval seating must have been uninterrupted with no gaps. After the magistrates ignored his order, Gracchus had the seating torn down the night before the show. By the middle of the next century, these elliptical stands seem to have had gaps that provided space for standing room behind fencing. Cicero speaks of his client Sestius receiving applause at a *munus* in the Forum from the seats and from spectators behind 'barriers'.[22]

By the 50s BC, architectural display had become another mode of competition available to givers of spectacles. In 58 BC the aedile M. Aemilius Scaurus organized *ludi* for which he built a fabulous wooden theatre. What was notable about Scaurus' temporary theatre was its scale and capacity. The elaborately decorated stage building which formed the backdrop of the action onstage was three stories high with 360 columns. The first storey was of marble, the second of glass and the third of gilded wood. Placed between the columns were 3,000 bronze statues. Pliny the Elder claims that its capacity was 80,000 people (a gross exaggeration, but its capacity must have been unusually large).[23] Pliny adds that Scaurus' dazzling building made the aspiring politician C. Scribonius Curio despair of ever surpassing Scaurus' achievement and making a lasting impression on the Roman people. Curio, however, used his own ingenuity and that of his architects to great effect. In 52 BC he presented a *munus* in honour of his father in a wooden amphitheatre that caused a great sensation. Curio's amphitheatre, like all preceding wooden entertainment venues in the Forum, was clearly temporary, but it was not taken down immediately after the *munus*, no doubt because of its special character. It was still in use in June, 51 BC, when a hostile crowd hissed the great orator Hortensius there.[24] (We do not know when it was finally dismantled.) By contrast, Scaurus' theatre, like most other temporary structures, was dismantled less than a month after its construction.[25] Curio had two semicircular wooden theatres built on a pivot. In the morning, two different dramatic presentations were given in these theatres positioned back to back. In the afternoon, the two sets of stands were swivelled about so that when they came together, they formed an oval surrounding a sandy central area (*arena*) for the gladiatorial combat.[26] Thus, the two theatres had been miraculously transformed in a matter of minutes into an amphitheatre. It would seem that this wondrous theatre/amphitheatre was as much part of the show as the gladiators. It was no doubt designed to surprise the spectators when the two theatres began to pivot. Pliny mentions that the pivoting began all of a sudden. The effect must have been like that of a thrill ride in a modern amusement park.

The people displayed the greatest madness of all in sitting on such an untrustworthy and unstable structure . . . hanging on a machine and applauding its own danger. Behold the whole Roman people, as if placed on two ships, is supported by two hinges and sees itself struggling, about to perish at any moment on machines that have fallen apart.[27]

Some spectators even continued to enjoy the ride after the first days of the *munus*, remaining in their seats as the device went through its scary transformation. The Roman people were enjoying their own fear. Curio had achieved his goal: a *munus* that would be long remembered, even longer than Scaurus' theatre.

In 46 BC, Julius Caesar built a temporary wooden structure for the *venatio* and gladiatorial combat he presented as part of his triumphal games. It was located in the Forum, like its many predecessors. Cassius Dio identifies it clearly as an amphitheatre.

He erected a hunting-theatre, which was also called an amphitheatre from its continuous seating all around without a stage. Both in honour of this [building] and his daughter [Julia], he presented the slaughters of wild animals and gladiator combats.[28]

Caesar was probably the author of the underground corridors dating from the first century BC, which have been discovered in the Forum with evidence of what may have been hoists to lift gladiators and animals from the subterranean area on to the Forum floor.[29] In this way, Caesar was able to avoid the dangerous risk of having gladiators and caged animals wait their turn outside the amphitheatre in the Forum.[30] An escape by armed gladiators and/or wild beasts would pose a serious threat to the safety of Roman citizens. Tertullian, in listing typical misfortunes experienced by mankind, mentions being killed by wild animals which have escaped from their cages in the midst of the city.[31] This underground area (*hypogeum*) remained in use until the Forum was repaved during the reign of Augustus and served as a storage area for the presentation of *munera*, just as they did later in amphitheatres.[32] The *hypogeum* was also a feature of amphitheatres in Italy (Capua and Puozzoli) and in the provinces (Trier in Germany, El Djem in Tunisia and Pula in Croatia). Trapdoors can still be seen in the surviving concrete floors of these amphitheatres.[33]

During the Republic and the early empire, the Circus Maximus, Rome's oldest and largest racetrack, was occasionally used for gladiator shows, but, after chariot racing for which it was originally designed, its most common use was for *venationes*.[34] It was not well suited for viewing gladiatorial duels because a pair of gladiators tended to be swallowed up by its vastness covering a rectangular space of approximately 10.7 acres. *Venationes* were better served because of the large number of animals often in action at the same time, but the site was still not ideal for that entertainment. As we have seen, Julius Caesar used the Circus Maximus for staged infantry battles during his triumphal games in 46 BC for which the site was more suitable.[35] The Forum, however, remained the primary site for gladiatorial combat throughout the Republic into the early empire both in Rome and in the rest of Italy in towns that lacked a permanent stone amphitheatre.[36] The last reported *munus* presented in the Forum was given by the future emperor Tiberius to honour his father in the 20s BC.[37]

While Romans were still watching gladiator shows in temporary amphitheatres in the Forum, permanent stone amphitheatres continued to be built outside of Rome, especially in Campania, the major centre in Italy for gladiatorial combat. Bomgardner lists ten amphitheatres built in Campania during the last century of the Republic. In this same period, there were also two amphitheatres built within a 60 mile radius north of Rome, two in Spain and one in Antioch (Syria).[38] Welch has plausibly argued that the architectural form of these Campanian permanent amphitheatres was derived from the temporary wooden stands in the Roman Forum. She also points out that the building of these permanent amphitheatres in Campanian cities was an architectural demonstration of their Roman sympathies.[39] The same could be said of the permanent amphitheatres that were built in the early imperial period throughout the western provinces, where the remains of 252 amphitheatres have been discovered.[40] Amphitheatres were also built in the eastern provinces but in much smaller numbers, perhaps twenty at the most.[41] For example, there was an amphitheatre at Corinth, whose origin can likely be traced to the re-foundation of the famous old Greek city as a Roman colony by Julius Caesar in 44 BC.[42] Caesar may have also been responsible for the amphitheatre at Antioch, which had a Roman garrison in the late Republic.[43] In general, however, the Greeks found it more convenient to use pre-existing stadia (originally built as sites of athletic games) and remodelled theatres for gladiator games and *venationes*.[44] In the theatre, the gladiators fought either on the stage or in the orchestra.[45] The Athenians held gladiatorial shows in the famous theatre of Dionysus where the plays of Aeschylus, Sophocles, Euripides and Aristophanes had been presented in the fifth century BC. The philosopher Apollonius (first century AD) warned the Athenians that they were alienating both Dionysus and Athena with the human slaughter that took place in the theatre.[46] Apollonius' contemporary Dio Chrysostom condemns the sacrilege of having gladiators fight in the orchestra where the Athenians placed a statue of Dionysus during his festival. He notes that there are even times when the fight reached the lowest rows of the theatre, splattering with blood the priest of Dionysus and other religious officials sitting in honorary seats.[47] The proximity of spectators to the fighting in the theatre could be dangerous for them. In Syracuse (Greek Sicily), a *retiarius* accidentally killed a spectator, a Roman equestrian. When the *retiarius* forced his opponent into the crowd in the lowest rows of the theatre, he missed with a thrust of his weapon and stabbed the equestrian instead.[48] Spectators in an amphitheatre enjoyed the protection of a high wall around the arena.

Statilius Taurus built Rome's stone amphitheatre in 30 BC in the Campus Martius as part of Augustus' building programme.[49] (There are no extant remains.) Welch speculates that, since the amphitheatre was completely destroyed in the great fire of AD 64, a good part of its interior was made of wood, the combination of wood and stone being a common construction technique of the late Republic and early empire.[50] Taurus, one of Augustus' most trusted generals, used the spoils of war from his victories in Africa (for which he received a triumph) to build the amphitheatre.[51] We do know some details about its maintenance staff. An inscription on the tomb of the Statilii announces that Charito, a custodian of the amphitheatre, was buried there.[52] Another inscription on the same tomb proclaims the presence of Menander, a doorkeeper of the amphitheatre.[53] Both of these men were likely Greek freedmen. (It was common for prominent families to make room in their monumental tombs for their freedmen and freedwomen.) In return for Statilius' generous gift to the Roman people, he received the honour of choosing one of the praetors each year.[54] Augustus must have been certain of his loyalty because the popularity that such a gift would bring to the donor could be a dangerous instrument in the hands of an ambitious man. Statilius' amphitheatre, however, failed to become a favoured site for *munera*. Imperial *munera* were only occasionally given there.[55] Cassius Dio tells us that Caligula did not like this amphitheatre, although he does not say why.[56] Welch suggests that the grand amphitheatre at Verona (still standing), perhaps built during the reign of Claudius, may have made the Roman amphitheatre look 'small and old fashioned'.[57] Caligula had just begun the construction of a new amphitheatre near the *Saepta* but it was not finished when he was assassinated. Claudius abandoned the project.[58]

From the time of Augustus until the dedication of the Colosseum in AD 80, a building in the Campus Martius called the *Saepta* served as a site for *munera*. The *Saepta* or, as it was sometimes called, the *Ovile* ('sheep corral'), was an unroofed enclosure in which Romans voted during the Republic. In 54 BC, Julius Caesar had planned to rebuild it, but we are not sure that he ever began the reconstruction.[59] In any case, its rebuilding was finished with surrounding porticos by the triumvir M. Aemilius Lepidus and later dedicated by Maecenas (26 BC), who decorated it with 'marble slabs and paintings'.[60] Its new official title was the *Saepta Julia*, in honour of Augustus. Even before popular elections were transferred to the Senate, the *Saepta* began to be used for spectacles, especially gladiator games and animal hunts. It was used for this purpose quite regularly during the reigns of Augustus, Claudius and Caligula. Its enormous size (covering about 8 acres) made it suitable for accommodating large crowds.[61] Seating must have been added to the *Saepta Julia*, but no remains of the building or seating have survived.

The *Saepta* remained the primary site for *munera* until the construction of a large wooden amphitheatre by Nero (dedicated in AD 57) in the Campus Martius. Neither the rectangular *Saepta* nor Taurus' undersized stone amphitheatre served the presentation of *munera* well. It is not certain whether Nero's amphitheatre, despite its wooden construction, was intended as a permanent amphitheatre or just a stopgap. Its magnificence, however, might argue for the former. Nero's amphitheatre was impressive enough to inspire a contemporary poet to write a description of it. That poet was Calpurnius Siculus, who incorporated into one of his *Bucolics* a description of a *venatio* given by Nero at the dedication of the new amphitheatre. The poet's theme is not just the *venatio* but the amphitheatre itself with its newly devised equipment. We see this new building through the eyes of a rustic named Corydon, who attended this *venatio* and upon his return home reports to his friend that Nero's amphitheatre was the most impressive thing he had seen in the big city. He mentions a conversation he had with an old man who sat next to him in the amphitheatre and the comparison the old man had made with past sites of spectacles: 'Whatever we have seen in prior years was cheap and tacky'.[62] Tacitus gives a backhanded compliment to Nero's amphitheatre, citing its massiveness:

> *[At this time] few things happened worthy of mention unless one likes filling volumes with praise of the foundations and wooden beams, with which Nero had constructed his huge amphitheatre in the Campus Martius.*[63]

Corydon is overwhelmed by the great height of the amphitheatre, noting that it 'almost looks down on the Tarpeian summit (the highest point of the Capitoline Hill)'.[64] Of course, one must allow for poetic hyperbole, but even so its height must have been impressive. The Capitoline Hill at its greatest height rises approximately 165 feet above the Forum; the Colosseum is 157.5 feet high.[65] Thus, even if Nero's amphitheatre was somewhat lower than the peak of the Capitoline Hill, it still would have been close to the height of the Colosseum.

There was, however, more to this amphitheatre than just its massive size. The old man sitting next to him points out to Corydon the luxurious adornments of the building: 'Look at how the gems decorating the wall (*balteus*) and the porticos adorned with gold compete with each other as they gleam in the sunlight'.[66] We know something about these 'gems' from another source. Pliny the Elder tells us that a certain Julianus, Nero's man in charge (*curator*) of gladiator games, sent a Roman equestrian in search of amber from Pannonia (modern western Hungary) to Germany's Baltic coast. This man was quite successful in his search and returned to Rome with large amounts, which were used to decorate the knots in the nets protecting the crowd from wild beasts, weapons, the stretchers for the dead and wounded, and other apparatus. There appears to be a small discrepancy when the old man refers to the knots in the nets as decorated with gold, but Pliny also mentions that amber was used on only one day of the spectacle; other valuable ornaments were used on other days.[67]

Other striking features of Nero's amphitheatre pointed out by Corydon were two devices to protect spectators from large predators, which might be able to climb the arena wall. Staged animal hunts could prove a danger to spectators as was demonstrated in a *venatio* given by Pompey in the Circus Maximus in 55 BC, when frenzied elephants almost broke down an iron fence that protected the spectators. This incident led Julius Caesar in 46 BC to have a circular trench (*euripus*) filled with water dug in the Circus

Maximus to keep dangerous large animals away from the crowd.[68] The most innovative safety device in Nero's amphitheatre was a large ivory cylinder (*rotulus*) that was attached horizontally to the wall surrounding the arena. With its revolving motion and slippery surface, it would have frustrated attempts of large cats to reach spectators sitting closest to the arena.[69] Corydon also mentions nets extending into the arena that were attached to elephant tusks projecting from the arena wall.[70] If, as it would seem, the nets were also intended as a safety device, the poet's use of *rotulus* in the singular and *retia* ('nets') in the plural may suggest an explanation of the redundancy. Since there apparently was only one *rotulus*, it would seem logical that this cylinder was attached to the arena wall immediately in front of the emperor's box for extra protection. Then one could assume that the nets extended around the rest of the arena wall to protect the other spectators. In fact, there might have been nets in front of the emperor's box in addition to the *rotulus*. Nero may have seen this device as a necessary security measure.[71] There is, however, a possibility that the nets served another purpose: to keep the animals, overwhelmed by the bright sun and the noisy crowd, from cowering against the wall where some spectators could not see them.[72] Scobie notes that there are stone sockets for fence posts in the arena of the Colosseum, 4 metres from the arena wall and 4¾ metres from each other, most likely for the purpose of spectator security.[73] He also points out that although some scholars have assumed that this fence had a *rotulus* and was attached to nets suspended from elephant tusks, there is no reason to believe that these features of Nero's amphitheatre ever appeared in the Colosseum.[74]

During the inaugural games of the Nero's amphitheatre, however, danger to the emperor came from a source other than wild animals. One of the features of these games was the enactment of the stories of Pasiphae and Icarus, but not as a means of executing criminals, as discussed earlier.[75] Nero had hired Greek youths to play the roles of Pasiphae and Icarus and promised them Roman citizenship in return for their work in the spectacle. After the enactment of Pasiphae's penetration by the bull came a representation of the fate of Icarus: the loss in mid-flight of the artificial wings made by his father Daedalus and his fall into the sea. When the actor playing Icarus was released from whatever device was keeping him airborne (perhaps a crane with a cable), it was no doubt intended that he would fall into a net or into a tank of water. Instead, he was released at the wrong time, and landed close enough to Nero to spatter him with blood. Suetonius seems to imply that this incident led Nero to preside over spectacles rarely, and when he did, to watch through small openings from a completely enclosed box. Only later, perhaps when he had regained his courage, did he sit on the open podium. Suetonius, however, does not clearly indicate that safety was the purpose of the enclosed box.[76]

Nero's amphitheatre had an underground storage area (*hypogeum*), which allowed animals to be released from their underground cages onto the arena floor through trap doors, as we have seen, a feature associated with gladiatorial combat and the *venatio* since the late first century BC. As noted in the previous chapter, Corydon notes the employment of trap doors through which trees were pushed up through the sand in a cloud of saffron spray to create an appropriately rustic setting for the animal hunt.[77]

Colosseum

When Martial composed his *Book of Spectacles*, he chose to open it with a paean to the grand new amphitheatre, known today as the Colosseum, comparing it favourably to the other wonders of the ancient world.

> *Let Memphis be silent about the barbarian splendour of the pyramids,*
> *And let Assyrian labour not boast of Babylon;*
> *Let the effeminate Ionians not be praised because of the temple of Diana,*
> *Let the altar crowded with horns allow Delos to exist in obscurity;*
> *Let the Carians not glorify Mausolus' tomb hanging in empty air.*
> *Let all work yield to Caesar's amphitheatre,*
> *Fame will speak of one work in preference to all of the above.*[78]

To be sure, Martial is guilty of poetic hyperbole, but his enthusiasm for the Colosseum is not unjustified. The structure was a marvel to all who saw it in its original state. When the eastern emperor, Constantius II (son of Constantine), first visited Rome in AD 358, he too was led to overstatement, awed by the monumental size of the Colosseum. He referred to 'the solid massiveness of the amphitheatre constructed of travertine from Tibur, whose summit human eyesight had to strain to see'.[79] The exaggeration represents well the emotional impact that the Colosseum must have had on those who saw it for the first time. Note that Martial refers to this building as 'Caesar's [i.e., the emperor's] amphitheatre' and not the 'Colosseum', a

Figure 27 Reconstruction of Colosseum with colossal statue of Nero on the far left and the *Meta Sudans* (fountain) in foreground right. Note the statues framed by the arches on the second and third levels and the masts for the awnings in their sockets. © Bettmann/Corbis

name unknown until the early Middle Ages. Its official name was the 'Flavian Amphitheatre' because it was built by the Flavian emperors, Vespasian and his two sons Titus and Domitian, but in practice it was referred to simply as 'the amphitheatre'. This is not surprising since it was the only amphitheatre in Rome and was unique in size and beauty throughout the whole empire. The later name 'Colosseum' has two possible origins: the colossal size of the structure itself or a colossal bronze statue (*colossus*) of Nero (Figure 27), estimated to be between 99 and 116 feet tall, that had stood near it in ancient times. This statue had originally stood by the entrance to Nero's Golden House (*Domus Aurea*).[80] After the great fire of AD 64, Nero appropriated the land on which he built his palace and installed a large artificial lake, which later would become the site of the Colosseum.[81] After the Golden House had been demolished and the lake drained and filled in, the colossal statue of Nero remained in place, but soon found itself in proximity to the new amphitheatre. It has been claimed that a famous poem attributed (wrongly) to the Venerable Bede dating from the eighth century AD may refer to the Flavian Amphitheatre under the name 'Colisaeus' (the colossal building).[82]

As long as the Colisaeus will stand,
Rome will also stand;
When the Colisaeus will fall,
Rome will also fall . . .

It is more likely, however, that *Colisaeus* refers to the statue and not the building. The word *colosseus* is in origin an adjective that adjusts its form to *colosseum* when it modifies a neuter noun such as *amphitheatrum*. The masculine noun *Colisaeus* of the 'Bede' poem, therefore, might better be interpreted as a medieval variant of *colossus*, classical Latin for 'a huge statue'. More recent opinion favors this interpretation.[83] Rossella Rea argues persuasively that the Colosseum was not referred to as the *Ampitheatrum Colosseum* until the tenth century AD.[84]

Once Vespasian had come to power after the civil wars that followed Nero's suicide, he decided to restore the land that Nero had appropriated to the rightful owners, the Roman people. Martial expresses his gratitude to Vespasian's son Titus for this dramatic change in Rome's landscape by comparing the glorious present with the terrible Neronian past:

Here where the gleaming colossus sees the stars from a closer distance
And high scaffolding increases in the middle of the road,
The hateful halls of the savage king [Nero] used to radiate light and
One home [the Golden House] then was occupying the whole city.
Here where the venerable mass of the remarkable amphitheatre
Is being erected, was the artificial lake.
Here where we wonder at the quickly built gift of bath buildings,
The haughty estate had taken away homes from the poor.
Where the Claudian portico unfolds extensive shadows,
Was the very edge of [Nero's] Palace.
Rome has been restored to itself and under your leadership, Caesar [Titus],
This area is now the delight of the people, which had been the private
pleasure of the tyrant.[85]

Nero had taken the path of the tyrant, making his extravagant home with its colossal statue an expression of his egotism and power, whereas Vespasian and Titus had followed the example of Julius Caesar, spending vast amounts of money for the benefit of the Roman people. Vespasian's generosity to the people is even more remarkable because of his well-known aversion to gladiator games.[86] The Colosseum, a structure for all the Roman people to enjoy, replaced Nero's Golden House, a blatant symbol of Nero's tyranny.

Just as was the case with Statilius Taurus' stone amphitheatre, the Colosseum was financed from the spoils of war. Considerable plunder had been taken by Vespasian and Titus from the Jewish war. A relief on the inside of Titus' triumphal arch shows numerous valuable objects taken from the temple of Jerusalem (for example, the great *menorah*). Vespasian dedicated much of this plunder to the goddess of Peace and deposited it in her new temple, which he had built. There were, however, many other valuable spoils of war that were awarded to Vespasian personally, which it was his right to sell for profit. The phrase *ex manubis* in the reconstructed inscription below refers to those spoils that he could have used to enrich himself but instead used to finance the building of the Colosseum, preferring the glory and the gratitude of the people.[87] No greater individual gift had been given to the Roman people either before or after the building of the Colosseum.

> IMP CAES VESPASIANUS AVG
>   AMPHITHEATRUM NOVVUM
> EX MANVBIS FIERI IVSSIT

> *The emperor Caesar Vespasian Augustus*
> *ordered that a new amphitheatre be constructed*
> *from the spoils [of the Jewish War]*[88]

The bronze letters of this inscription were originally attached to a block of marble found in the Colosseum. The letters were later removed and replaced in the fifth century AD with another inscription incised in the marble. The nails holding the original bronze letters left holes that, in their arrangement, gave clues to the words of the original inscription.[89] An interpretation of these holes suggests that a 'T', an abbreviation for Titus, was squeezed later into a separating space in the first line of the above inscription between the abbreviations meaning 'the emperor Caesar' (IMPTCAES VESPASIANUS AVG) after Vespasian's death to give his son Titus credit for his completion of the Colosseum.[90]

At just about the same time as the construction of the Colosseum, another amphitheatre of significantly smaller scale was built in a small town in central Italy called Urbs Salvia (modern Urbisaglia) by a certain L. Flavius

Silva Nonius Bassus, no doubt also from the spoils of the Jewish war. Silva, during his governorship of Judaea, was the commander of a Roman army that besieged and took Masada. An inscription details his distinguished career, ending with the consulship and his service as a pontifex, one of a board of the chief religious officials at Rome, and credits him with the building of the town's amphitheatre on his own property and at his own expense.[91] It must have been quite small. Only 650 seats were allocated to the common people of the town, who must have been considerably more numerous than the elites.[92] Nonetheless, it must have been received with great enthusiasm in Urbs Salvia. It was a sign of the town's Romanness, in the way that a gymnasium was essential to the identity of a Greek city. The Romans valued the amphitheatre at least as much as any other public building, and perhaps even more. Coleman calls attention to an inscription praising a wealthy patroness that puts building an amphitheatre on the same level as constructing a temple: 'Ummidia Quartilla, daughter of Gaius, built an amphitheatre and a temple for the citizens of Casinum (near modern Cassino) at her own expense'.[93]

In addition to its overwhelming size, the Colosseum was an artistic success: a marriage of outer graceful beauty and symmetry with inner order and functionality. The exterior façade consists of three stories of superimposed arcades with each storey consisting of eighty arches, and a fourth storey at the top with windows instead of arches. Engaged columns (pilasters) with capitals of three different architectural orders divide the arches from each other. On the bottom level, the columns have Tuscan capitals (an Italic version of the Greek Doric order), on the second, Ionic capitals, and the third, Corinthian capitals. The arches on the second and third stories served as frames for statues, which have long disappeared, removed by looters over the centuries. On the fourth storey, the windows are framed by pilasters of the Corinthian order and are positioned over every other arch on the third level (Figure 27).

When the Colosseum was dedicated in AD 80, it most likely did not have this fourth storey, which was a later addition, probably during the reign of Domitian.[94] The fourth storey appears on a coin of Titus, but this may just represent what the Colosseum was supposed to look like when it was finally finished. The eighty arches on the ground floor served as entrances.[95] Seventy-six of these arches had numbers inscribed above them, which were essential for helping spectators to find their seats. The four entrances

Figure 28 Bas-relief (detail) from the tomb of the Haterii in Rome depicting the Colosseum with three stories of arcades without the windowed fourth storey added later. Vatican, Museo Gregoriano Profano/Scala London

without a number were special points of entry, each at the ends of the amphitheatre's major east/west and minor north/south, axes. Seats at both ends of the minor axis provided the best vantage points in the amphitheatre.[96] In a bas-relief on the tomb of the Haterii from the late first century AD depicting the Colosseum (Figure 28), we see at ground level a monumental entrance shaded by a porch with a pediment surmounted by four horses, which were no doubt pulling a chariot with a driver (not visible). The bas-relief gives us no idea on which end of the north/south axis this entrance was, but the coin of Gordian III (Figure 29) shows the entrance portico (on the right) and gives two reference points, Domitian's *Meta Sudans*, a monumental fountain, and Nero's colossal statue. We know that these two monuments were located at the west end of the Colosseum.[97] Since, on the coin, the fountain and the colossus are to the left of the entrance portico, the porch and pediment must have been on the south end of the minor axis of the amphitheatre. The presence of an underground tunnel near the south entrance leading into the lowest seating of the Colosseum confirms that this was the side on which the emperor entered the building, at first through the above-ground access and then later (perhaps beginning with the reign of Domitian) through the tunnel.[98] His final destination would have been his box on the podium, of which there are no surviving remains. This underground passageway may have been the place where Commodus was almost

Figure 29 Coin of Gordian III depicting the Colosseum with fourth level. Note also the *Meta Sudans* (fountain) and the colossal statue of Nero on the far left and the monumental entrance on the far right. In the arena, a bull fights an elephant. The large human figure opposite the fighting animals represents Gordian. © The Trustees of the British Museum

assassinated on his way into the Colosseum, for which reason the tunnel is popularly called 'Commodus' passageway' (*cryptoporticus*).[99] The north entrance may have been for other important personages such as the praetors and (later) quaestors who sponsored the annual *munus*. Suetonius tells us that Augustus had assigned reserved seats to the Vestal Virgins on the other side of the arena from the 'praetor's tribunal'. This tribunal may be the box in which the presiding magistrates sat.[100] The question is, where is this tribunal in reference to the emperor's box? Is it opposite the emperor's box or on the same side? Sorry to say, there is no definitive evidence of the tribunal's exact location. I would opt for the tribunal being opposite the emperor's box, which would put the Vestal Virgins on the south side somewhere near the emperor, as in Gérôme's painting. My feeling is that Augustus would have wanted to give at least the appearance of the praetors' independence by placing them on the other side of the arena from himself. Intuition, however, is not a very strong argument.

Although there is no evidence, it is likely that the entrances on the east/west major axis were the points of access for gladiators, *venatores* and wild animals, at least until the Colosseum was connected with the *Ludus Magnus* by an underground passageway.[101] Rossella Rea and Silvia Orlandi claim that the *pompa*, which began the gladiator show, entered through the entrance of the western end of the major axis. This is certainly possible, but cannot be proved or disproved.[102]

Seating assignments

The seating assignments for the upper classes in the Colosseum, or, for that matter, any other amphitheatre or theatre in Rome, Italy or the provinces, were the result of practices that began to be formulated in the early second century BC. Not surprisingly, senators, the most prestigious class of citizens at Rome, were first to be singled out for priority seating at spectacles. P. Scipio Africanus, the conqueror of Hannibal, had set the precedent at *ludi* he sponsored in 194 BC during his second consulship.[103] From that time, senators had the best seats, closest to the action, in the orchestra of the theatre or in lowest part of the amphitheatre. In 67 BC, a law of Roscius Otho, a tribune of the people, confirmed the right of the equestrians, the other elite class in Rome, to sit in the first fourteen rows above the orchestra of the theatre or immediately behind the senators in the amphitheatre.[104] The seating privilege for the equestrians may have been customary (not legally prescribed) prior to Roscius' law, but it had been disregarded since Sulla's rise to power (late 80s BC).[105] (Sulla was a notorious enemy of the equestrian class.) A seat, however, was not guaranteed to every equestrian at every show. The equestrians were a much larger class than the senators. Seneca, an equestrian, points out that if all the places were taken when he arrived, he was out of luck. He had the right to sit in the equestrian section, but only if space was available.[106] A famous anecdote confirms the problem of overcrowding in the equestrian section. Augustus, annoyed by an equestrian drinking in his seat, sent him a message: 'If I want to have lunch, I go home'. The quick-witted equestrian retorted: 'You are not afraid of losing your seat'.[107] The problem of overcrowding in the equestrian section was occasionally exacerbated by unauthorized people sitting in this section. This was a problem that did not plague the senators' section. Most likely any interloper would have been prevented from even entering

the senatorial seating area (*cavea*) by ushers who could recognize senators at sight. No doubt many Romans envied the senators their seats, but
also realized that sitting in their section was an unrealizable dream.[108]
There is only one recorded example of what may have been unauthorized
sitting in the senators' section. In the early 20s AD, there was an unpleasant
incident at a *munus*, in which a young noble named L. Sulla refused to give
up his place to a certain Domitius Corbulo, who was an ex-praetor and
therefore a senator of note.[109] As E. Rawson points out, it is not clear what
Sulla's status was.[110] If he had not yet been elected to the quaestorship,
which was the qualification for entry into the Senate, he was indeed a tres-
passer. But since the quaestorship was held early in a man's political career
(early 30s, which still might be called 'young'), Sulla might have held this
office and therefore had a right to his seat. In this case, it would have been
just a matter of a younger man not giving due respect to an older and more
distinguished man. Another possibility is that the seating regulations for
some special reason were not in effect for this show. Even when Roscius' law
of the fourteen rows was enforced, interlopers found it easier get into the
equestrian section. In 41 BC, Octavian, fresh from his victory the previous
year over Brutus and Cassius at Philippi, ordered a soldier removed from the
equestrian rows. A nasty rumour circulated that Octavian had this soldier
tortured and put to death, outraging soldiers present at the show. They
threatened Octavian's life, but he was saved by the sudden appearance of
the soldier, who showed no evidence of physical injury.[111]

At some point between the death of Augustus (AD 14) and the reign of
Domitian (AD 81–96), the Roscian law stopped being enforced and it was
every man for himself, with equestrians competing with the common
people. As part of his policy of improving public manners, Domitian decided to enforce the Roscian law again and banned the common people
from sitting among the equestrians.[112] A favourite *topos* of Martial was the
attempt of various lower-class persons to circumvent Domitian's decree.
Martial makes fun of the dogged attempts of a certain Nanneius, who got
used to sitting in the first row of the equestrian section when the law was in
abeyance. After having been chased out of his seat twice by an usher, he hid
behind two spectators by crouching down between two rows and watched
the show with a hood over his head. Soon he was discovered again by the
usher and made his way out into the aisle where he half sat on the very end
of the bench, trying to convince the annoyed equestrians he was sitting (and

therefore belonged in their section) and the usher that he was only standing in the aisle.[113] Martial credits another usher with removing the haughty Naevolus from a seat immediately behind the equestrian seating where Martial was entitled to sit because of his position as a 'tribune'.[114] 'Tribune' here probably refers to the position of *viator tribunicius* ('a tribunicial messenger'), whose primary duty was to summon people to appear before a magistrate. The *viator tribunicius* was one of the public servants (*apparitores*) who, like scribes and lictors, were assistants to magistrates or performed other public duties. Another interloper named Bassus proudly wore green garments as he sat in the equestrian section in the pre-Domitianic era, but as soon as the equestrian seating regulations were enforced again, he began to wear cloaks richly dyed with aristocratic colours (scarlet and purple) to make the usher think that he was rich enough to be an equestrian. Martial tells Bassus in a poem that there is no cloak that would qualify him for equestrian seating.[115] The ushers were no doubt slaves, but citizens were expected to obey their orders and could be penalized for occupying an unauthorized seat, perhaps with a fine.[116]

An incident that occurred outside Rome spurred Augustus to affirm clearly the order of seating that would apply in all theatres and amphitheatres.[117] A senator was unable to find a seat at a show in Puteoli and no one was willing to give up his place to this eminent visitor. Augustus therefore decided to restore the privileges of rank in the theatre and amphitheatre that had ceased to be observed in the late Republic. In the late 20s BC he issued his famous *Lex Iulia Theatralis* that guaranteed senators priority seating anywhere in the empire and added seat assignments for other groups.[118] Interestingly, Suetonius, our primary source for the *lex*, does not mention reserved seating for equestrians, but his account probably was not meant to be exhaustive, because we know of other seating assignments that are not mentioned by the biographer (see below). Augustus' seating divisions were meant to reflect the various social segments of the Roman people arranged in hierarchical order. In this way, Augustus tried to remedy the first-come, first-served seating policy that apparently had prevailed since the chaotic times of the civil wars: '[Augustus] reformed and regulated the [Romans'] disorderly and haphazard manner of watching a spectacle'.[119] The rest of his reforms listed by Suetonius have to do with the seating of soldiers, plebeian husbands, boys and their pedagogues, and women of all classes.[120] The poet Statius sums up the Augustan seating hierarchy succinctly from the highest part of the theatre or amphitheatre to the lowest: 'small boys, women, plebeians, equestrians, senators' (*parvi, femina, plebs, eques, senatus*).[121] In all likelihood, the small boys and women were together in the same (highest) level, which they shared with the poorest citizens. As we shall see below, well-off plebeians sat in the middle level. The equestrians sat in the lowest section of the amphitheatre proper, just above the senators, who sat on a podium, a platform that extended out into the arena and encircled it.

Each of the three levels of the amphitheatre was divided into wedges (*cunei*), blocks of seating bordered vertically by staircases and horizontally by walkways.[122] For example, one wedge was for plebeian husbands. Unmarried men (and women) may have been banned from spectacles, at least during the reign of Augustus.[123] Another wedge consisted of young boys wearing the *toga praetexta*, a white garment with a broad purple border that was also the official dress of the senatorial class.[124] Immediately adjacent to this section of young boys was another wedge filled with their *paedagogi*, slaves who took care of their young charges, serving as a protective escort outside the home and as a teacher inside. These *paedagogi* were the only slaves who, because of their important duties, had special seating.[125] The fact that the fathers of these boys could afford to provide them with a personal slave indicates that these boys were children of the upper classes and of well-to-do plebeians. The plebeian fathers of these boys sat on the same level as their sons in different wedges, wearing the *toga virilis* ('a man's toga', white with no stripe). Male children of the poorest citizens sat with their fathers, whom Augustus excluded from the middle level because they wore a dark-coloured cloak or tunic, the characteristic clothing of the poor.[126] Thus, the podium where the senators sat, wearing white togas with broad purple stripe, the first seating level reserved for equestrians clad in white togas with narrow purple stripe, and the next level up where plebeians sat wearing the white *toga virilis*, would have presented a sea of white-clad Romans. This is exactly what Siculus' Corydon, whose first visit to Nero's famous wooden amphitheatre was discussed earlier in this chapter, saw as he walked up past the sections reserved for the equestrians and *plebs* on his way to the highest seating level.[127] This sight must have pleased Augustus immensely, especially when one considers Augustus' sarcastic reference to Roman citizens dressed in dark clothing at a political meeting as 'the togaed race', a quote from Virgil.[128] Augustus believed that the proper dress for a

Roman citizen at a public function was the toga. Not every successor to Augustus agreed with this policy. Claudius allowed senators to dress as ordinary citizens and to sit where they liked, although the podium was still reserved for them.[129] By the beginning of the second century AD, Romans seem to be abandoning the toga. Juvenal complains that 'in a great part of Italy, if we admit the truth, no one wears the toga except a corpse'.[130] The annual December *munus* posed a dress problem for those spectators who were sufficiently well off to own a toga. The toga, not a very substantial garment, was quite adequate in warm weather, but something more was required in December, when, in Italy, the weather could turn cold and it could even snow. In such weather, the equestrians often wore a scarlet or purple cloak, but these colours violated Augustus' 'all-white' rule. Martial recommends that the civic-minded thing to do would be to wear a white cloak.[131] On one occasion a certain Horatius showed up at the amphitheatre wearing a black cloak, while all the plebs, equestrians, senators and the emperor himself (Domitian) were wearing white. Martial points out that during the show Horatius' cloak became white when it snowed.[132]

During the Republic and the early part of Augustus' reign, the ability of women to sit wherever they pleased amid the male spectators is a good example of what Augustus called the Romans' 'disorderly and haphazard manner of watching a spectacle'. Thus, Augustus restricted seating at *munera* for women (probably upper class) 'to a higher place', no doubt wedges of the highest level of the amphitheatre, where they sat on chairs or benches with backs (*cathedrae*), perhaps as compensation for their remote location.[133] Calpurnius' Corydon, as a poor man (possibly a slave) and an out-of-towner, had to climb to the highest part of the *cavea* where he found himself sitting near the women's section.[134] Before the Augustan seating reform, the presence of women among men certainly encouraged flirtation, which may have concerned Augustus, who was very much concerned with the sexual behaviour of his subjects, issuing stern legislation on adultery in 18 BC. He exiled both his daughter and granddaughter (both named Julia) for adulterous behaviour and the poet Ovid, probably for the loose sexual behaviour he condoned in his poetry. Plutarch includes an anecdote about Sulla in his biography of the dictator, demonstrating how his interest was piqued by the flirtatious behaviour of a woman sitting near him at a *munus*. Her name was Valeria, a beautiful divorced woman, whose father and brother were members of the senatorial class. She decided to take the initiative with the great man, and as she moved along a row to reach her seat, put her hand on his shoulder and 'innocently' picked a tuft of material off his cloak. She then said to the dictator: 'It's no big deal, dictator, but I wanted to share in your success'. Sulla was left speechless but not offended by her behaviour. After investigating her background and character, he married her.[135] Naturally, young men used the opportunity provided by the presence of women nearby to take the initiative. As we had seen earlier, Ovid in his advice to male readers on how to meet girls, advises them to ask to borrow a programme from a girl and then to touch her hand as she gives it to him.[136] Ovid reveals the romantic atmosphere of the amphitheatre with his poetic imagery:

> *The boy Cupid has often fought in that arena and the man who has watched the infliction of [real] wounds is himself wounded [by love] . . . . Wounded he moaned and felt the winged arrow and becomes part of the munus he is watching.[137]*

Augustus' placement of women in the upper part of the amphitheatre, however, did not stop flirtations. Men in the lower part of the auditorium could still make eye contact with women at the top. Girlfriends in the women's section kept an eye on their lovers below and were moved to jealousy when they caught them eyeing another woman. Propertius' beloved Cynthia, outraged by his unfaithfulness, requires that he stop looking back at the highest part of the amphitheatre as a condition of reconciliation.[138] Ovid complains that he is so tired of his girlfriend's jealous accusations that he, in order to antagonize her, turns his head to exchange silent but provocative glances with another woman in the highest part of the amphitheatre.[139] Perhaps Ovid and Propertius on these occasions were sitting in the small amphitheatre of Statilius Taurus, in which it might have been possible for someone sitting in a lower part of the structure to catch the eye of a spectator in the upper levels. In the huge Colosseum, however, interchanges at a distance between male and female spectators would have been much more difficult, if not impossible.

Not all women sat in these upper reaches. As we saw earlier in this chapter, Augustus provided reserved seating to the Vestal Virgins, probably on the podium. After the reign of Augustus, other prominent women joined the Vestals in this special seating. Tiberius decreed that his mother Livia, now enjoying the title of Augusta, sit with the Vestals whenever she chose to attend a spectacle.[140] Caligula gave the same privilege to his grandmother Antonia (the younger daughter of Marc Antony and niece of Augustus) and to his sisters, while Claudius did the same for his wife Messalina.[141]

The Vestals were not the only religious officials to have preferred seating. That privilege was also enjoyed by a college of twelve priests called the Arval Brothers ('Brothers of the Field') who had charge of the cult of Dea Dia, a goddess who presided over the fertility of the fields. An inscription entitled *Public Transactions of the Arval Brothers*, dating from AD 80, the very year in which the Colosseum was dedicated, contains a record of the spaces reserved for this religious college in the three seating levels of the Colosseum above the podium.[142] The inscription mentions three levels of seating in which the Arval Brothers were given seats and gives the levels the following names: *maenianum primum* ('first level'), the *maenianum summum secundum* ('the highest part of the second level') and the *maenianum summum in ligneis* ('the highest level in wood'). The name *maenianum summum secundum* must presume the existence of a *maenianum imum secundum* ('the lowest part of the second level'), which is not mentioned because the Brothers were not assigned seats there.[143] These four levels will be discussed further below.

The Arval Brothers were granted space in the lowest level (*maenianum primum*) where the equestrians sat (just behind the podium), totalling a length of 42.5 Roman feet (approximately 41.8 modern feet) in eight contiguous rows. (Note that seats in the Colosseum were not numbered, so that seating was assigned by overall space rather than by individual seats). Perhaps space was reserved in this level for Brothers who were members of the equestrian order to make sure that seats were always available. Evidence from other amphitheatres in which individual seats are marked by lines etched in the stone enables us to estimate how many persons would have been accommodated in 42.5 Roman feet of seating. The average space allocated per person in these other amphitheatres is 15.7 inches, which means that the 42.5 feet would have held about 32 jam-packed persons. If 15.7 inches sounds too small, one must remember that the average height of an adult male in ancient Rome was only 5.5 feet. The larger average size of modern men and women requires wider seats.[144] Other seats reserved in the name of the Arval Brothers were in the *maenianum summum secundum*, consisting of 22.5 Roman feet (21.12 modern feet) in one row of one wedge and in the *maenianum summum in ligneis*, 63.5 Roman feet (62.4 modern feet) in four rows of one wedge. With this amount of space reserved, it is evident that the allotted seats were occupied by more than just the twelve Arvals. Obviously, the best seats in the *maenianum primum* would be occupied by Arval Brothers themselves, perhaps along with other male members of their families.[145] Their various assistants (attendants, servants, scribes and so on) would no doubt have sat in the *maenianam summums secundum*, while the large amount of space reserved in the *maenianum summum in ligneis* in the upper reaches of the Colosseum might accommodate the college's slaves and wives.[146] It should also be noted that just about every religious college enjoyed reserved seating in the *maenianum primum*.[147] Moreover, inscriptions inside the Colosseum on the anterior facing of rows give evidence of reserved seating for other groups such as the citizens of Gades (Cadiz) in Spain, and in the late empire even for specific senators and their families.[148]

Access to the Colosseum and other entertainment venues was not limited to Roman citizens. The Romans wanted to impress foreign dignitaries with their various spectacles, especially gladiatorial games. Augustus did not allow foreign ambassadors of independent and allied nations to sit among the senators because they were sometimes freedmen, probably banishing them to sit in the upper reaches of the *cavea*.[149] After his death, however, that policy changed. When Frisian ambassadors came to Rome during Nero's reign, the Roman authorities, wanting to impress them 'with the greatness of the Roman people', invited them to attend a spectacle at Pompey's theatre.[150] When the Frisians noticed men in foreign dress sitting in the senators' section, their Roman hosts explained that only ambassadors from nations noted for their courage and friendship to Rome were given this honour. The naïve Frisians announced that no nation surpassed them in war or in loyalty to the Romans, entered the senatorial area, and sat down. The Roman spectators were charmed by the Frisians' impulsive and unsophisticated behaviour.[151]

Martial in his *Book of Spectacles* pointed out to the emperor Titus some representative foreign nationals present at the grand opening of the Colosseum, sporting their native dress and speaking their strange-sounding languages: Thracians, nomadic Sarmatians famous for drinking horses' blood (the northern Black Sea and Danube areas), Egyptians, Britons, Arabs, Sabaeans (modern Yemen), Cilicians (modern southern Turkey), Sygambrians (a Germanic people) and Ethiopians, the last two groups with dramatically contrasting hairdos.[152] The poet gives us no clue as to the status of the peoples he mentions here. They could be either foreign envoys who were sitting with the senators or ordinary foreign visitors in the upper reaches of the *cavea*. In any case, Martial uses the exotic names and customs of these visitors to this new architectural symbol of Roman greatness to highlight the vastness of the Roman empire.[153] Cassius Dio adds Macedonians, Greeks, Sicilians, Epirots, Asiatics, Iberians and Carthaginians to Martial's list.[154]

Individual Romans such as winners of the *corona civica* ('civic crown') were honoured with special seating in the theatre and the amphitheatre. These men were war heroes who had saved the life of a fellow Roman citizen while killing an enemy.[155] As they entered the theatre or amphitheatre, the senators rose in their honour and they took their place immediately behind the senators.[156] In the late Republic, one example of honorary seating was actually outside the temporary amphitheatres built in the Forum! A statue of the Republican hero Ser. Sulpicius Rufus was placed on the Rostra (speaker's platform) in the Forum and his descendants were given seats in perpetuity within a circle of diameter of 10 feet around the statue.[157] It would seem impossible that these honorary seats outside the tiered stands could provide a good view of the action in the arena. At the time this honour was decreed, a new Rostra had been built by Julius Caesar (11.5 feet high as preserved today) just before his assassination. Although we do not know how high the seating was in these temporary structures, it must have been higher than 11.5 feet. Welch suggests two possibilities: (1) seating of irregular heights at various points in the oval, which would allow the Sulpicii sitting on the Rostra to look into the arena at the same level as the best seats, or (2) only the long sides of the oval had high seating (perhaps as much as 33 feet high), while the short ends had low stands which would have given the Sulpicii a good view of the arena.[158] An even earlier award of honorary seating took place in the early second century (184 BC). A member of the Maenian family sold his house, which looked down into the Forum (with a good view of any entertainment given there) to make way for the building of the Basilica Porcia. In compensation for having lost an excellent vantage point, he and his descendants received the right to special seating in a balcony attached to the Maenian Column, a Forum landmark, which honoured his famous ancestor C. Maenius (fourth century BC), from whose name was derived the word *maenianum* ('seating level').[159] The sources point out that the main purpose of this seating was a good view of gladiator shows in the Forum.[160] The seating must have been high enough to overlook temporary wooden stands. Outside of Rome, a more typical example of honorary seating is that of Cupiennius Satrius, who had the right to sit opposite the box of the *editor* on the other side of the arena in the amphitheatre at Cumae.[161]

Distribution of seats

Tickets were required for access to the Colosseum. These tickets were small pieces of lead, wood or bone called *tesserae*, which were distributed free of charge, probably by means of the patron/client system.[162] None of these *tesserae* have survived. Incised on each ticket must have been a number from I to LXXVI corresponding to one of the seventy-six entrance arches available to the public. The ticket also must have specified level, wedge and row number. It seems logical that *munerarii* (including the emperor) were significant distributors of blocks of seats to their friends and supporters. The recipients of these seats no doubt shared their bounty with their friends, supporters and dependants, resulting in a 'trickle-down effect' to the lowest members of society.[163] As Rawson has shown, an important source of these tickets during the Republic was the magistrates and members of important religious boards.[164] Cicero reports a conversation he had with Clodius about the allocation of tickets to clients. Cicero had not been in the habit of distributing tickets, even to the Sicilians, his clients, on whose behalf he had prosecuted their infamous governor Verres for extortion. Clodius, who, like Cicero, had served as a quaestor in Sicily, announced his intention as their new patron to do so. His only problem was that his source of tickets, his sister Clodia, had been stingy with them, although she had a large allocation from her husband, the consul Metellus Celer. Clodius complains that she gave him 'only one foot of space'.[165] In his *Defence of Murena*, Cicero mentions that a client of his had received space (*locus*, literally 'a place') from one of the Vestal Virgins, a relative.[166] Rawson convincingly argues that the *locus* given by the Vestal Virgin to Cicero's client (like the *locus* desired by Clodius) is actually a block of seats, which he will in turn distribute to others.[167] Ticket brokers called *locarii* (from *locus*) also played a role in the distribution of tickets, but at a cost. They probably bought seats directly from the *editor* and from those who had received them without cost, and resold them.[168] Martial calls the famous gladiator Hermes 'the wealth of ticket brokers' because people were willing to pay the *locarii* large amounts of money to see him in action.[169] It should also be noted that the average citizen could not count on being able to attend shows in the Colosseum on a regular basis. Without a connection to an important person, tickets must have been quite hard to get. They must have been relatively scarce when one takes into account the amount of space reserved for the upper classes and the competition for the rest of the seats among a population of approximately 1 million people.[170] The average citizen had a much better chance of getting into the Circus Maximus, the enormous confines of which could accommodate 25 per cent of the city's populace, whereas the Colosseum could hold only 5 per cent.[171]

Entry and exit

Most important in the construction of any entertainment venue, whether ancient or modern, are provisions for allowing spectators to get to their seats and back to the exits as easily and quickly as possible. It is not difficult to see how crucial a problem this is in a building like the Colosseum, which had a capacity most realistically estimated at 50,000 spectators. This problem was solved by a system of circuit corridors intersected by radial passageways under the seating area (*cavea*). There were concentric corridors that made a circuit around the whole arena (indicated by A, B, C and D in Figure 30), leading spectators to their seats. Since all the seating has long since vanished from the Colosseum, the reconstructions of the *cavea* that appear in various modern texts are really educated guesses that are more or less convincing. The senators had the best seats closest to the action and sat on a podium, a platform interrupted on the opposite sides of the minor axis by the emperor's and the *editor*'s boxes.[172] Suetonius identifies the podium as the location of Nero's box in his wooden amphitheatre.[173] The Colosseum as a successor to Nero's structure no doubt would have had one too. Juvenal also mentions a podium in an unidentified amphitheatre, which, it would be safe to assume, was the Colosseum. The senators and other distinguished spectators, as suited their status, had easy access to their seats on the podium. They could walk straight from their assigned entrance through a radial corridor to the innermost circuit corridor A and then up a short

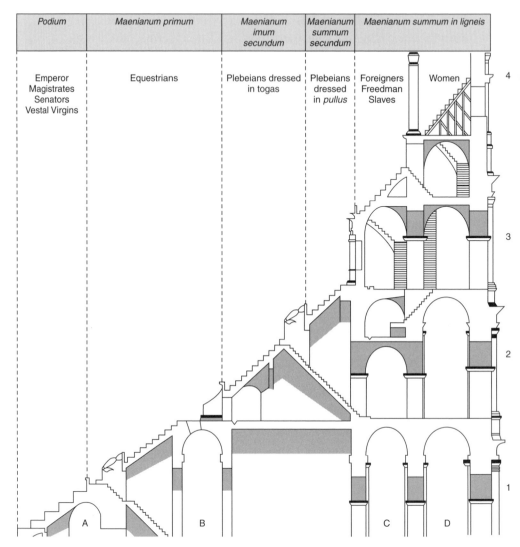

Podium	Maenianum primum	Maenianum imum secundum	Maenianum summum secundum	Maenianum summum in ligneis	
Emperor Magistrates Senators Vestal Virgins	Equestrians	Plebeians dressed in togas	Plebeians dressed in *pullus*	Foreigners Freedman Slaves	Women

Figure 30 Cutaway of Colosseum

number of steps through an entrance (*vomitorium*) on to the podium. Seating for the senators consisted of moveable wooden benches without arms or backs called *subsellia*.[174] These benches were made more comfortable by the use of cushions.[175] The next level up was assigned to the equestrians, who proceeded straight from their assigned entrance through a radial passageway to circuit corridor B and used stairs to reach the their part of the *cavea.*[176] In order to reach the next level, which was assigned to plebeians wearing the toga (*maenianum imum secundum*), spectators had to go to the second floor of the amphitheatre, accessed by stairs which connected with circuit corridors B and C on the ground floor. The *maenianum summum secundum* was likely the seating assigned to citizens of lower status who wore a dark cloak called the pullus. The next section up (*maenianum summum in ligneis*) was cut off from the lower part of the *cavea* by a wall nearly 16.5 feet high by means of which the spectators in this section were literally and figuratively kept in their place.[177] These two *maeniana* could only be reached from the outer corridors on the second floor.[178] Who sat in the *maenianum summum in ligneis*? Given the lack of definitive evidence, scholars have had to resort to informed conjecture. Connolly and Rea assign it to the lowest elements of Roman society, a plausible suggestion.[179] This group would have included freedmen and slaves, but foreign tourists probably also sat in this area. On the other hand, Bomgardner reserves this section for women, arguing that 'respectable wives and daughters of Roman citizens' sat on this level, protected by a portico from a working-class woman's telltale suntan.[180] Although nothing of the portico has survived, there is reliable evidence of its existence. It is evident on a coin depicting the Colosseum and Cassius Dio vaguely reports that the 'uppermost circumference' (i.e., the portico) of the amphitheatre was hit by lightning and caught fire. It does seem reasonable to place women at the highest part of the Colosseum, since Augustus had ordered women to sit in 'a higher location'.[181] On the other hand, they probably would not have needed a portico to avoid a suntan. The awnings would have kept them well shaded. Bomgardner's other argument, however, is more compelling. He talks of the more effective segregation of 'ladies of quality' in the colonnade. Indeed, if Augustus' main concern in moving women to the higher regions of the amphitheatre was, in Bomgardner's words, 'purdah', the colonnade would have been the best way of accomplishing that purpose. A colonnade would have provided the most privacy and perhaps better accommodated the special chairs (*cathedrae*) that women enjoyed in the amphitheatre.[182] Moreover, the colonnade would seem to be too impressive a structure for the common people, slaves and foreigners some scholars place there. It would seem logical to identify this colonnade with the *maenianum summum in ligneis*, mentioned only in the Arval Brothers inscription discussed earlier, which dates from the opening of the Colosseum in AD 80. If, however, the Chronography of 354 is correct that the attic storey was built under Domitian (AD 81–96), then it would seem that colonnade had been built after AD 80. What, then, did *maenianum summum in ligneis* refer to in the year of the Colosseum's dedication? Here is a possible answer. Without the colonnade, the original *maenianum summum in ligneis* would have been the highest seating area in the *cavea* of the newly dedicated Colosseum, made of wood in contrast with the marble seating below (*maenianum primum, maenianum imum secundum, maenianum summum secundum*). Women, fulfilling the order of Augustus, would have sat in this area among their social inferiors. When Domitian added the attic storey sometime later, it took the form of a wooden colonnade, reserved for women and sharing the same name with their pre-Domitianic location. While women enjoyed the covered portico, their former seating companions remained in the uncovered section immediately below.

Awnings

One very important feature, not just of the Colosseum but of all Roman amphitheatres (and theatres) was the use of awnings (*vela*) to protect the spectators from the hot Italian sun, especially during the late spring and summer. When Caligula was in a particularly vile mood and the sun was burning with special intensity, he would order the awnings rolled back and not allow any spectator to leave the amphitheatre (perhaps that of Statilius Taurus).[183] The very fact that Caligula chose this particular punishment shows how important awnings were to the enjoyment of the show. As we have seen, the promise of awnings was frequently a feature of the advertisement of a *munus*. Awnings were first employed by Q. Lutatius Catulus in his dedication of the Capitolium in 69 BC.[184] Julius Caesar made spectacular use of *vela* for a *munus* during his triumphal games in the Forum in 46 BC. Caesar completely covered with a silk awning the open plaza of the Forum and the *Via Sacra* ('Sacred Way') from his house all the way up the Capitoline Hill.[185] It was reported that the crowd seemed to have enjoyed the awnings more than the gladiator show.[186] Augustus followed the example of his adoptive father when he covered the whole Forum with awnings for a show given by his nephew Marcellus as aedile. These awnings were left in place for the whole summer.[187] The first century BC poet Lucretius describes the colourful effects of awnings.

. . . awnings yellow, red, and purple [cast colours]; when stretched over great theatres, they flap and flutter, hanging from masts and beams. For they cover the audience in the tiers beneath with colourful shadows . . . and make them seem to vibrate as they are bathed in colours.[188]

These effects must have contributed greatly to the holiday atmosphere of the spectacle. Nero was in the habit of using awnings whose colour imitated that of a dark blue sky with stars. These awnings were decorated all over with stars that stood out against the azure background.[189] Nero's megalomania was evident in the decoration of the awnings for Tiridates' coronation as king of Armenia. He had a figure representing himself riding in a chariot embroidered in the centre of the awning, identifying himself with the sun god (*Sol*), who in myth rode a chariot across the sky during the day. This identification served as a reminder to Tiridates and the Roman people of Nero's overwhelming power. This theme seems also to have been prominent in Nero's Colossus, which wore the radiate crown of the Sun god.[190]

On the fourth storey's outer wall, behind the seating for women, were positioned the poles that supported the awnings of the Colosseum. These masts were held in place by sockets between the windows in the outer wall (Figure 27). There is evidence of stairs on the inside of the north-west outer wall to the top of the Colosseum. They were likely used by the sailors from the imperial fleet at Misenum on the Bay of Naples, who were responsible for setting up and taking down these massive awnings. They were quartered near the Colosseum in the *Castra Misenatium* ('Camp of Misenates'). Their experience with ship sails naturally qualified them for this job.[191] It is estimated that as many as a thousand men were required to take care of the task of furling and unfurling the awnings. The task cannot have been easy, and must have required great effort and cooperation. There were occasions when it was impossible to set up the awnings. Wind, snow and probably rain were factors that could cause the sailors to leave the awnings furled. Even after the awnings had been spread out, it must have been necessary on some occasions to draw them back quickly when winds arose suddenly or it began to rain or snow.[192] This would have had to be done relatively quickly before the awnings were damaged. Norma Goldman posits that the 'quick maneuverability' of the awnings would have saved the day in such circumstances.[193] On one occasion, the sailors were given another task to perform by Commodus, which they fortunately never had to carry out. Commodus, who was used to fawning applause for his performances as a gladiator, suddenly had an attack of paranoia that made him think that the crowd's tepid response indicated their contempt. He immediately commanded the sailors to kill the spectators and ordered the city of Rome to be burned, but was eventually convinced by his praetorian prefect to rescind both orders.[194]

In the absence of awnings, Martial urges spectators to use umbrellas to protect themselves.[195] Even when the awnings were unfurled, at midday they protected only the higher seats, while the senators on the podium were exposed to an unfiltered blazing sun that made enjoyment of the show all but impossible.[196] This may have not been a serious problem, since it is likely that most senators left the amphitheatre at noon to take lunch. For those who stayed to watch the *meridianum spectaculum*, broad-brimmed hats allowed comfortable viewing.[197]

Most likely the awnings of the Colosseum were supported by radial ropes coming from the 240 vertical masts that crowned the amphitheatre. These ropes would have been attached to an elliptical rope high above the centre of the arena, forming a circular opening (*oculus*, 'eye') through which the sun shone.[198] Pliny the Elder mentions that Nero's awnings were held in place by ropes.[199] Another method of rigging was used in the amphitheatre in Pompeii. The awnings were supported by poles projecting horizontally from the rim of the amphitheatre.[200]

Hypogeum

The subterranean area of the Colosseum (*hypogeum*, 'underground') is a two-storey structure which is actually a bit larger than the arena. It is difficult to generalize about this area because of the regular changes it underwent throughout its history. Some of what we see today dates from late antiquity (as late as the fifth century AD).[201] An underground tunnel from the *Ludus Magnus* provided access to the *hypogeum* from the east side of the amphitheatre. Also connecting with the *hypogeum* are two staircases leading down from the west entrance and two passageways that led to the podium, one on each end of the minor north/south axis.[202] The *hypogeum* was used as a staging area for gladiators, hunters and animals before their entry into the arena. Scenery and other stage properties were also kept there. It is generally assumed that this area did not exist when the Colosseum was inaugurated in

AD 80 and was added later by Domitian.[203] One reason for this assumption is that during the inauguration of the building, the emperor Titus flooded the arena for a *naumachia* and other water displays. The existence of a *hypogeum* at this time would have made the water shows impossible, because the basin could not be kept watertight.[204] What can be seen today are thirty-two vaulted hollow spaces arranged around the edge of the ellipse, three circuit corridors adjacent to the ringside of the arena, and two straight parallel walls on either side of a wide central corridor. The vaulted cavities were likely temporary storage pens for animals. The vertical shafts attached to the four straight walls flanking the central corridor must have housed elevators to raise gladiators and/or animals to the arena floor. Caged animals were raised to a space just below the arena floor and then released to be driven up small ramps by men with torches through trapdoors into the arena.[205] Since the arena floor of the Colosseum no longer exists, there are obviously no indications of the locations of the trapdoors. There is, however, a well-preserved system of trapdoors in the amphitheatre in Capua Vetere, which has a substructure similar to that of the Colosseum. This system has a total of sixty-two trapdoors, including six of double size. The larger Colosseum would have had even more.[206] The narrowness of the shafts, however, poses a puzzling problem, as yet unsolved. They could only have accommodated smaller animals such as boar, dogs and medium-sized cats. Large beasts would have had to be brought into the arena in some other way.[207]

The Colosseum from late antiquity to the present

The Colosseum served Rome uninterruptedly for 137 years before there was a break in service. In AD 217, lightning struck the Colosseum causing a fire that left the building in need of extensive repairs. The natural disaster was itself a spectacle worthy of the Colosseum. Cassius Dio, who most probably viewed at least the results of the disaster, gives his description of the event:

> *The hunting theatre [Dio's term for the Colosseum] on the very day of the Vulcanalia [the festival of Vulcan, the fire god] having been struck by lightning was engulfed in such a conflagration that the circumference of the top of the building and the arena floor were completely destroyed by fire and as a result of this the rest of the building was ravaged by fire nor could human effort fight it although the city used all of its water resources, nor was a very*

heavy and violent downpour able to have any effect. Thus both sources of water could not counteract the power of the thunderbolts and to a degree also caused a significant amount of damage. As a result gladiatorial shows were held for many years in the stadium.[208]

The lightning must have first struck the wooden colonnaded seating, which, having caught fire, fell down over the lower seating area of the auditorium, finally reaching and setting fire to the wooden arena floor. The superheated stone of the structure and marble covered seating in the auditorium also suffered damage, being converted by the process of calcination into granulated bits and pieces.[209] Once the fire ravaged the wooden arena floor, it must have raged through all the wooden equipment in the substructure under the arena. The Colosseum was not reopened and rededicated until AD 222 under Alexander Severus, but the restoration was by no means complete and would not be finished for another fifteen years.[210] In the fifth century, there were three earthquakes that did serious damage to the Colosseum (AD 429, 443, and 484 or 508). The first two caused blockage in the sewers, thereby flooding the *hypogeum*. The third was disastrous. Besides dangerously weakening the whole structure, the earthquake brought down the colonnade at the top of the amphitheatre again (no doubt the most vulnerable part of the seating area), which caused grave damage to various parts of the *cavea*.[211] The debris from the colonnade was moved into the *hypogeum*, no doubt making it difficult, if not impossible, to take advantage of this underground chamber in the presentation of shows.

With the disappearance of gladiatorial combat in the fifth century and the *venatio* in the sixth, the Colosseum ceased to be a site for public entertainment, with one notable exception. In 1332, a bullfight was given in honour of Ludwig the Bavarian, who was visiting Rome.[212] The bullfight was very similar to the *venatio*, with the human participants carrying a single spear much like the ancient *venator*. Gibbon gives the final score of this contest. It was a clear-cut victory for the bulls, which had killed eighteen of their human opponents and wounded nine. In contrast, humans had killed only eleven bulls.[213] Although it would be easy to suppose that this bullfight was an attempt to restore the Colosseum to one of its original functions, such an assumption would be incorrect. In the fourteenth century, it was not known that the Colosseum in antiquity had been the venue for bloody spectacles. In fact, it was not until the next century that scholars such as Flavio Biondo and Poggio Bracciolini finally discovered the Colosseum's original *raison d'être*. The only reason that the amphitheatre had been chosen for this bullfight was the availability of space and seating.

Left without a purpose and having suffered structural damage from earthquakes, the Colosseum became an abandoned building subject to the depredations of all those who sought to use it for their own purposes. From the sixth to the ninth century, craftsmen had shops in the seating area and people lived either inside the building or in shacks built against the outer walls. Beginning in the twelfth century, the Frangipane family appropriated part of the Colosseum for use as a fortress during civil wars for the better part of a century. The Colosseum was also a valuable source of raw materials. There were 100,000 cubic feet of travertine stone in the Colosseum, which could be reused in construction or converted to quicklime, a hardening agent in plaster and mortar. There were also large amounts of marble and tufa, two other valuable stones. Moreover, there was a great deal of metal, a scarce resource in the Middle Ages, to be salvaged from the Colosseum. Already in the fourth century, lead pipes were being taken from the building, cutting off water from the latrines and fountains.[214] The greatest amount of metal in the Colosseum was in the form of 300 tons of iron clamps that held blocks of stone together.[215] The holes that these clamps made in the stone are still evident on the outer façade of the Colosseum. The recycling of stone and metal from the Colosseum, however, was not just the result of informal looting; permissions to take building materials from the amphitheatre were sometimes given, sometimes sold, to builders by the authorities. The earliest record we have of this practice is an inscription dating from the late fourth century that was found in the Colosseum in which the emperor Theodosius I granted permission to a senator named Gerontius to take stone from the amphitheatre.[216] The Romans were very practical and quite unsentimental in this matter. For them, the past should serve present needs. This attitude can be seen in a letter from the ruler Theodoric in response to a request that the city of Catania (Sicily) be allowed to use stones from an amphitheatre to fortify the city walls:

> *The stones from the amphitheatre in ruins because of its antiquity, which you suggest contributes nothing to the beauty of the city except to display ugly ruins, we grant you permission to put to public use, so that which cannot be of any use if it lies on the ground may be incorporated into the city walls.*

Therefore, confidently do whatever is necessary to strengthen and beautify the walls and be assured that whatever you do will be pleasing to us if the charm of your city is more evident.[217]

Once the Church became one of three primary owners of the Colosseum in the fourteenth century, popes were not reluctant to make a tidy profit by selling these permissions.[218] In spite of the protests of scholars, popes themselves engaged in wholesale quarrying of the Colosseum for their pet projects. For example, Pope Nicholas V (1447–1455) took huge amounts of stone from the amphitheatre to construct St Peter's Basilica. Pope Pius II (1458–1464) recycled tons of stone for the building of the Palazzo di Venezia, the first of the great renaissance *palazzi*, and the restoration of the Basilica of San Marco, which was incorporated into the palazzo.[219] Other popes saw additional uses of the Colosseum. Sistus V (1585–1590) planned to build a spinning mill in the amphitheatre, but that project fell through. Instead, some workers installed a glue factory in the second level of seats. Clement XI in 1700 ordered that a manure dump be created in the Colosseum, which was used to produce saltpetre (potassium nitrate), the primary ingredient in gunpowder. This dung heap, the corrosiveness of which did great damage to the travertine pillars on the first level, was still in place at the beginning of the nineteenth century.[220] The smell must have been horrendous.

In the Middle Ages, legends developed around the Colosseum that were a jumble of misinformation. The main source of these legends was a medieval guide for pilgrims called *The Wonders of the City of Rome* (*Mirabilia Urbis Romae*) written in the eleventh century. The *Mirabilia* claims that the Colosseum in ancient times was a round temple with a domed roof. In the centre of the arena stood a colossal statue of Apollo holding a sphere as a symbol of Rome's domination of the world. This statue seems to be a distorted memory of Nero's colossal statue depicting him as the Sun god that in ancient times had stood just outside the Colosseum. The author of the *Mirabilia*, undoubtedly concerned that this information contradicted what medieval pilgrims actually saw when they visited the Colosseum, added the explanation that Pope Sylvester (314–335), a zealous enemy of paganism, destroyed the temple and put the head and hand of the statue in front of the Basilica of St John Lateran.[221] The Colosseum also acquired in the popular mind an otherworldly aspect that made it into a magical and sinister building in which demons regularly gathered, especially at night. Among these demons were the pagan gods whom Christians associated with ancient Roman spectacles.[222] As late as the sixteenth century, the Florentine artist Benvenuto Cellini, along with some friends and a priest expert in necromancy, went to the Colosseum on two occasions to use sorcery to win back his girlfriend. On the second occasion, the necromancer was apparently so successful in summoning thousands of demons from hell that Cellini's friends were panic stricken. The demons, however, were put to immediate flight when one of Cellini's group suffered a huge intestinal explosion.[223] The otherworldly character of the Colosseum is also reflected in the medieval legend of Virgil as its architect, an anachronism since the poet died almost a full century before the building of the Flavian Amphitheatre. In the Middle Ages, however, Virgil was better known as a great magician, necromancer and prophet than as a poet. The powers of this fanciful 'Virgil' were great and were used against the forces of darkness.[224]

In the sixteenth century, the Church began to see the Colosseum in a different light as a sacred place where martyrs had provided their fellow Christians with edifying examples of religious belief. Pius V (1566–1572) decided not to demolish the Colosseum so that pilgrims could take home as a relic earth that, as it was believed, had absorbed the blood of martyrs.[225] The problem with this belief is the lack of any substantial evidence that Christians had been martyred in the Colosseum. The Christian conviction that St Peter had been executed in the Colosseum is contradicted by the fact that Peter had been martyred over a decade before the amphitheatre was built. The tradition that Ignatius of Antioch was the first Christian martyred in the Colosseum during the reign of Trajan is not supported by any reliable evidence. On the other hand, despite the lack of evidence, it seems logical that at least some Christians were martyred in the Colosseum's arena.[226] Historical accuracy mattered little to devout Christians. Many an amphitheatre throughout the Roman world had witnessed the ultimate testimony of Christian martyrs to the strength of their faith. Since the Colosseum was the largest and most famous amphitheatre in the empire, it was a convenient symbol, not only of Roman persecution but also of the defeat of paganism.

The earliest reliable connection between Christianity and the Colosseum was in the late fifteenth century when a passion play began to be presented annually in the arena on Good Friday, a tradition which continued until the middle of the next century.[227] In the early sixteenth century, a small chapel of Santa Maria della Pietà was built in the eastern part of the arena. Pope Clement X (1670–1676) planned a more ambitious church in honour of the martyrs to be built in the middle of the arena. It was to be designed by the famous architect Gian Lorenzo Bernini, the designer of the piazza and colonnades of St Peter's, but Clement's plan was never realized.[228] He, however, was still determined to proclaim the Colosseum a Christian shrine. He installed a cross at the top of the Colosseum and dedicated the amphitheatre to the martyrs that purportedly had died there. This dedication was proclaimed by a painted announcement that was eventually replaced a century later, when Pope Benedict XIV set up an inscription in marble on the western exterior wall of the Colosseum, which can still be seen today.

> *The Flavian Amphitheatre renowned for its triumphs and spectacles, dedicated to the gods impiously worshipped by the pagans, rescued from vile superstition by the blood of martyrs. Lest their courage be forgotten, Pope Benedict XIV in the jubilee year of 1750 in his tenth year as Pope had rendered in marble the notice painted on the whitewashed walls [of the Colosseum] by Pope Clement in the jubilee year of 1675 but made illegible by the ravages of time.*

Benedict placed a large cross in the centre of the arena, which became a huge tourist attraction.[229] Clement XI in 1720 installed Stations of the Cross around the edge of the arena in the form of small shrines.[230] The cross and Stations of the Cross remained in place until the last quarter of the nineteenth century when they were removed to allow archeological excavation.[231]

Popes occasionally sponsored efforts to clean up the Colosseum with a view to the restoration of the structure. For example, under Pope Pius VII (1800–1823), the manure pile, which had been in the Colosseum since the seventeenth century, was finally removed. There was also papal concern about the northern exterior wall, which was in danger of collapsing after an earthquake in 1803. The southern section of the exterior wall had already collapsed in an earthquake in 1349. Thus, a brick buttress was built to support the east side of the wall, and was finished in 1820. Under Pope Leo XII, a second buttress on the west side was completed in 1826.[232] Both buttresses are still visible today. Moreover, the use of the Colosseum as a quarry for building materials was no longer tolerated. Clement XI (1700–1721) was the last pope to remove stone from the Colosseum.[233]

The Colosseum remained primarily a religious shrine until the second half of the nineteenth century, when the general view of the building went through a significant change. The amphitheatre was now generally considered an archeological site important to the understanding the history and culture of ancient Rome. In 1870 the Office of the Superintendent of the Excavation and Preservation of Monuments was created, which supervised archeological efforts in the Colosseum with varying results until 1968, when the Office of Archaeological Superintendency of Rome took over, ushering in an era of scientific archaeological research.[234]

The Colosseum, a great tourist attraction since the Middle Ages, became even more popular in the nineteenth century, due in great part to Lord Byron's impassioned description of the amphitheatre in the moonlight in his *Manfred*. This passage inspired many a tourist to experience the Colosseum as he had described it. It became almost mandatory for nineteenth and early twentieth century tourists to visit the Colosseum at night. In the *Marble Faun*, Nathaniel Hawthorne comments on the influence of this passage:

[A light] indicated a party of English or Americans paying the inevitable visit by moonlight, and exalting themselves with raptures that were Byron's, not their own.

In *Manfred*, Lord Byron created a romantic vision of the Colosseum, revealing a mysterious beauty in ruin and decay. Note Byron's reference to the Colosseum as 'the gladiators' bloody Circus', which confuses the amphitheatre with the Circus Maximus:

I do remember me, that in my youth,
When I was wandering, – upon such a night
I stood within the Coloseum's wall,
Midst the chief relics of almighty Rome.
The trees which grew along the broken arches
Waved dark in the blue midnight, and the stars
Shone through the rents of ruin; from afar
The watchdog bay'd beyond the Tiber; and
More near from out the Caesars' palace came
The owl's long cry, and, interruptedly,
Of distant sentinels the fitful song
Begun and died upon the gentle wind.

Some cypresses beyond the time-worn breach
Appear'd to skirt the horizon, yet they stood
Within a bowshot. Where the Caesars dwelt,
And dwell the tuneless birds of night, amidst
A grove which springs through levell'd battlements,
And twines its roots with the imperial hearths,
Ivy usurps the laurel's place of growth; –
But the gladiators' bloody Circus stands,
A noble wreck in ruinous perfection!
While Caesar's chambers, and the Augustan halls
Grovel on earth in indistinct decay. –
And thou didst shine, thou rolling moon, upon
All this, and cast a wide and tender light,
Which soften'd down the hoar austerity
Of rugged desolation, and fill'd up,
As 'twere anew, the gaps of centuries;
Leaving that beautiful which still was so,
And making that which was not, till the place
Became religion, and the heart ran o'er
With silent worship of the great of old, –
The dead, but sceptred sovereigns, who still rule
Our spirits from their urns. –
'Twas such a night!
'Tis strange that I recall it at this time;
But I have found our thoughts take wildest flight
Even at the moment when they should array
Themselves in pensive order.

Hawthorne recognized the difference between the real Colosseum and Byron's vision and preferred the well-defined grandeur of the former to the vagueness of the latter:

Within, the moonlight filled and flooded the great empty space; it glowed upon tier above tier of ruined, grass-grown arches, and made them even too distinctly visible. The splendor of the revelation took away that inestimable effect of dimness and mystery by which the imagination might be assisted to build a grander structure than the Coliseum, and to shatter it with a more picturesque decay. Byron's celebrated description is better than the reality.

It should also be noted that Byron's description inspired a scene in which Hawthorne's characters paid a nocturnal visit to the Colosseum, an episode also found in Henry James' *Daisy Miller* and Edith Wharton's *Roman Fever*.[235]

In the twentieth and twenty-first centuries, the Colosseum has remained an object of archaeological research and the most popular of all ancient tourist attractions in Rome. Its only deviation from these functions was its use as a place of political assembly and as a shelter and arms depot by German paratroopers during the Second World War. Ironically, in 1999, the Colosseum, a place of violence and death in the ancient world, became a symbol of mercy and life. Amnesty International with the support of the Pope has instituted the practice of lighting up the Colosseum whenever a country decides to suspend or abolish the death penalty.[236]

Chapter 7

Gladiators in Film

With the appearance of Ridley Scott's *Gladiator* (2000), the topic of gladiators in film has evoked a lively interest among scholars. For example, just after the release of the film, Marcus Junkelmann wrote a short but penetrating appraisal of the film's portrayal of gladiators and gladiatorial combat in his *Das Spiel mit dem Tod* (*Death Game*) along with a few paragraphs on Stanley Kubrick's *Spartacus* (1960). Four years later, *Gladiator: Film and History*, edited by Martin Winkler, was published. The book is devoted entirely to Scott's *Gladiator*, examining and evaluating not only the film's depiction of gladiatorial combat but also the representation of the history of the period in which it is set. Other parts of the book investigate the meaning of the film for twenty-first century America. Most recently, Fik Meijer, in his book *The Gladiators* (2005), included a brief chapter on the same two films as Junkelmann. This chapter will revisit these two films, but will also include a discussion of major Hollywood films that contain gladiatorial scenes made before *Spartacus* and *Gladiator*, beginning with Cecil B. DeMille's *The Sign of the Cross* (1932). It is my intention to examine how these films have influenced each other and to estimate how accurately their creators have represented gladiatorial combat. There are, however, limits to the historical criticism that one can apply to 'sword and sandal' films. In general, film makers can be credited with getting the large picture right and occasionally showing concern for accuracy in details. One cannot expect an entertainment medium, which above all aims at commercial success, to maintain a scrupulous adherence to historical authenticity, especially when it comes to finer points. After all, these films are not scholarly documentaries. It would be a mistake to probe too far into historical minutiae in judging them. On the other hand, there is a point at which the accumulation of historical errors begins to diminish the re-creation of the spirit of any past era. Films with an historical setting have a responsibility to represent the past as accurately as possible, and when they insert fictional events and characters, to do it at least plausibly.[1] After all, film has the power to bring history to life and thus to convince. Historical accuracy is especially important for a film like *Gladiator*, whose director, although he warned that his intention was to represent the spirit of the times rather than the letter, promised a scrupulous concern for historical truth.[2] Moreover, the avoidance of historical errors is not incompatible with the creation of a dramatically interesting and enjoyable film. Film makers must remember that they have a special responsibility when they undertake historical subject matter, especially because the average cinemagoer generally assumes that what appears on the screen is at least a reasonable approximation of the period it represents. Historical accuracy in films is not an impossible ideal to attain, but it does require attention to the recommendations of a knowledgeable consultant. Unfortunately, this is an area where film makers often fall short, as in the case of *Gladiator*. It is a disservice to the viewer of a film to flout flagrantly the expectation of historical accuracy. As Kathleen Coleman points out:

> . . . *for those viewers whose reception of history begins and ends with the version presented on screen, Hollywood's Rome is not a palimpsest but an original and ineradicable document.*[3]

Moreover, historical errors in films mislead not only the average cinemagoer but also other film makers, who often naïvely repeat them in their own films.[4]

I will attempt to judge these films fairly, but I have no doubt that at least some of my criticisms will strike the reader as nitpicking, an activity scholars find hard to resist.

The Sign of the Cross (dir. DeMille, 1932)

The Sign of the Cross, the earliest of the films discussed in this chapter, apparently had ambitions of historical authenticity and in fact succeeds in this area to a certain degree. Before the film's depiction of a *munus* sponsored by Nero, it displays an advertisement (*edictum*) for the show in the style of real *edicta*, written in (mostly) grammatical Latin and, with a fade to English, translates it for the audience. This promising beginning seems to augur further historical accuracy, but some confusion follows. The advertisement promises overall sixty pairs of gladiators, thirty 'of the Thracian School' and thirty 'of the School of Murranus'. When these gladiators appear in the arena, we see helmeted gladiators who must be the gladiators from the Thracian school mentioned in the *edictum*. The helmetless gladiators carrying a trident and a net, whom we clearly recognize as *retiarii*, must belong to 'Murranus' School'. We then hear two voices from the crowd, one announcing a bet on a particular *thraex*, and the other, on his opponent, whom he wrongly calls a Gaul. As we have seen, the Gaul had long disappeared from the arena by the reign of Nero (the period of this film) and, although we know almost nothing about this gladiatorial type, he certainly would not have been similar to *retiarius*, the most distinctive of all gladiators. The two spectators are wrong on both counts. The prominent angular crest on the helmets of the '*thraeces*' indicates that they are really *murmillones*; as we have seen, the helmet of the *thraex* had a projecting finial representing a griffin. The mention of a 'Thracian school' is also misleading because gladiatorial schools did not teach just one style of fighting, but all the major styles. The makers of *Sign* had probably chosen these two types of gladiator because of Gérôme's famous painting *Pollice Verso*, which shows a *murmillo* standing over the body of a *retiarius* (Figure 24), but they apparently did not know their correct names. In fact, the choice of the *murmillo* as an opponent of the *retiarius* is not historically incorrect, but in this film, and even in the painting, the *murmillo* fighting a *retiarius* is an anachronism. By the reign of Nero, the *murmillo* had been replaced as the regular opponent of the *retiarius* by the *secutor*, whose head was completely covered by a bowl-like helmet. The *murmillo/retiarius* pairing is even more anachronistic in Gérôme's painting, the setting of which is the Colosseum (dedicated in AD 80).[5] The *secutor* has been consistently ignored by film makers in favour of the *murmillo*. The cause of this omission is not that the *secutor* was unknown outside of scholarly circles. As early as 1913, George Bernard Shaw's play *Androcles and the Lion*, set in the mid-first century AD, included a *retiarius* and a *secutor* as characters and paired them in a match.[6] Chester Erskine's film adaptation of the play (1952), set in the reign of Antoninus Pius (AD 138–161), pays lip service to the pairing of the *retiarius* and the *secutor*, but inexplicably, when these *secutores* appear on screen, their helmets clearly identify them as *murmillones*. There is, however, more at stake here than just historical accuracy. The *secutor*, whose face, with the exception of his eyes, was completely hidden by his helmet, was an ominous, almost inhuman figure, whose presence in film could have significantly enhanced the drama of duels with the *retiarius*.

Beginning Nero's *munus* with gladiatorial combat and not the usual morning *venatio* is another error. Whoever recommended that the film's *munus* should begin with gladiators may have been misled by the order of events given in surviving *edicta*, which is not chronological, but according to importance. *Edicta* mention the number of gladiator pairs first, while the *venatio* appears along with mention of awnings: *venatio et vela erunt* ('there will be a *venatio* and awnings').[7] Of course, DeMille probably wanted the gladiators to appear first for effect, notwithstanding the requirements of history. The gladiators, represented by the voice of one man, give the famous, but, as we have seen, erroneous, greeting to the emperor: 'Hail, Caesar, we who are about to die, salute thee'. This error ranks in popularity and frequency with the use of the thumbs-up gesture for approval and thumbs-down for disapproval. These misrepresentations, however, seem to be impervious to criticism. No gladiator film has been able to avoid them. In the mind of film makers, and therefore of cinemagoers, they have achieved the status of unassailable truth.

When combat starts, all sixty pairs fight at the same time. Group fights did take place in the arena on occasion but never in these large numbers.[8] One hundred and twenty combatants are more appropriate to a staged infantry skirmish, but, as we have seen, valuable professional gladiators never took part in these battles, for which *editores* used convicts and prisoners of war. The largest group fight involving gladiators we hear of consisted of ten gladiators: five pairs of *retiarii* and *secutores*.[9] Although Suetonius and Cassius Dio mention large-scale group fights among gladiators involving even larger numbers than the group fight that appears in *Sign*, these combats consisted not of professionally trained fighters, but of amateurs.[10] Sixty pairs would normally have been presented in individual duels and probably spread out over a five-day period. No *editor* would have wanted to waste his money by presenting so large a number of professional fighters at once in a chaotic situation where the skills of the fighters and the drama of each match could not be fully appreciated. This is especially true of a contest between a sword fighter and a *retiarius*, which had the possibility of a greater variety of action than any other gladiator combination. It is not hard to explain why DeMille substituted group fights for individual duels. For the opening of the *munus*, he must have wanted as much action as possible crammed into the arena, preferring a motion-filled frame to the deliberate movements of one duelling pair.

The rest of the amphitheatre scene involves a *venatio* with *ad bestias* executions and men fighting animals interlarded with two athletic events (boxing and wrestling). In the film's *venatio*, there is nothing that did not, or could not, have taken place in ancient times, except for a nearly naked girl tied to a herm with a Pan's head who is approached threateningly by a gorilla, an ape unknown in Roman times.[11] Unfortunately, the unconvincing gorilla suit makes the scene more laughable than scary. The next event, a *gregatim* gladiatorial combat between women dressed as Amazons and dwarf gladiators (they are called 'barbarian women' and 'pygmies' in the *edictum*), is anachronistic in a film set in the reign of Nero, but forgivably so (this novelty was a creation of the later emperor Domitian). The film captures well the grotesque quality of this fight, although one might question why it is presented during the *venatio*. The end of the film brings us back to the *venatio* when one hundred Christians, including the converted hero (Frederic March) and the heroine (Elissa Landi), enter the arena to face the lions.

The Last Days of Pompeii (dir. Schoedsack, 1935)

The Last Days of Pompeii demonstrates the same predilection for group combat as *Sign*. Combat scenes in the arena start with a *gregatim* fight, in which the hero, Marcus (Preston Foster), participates. He sufficiently distinguishes himself to be promoted to fighting individual duels, but the film shows little interest in this format and presents only brief snippets of duels. In these the hero distinguishes himself as a skilled gladiator. The film uses the format of ancient programmes (*libelli*) listing the gladiator pairs by name (a nice touch) to introduce each stage of Marcus' rise to prominence in the arena. The *libelli* in *Last Days* put to shame the curious representation of a *libellus* in Ridley Scott's *Gladiator*. In Scott's film, a man looks at a programme that has a picture of two fighting gladiators with the title *Gladiatores* at the top and the word *violentia* at the bottom. What use such a 'programme' could have been to any spectator is beyond me. *Demetrius and the Gladiators* does not display a *libellus* on screen, but one of the characters shows a *libellus* to another as proof that Demetrius will fight the next day, an accurate representation of its purpose. *Last Days* also presents an advertisement (*edictum*) for a gladiator show in Latin, but does *Sign* one better by using a real *edictum* (in its original Latin and not translated), appropriately for this film, from Pompeii.[12]

It is clear that the makers of *Last Days* naïvely assumed that gladiatorial combat in ancient Rome was conducted organizationally just like modern boxing. In Marcus' first appearance in an individual bout, he and his opponent are listed as the first fight or, as it would be called in today's boxing vernacular, 'a preliminary bout'. In the next *munus*, Marcus and his opponent are placed at the top of the 'undercard', fighting just before the 'main event'. Marcus' next bout is 'the main event', and after his victory in this fight he is hailed as a 'champion'. After his victory, a *munerarius* throws him a crown, which, as we have seen, was a special prize added to the palm branch and cash, rewarding an outstanding performance. It was not, however, symbolic of winning a championship, like a boxing champion's belt. When he is defeated in his next fight, his opponent, Murmex of Carthage, is hailed as the new 'champion'. The idea of a gladiator 'champion' is of course an anachronism, but the idea has had a long life in gladiator films, as we shall see later. In gladiatorial combat, one gladiator did not reign as champion over all the rest until he was defeated, as in modern boxing. The Romans kept won–lost records, but not to establish an overall ranking system.

The last combat scene in the film returns to the mêlée format, but appropriately so, since it is no doubt intended as a mass capital punishment in which the participants execute each other in the course of the fight. The combat is at least plausible, if unusual, in which a ragtag group of barbarian cavalrymen (Germanic warriors?) fight Christians armed with shields and spears. In this scene, the film commits its worst solecism, although it has nothing to do with gladiatorial combat. The cavalrymen enter the arena between the legs of a colossal statue of a naked gladiator wearing a helmet and modestly holding a sword in front of his crotch. This statue vies in its absurdity with the crouching gargoyle-like statue at one end of the racetrack infield in William Wyler's *Ben Hur* (1959). Both of these ridiculous representations have nothing to do with real Roman art. *Last Days*, however, is to be praised for its depiction of a poor man who, having lost his wife and child, decides that money is the key to happiness and becomes a volunteer gladiator (*auctoratus*) to make his fortune as did so many bankrupts in antiquity. The film emphasizes his growing wealth by showing his accumulation of gold coins (*aurei*), the currency with which real gladiators were rewarded.[13]

Demetrius and the Gladiators (dir. Daves, 1954)

One of the most accurate portrayals of gladiatorial combat can be found in Delmer Daves' *Demetrius and the Gladiators* (1954), a film that was not a great dramatic success. Perhaps the film is almost too determined to provide an historically accurate depiction of gladiators to its audience. In this mission at least, it succeeds admirably. Early in the movie, we see the Christian Demetrius (Victor Mature) in court where he is condemned to a gladiatorial school (*ad ludum*) for assaulting a *decurion* of the Praetorian Guard. As we have seen, those who incurred this penalty were an important source of gladiators in ancient times. Demetrius, along with other convicts, is welcomed to the gladiatorial school by its gruff chief *doctor*, Strabo (Ernest Borgnine), who tells them how lucky they are to have been enrolled in the school of Claudius (the future emperor).[14] The reasons for their good luck provide an opportunity to give some information about gladiators to the audience: the excellent quality of their medical care, good nutrition, the admiration of young women, and the possibility of winning fame, fortune and even freedom by excellent performances. The training at the school itself is accurately depicted. Some trainees practise their sword strokes on the *palus*, while other more experienced gladiators engage in practice duels with wooden or real swords. Action in the arena comes when Claudius (Barry Jones) presents a birthday *munus* for his nephew, the wonderfully evil emperor Caligula (Jay Robinson). The *munus* takes place in an impressive amphitheatre, but the makers of this film avoid the anachronism of suggesting that it was the Colosseum, which was not built until thirty years later. The amphitheatre is identified as a private arena that is part of Caligula's palace complex. There is no record of such an amphitheatre, but it is a plausible invention given Caligula's predilection for gladiators.[15]

On the night before each of the two days of the *munus*, Messalina, Claudius' wife (Susan Hayward), sponsors a *cena libera* (in the film simply referred to as 'a special entertainment') with gourmet foods, the finest wine, prostitutes and gambling. On the first day of the *munus*, there is an impressive procession (*pompa*) of the gladiators (certainly the best in film) into the arena accompanied by musicians playing various kinds of horns. The only blemish is the absence of the sponsor of the show (Claudius) from the parade. As in *Sign* and *Last Days*, the combat begins with a group gladiatorial fight. *Demetrius*, however, avoids creating a large crowd scene of gladiatorial pairs in the arena in the manner of the two earlier films. The *gregatim* fight consists of six pairs of *murmillones* and *retiarii*, only one more pair than the historical group fight mentioned earlier. The only misrepresentation in this combat is that the *retiarii* wear metal caps, whereas real *retiarii* did not wear a helmet.

The next event is a duel between Demetrius and the Nubian Glycon (William Marshall).[16] They both wear a *murmillo*'s helmet, although the *murmillo* was not one of those gladiators who fought an opponent of the same category. The choice of pairing two *murmillones* was probably forced on the film by the desire for variety, since Demetrius as a *murmillo* will later fight a *retiarius*. One, however, should not press this issue too far. As far as 'sword and sandal' films are concerned, there are only two types of gladiator: the *murmillo* and the *retiarius*. The existence of the *thraex* is sometimes acknowledged, but this gladiator type is rarely represented. The film maker's concern for authenticity of pairing in any of these films seems to be satisfied if they follow the example of Gérôme's painting.

Demetrius defeats Glycon, but refuses to obey Caligula's decision to kill his opponent, explaining that he, as a Christian, cannot kill another human being. Caligula releases Glycon, but angered by Demetrius' disobedience, requires that Demetrius fight tigers, all of which he kills. The Romans did not mix gladiatorial combat with the *venatio* and killing tigers was a *venator*'s job, but this abnormality is at least plausible, given Caligula's quirky character and the fact that this was a private performance. On the next day, although Demetrius was not scheduled to fight, he rushes out against Strabo's orders to fight the famous *retiarius* Dardanius (Richard Eagan), who the night before at the *cena libera*, had accidentally killed

Demetrius' girlfriend (Debra Paget). After Demetrius kills Dardanius, events depart even further from historical precedent. Strabo, urged on by Glycon, sends out four more gladiators to fight Demetrius, three of whom fight him all at once.[17] Demetrius kills all of them. The obvious purpose of this display of slaughter is to show graphically how much he now enjoys combat and killing. It also emphatically demonstrates his rejection of Christianity, a renunciation that he declares openly to Caligula in the arena after his victories. This contest between one gladiator and a group of gladiators is the one significant mistake that this film makes. There is no evidence for such a contest and it does not seem possible that one gladiator could defeat three fully armed opponents who attack him at the same time. At least the film suggests to the audience that such a fight is unusual, when one of the gladiators sent out to fight Demetrius protests to Strabo: 'You can't get me out there. You know the rules!' Strabo answers: 'We've changed the rules!'

Spartacus (dir. Kubrick, 1960)

Six years later, Kubrick's *Spartacus* admirably follows in the footsteps of *Demetrius* in its concern for historical accuracy. The film starts by explaining Spartacus' path to the gladiatorial school. After having been sold into slavery in the mines of Libya, he was purchased by the owner of a Capuan gladiator school, Lentulus Batiatus (Peter Ustinov). Spartacus' slavery in the mines is an invention of the screenwriters, but perfectly legitimate in this historical context. With few exceptions, the Capuan scenes at Battiatus' gladiator school show an acute awareness of the historical sources. Like Strabo, the trainer in *Demetrius*, Batiatus delivers a speech to the newly arrived slaves (including Spartacus) that accurately outlines the advantages of becoming a gladiator (sex, massages, decent chance of survival, possible freedom, and so on). Admittedly, the training scenes in the school are overdone, especially in comparison with the simpler and more realistic rendering of a school in *Demetrius*. Oddly, the training scene at the *ludus* omits practice at the *palus*, which was appropriately included in *Demetrius*. The makers of *Spartacus* apparently wanted something more exciting and eye-catching. What we see are elaborate training machines, for which there is no historical evidence. These machines give the impression of noisy and frenetic activity, heightened by similar qualities in Alex North's musical score. For example, there is a revolving dummy head and torso with shield on one arm and a ball and chain attached to the other, and a rotating pole with a bar at shin level and another at head level. The apparent purpose of both machines is to practise the timing of ducking quickly under an opponent's sword swings. On the other hand, the practice matches with wooden swords and the offensive and defensive exercises by the numbers are on a solid historical footing. Best of all, the training scenes, like those in *Demetrius*, give a good overall impression of the professionalism of the gladiators. As Batiatus' chief *magister* says: 'We expect more than simple butchery'.

Visitors to the school from Rome provide an excuse to show gladiators in action. M. Licinius Crassus (Laurence Olivier), accompanied by a female friend, her brother and his fiancée, requests a private display of two gladiator pairs fighting to the death to celebrate the couple's upcoming marriage. Both Crassus and Batiatus are historical personages, but there is no evidence that Crassus ever made such a visit. It is, however, a perfectly plausible fiction. Batiatus, ever concerned with his profits, characteristically objects to the cost of losing two gladiators whom he has trained and maintained. When Crassus, the richest man in Rome, immediately overwhelms Batiatus' objection with his extravagant offer of 25,000 sesterces, the audience realizes what big business the gladiator industry was. The scene in which the two women pick out four gladiators for the two contests emphasizes the powerful sexual attraction of gladiators that is so well attested in the sources. As they look over the various gladiators, the women behave like children in a candy store, leering and whispering in each other's ear, with one woman requesting that the gladiators they choose wear no more than modesty requires.

When it is announced that there will be a fight to the death, Crixus (John Ireland), Spartacus' (Kirk Douglas) closest friend, expresses his fear that he might be matched against him, a real problem that gladiators in the same troupe had to face frequently. Spartacus' response is a reiteration of the gladiator code: if they are paired, they will both try to kill one another. As it turns out, Spartacus is paired not with Crixus but with an Ethiopian *retiarius* named Draba (Woody Strode).[18] It is easy to criticize the pairing of these two gladiators. It is not clear what kind of gladiator Douglas is supposed to represent because he lacks most of the typical gladiatorial armour (except for a small circular shield and a *manica*) that would help us identify the type. Junkelmann is no doubt correct when he suggests that Douglas was intended to represent a *thraex*, since he was an ethnic Thracian.[19] Fik Meijer agrees, but also rightly points out that Spartacus' small round shield and straight sword were not typical implements of the *thraex*.[20] Junkelmann concludes that Douglas should have been outfitted as a *murmillo*, an early opponent of the *retiarius*, but even this adjustment would not have solved the problem entirely. The *retiarius* as a gladiator type did not exist in the period in which this contest is depicted as taking place (73 BC), but only first appeared in the early empire. Douglas' lack of a helmet is also a problem; only the *retiarius* fought without a helmet. The historical inaccuracy here, however, can be forgiven. Kirk Douglas is the star of the film and the drama of the fight would have been lessened if his expressive face had been obscured by a helmet.[21] Actually, since the two duels are part of a private show, perhaps one should not expect the participants to follow the regular practices of the public arena. The fight between Draba and Spartacus is one of the best representations of gladiatorial combat available in any gladiator film. In this combat, we get the sense of two trained professionals applying offensive and defensive techniques in their quest for victory. Despite its small mistakes, *Spartacus* in its gladiatorial scenes has come close to the ideal of historical films: historical accuracy combined with impressive dramatic power.

Barabbas (dir. Fleischer, 1962)

The best candidate as the film with the least historically informed gladiator scenes is Richard Fleischer's *Barabbas*. The first glimpse we get of a gladiatorial show is a chaotic scene in a large arena jam-packed with participants of indeterminate types.[22] The influence of *Sign*'s sixty pairs of gladiators is evident, but *Barabbas* goes one better with what looks like a hundred or more pairs of gladiators fighting on what can only be described as a trident-shaped bridge, partly over burning liquid (probably flaming oil on water) and partly over a den of lions. Gladiators push each other off the bridge into the fire or into the midst of hungry lions. It seems safe to assert that a *munus* even remotely like this one never took place in ancient times. If the gladiatorial combat on the bridge were not enough, there is also a battle going between a much smaller number of dwarfs and female gladiators (also undoubtedly inspired by *Sign*) on what appears to be a representation of a hillside village. Finally, there is a modern circus ring with six elephants going through their paces! This awkward combination of an absurdly massive group combat with the *venatio* is a real distortion of the historical *munus*.

In the gladiator school, there is the normal swordplay practice, but no hint of a *palus*. The film makes much of the revolving dummy torso taken from *Spartacus*. Other unhistorical training machines concocted for *Barabbas* show little relevance to gladiatorial combat beyond general physical conditioning. The training of the *retiarii*, who practise the net-throw with *both* hands, is a notable howler. The real *retiarius* threw the net with his *right* hand while he held the trident in his left. Later, the film reveals the impossibility of this technique in what is the most accurately depicted gladiatorial scene in the film: a fight between the popular pairing of *murmillo* and the *retiarius* Sahak (Vittorio Gassman), who properly fights with the trident in his left hand and the net in his right. This duel is part of a *gregatim* fight on a smaller scale than the first group combat. The film, however, ignores the role that the *editor* (Nero) should play in the life or death decision for a losing gladiator, only to acknowledge it later in the film. In this group combat, a gladiator, not waiting for the decision of the emperor, dispatches his opponent as soon as the crowd gives the thumbs-down signal. Also with no signal from the emperor, Sahak ignores the demand of death for his opponent from the crowd and simply walks out of the arena with impunity.

On the second day of the show, there is a showdown in the arena between Barabbas (Anthony Quinn) and his nemesis, the famous gladiator Torvald (Jack Palance).[23] The confrontation, however, is a bizarre concoction that has nothing to do with real gladiatorial combat, departing completely from historical precedent.[24] In this contest, Torvald, driving a chariot and carrying a net, faces three men (the third of whom is Barabbas), each with a spear, one at a time. The first two miss Torvald with their spear-throw as he charges at full speed at them. He catches both in his net, dragging one to his death and running over the other. Barabbas, however, is more successful. He uses his spear to get the net away from Torvald and captures him in it. Torvald is injured badly as his own chariot drags him in the net. *Barabbas* at least avoids gross errors at the end of this climactic scene. Barabbas looks to the crowd which gives the thumbs-down signal and then to the emperor, who does the same. Barabbas kills Torvald with a sword, and as a result, receives the *rudis*, released from his obligation to fight the arena ever again.

Gladiator (dir. Scott, 2000)

Ridley Scott's *Gladiator* seemed poised to redeem the historical inaccuracies of previous gladiator films. The digital re-creation of the Colosseum in fact is a great success, showing the result of careful research and presentation. The makers of the film initially showed such concern for historical correctness that they hired one of the best available consultants, Kathleen Coleman of Harvard University. Unfortunately, they did not take advantage of her expert services.[25] The result is numerous errors that could easily have easily been avoided with Coleman's help. One prominent mistake is the claim by one of the characters in the film that Marcus Aurelius had banned gladiatorial combat. As we have seen, when Aurelius served as *editor*, he did require that gladiators fight with blunted weapons, but any objection that Aurelius had to this kind of spectacle did not prevent his making sure that *munera* would be given at Rome during his absence on the Danube frontier.[26]

There are five arena scenes in *Gladiator*, two in Zucchabar, a non-existent Roman 'province' in North Africa, and three in the Colosseum in Rome.[27] From the beginning the film reveals itself incapable of avoiding the traditional cinematic preference for group fighting, dating back to the *Sign of the Cross*. The first three combat scenes in *Gladiator* involve *gregatim* fighting. We do not see a gladiatorial duel until the last two events. In the first North African episode, things seem to get off to a good start. We see three gladiators warming up, an historical practice of gladiators before combat (*prolusio*), but the film's problems with historical accuracy quickly come to the fore. Junkelmann's characterization of the armour in *Gladiator* as 'pure fantasy à la Conan the Barbarian' is blatantly evident in this scene.[28] The first gladiator, wearing a steer's head instead of a helmet, waves a sword while the two other helmeted gladiators brandish medieval weapons: one wields a mace and the other a flail.[29] These three are part of a group of gladiators who will take on the hero Maximus (Russell Crowe) and his comrades, who are given weapons but not gladiatorial armour. They are chained together, which suggests that they are *damnati*, but they do not fight each other as *damnati* normally do. Instead they find themselves required to fight a group of professional gladiators, including the three mentioned above and a *retiarius*, who wrongly wears a helmet. Professional gladiators would have never been required to fight a group of untrained *damnati*.

The second combat in Zucchabar is even odder. Maximus, outfitted not as a gladiator but as a soldier with a corselet, is matched against five gladiators, who do not attack as a group, but one at a time. Their good manners allow Maximus to kill all five. This fight is a familiar staple of many a martial arts movie, and utterly alien to the Roman arena.[30] This scene is reminiscent of the one discussed earlier in *Demetrius*, in which the hero kills five opponents one after the other. The important difference is that *Gladiator* offers this scene without comment, giving the false impression that a contest of one gladiator against multiple opponents is a normal practice in the arena.[31]

The next arena event is the re-creation of the battle of Zama, the decisive contest in the second Punic War, which takes place in the Colosseum. Battle re-creations were popular as the film suggests, but, as mentioned earlier, trained gladiators did not take part in them. The film at least recognizes the problem. When Proximo (Oliver Reed), Maximus' *lanista*, comments on this misuse of his men, the film attempts a plausible explanation.[32] A representative of the emperor points out to Proximo that they are needed because of a scarcity of convicts. The substitution of gladiators for convicts in this case is not that objectionable because the actual battle is not on the scale of the massed infantry skirmishes given by Julius Caesar, Augustus and Claudius, but a relatively small fight on the dimensions of the typical gladiator *gregatim* contest.

Another problem is the involvement of the Roman army in this spectacle. Generally, staged battle enactments were between armies about whom the Roman audience could be neutral, probably because spectators undoubtedly would be displeased to see fighters representing the Romans lose a battle to an enemy. There is a comment from Commodus (Joaquin Phoenix) on this second oddity, when the 'Romans' lose the battle to the Carthaginians. Could the makers of this film be indulging in an in-joke, anticipating pedantic concerns about historical accuracy? Among all recorded battle re-creations, there was only one that involved the Roman army: Claudius' troops storming a British town. On that occasion, history was repeated with a Roman victory. No emperor, not even Commodus, would have tolerated even the possibility of a Roman loss. The film descends into complete nonsense when 'the Roman legionnaires' come into the arena to face Maximus and his men portraying 'the barbarian horde' (i.e., the Carthaginians). The Roman army turns out to be what appears to be female chariot fighters (*essedariae*) using bow and arrows and spears), a form of warfare that was used by the Britons against the Romans in Caesar's day but never employed by the Romans. The armament of the Maximus' comrades with their pointed helmets and chain mail seems acceptable as a generic representation of the Cartagians, but Maximus' armor vaguely suggests that of a Roman soldier.

Another problem in this scene is the apparent confusion of the amphitheatre with the Roman circus (racetrack). For this skirmish, the arena is set up almost as a racetrack outlined by bullet-shaped pillars on which chariots run circling Maximus and his men who are located in the 'infield'. These pillars resemble *metae* or 'goals', which did not outline the ancient racetrack as here, but in groups of three marked both ends of the infield of a Roman racetrack. Of course, the biggest mistake is placing the *metae* in the amphitheatre at all.[33] Chariot racing took place in a structure called a *circus* (for example, the Circus Maximus), not in an amphitheatre. This confusion perhaps can be traced back to the arena scene in Mervyn Leroy's *Quo Vadis?* (1951), which, for some unfathomable reason, merges the amphitheatre and the Circus Maximus into one structure. In that film, Nero has Christians thrown to the lions in the arena of a huge stone amphitheatre that has a vast built-up infield, suggesting a racetrack. The viewer can see only one end of the infield, on which are clearly visible three conical pillars topped with egg-like objects, an excellent representation of the *metae*. Presumably, three more *metae* would have been located at the other (unseen) end of the infield.

The final two gladiatorial events in the Colosseum at last present Maximus in a duel, but even these two contests are marred by historical inaccuracy. The first duel is between Maximus and Tigris of Gaul, who is announced as 'the only undefeated champion in Roman history', returning after five years in retirement. The return from retirement has a solid historical basis: *rudiarii* often went back to the arena, lured by substantial cash payments. I have already discussed the anachronism of the 'champion gladiator', which also appears in *Quo Vadis? Gladiator* wanders even further from history when the match turns into a combination of gladiatorial combat with the *venatio*, obviously inspired by the same scene in *Demetrius and the Gladiators*. As Tigris and Maximus fight, arena attendants release tigers on chains through trapdoors. One tiger attacks Maximus, who kills it. Another problem with this contest is the weapon that eventually determines victory. Tigris has a second weapon, a battleaxe in his left hand.[34] When he drops it, Maximus (on the ground) picks it up and drives it into Tigris' foot. The Roman army on occasion did use battleaxes, but there is no evidence of gladiators using them in the arena. The quality of the fighting in this duel (and throughout the film) reveals nothing of the gladiator art, but is blatantly, to borrow Allen Ward's appropriate phrase, of the 'flail and hack' school.[35] The second duel is the climactic event in the film in which Maximus kills Commodus and then dies of a wound inflicted by a dagger which Commodus had treacherously concealed in his corselet. There is nothing wrong with screenwriters concocting a gladiatorial match between an historical character (Commodus) and a fictional character (Maximus) as long has it has historical plausibility. This quality is sorely missed, however, in this scene. First, the idea that the Romans would tolerate the determination of who would rule the empire by victory in a gladiator match is patently ridiculous. Moreover, although Commodus loved gladiatorial combat and performed as a gladiator both in private and in public, the likelihood that he would have voluntarily faced a 'champion' gladiator in a match with real weapons is non-existent. As we have seen, when Commodus used real weapons, he fought servants in his palace, wounding some and killing some of these easy victims. When he appeared in public as a gladiator and fought real gladiators, he used a wooden sword while his professional opponents were limited to some kind of wooden stick. This mistake is due to the fact that *Gladiator*, which is practically a remake of *The Fall of the Roman Empire* (dir. Mann, 1964), adopts portions of the plot of that film almost as if it were a real historical source. The climax of *The Fall* is a duel (with spears and not swords) between Commodus (Christopher Plummer) and Livius (Stephen Boyd), Marcus Aurelius' adopted son (like Maximus, a fictional character) and his preference as successor. Both Livius and Maximus kill Commodus in their respective duels, but do not succeed him.[36] Both films wisely stop short of revising history that drastically.

In all fairness, however, it should be pointed out that *Gladiator* did capture the big picture in its representation of the life of a gladiator. Perhaps the most significant success is the film's emphasis on the redemption that was available to the gladiator as illustrated in the fictional story of Maximus.[37] After Marcus Aurelius designated Maximus as his successor, the jealousy of Commodus, who had naturally expected to succeed his father, led him to have Maximus' wife and son murdered and condemn Maximus to a life of slavery.[38] Maximus, however, takes advantage of the opportunity to redeem himself through his courageous performances as a gladiator and reaches a point where he can again challenge Commodus for the throne. To be sure, such an extreme reversal of fortune would have been unlikely in real life, but it is only an exaggeration of a basic truth about the life of a gladiator, which offers, however remote, the possibility of redemption. Maximus, with his death, falls tragically short of complete success, but distinguishes himself as a courageous hero, willing to risk his life, no matter what the odds, to fulfil the demands of martial virtue.

Notes

Preface

1 Donald Kyle in his *Spectacles of Death in Ancient Rome* (London and New York) ix reports that he took a similar path to this topic.
2 The *Interactive Ancient Mediterranean* website provides useful information about the format of references to ancient authors and lists of abbreviations: http://iam.classics.unc.edu/main/help/A.html.

Chapter 1 Cultural Context and Origins of Gladiatorial Combat

1 This dream, like her two other dreams, are found in a work of anonymous authorship called the *Passio Perpetuae et Felicitatis* (*Passion of Perpetua and Felicity*) 4; 7; 10. Most scholars agree that the accounts of these three dreams were written by Perpetua herself. See Robert Rousselle, 'The Dreams of Vibia Perpetua: An Analysis of a Female Christian Martyr', *The Journal of Psychohistory* 14 (1987) 194. Although Thomas Heffernan (*Sacred Biography: Saints and their Biographers in the Middle Ages* (New York, 1988) 200; 202) places the *Passion* 'within a sphere of textual/historical indeterminacy', he nonetheless says that Perpetua's dreams are probably genuine. For introduction, Latin text and English translation of the *Passion*, see Herbert Musurillo, *The Acts of the Christian Martyrs* (Oxford, 1972) xxv–xxvii and 116–19 (10).
2 See Georges Ville, *La Gladiature en occident des origines à la mort de Domitien* (Paris, 1981) 276, n. 107. Perpetua calls this figure a *lanista* ('owner-trainer of gladiator troupe'), which Ville says is an incorrect use of the word, although he does point out that *lanista* may have had the metaphorical meaning of 'referee' as seems to be the case in a passage from Cicero's thirteenth *Philippic* (40). Peter Dronke's identification (following von Franz) of this figure as an African priest of Saturn and his rod as the wand of Hermes is much less convincing. See his *Women Writers of the Middle Ages: A Critical Study of Texts from Perpetua (+203) to Marguerite Porete (+1310)* (Cambridge, 1984) 14. The outfit of the

lanista most closely resembles that of a referee of a gladiator match, as can be seen most clearly in Figures 18 and 23 in Chapter 3.

3 See Brent Shaw, 'The Passion of Perpetua', *Past and Present*, 139 (May 1993) 28, n. 63.

4 Shaw ('Passion', 28, n. 62) says that the Egyptians were the most hated ethnic group in the ancient world and interprets Perpetua's description of the Egyptian ('foul in appearance') as referring to the dark skin of Egyptians, which he sees as a racist satanic reference. Jan Den Boeft and Jan Bremmer ('*Notiunculae Martyrologicae II*' *Vigiliae Christianae* 36 (1982) 390) also connect the Egyptian with the Devil. They point out that the popular image of the Devil in the early third century AD was black skinned. Joyce Salisbury (*Perpetua's Passion: The Death and Memory of a Young Roman Woman* (New York, 1997) 110) omits any reference to skin colour (as does Perpetua) and suggests that Perpetua's demonizing of the Egyptian derives from his homeland's association with pagan wisdom.

5 See Dronke, *Women Writers*, 15. Tertullian, speaking on behalf of martyrs, notes the irony of a martyr's victory: 'Therefore we have conquered, when we are put to death; we go forth [to victory], when we are defeated' (*Apol.* 50.3).

6 *Pass. Perpet. et Felic.* 10.13–14. The gladiator seems to have been an important symbolic figure for pagan dreamers in the Greco-Roman world. Artemidorus in his *Interpretation of Dreams* discusses what dreams of fighting various types of gladiator meant. In all instances but one, the gladiator type in the dream provides a forecast of the kind of wife the dreamer will marry. For example, if he dreams of fighting a *thraex* ('Thracian'), he will marry a wife who is wealthy, cunning and ambitious. According to Artemidorus, her wealth is indicated by the fact that the *thraex* was covered with armour. The wife is cunning because the *thraex*'s sword is not straight, and ambitious because the *thraex* always moves forward (2.32).

7 See Daniel Boyarin, 'Martyrdom and the Making of Christianity and Judaism', *Journal of Early Christian Studies* 6.4 (1998) 615 and n. 119; C. Barton, 'Savage Miracles: The Redemption of Lost Honor in Roman Society and the Sacrament of the Gladiator and the Martyr', *Representations* 45 (Winter 1994), 56–8; Leonard Thompson, 'The Martyrdom of Polycarp: Death in the Roman Games, *Journal of Religion* 82.1 (2002) 42–3; Salisbury, *Perpetua's Passion*, 55.

8 This translation is from Musurillo, *Acts*, 75.

9 'Passion', 29.

10 *Ad martyr.* 3.3–5. Eusebius, a fourth century AD historian of the early Church, compares the martyr Porphyrios to a pancratiast (*De martyribus Palaestinae* 11.19).

11 Petron. 117.5.

12 *Pass. Perpet. et Felic.* 18.2.

13 Pliny. *HN* 11.144. The power that a fixed gaze can exert over an opponent can be seen in Mucius Scaevola's intense stare at the Etruscan king Porsenna as he held his hand in a fire to demonstrate his contempt for pain (Plut. *Public.* 17.24). See Barton, 'Savage Miracles', 48–9.

14 Actually, the *Passion* merely says 'in the usual place', which scholars have assumed (rightly) to be the *spoliarium*. David Bomgardner ('The Carthage Amphitheatre: A Reappraisal', *AJA* 93.1 (1989) 89–90; 102) places the *spoliarium* in a subterranean chamber of the amphitheatre. The same is true of the *spoliaria* at Capua and Puteoli. At Rome and Praeneste, the *spoliarium* seems to have been a separate facility. See, Donald Kyle, *Spectacles of Death in Ancient Rome* (London, 1998) 158–9.

15 Sen. *Ep.* 93.12.

16 *Ep.* 30.8.

17 Another important 'gladiatorial' painting of the period is Simeon Solomon's *Habet!* (1865), which was inspired by contemporary interest in gladiators and Roman life. It depicts six aristocratic women, a female slave, and a child watching a gladiator match (unseen). The title refers to the shout of the Roman crowd when a gladiator wounded his opponent. The painting shows the different reactions (including a dead faint) of these spectators to this important moment in a match. The painting was forgotten after it was sold at Christie's in 1891 and only resurfaced in a private collection in the early 1990s. See Elizabeth Prettejohn, ' "The monstrous diversion of a show of gladiators:" Simeon Solomon's *Habet!*', in Catherine Edwards (ed.), *Roman Presences: Receptions of Rome in European Culture, 1789–1945* (Cambridge, 1999) 157, n. 1.

18 Margaret Malamud, 'Roman Entertainments for the Masses in Turn-of-the-Century New York', *CW* 95 (Fall 2001) 50–4.

19 *Ep.* 6.34.

20 Funeral *munera* did not necessarily take place at the time of the funeral and burial. In many cases, they were given some time afterwards, sometimes even years later. See F. Meijer, *The Gladiators: History's Most Deadly Sport*, trans. Liz Waters (New York, 2005) 26.

21 *La Gladiature*, 72–8.

22 Aristocratic *editores* looked upon the expense of producing a *munus* or any other spectacle as a civic responsibility in keeping with their high status in society: a gift pure and simple to their fellow citizens. We do hear of *munera* being used as a source of revenue outside of Rome in Cirta (Numidia) (*CIL* VIII.6695), probably by the state. Vitruvius mentions that charging for luxury seating in balconies attached to the upper part of public buildings (ancient sky boxes?), produced revenue for cities in Italy (*De arch.* 5.1.2) There are reports of Caligula charging for seats at spectacles, but this may have only been an emergency measure in a time of state bankruptcy (Cass. Dio 59.14.1; Suet. *Calig.* 26.4; 38). Imperial legislation of AD 177–180 mentions *munera assiforana* ('gladiator shows for profit') but these were small-time affairs given by travelling troupes of gladiators, much like a modern carnival (*ILS* 5163.29).

23 For tomb paintings, see Ville, *La Gladiature*, 20–35. Campania extended west from central Italy to the coast of southern Italy, including such famous cities as Capua, Cumae and Naples.

24 *Pun.* 11.51–4. See also Livy 9.40.17 and Strabo 5.4.13.

25 See W. G. Runciman's review article of K. Hopkins' *Death and Renewal*, 'The Sociologist and the Historian', *JRS* 76 (1986) 260.

26 Tac. *Hist.* 2.95.

27 See Ludwig Friedländer, *Roman Life and Manners under the Early Empire*, seventh enlarged and revised edition of *Sittengeschichte Roms*, trans. J. H. Freese and Leonard A. Magnus, II (London and New York, 1908–13) 42.

28 'The Contagion of the Throng: Absorbing Violence in the Roman World', *Hermathena* 164 (1998) 78–9.

29 Epict. *Dissertationes ab Arriano digestae* 3.15.5; *Ench.* 29.3.

30 *Das Spiel mit dem Tod: So Kämpften Roms Gladiatoren* (Mainz am Rhein, 2000) 11.

31 *Pis.* 65.

32 *Fam.* 7.1.1–3.

33 Cicero had attended these games, but probably only to avoid giving offence to Pompey.

34 *Att.* 2.1.1. In this passage, Cicero is no doubt alluding to Lucilius, a second century BC satirist, who reports that he left Rome to avoid the city while a *munus* in memory of the great general Metellus Macedonicus was going on. See *Remains of Old Latin*, ed. and trans. E. H. Warmington (Cambridge, MA, 1938) 3, 636–7.

35 2.41. Cicero's indecision may be purely rhetorical here, because it suits his argument at this point.

36 For example, Lucian, *Demon.* 57 and *Anach.* 37; Philostr. *VA* 4.22; Plut. *De soll. an.* 959 C.

37 Cass. Dio 71.29.3.

38 *Senatus Consultum de sumptibus ludorum gladiatorum minuendis, ILS* 5163.

39 Hor. *Sat.* 2.6.44.

40 *Dial.* 29.3.

41 *De spect.* 12.1–4. Servius, a fourth century AD commentator on the works of Virgil, notes the same 'progress' claimed by Tertullian from human sacrifice at the tomb to the less cruel practice of gladiatorial combat (*ad Aen.* 10.519).

42 *Blood in the Arena: The Spectacle of Roman Power* (Austin, TX, 1997) 205–10. See also Lintott, *Violence in Republican Rome* (Oxford, 1968) 40 and Peter Connolly, *Colosseum: Rome's Arena of Death* (London, 2003) 68–9.

43 *Emperors and Gladiators* (London and New York 1995) 34.

44 See also Donald Kyle, *Spectacles of Death*, 40 and D. S. Potter, 'Entertainers in the Roman Empire', in D. S. Potter and D. J. Mattingly (eds), *Life, Death, and Entertainment in the Roman Empire* (Ann Arbor 1999) 305–7.

45 *Blood*, 110.

46 *Ibid.* 4.

47 David Magie, *Roman Rule in Asia Minor, to the End of the Third Century after Christ* (Princeton, NJ, 1950) 1, 127.

48 J. E. Lendon has presented telling objections to Futrell's theories in his review article 'Gladiators' in *CJ* 95.4 (2000) 402–4.

49 *Conquerors and Slaves* (Cambridge, 1978) 208.

50 *Rituals and Power: Roman Imperial Cult in Asia Minor* (Cambridge, 1984) 89.

51 *Blood*, 213. See Edmondson, 'Dynamic Arenas: Gladiatorial Presentations in the City of Rome and the Construction of Roman Society during the Early Empire', in W. J. Slater (ed.), *Roman Theater and Society* (Ann Arbor, MI, 1996) 72; Skinner, *Sexuality in Greek and Roman Culture* (Malden, MA, 2005) 210.

52 See also Kyle, *Spectacles of Death*, 43; Meijer, *The Gladiators*, 24.

53 M. Clavel-Lévêque, *L'Empire en jeux: espace symbolique et pratique sociale dans le monde romain* (Paris, 1984) 79.

54 Michael Poliakoff, *Combat Sports in the Ancient World: Competition, Violence, and Culture* (New Haven, CT, 1987) 155.

55 Val. Max. 2.4.6.

56 *Gryphus*, 36–7; Serv. *ad Aen.* 3.67. Ausonius' identification of these gladiators as *thraeces* (Thracians) is anachronistic. The *thraex* did not exist at this very early period. See Futrell, *Blood*, 22.

57 Serv. *ad Aen.* 10.519.

58 Cic. *Pis.* 19.

59 *Gryphus* 37.

60 *Spectacles of Death*, 47–9.

61 'Gladiators and Blood Sport', in Martin Winkler (ed.), *Gladiator: Film and History* (Malden, MA, 2004) 80.

62 Frag. 84.6–7.

63 *La Gladiature*, 2.

64 For example, see Potter, 'Entertainers in the Roman Empire', in Potter and Mattingly (eds), *Life*, 305; Jean-Claude Golvin, *L'Amphithéâtre romain: essai sur la théorisation de sa forme et de ses functions* (Paris, 1988) 15; Keith Hopkins and Mary Beard, *The Colosseum* (Cambridge, MA, 2005) 119.

65 *Op.* 654–7.

66 Mark Golden, *Sport and Society in Ancient Greece* (Cambridge, 1998) 91–3.

67 *Il.* 23.798–825.

68 *Sport and Society*, 92–3.

69 It has been suggested that the gladiators used in the first *munus* were prisoners of war who marched in D. Junius Brutus Pera's triumphal procession. See *RE* 10.1 (1914): 1026, 59. No record of Pera's political and military achievements has survived, but to be honoured in this public and novel way indicated that he was a man of importance, who probably had distinguished himself in war and politics, the only careers open to a Roman noble. All we can say for certain is that he belonged to one of the most prominent aristocratic families of the Roman Republic. His son Decimus, one of the givers of the *munus* in his honour, two years before the funeral had been a consul and had been granted the great

honour of a triumph for his victories in northern and southern Italy. Other notable members of the Junian family: L. Junius Brutus, an ancestor who, according to legend, played an important role in the creation of the Republic; M. Junius Pera, a descendant of Pera, who, later in the third century, was appointed to the office of dictator, a constitutional magistracy of limited duration, which was given in times of crisis to Rome's most trusted citizens; and M. Junius Brutus, leader of the assassins of Julius Caesar.

70 'Das Ende der Gladiatorenspiele', *Nikephoros* 8 (1995) 151.

71 *La Gladiature*, 9–19.

72 Johan Huizinga *Homo Ludens: A Study of the Play Element in Culture* (New York, 1970) 26, 30, 32, 47.

73 Allen Guttmann, 'Roman Sports Violence', in Jeffrey Goldstein (ed.), *Sports Violence* (New York, 1983) 9.

74 Pierre Cagniart, 'The Philosopher and the Gladiator', *CW* 93 (2000) 607–10.

75 Sen. *Ep.* 7.3–4.

76 *Homo*, 40–1.

77 *Death and Renewal* (Cambridge, 1983) 29.

78 'Contagion', 70.

79 *Violence*, 36.

80 Livy 28.20.6–7. It should be noted here that even in modern times the killing of non-combatants has been seen as an unpleasant necessity when in World War II the Allies bombed German cities and the Americans dropped atom bombs on Hiroshima and Nagasaki.

81 Polyb. 6.38.1–4. The word 'decimation' comes from *decimus*, 'tenth'.

82 Plut. *Crass.* 10.2.

83 Ulp. *Dig.* 50.17.32.

84 *Cod. Theod.* 2.25.1.

85 *SHA Hadr.* (Aelius Spartianus) 18.8.

86 The usual site of abandonment of slaves was an island in the Tiber dedicated to Aesculapius, the god of healing (Suet. *Claud.* 25.2). As inhuman as this abandonment was, at least the reason why masters abandoned their slaves on Aesculapius' island seems to have been their hope that this healing god would cure their illnesses and infirmities.

87 Modest., *Dig.* 48.8.11.1–2.

88 Tac. *Ann.* 14.42–5.

89 *Ep.* 3.14. American slave owners could be as cruel as the Romans. During the Revolutionary War, one slave owner punished a 15-year-old girl for seeking independence with the British army, with eighty lashes, which he followed up by putting hot embers into her wounds (*The New Yorker*, Jill Lepore, 'Goodbye Columbus', 8 May 2006, 74.) Although the Romans never abolished slavery even in Christian times, Roman law eventually outlawed traditional practices that were considered inhumane.

90 *Slavery and Social Death: A Comparative Study* (Cambridge, MA, 1982) 337.

91 See Friedländer, *Roman Life*, II. 78.

92 See Lintott, *Violence*, 43–4. This attitude seems to be related to the principle of law that lower-class citizens deserve harsher punishment than the upper classes for the same crime. Seventeenth century England was not that different from ancient Rome in this regard. See Thomas Macaulay, *The History of England, from the Accession of James the Second*, I, ch. 3.

93 *Clem.* 2.5.1. See Magnus Wistrand, *Entertainment and Violence in Ancient Rome: The Attitudes of Roman Writers of the First Century* A.D. (Gothenburg, Sweden, 1992) 19–20.

94 *Emperors*, 92–3.

95 *Ibid.* 35.

96 *Entertainment*, 15–16 and 18–20. See also Katherine Welch ('The Roman Arena in Late-Republican Italy: a New Interpretation', *JRA* 7 (1994) 80), who calls martial virtue 'a key ingredient of the Roman self-image'.

97 *Leisure and Ancient Rome* (Cambridge, MA, 1995) 35.

98 2.10.2–13. In Polybius' version of the story (6.55.3), Horatius is killed.

99 Livy 2.12.13–15. This story explains the origin of Mucius' cognomen Scaevola ('Lefty').

100 Hor. *Carm.* 3.5.13–56.

101 Livy 8.9.6–14.

102 See Keith Hopkins, *Death*, 29, who views the arena as an image of the battlefield.

103 *Emperors*, 36–7.

104 'Single Combat in the Roman Republic', *CQ* NS 35.2 (1985) 392–410.

105 *Tusc. Disp.* 2.41. Cicero is undoubtedly indulging in hyperbole in this passage. Indeed, gladiators were taught to be courageous, but it stands to reason that there were some who did not live up to Cicero's high standards.

106 51.7.2–6.

107 Plut. *Cic.* 48.3–4.

108 *Ep.* 30.8.

109 *Ep.* 26.10; 70.6; 77.6; *Ira* 15.4; *Tranq.* 11.4; *Q Nat.* 2.59.3; 6.32.4. See Cagniart, 'The Philosopher and the Gladiator', 611–18.

110 *Pan.* 33.1. For gladiatorial combat as stimulation to virtue for young men in the Greek east, see Livy 41.20.12.

111 *Max et Balb.* 8.7.

112 'Les Jeux de gladiateurs dans l'empire chrétien', *Mélanges d'archéologie et d'histoire* 72 (1960) 304–5.

113 *Tranq.* 3.2; 11.4.

114 Sen. *Prov.* 2.8.

115 Livy 9.40.17.

116 Quint. *Decl. Min.* 305.17.

117 The Gauls had sacked Rome in 390 BC and remained a danger until they were defeated by Julius Caesar in the middle of the first century BC. By the imperial period they were thoroughly romanized.

118 In Latin, the name of this gladiatorial type was spelled *thraex* or *threx* to differentiate the gladiator from an ethnic Thracian (*Thrax*).

119 Flor. *Epit.* 2.8; Oros. *Hist. adv. pag.* 5.24.

120 Cass. Dio 68.32.2.

121 *ILS* 5085.

122 As Carlin Barton ('Savage Miracles', 52) points out, '[gladiators] inspired both worship and disgust, emulation and loathing, sympathy and revulsion'.

123 *The Game of Death in Ancient Rome* (Madison, WI, 1995) 10.

124 41.20.11–13.

125 Quint. *Decl. Min.* 279.8.

126 August. *Conf.* 6.8.

127 Plin., *Ep.* 1.8.10 and Sen. *Tranq.* 2.14.

128 *Publ. Spect.*, 5.

129 Suet. *Claud.* 34.1–2.

130 *Pass. Perpet. et Felic.* 21.7.

131 *De spect.* 21.4.

132 *Resp.* 439e–440a. See K. M. Coleman, 'Fatal Charades: Roman Executions Staged as Mythological Enactments', *JRS* 80 (1990) 58.

133 *The History of England*, I, ch. 3.

134 *Roman Life*, IV, 192–3.

135 'The Martyrdom of Polycarp', 30–1.

136 45.6.

137 *Tranq.* 2.13.

138 Livy 39.42.8–12.

139 Dio Chrys. *Or.* 31.122 and S. R. F. Price, *Rituals and Power*, 88.

140 *Tox.* 59.

141 *Panegyr.* 34.4.

142 As, for example, the heavy-handed censure of gladiatorial combat found throughout Michael Grant's *Gladiators: The Bloody Truth* (New York, 2000, reprint of 1971 edition): 'The constant recurrence of this bloodthirstiness throughout long centuries is one of the most appalling manifestations of evil that the world has ever known' (105).

143 Quoted by Elizabeth Prettejohn, 'The monstrous diversion of a show of gladiators: Simeon Solomon's *Habet!*', in C. Edwards (ed.), *Roman Presences*, 171. See also Christopher Kelly, 'Corruption', in Simon Hornblower and Antony Spawforth (eds), *Oxford Classical Dictionary*, 3rd edn (Oxford, 1996) and Bomgardner, *The Story of the Roman Amphitheatre* (London, 2000), 226–7.

144 'The Ideology of the Arena', *Classical Antiquity* 15 (1996) 122–3.

145 Wistrand, *Entertainment*, 15 and Meijer, *The Gladiators*, 8.

146 See 'Violence in Media Entertainment', 'http://www.media-awareness.ca/english/issues/violence/violence_entertainment.cfm.

147 'Contagion', 80.

148 There was also a big-game fishing component to the show; http://sports.espn .go.com/outdoors/tv/columns/story?columnist=gowdy_curt&page=g_col_ gowdy_sportsman. Ancient fans of the *venatio* clearly had the advantage in the matter of excitement over the viewers of this TV show. The ancient arena hunter clearly put himself in much greater danger than the modern hunter, whose high-powered rifle virtually assures success with minimum risk.

149 *Get Wild with Cindy Garrison* on ESPN 2. See http://sports.espn.go.com/ espn/print?id=2251147&type=story. Bullfighting, most likely a direct descendant of the *venatio*, seems to be approaching its last days, even in Spain.

Chapter 2 Recruitment and Training of Gladiators

1 *Tusc.* 2.41.

2 Cicero calls these convicts *sontes*, a group elsewhere in this book referred to as *noxii* or *damnati*. All three words are synonymous.

3 Plin. *Ep.* 10.31.2. See Magie, *Roman Rule*, II, 604–5. A public slave was owned by the state rather than by a private individual.

4 Ulp. *Dig.* 48.19.8.11–12.

5 Suet. *Vit.* 12.1.

6 Ville, *La Gladiature*, 240.

7 The Romans connected the word *lanista* with *lanius* ('butcher'), a term of Etruscan origin.

8 *Ben.* 6.12.2.

9 87.15. See Juv. 3.156–8.

10 *Spartacus: A New Edition with a Special Introdution by the Author* (Armonk, NY, 1996) 170.

11 See Chapter 3 ('Spartacus: Testing the Strength of the Body Politic') in Maria Wyke's *Projecting the Past: Ancient Rome, Cinema and History* (New York, 1997) 34–72 for a thorough discussion of the novels, plays and films that Spartacus has inspired.

12 Flor. *Epit.* 2.8.

13 *Ibid*; Oros. *Hist. adv. pag.* 5.24.

14 *Leg. Agr.* 2.95.

15 *ILS* 5062.

16 *B Civ*, 1.14.116.

17 *Crass.* 8–9.1. Well over a century later during Nero's reign, there was an attempted breakout at a school in Praeneste (modern Palaestrina, just east of Rome), which was put down by its military guard. Ville (*La Gladiature*, 284, n. 134) points out that, since this school had a military guard, it was probably an imperial gladiatorial school (private gladiatorial schools had no such protection). Like the rebellion of Spartacus, the Praenestine breakout indicates that the school contained convicts and prisoners of war kept under lock and key.

18 *Crass.* 8.1; *Mor.* 997 C.

19 Other Greek intellectuals took a similarly dim view of gladiatorial combat, for example Demonax (Lucian, *Demon.* 57). See also Dio Chrys. *Or.* 31.121. Both sources are contemporary with Plutarch. See Robert, *Les Gladiateurs*, 239–48.

20 Plut. *Crass.* 9.9–11.11. For the crucifixion of Spartacus' army, see App. *B Civ.* 1.14.120. For distance between crosses, see Brent Shaw, *Spartacus and the Slave Wars: A Brief History with Documents* (Boston, 2001) 144, n. 8. Plutarch does not mention this punishment, but credits Pompey, who had just arrived from Spain, with slaughtering the remainder of Spartacus' army (*Crass.* 11.11).

21 These two fighters no doubt belonged to the category of gladiators called *equites* ('horsemen').

22 Shaw, *Spartacus*, 15.

23 *Crass.* 8.2. See Shaw, *Spartacus*, 131. Batiatus' official Roman name was probably Cn. Cornelius Lentulus Vatia. The name Batiatus only appears in Plutarch, a Greek source, which substitutes *B* for *V* and adds a suffix. The confusion of *B* and *V* is a familiar linguistic phenomenon in the empire. See E. H. Sturtevant, *The Pronunciation of Greek and Latin: The Sounds and Accents* (Chicago, 1920) 87; 142–3.

24 J. A. Crook, *Law and Life* (Ithaca, NY, 1967) 83 and C. Edwards, 'Unspeakable Professions', 67.

25 Crook, *Law*, 83–5.

26 'Unspeakable Professions', 67. See also Ville, *La Gladiature*, 462–3.

27 Hor. *Epist.* 1.18.36.

28 11.20.

29 Sen. *Con.* 10.4.18. Tacitus also reports that towns throughout Italy offered lavish compensation to equestrian youth as an inducement to fight in the arena (*Hist.* 2.62).

30 Sen. *Ep.* 99.13.

31 Quint. *Decl. Min.* 260.22.

32 *Tib.* 35.3.

33 *La Gladiature*, 227.

34 See Manil. 4.224–9 and Tert. *Ad mart.* 5.1. Wiedemann (*Emperors*, 109), however, is sceptical about the boredom motive. He proposes that peacetime longing for warfare may be more of literary commonplace that a real-life motive.

35 C. Barton, *The Sorrows of the Ancient Romans: The Gladiator and the Monster* (Princeton, NJ, 1995) 38. See Katherine Welch's criticism of Carlin's arguments in *Journal of Social History*, 27 (1993) 2, 430–3.

36 *Roman Society from Nero to Marcus Aurelius* (New York, 1956) 242.

37 Juv. 11.5–8.

38 Ville, *La Gladiature*, 250.

39 Quint. *Inst.* 8.5.12. See also Sen. *Clem.* 2.6.2.

40 *Pont.* 1.5.37–8; *Trist.* 2.1.17.

41 28.21.2.

42 Petron. 117.5. See also Hor. *Sat.* 2.7.58–9.

43 Sen. *Ep.* 37.1–2. See Ville, *La Gladiature*, 247–51.

44 Sen. *Apoc.* 9.3.

45 See Ville, *La Gladiature*, 255.

46 Val. Max. 2.3.2.

47 *Att.* 7.14.2. I have adopted Shackleton Bailey's (*Cicero's Letters to Atticus*, 4 (Cambridge, 1968) 18) reading of CIƆ (1,000), rather than the commonly accepted IƆƆ (5,000). The text says 'shields' (*scutorum*) rather than 'gladiators'. I heartily agree with SB (138, n. 5) that it is hard to believe that Caesar's *ludus* housed 500 gladiators, much less 1,000 or 5,000, but SB thinks *scutorum* could have its normal meaning and not be metonymy for 'gladiators'. This leads him to a translation that does not make sense: 'There were 1,000 shields in the establishment and they were said to be going to break out.' Interpreting shields as 'gladiators' seems to me to be the only way of making sense of the Latin.

48 Gaius *Inst.* 3.146. This evidence is late (Gaius is second century AD and Ulpian, third century), but it most likely that these rules were already in effect in the late Republic. See D. Potter, 'Gladiators and Blood Sport', in Martin Winkler (ed.), *Gladiator: Film and History* (Malden, MA, 2004) 79.

49 *Att.* 4.8.2.

50 *Oct.* 37.3.

51 Cyprian, *Ad Donat*, 7. See also Tert. *De spect.* 12.3.

52 Juv. 6.247–9.

53 45.12.

54 Suet. *Iul.* 26.3.

55 Tert. *Ad martyr.* 1.2.

56 Sen. *Ep.* 22.1.

57 *Les Gladiateurs*, 304.

58 Quint. *Inst. Orat.* 10.5.20.

59 A Roman foot was equivalent to approximately 11.6 inches.

60 *Mil.* 1.11. Quintilian in a simile describes a four-step process for gladiatorial combat which involves a series of feints countered by parries, which is then repeated (*Inst.* 5.13.54).

61 5.24.2–3.

62 *ILS* 5091; 5099; 5103; 5110; 5116.

63 J. D. Duff (*Fourteen Satires of Juvenal* (Cambridge, 1957) 233 *ad loc.*) suggests that this is the armament of a Samnite gladiator, but by Juvenal's day (early second century AD) the Samnite had long disappeared from the arena.

64 Juv. 6.256–8.

65 6.82–105.

66 We hear of a *ludus*, in Rome or Capua, owned by a certain C. Aurelius Scaurus, from which P. Rutilius Rufus (consul in 105 BC) hired arms experts to train his soldiers (Val. Max. 2.3.2.). See Ville, *La Gladiature*, 273, n. 98. In the late first century, Horace mentions the school of a certain Aemilius that was famous

enough to be used as a landmark in Rome (*AP* 32). For the possible danger that the presence of many gladiators in Rome posed during the Catilinarian conspiracy, see Sall. *Cat.* 30.7.

67 Friedländer, *Roman Life*, II, 56. For Ravenna, see Strabo 5.1.7.

68 Ps. Quint. *Decl. Mai.* 9.5.19.

69 11.20. See also Cypr. *Ad Donat.* 7.

70 Plin. *HN* 18.72.

71 *Hist.* 2.88.

72 See Suet. *Aug.* 42.3 and Cass. Dio 55.26.1.

73 Ps. Quint. *Decl. Mai.* 9.21.

74 Luciana Jacobelli, *Gladiators at Pompeii* (Los Angeles, 2003) 66.

75 6, Ox. 13.

76 Ps. Quint. *Decl. Mai.* 9.21. See *Ergastulum* in William Smith, *A Dictionary of Greek and Roman Antiquities* (London, 1875) http://penelope.uchicago .edu/Thayer/E/Roman/Texts/secondary/SMIGRA*/Ergastulum.html.

77 Plut. *Crass.* 8.4.

78 Jacobelli, *Gladiators*, 19.

79 The nature of the profession ensured that most of these unions would be temporary.

80 5.24.10.

81 See Valerie Hope, 'Fighting for Identity: The Funerary Commemoration of Italian Gladiators', in Alison Cooley, *The Epigraphic Landscape of Roman Italy* (London, 2000) 104. Wife sets up memorial for gladiator husband: *ILS* 5090; 5095; 5098; 5100; 5101; 5102; 5104; 5107; 5112; 5115; 5120; 5121; 5122; 5123. Reversal: *ILS* 5125. *Contubernalis* Euche: *ILS* 5096.

82 *Claud.* 21.5.

83 *ILS* 5115.

84 *Apol.* 98.

85 Ps. Quint. *Decl. Mai.* 9.21.

86 *Ibid.* 9.5.

87 See Robert, *Les Gladiateurs*, 29 and Marcus Junkelmann, '*Familia Gladiatoria*: The Heroes of the Amphitheater', in Eckart Köhne and Cornelia Ewigleben (eds), *The Power of Spectacle in Ancient Rome: Gladiators and Caesars* (Berkeley, CA, 2000) 32–3. Ville (*La Gladiature*, 324, n. 217) points out that the hierarchical ranking for each type of gladiator in the *ludus* did not exist until after the reign of Domitian (AD 81–96). Carter (Gladiatorial Ranking and the 'SC de Pretiis Gladiatorum Minuendis' (*CIL* II 6278 = *ILS* 5163) *Phoenix* 57.1/2 (2003) 90) suggests the possibility of the existence of a sixth, and even an eighth *palus* in some schools.

88 *Les Gladiateurs*, 30–1.

89 Inscriptions 16, 35, 89, 179, 293, 298 in Robert, *Les Gladiateurs*. See Cass. Dio 72.22.3.

90 See Ville, *La Gladiature*, 304, n. 184.

91 *ILS* 5107.

92 Cass. Dio 72.22.3.

93 Herodian 1.15.9.

94 Cass. Dio 72.19.2.

95 Cass. Dio 72.22.3. For Hercules and gladiators, see Hor. *Epist.* 1.1.5.

96 *ILS* 5085; 5087; 5088; 5089; 5095; 5101; 5115; 5118; 5120.

97 Ville, *La Gladiature*, 266–7.

98 For example, *ILS* 5113; 5118; 5124.

99 *ILS* 5108. Much of what we know about gladiators comes from their epitaphs.

100 *Les Gladiateurs*, 147.109.

101 *ILS* 5126.

102 *ILS* 5108a; 5110.

103 *ILS* 5086; 5121.

104 *ILS* 5123.

105 Quint. *Inst.* 2.17.33. As we shall see in Chapter 7, the film *Spartacus* deals with the issue of members of the same gladiatorial troupe fighting each other in the arena.

106 *Dial.* 4.8.2.

107 *Phil.* 6.13.

108 *ILS* 5124.

109 See Wiedemann. *Emperors*, 119.

110 6. Ox. 8–9.

111 8.200–01.

112 Susanna Braund, *Juvenal Satires: Book I* (Cambridge, 1996) 159.

113 22.123–25.

114 6. Ox. 12–13.

115 M. D. Reeve, 'Gladiators in Juvenal's Sixth Satire', *CR* NS, 23.2 (1973) 125.

116 *Q Nat.* 7.31.3. S. Cerutti and L. Richardson ('The *Retiarius Tunicatus* of Suetonius, Juvenal, and Petronius', *AJP* 110.4 (1989) 590) argue that the segregation reported by Juvenal and Seneca refers to one and the same part of the school, as does Susanna Braund, *Juvenal Satires*, 159). For the opposite opinion, see S. G. Owen, 'On the *Tunica Retiarii* (Juvenal II. 143 ff.; VIII. 199 ff.; VI. Bodleian Fragment 9 ff.)', *CR* 19.7 (1905) 355–6.

117 *CIL* XIV.3014.

118 This house was first discovered in 1890 and was finally excavated in 1899. See Ville, *La Gladiature*, 297, n. 165.

119 *CIL* IV.4420.

120 *CIL* IV.283.

121 *CIL* IV.4342; 4345.

122 *CIL* IV.4353; 4356.

123 *De spect.* 22. See *CIL* IV 4342; 4345; 4353; 4356.

124 2.32.

125 *The Colosseum*, 83.

126 126.5–6.
127 Rumour had it that her son Commodus was actually fathered by a gladiator (*SHA Marc.* (Julius Capitolinus) 19.2). See also Tac. *Ann.* 11.21; Plut. *Galb.* 9.2.
128 6.104–12. As Tertullian points out, the denizens of the arena (and no doubt women attracted to them) considered scars essential to their sexual magnetism (*Ad mart.* 5.1).
129 Ville, *La Gladiature*, 298.
130 Jacobelli, *Gladiators*, 49; 67.
131 *Ibid.* 67.
132 The name was still appropriate, because Octavian was adopted by Caesar in his will and thus received the surname of *Julius.*
133 *Ner.* 30.2. Victorious generals made huge profits when they sold the portion of the spoils that were awarded to them personally. The rest of the spoils were dedicated to the gods.
134 *HN* 11.144. Ville (*La Gladiature*, 281, n. 124), claims that twenty is too small to be the total number of gladiators in Caligula's school or in any imperial school. Perhaps so, but this count may have been taken after Caligula's auction of gladiators (Suet. *Calig.* 38.4).
135 Plin. *HN* 11.245.
136 Suet. *Calig.* 32.2.
137 Tac. *Ann.* 11.35. A *procurator* was an employee and representative of the emperor in various administrative capacities.
138 See Wiedemann, *Emperors*, 170.
139 *ILS* 1428. The adjective *matutinus* means 'morning'. Since beasts hunts (*venationes*) regularly took place in the morning, the school for hunters received the official name of 'the Morning School' – its unofficial name may have been *ludus bestiariorum* or *ludus bestiarius* ('beast fighters' school'). See Sen. *Ep.* 70.20; 22 and Ville, *La Gladiature*, 281.
140 *ILS* 1412.
141 *ILS* 1420. This was the triumphal procession that was represented so splendidly in the film *The Fall of the Roman Empire.*
142 See Ville, *La Gladiature*, 284–7 and Wiedemann, *Emperors* 170–1.
143 *ILS* 9014; 1396.
144 *CIL* IV.1190; 2508. See Jacobelli, *Gladiators*, 45–6.
145 Wiedemann, (*Emperors*, 17) wrongly calls Ampliatus a *lanista.* See Marcus Junkelmann's review of Wiedemann in *Plekos* 4 (2002) 40.
146 *CIL* IV.1182. It is probably the tomb of Umbricius Scaurus, but there are other interpretations of the evidence. See Jacobelli, *Gladiators*, 92.
147 See Ville, *La Gladiature* 289, n. 146.
148 Suet. *Calig.* 38.4.
149 *ILS* 5084.
150 John Scarborough, 'Galen and the Gladiators', *Episteme* 5 (1971) 102.

151 Aul. Gell. *Att. Noct.* 12.5.13.
152 See Vivian Nutton, 'The Chronology of Galen's Early Career', *CQ* 23. 1 (1973) 164. Roman Asia was not the continent, but a large province that occupied approximately the western half of modern Turkey. The high priest of the province of Asia was sometimes referred to as the 'Asiarch'.
153 Gal. *De alimentorum facultatibus* (Kühn) 6.529–30. See Scarborough, 'Galen', 102–3.
154 Gal. *De compositione medicamentorum* (Kühn) 13.600. See Scarborough, 'Galen', 107–11 and Vivian Nutton, 'Chronology', 163.
155 See Robert, *Les Gladiateurs*, 117.61.
156 *ILS* 5152.
157 Sen. *Dial.* 1.4.4.
158 *Diss.* 1.29.37.
159 Suet. *Dom.* 4.1. See Sen. *Ep.* 7.4 and G. Lafaye, 'Gladiator', in C. Daremberg, E. Saglio and M. Pottier (eds) *Dictionnaire des antiquités greques et romaines d'après les textes et les monuments* (Paris, 1896) 1590.
160 Cass. Dio 67.8.4.
161 Suet. *Dom.* 4.1.
162 *Ibid.*
163 See Ville, *La Gladiature*, 400.
164 *ILS* 5163.34; Epict. *Dissertationes* 2.24.23. See also C. Barton, *Sorrows*, 80.
165 Suet. *Dom.* 17.2.
166 *ILS* 5128; 5129; 5130; 5131; 5132.
167 Amanda Claridge *Rome: An Oxford Archaeological Guide* (Oxford, 1998) 283.
168 *ILS* 6087.70 (Urso charter). The *duoviri*, the chief executive magistrates of Urso, were allowed to supplement their personal expenditure with up to 4,000 sesterces from public monies. For Aurelius' legislation, see *ILS* 5163.
169 Cass. Dio 54.2.4.
170 Suet. *Tib.* 34.1.
171 The giving of a *munus* in the provinces was seen as means of displaying loyalty to Rome. The Athenians, influenced by the adoption of gladiatorial shows by the Corinthians, introduced them into their city. The philosopher Demonax tried to convince the Athenians not to follow the Corinthians in this regard. He sarcastically told the Athenians not to vote in favour of this proposal if they did not first demolish their famous Altar of Pity (Lucian, *Demon.* 57).
172 Most *munerarii*, however, were not reluctant to impoverish themselves; for example, a certain Tertullus of Sagalassus (north-west Turkey), who put 'his country before his possessions'. See Robert, *Les Gladiateurs*, 142. 98.6.
173 *ILS* 5163.16–18. See James H. Oliver and Robert E. A. Palmer, 'Minutes of an Act of the Roman Senate', *Hesperia* 24.4 (1955) 320–49.
174 A fragmentary copy of this inscription, inscribed in marble, was found in the city of Sardis in the province of Asia. Michael Carter ('Gladiatorial Ranking', 84) writes of both inscriptions: 'Surviving inscriptions of the same decree

found at opposite ends of the Empire . . . do indicate that the decree had universal importance and application'.

175 *SHA Marc.* (Julius Capitolinus) 23.5. See Grant, *Gladiators*, 51.
176 Michael Carter, 'Gladiatorial Ranking', 86. This sales tax was probably intended to finance the war against German tribes on the northern border of the empire.
177 *Story*, 209–10.
178 Fergus Millar (*The Emperor in the Roman World: Economy, Society and Culture* (Ithaca, NY, 1977) 195), argues that the tax was not removed, but prices were drastically reduced, causing a corresponding reduction in taxes. Carter ('Gladiatorial Ranking', 86, n. 15) rejects Millar's interpretation, pointing out that: 'It seems clear from the text . . . that the revenue abandoned was derived from a *vectigal* ["tax paid to the state"].
179 Carter ('Gladiatorial Ranking', 88, n. 17), however, points out that although there is general agreement that that *munera assiforana* were given for profit, the evidence that *lanistae* were *editores* is weak. He also speculates that the limitation in cost for these shows below the level of the non-profit games may have been designed to prevent competition 'in grandeur' with the shows of the priest of the imperial cult.
180 *ILS* 5163.29.
181 'Gladiatorial Ranking', 95–8.
182 *ILS* 5163.29–35. Note that these price limitations did not apply to *munera* given by the emperor.
183 45.6.
184 See Bomgardner, *Story*, 230–1 for the different numbers of gladiators possible in *munera* of various price ranges according to the legislation's guidelines. Bomgardner assumes that the prices mentioned in the legislation are lease rates.
185 'Gladiatorial Ranking', 106–8.
186 *Ibid.* 101–3.
187 *Ibid.* 100–1.
188 *ILS* 5163.9–10.
189 *ILS* 5163.55–58. The text of the inscription actually says that provincial procurators could charge only six gold coins (*aurei*) per man. Cassius Dio says that one *aureus* was equivalent to 100 sesterces (55.12.4).
190 *Minutes*, 324–6.
191 *Acts*, xx–xxi. See J. F. Matthews' review of *Marcus Aurelius* by A. Birley, *JRS* 58.1/2 (1968) 263; Robert M. Grant, *Augustus to Constantine* (1970) 93–4. Michael Carter, however, recently referred to Oliver and Palmer's thesis as the 'prevailing scholarly opinion' in his review of *Blood in the Arena: The Spectacle of Roman Power* by Alison Futrell, *Phoenix* 53.1/2 (1999) 157.
192 *ILS* 5163.59–61.
193 See Bomgardner, *Story*, 210.
194 Symm. *Relat.* 8.3.

Chapter 3 Gladiator Games in Action

1 *De arch.* 10.pr.3.
2 Not all *edicta* advertise gladiator games. For example, Cn. Alleius Nigidius Maius, a leading citizen of Pompeii, on at least on two occasions gave shows that included a *venatio* and Greek athletic contests, but no gladiatorial fights. Athletes who appeared in Roman spectacles would most likely have been practitioners of combat sports (boxing, wrestling and pankration) and not of the track and field sports (foot-racing, jumping, javelin, discus).
3 *CIL* IV.1181.
4 *CIL* IV.1180.
5 For example, *CIL* IV.1179.
6 Before the linking of the *venatio* with gladiatorial combat in the *munus*, we hear of gladiator matches starting at dawn (Hor. *Epist.* 2.2.98).
7 See *CIL* IV.1180; 1183; 1184; 1186; 1189; 7993; 7994.
8 *CIL* IV.1989; 3881; 3882.
9 *CIL* IV.1181; 9980.
10 For example, *CIL* IV.1177, 1180; 1181; 1184; 3883. See more on the *sparsio* later in this chapter.
11 *CIL* IV.7993.
12 Ville, *La Gladiature*, 401.
13 *CIL* IV.3884.
14 The dates given as April 8 to 12 are a modernization. What the Latin says is the day before and the third, fourth, fifth and sixth days before the Ides of April (13 April). The Roman system of giving dates involved counting backwards from three key days in the month: the Kalends (first day), the Nones (5th or 7th, depending on month), Ides (13th or 15th, also varying with the month). For us the next day in a reverse series would be the second day before the Ides of April, but the Romans always counted both ends of a series, so April 11 for them was the third day before the Ides and so on. The *pr* in the inscription is for *pridie* ('the day before').
15 *CIL* IV.1189.
16 There is another term used in inscriptions, *plena* ('full'), which is probably synonymous with *legitima* in this context. See Ville, *La Gladiature*, 399.
17 *SCR* is abbreviation for *scribit* ('painted'), *SING* is short for *singulus* ('all by himself') while *AD LUNA[M]* means 'by the light of the moon'.
18 *CIL* IV.1179.
19 See Ville, *La Gladiature*, 396.
20 77.6.2.
21 *CIL* IV 1179.
22 5.24.8.
23 Ville, *La Gladiature*, 397.
24 45.11.
25 Ville, *La Gladiature*, 397.

26 *AE* 1961, 140; 1969–70, 183.

27 Sen. *Ep.* 7.4.

28 Ville, *La Gladiature*, 326. See Juv. 6.248; Ov. *Ars am.* 3.515; Tac. *Dial.* 34.5; Livy 40.6.6 (reading *rudibus*, rather than *sudibus* ('stakes'). See also *Livy The Dawn of the Roman Empire: Books 31–40*, trans. J. C. Yardley (Oxford, 2000) 583, note on 'wooden stakes'.

29 Suet. *Claud.* 21.5; Calp. Flacc. 52; Quint. *Decl. Min.* 302. When an *auctoratus* received the *rudis*, he was released from his voluntarily assumed obligation to perform in the arena and resumed his status as a freeman. When a slave received the same release, he remained a slave (Ville, *La Gladiature*, 328. See Tert. *De spect.* 21.4).

30 There is also a *secunda rudis*. He probably served as the second referee we sometimes see in ancient depictions of gladiatorial combat. See Figures 12 and 18.

31 See Robert, *Les Gladiateurs*, 138.90. This inscription is accompanied by a depiction of a *summarudis* dressed in a tunic and holding a stick in his hand in the act of refereeing a match.

32 Ville, *La Gladiature*, 372.

33 Suet. *Tib.* 7.1.

34 Livy 44.31.15.

35 See Martin Winkler's quotation of Lewis Mumford (*The City in History: Its Origins, Its Transformations and its Prospects* (New York, 1961) 229–30) in 'Gladiator and the Colosseum: Ambiguities of Spectacle', in Winkler (ed.), *Gladiator: Film and History*, 96.

36 *CIL* X; X.4643; 6090X; *AE* 1927, 124; 1975, 255; *FIRA*, 2.557.

37 *CIL* X.4643.

38 *CIL* X.6429.

39 *AE* 1969–70, 183.

40 *Dial.* 10.16.3.

41 4.13.

42 45.7–8. See Wistrand, *Entertainment*, 24.

43 Suet. *Iul.* 39.4.

44 Plass (*Game of Death*, 52) sees the *cena libera* as a mediation between the living and the dead, the hospitality of which provides a dramatic contrast with the violence to occur the next day.

45 *Mor.* 1099B.

46 For the *cena libera* as compensation, see Ville, *La Gladiature*, 366. M. Z. Brettler and M. Poliakoff ('Rabbi Simeon ben Lakish at the Gladiator's Banquet: Rabbinic Observations on the Roman Arena', *The Harvard Theological Review* 83.1 (1990) 93–8) question Ville's theory, finding it impossible to explain why *editores* felt obliged to give compensation, especially to *damnati*. The authors discuss the *cena libera* in the light of the human sacrifice theory of the origin of gladiatorial combat, arguing that prisoners and captives do not make suitable victims for funeral ritual. Citing Karl Meuli, *Der griechische Agon: Kampf und*

Kampfspiele in Totenbrauch, Totentanz, Totenklage, und Totenlob (Cologne, 1968) 49, they argue that the *libera cena* as a purification ceremony makes the victims more worthy by temporarily raising their status.

47 The five revellers may in fact represent the five associations (*sodalitates*) of *venatores* in North Africa, among whom are the famous Telegenii, the Pentasi and perhaps the Leontii. See Katherine Dunbabin, *The Mosaics of Roman North Africa* (Oxford, 1978) 78–83. See plate xxvii.69 in Dunbabin.

48 Tert. *Apol.* 42.5. See Junkelmann, '*Familia Gladiatoria*', in Köhne and Ewigleben (eds), *The Power of Spectacle*, 64.

49 Plut. *Mor.* 1099 B. A gladiator who had slaves could have been an *auctoratus*, but some slave gladiators were wealthy enough to afford their own slaves. We have the example of an *essedarius* ('chariot-fighter') named Porius who celebrated a victory by manumitting a slave. When the crowd vigorously applauded Porius' generosity, Caligula experienced a fit of jealousy because the people were lavishing their respect upon Porius rather than on himself, the emperor. The incident ended comically with Caligula tripping on the hem of his toga as he rushed down the steps (Suet. *Calig.* 35.3). Porius' name is Greek, indicating that he is probably either a slave or a freedman. For slaves as slave owners, see Plaut. *Asin.* 433–4; Hor. *Sat.* 2.7.79; Mart. 2.18.7; Paul. *Dig.* 9.4.19.2; Ulp. 15.1.17.pr. A slave's slave was called a *vicarius*. See also Beryl Rawson, 'Family Life among the Lower Classes at Rome in the First Two Centuries of the Empire', *CPh*, 61.2 (1966), 75.

50 *Pass. Perpet, et Felic.* 17.1–2.

51 In Figure 4, the top panel is divided into two segments, one on top of the other, to fit the format of the page.

52 See Junkelmann, '*Familia Gladiatoria*', in Köhne and Ewigleben (eds), *The Power of Spectacle*, 65.

53 The toga was worn only by Roman citizens on official occasions. Note that the musicians, who are probably slaves, are wearing tunics. The lictors carry the *fasces*, symbolic bundles of rods and axes that represent the magistrate's power to punish with flogging or with death.

54 The best modern depiction of a *pompa* is in the film *Demetrius and the Gladiators* (dir. Daves, 1954).

55 The blacksmiths are very small, but that is probably due to the limitations of space in the panel.

56 Suet. *Tit.* 9.2. Cassius Dio tells practically the same story about a later emperor, Nerva (68.3.2).

57 Third century emperors used gladiators in processions of other kinds, probably because of their impressive appearance with their bejewelled armament and plumes. Gallienus (AD 259–68) commemorated the tenth anniversary of his rule with a parade including 1,200 gladiators, while Aurelian (AD 270–275) celebrated a triumph with a procession including 1,600 gladiators (*SHA Gallien.* (Trebellius Pollio) 8.3 and *Aurel.* (Flavius Vopiscus Syracusius) 33.4).

58 For gladiators' participation in the *pompa*, see Ps. Quint *Decl. Mai.* 9.6 and Robert, *Les Gladiateurs*, 174–6.171.9.

59 3.59.

60 *Tox.* 58.

61 Cass. Dio 44.16.2; Appian, *B Civ.* 2.17.118; Vell. Pat. 2.58.

62 Even after the *venatio* became a regular feature of the *munus*, on occasion it was given in the Circus Maximus in connection with chariot races. For example, Caligula was fond of combining chariot races with animal hunts, by presenting *venationes* between races (Suet. *Calig.* 18.3). Cassius Dio says that Claudius adopted this practice at least on one occasion, presenting bear hunts, athletic contests and Pyrrhic dances (war dances) between chariot races (60.23.5) Suetonius adds that Claudius frequently used this hybrid format in circus games on the Vatican hill, inserting a *venatio* every five races (*Claud.* 21.2).

63 The word *venatio* is related to 'venison', which originally meant 'the flesh of a hunted animal'.

64 See Juv. 4.100–1.

65 Apul. *Met.* 4.13. The importance of swiftness for the hunter also explains the short tunic. Any article of clothing longer than this was liable to impede the progress of the hunter in various ways as he raced through the forest. Once the prey had been cornered by the dogs, the hunter would dispatch it with one of his two spears.

66 Sen. *Dial.* 10.13.6. Before this occasion lions in the arena had always been chained.

67 Plin. *HN* 8.131.

68 *Ibid.* 8.20.

69 Strabo 17.1.44.

70 Ulp. *Dig.* 48.19.8.11.

71 Cic. *Sest.* 135.

72 *Q Fr.* 2.5.3.

73 45.11. See also Cic. *Vat.* 40; Tert. *De anim.* 57.5.

74 '*Familia Gladiatoria*', in Köhne and Ewigleben (eds), *The Power of Spectacle*, 71.

75 *Ep.* 70.20; 22.

76 Ulp. *Dig.* 48.19.8.11.

77 See Roland Auguet, *Cruelty and Civilization: The Roman Games* (London, 1994) 89–90; 93.

78 Plin. *HN* 33.53.

79 *Claud.* 34.2.

80 *Ben.* 2.19.1.

81 *Apol.* 9.5; 42.5.

82 Whipping and torches were also used to force reluctant gladiators to fight.

83 *Dial.* 5.43.2.

84 See Salvatore Aurigemma, *I Mosaici di Zliten* (Rome, 1926) 188.

85 14.53; *Spect.* 11; 21; 22. The numbering of the poems in Martial's *Book of Spectacles* used in this book is that of D. R. Shackleton Bailey in the first volume of his *Loeb Classical Library* translation of Martial (Cambridge, MA, 1993).

86 Ov. *Met.* 11.25–7.

87 Symm. *Ep.* 2.77.

88 11.69.

89 *I Mosaici*, 186; 188.

90 Varro *Rust.* 3.13.1–3. Hortensius' dinner guests had a view of his park and enjoyed watching a servant dressed as Orpheus summon the animals by blowing his horn. Roman elites also enjoyed keeping fish ponds and aviaries.

91 *Ner.* 31.1.

92 *SHA Gord. Tres* (Julius Capitolinus) 33.1. Procopius mentions that there was a *vivarium* in Rome just outside the Praenestine Gate (*De bell.* 5.22.10). Animals were kept in this area and attended by *magistri* (trainers) until they were transported to the amphitheatre (*CIL* VI.130).

93 Wiedemann (*Emperors*, 64) says that 'in a pre-industrial world, any sign of control over the natural world is reassuring to society at large'.

94 2.5.33. A poem in the *Anth. Palat.* (7.626) says practically the same thing. See Edmondson, *Dynamic Arenas*, 72–3.

95 Themist. *De Pace* 140.2–4.

96 *Ep.* 41.6.

97 *SHA Gord. Tres* (Julius Capitolinus) 3.7.

98 The naturalist Pliny the Elder enthusiastically makes this claim for elephants, calling their intellectual and emotional capacity closest to that of human beings. Pliny, however, in the examples that he presents to support his claim, indulges in gross anthropomorphism, noting the elephant's religious tendencies (*HN* 8.1).

99 J. M. C. Toynbee, *Animals in Roman Life and Art* (Ithaca, NY, 1973) 21.

100 4.40.

101 Cass. Dio 66.25.1; 68.15.1.

102 Theodoric, an Ostrogoth, relied on Cassiodorus to ghost-write his letters in polished Latin. It is impossible to know where Theodoric ends and Cassiodorus begins in these thoughts on the *venatio*, but I think it is safe to assume that the two men, as Christians, were in agreement on this matter. See James O'Donnell, *Cassiodorus* (Berkeley, CA, 1979) 96.

103 Cassiod. *Var.* 5.42.2. Theodoric expresses distaste for the *venatio*, but never questions the political value of these shows.

104 *Var.* 5.42.6–10. The phrase 'four panels that rotate around a central pole' is my simplification of Cassiodorus' vague description of this device. S. J. B. Barnish (*The Variae of Magnus Aurelius Cassiodorus Senator* (Liverpool, 1992) 92) translates the phrase more literally: 'angled screens, fitted in a rotating four part apparatus'.

105 *Rust.* 3.5.
106 See 'Cochlea' in William Smith, *A Dictionary of Greek and Roman Antiquities* (London, 1875). (http://penelope.uchicago.edu/Thayer/E/Roman/Texts/ secondary/SMIGRA/home.html.
107 See figures 1687–8 in E. Saglio, 'Cochlea', in Dar.–Sag., *Dictionnaire*, 1265.
108 9.533.
109 See George Jennison, *Animals for Show and Pleasure in Ancient Rome* (Manchester, 1937) 180.
110 *Ibid.*
111 One is reminded of the two wooden walls (*burladeros*) at opposite ends of the arena in modern bullrings, from behind which *toreros* taunt the bulls. See Terin Tashi Miller, 'On Bullfighting'. http://www.lostgeneration.com/article6.htm.
112 See Dunbabin, *Mosaics*, 76; plate XXVI.65 (Khanguet el-Hadjaj) in which a man coming out of a door seems to be trying to get the attention of animals, which will be lassoed by the man standing nearby. Another 'teaser' of wild beasts in the arena was the tree-climber (*arborarius*), who used this method of escape. Robert (*Les Gladiateurs*, 327) suggests that he was paired with a bear to introduce more risk into this event since a bear is also a tree-climber.
113 A. Chastagnol, *Le Senat romain sous le règne d'Odacre: recherches sur l'epigraphie du Colisée au V*ᵉ *siècle* (Bonn, 1966) 20–2.
114 See figure 98 in Peter Brown's *The World of Late Antiquity* AD *150–750* (London, 1973). See also *Porphyrius the Charioteer* (Oxford, 1973) 228–9 and Bryan Ward-Perkins, *From Classical Antiquity to the Middle Ages: Urban Public Building in Northern and Central Italy* AD *300–850* (Oxford, 1984) 114.
115 Cass. Dio 37.46.4.
116 Sen. *Ep.* 7.3–4.
117 See Hopkins and Beard, *The Colosseum*, 73.
118 *CIL* IX.3437 (Peltuinum) and *ILS* 5063a (Beneventum).
119 See Lucian, *Tox.* 59.
120 The Athenians also armed criminals such as adulterers, male prostitutes, burglars and kidnappers, and forced them to fight as gladiators (Philostr. *V A* 4.22).
121 *Ep.* 7.3–4. Seneca elsewhere condemns these fights: 'A human being . . . is led out [into the arena] naked and defenceless and the spectacle is no more than a man being killed'. Some scholars, such as Otto Kiefer (*Sexual Life in Ancient Rome* (New York, 1993) 102–3), have mistaken this passage as a reference to trained gladiators, but although gladiators might loosely be described as naked, they had protective armour.
122 Salisbury, *Perpetua's Passion*, 130.
123 Suet., *Claud.* 34.2. See also Cass. Dio 60.13.4.
124 Cass. Dio 60.13.3. See Ville, *La Gladiature* 134–5.
125 Sen. *Ep.* 14.5. See also Juv. 1.155–7. Tertullian reports seeing a man volunteer to wear the *tunica molesta* for a price in order to show his contempt for fire (*Ad nat.* 1.18.10). This man seems to be a precursor of the modern fire-eater.

126 Suet. *Vit.* 17.1–2.

127 Plin. *Pan.* 34.3.

128 *AE* 1975, 255.

129 Wiedemann. *Emperors*, 71. The placard was also used to humiliate Attalus in the amphitheatre of Lyons in AD 177. Attalus, because he was the most well-known of the *damnati*, was forced to walk around the arena behind a sign, which read: 'This is Attalus, the Christian' (Euseb. *HE* 5.1.44).

130 *Ad nat.* 1.10.47.

131 Ville, *La Gladiature*, 425

132 *Ad nat.* 1.10.47.

133 The picture of Tertullian and his friends enjoying themselves at the *meridianum spectaculum* seems at odds with his strong Christian stance in his writings, but his attendance at the amphitheatre was no doubt before his conversion to Christianity. It should be noted, however, that Tertullian shares a fixation with Seneca and various Christian writers. As Barton ('Scandal of the Arena', *Representations*, 27 (1989) 29, n. 49) comments, Tertullian is 'fascinated and obsessed with the violence he often decries'.

134 Bomgardner, *Story*, 137.

135 *Ad nat.* 1.10.46. See also *Apol.* 15.5. Ville (*La Gladiature*, 378) believes that these two 'gods' were also employed at the *ad bestias* executions.

136 Junkelmann, *Das Spiel*, 141.

137 Fabian Kanz and Karl Grossschmidt, in their valuable study of the head injuries of gladiators ('Head Injuries of Roman Gladiators', *Forensic Science International* 160 (2006) 214), trace four head traumata of either round or square shape to the hammer of Dis Pater.

138 *Das Spiel*, 141.

139 *La Gladiature*, 377.

140 Vitr. 1.7.1, Mart. *Spect.* 26.3.

141 *ILS* 2088; 2096; 3739.

142 *ILS* 3628.

143 *ILS* 3744.

144 Robert, *Les Gladiateurs*, 182–3.179.

145 Nick Bateman, *Gladiators at the Guildhall: The Story of London's Roman Amphitheatre and Medieval Guildhall* (London, 2000) 34.

146 *ILS* 5121.

147 *ILS* 3742; 3743. See Bomgardner, *Story*, 137.

148 Robert, *Les Gladiateurs*, 87–90.24.

149 *Blood*, 110, 114, 118.

150 See Ov. *Ib.* 47–9 (I read *velitis*, 'a light-armed gladiator', instead of *militis* ('soldier'). It may have been during the *prolusio* that new *auctorati* were subjected to a gauntlet as an initiation ceremony (Sen. *Apoc.* 9.3).

151 Ov. *Ars am.* 3.515.

152 *Ep.* 117.25.

153 *De Or.* 2.317.

154 *Ibid.* 2.325.

155 Ps. Quint. *Decl. Mai.* 9.6; Petron. 36.6. See Ville, *La Gladiature*, 408.

156 Ovid in his *Ibis* (47–9), speaking of a gladiator in the *prolusio*, uses the verb *calefacere*, which can mean both 'to warm up' and 'excite the emotions'. Perhaps Ovid wants both meanings to apply.

157 *Tusc.* 4.48. Cicero is quoting the second century BC satirist Lucilius.

158 Besides gladiators, the *lanista* provided other necessities for the *munus*: arms, a herald, musicians, a flogger (for reluctant gladiators) and arena attendants.

159 Cic. *Phil.* 2.97.

160 *Fam.* 2.8.1.

161 *SHA Claud.* (Trebellius Pollio) 5.5.

162 *Ars am.* 1.167.

163 See Junkelmann, '*Familia Gladiatoria*', in Köhne and Ewigleben (eds), *The Power of Spectacle*, 64; Ville, *La Gladiature*, 364.

164 The *acta diurna* were first published by order of Julius Caesar in 59 BC during his first consulship. They contained proceedings of the Senate, news about notable people (births, deaths, marriages, divorces), and other noteworthy events (Suet. *Iul.* 20.1). There is a parody of the *acta diurna* in Petronius' *Satryicon* (53). Trimalchio, the central character, has so much property that, like an inhabitant of a city, he needs a newsletter to keep him informed of events. Here is a sample: 'June 25: on the Cumaean estate which belongs to Trimalchio there were born thirty slave boys and forty slave girls; five hundred thousand pecks of wheat were removed from the threshing floor and put into the storehouse; five hundred cattle were tamed. On the same day: the slave Mithridates was crucified for cursing the *genius* ['spirit'] of the master. On the same day: ten million sesterces were put into the money chest because they could not be invested. On the same day: There was a fire in the gardens at Pompeii, which started with the house of the steward Nasta'.

165 *CIL* IV.2508. See Lafaye, 'Gladiator', in Dar.–Sag., *Dictionnaire*, 1597.

166 Grant, *Gladiators*, 57.

167 *Gladiators*, 7.

168 Fest., *Gloss. Lat.* 285.12–16; '*Familia Gladiatoria*', in Köhne and Ewigleben (eds), *The Power of Spectacle*, 37.

169 *Epist.* 2.2.98.

170 Livy 9.40.3.

171 *Sest.* 126.

172 Junkelmann, '*Familia Gladiatoria*', in Köhne and Ewigleben (eds), *The Power of Spectacle*, 37; 47.

173 *Orig.* 18.53.

174 While the position of the *equites* in the gladiatorial programme was fixed, *editores* regularly varied the sequence of other paired gladiator types.

175 Junkelmann, 'Familia Gladiatoria', in Köhne and Ewigleben (eds), The Power of Spectacle, 47–8.

176 Robert (Les Gladiateurs, 67) points out that the essedarius ('chariot fighter') was also depicted fighting on foot.

177 See Junkelmann, 'Familia Gladiatoria' in Köhne and Ewigleben (eds), The Power of Spectacle, 38.

178 Sest. 126; 134.

179 Junkelmann, 'Familia Gladiatoria', in Köhne and Ewigleben (eds), The Power of Spectacle, 37.

180 Prov. Cons. 9; Phil. 6.13.

181 Sen. Controv. 3. pr.10. See also Jacobelli, Gladiators, 50.

182 Emperors, 30. See Cass. Dio 72.19.2.

183 'Note sur une lampe représentant deux gladiateurs', Phoenix, 57.1/2 (2003) 141–2.

184 Das Spiel, 128. For example, see ILS 5105.

185 'Familia Gladiatoria', in Köhne and Ewigleben (eds), The Power of Spectacle, 51–2.

186 Ibid. 52.

187 Aurigemma, I Mosaici, 170, figure 101.

188 Grant, Gladiators, 57.

189 Gloss. Lat. 285.12–16.

190 See Val. Max. 1.7.8 for a murmillo paired with a retiarius.

191 Adv. nat. 6.12.2.

192 Aequoreus (CIL X.1927). See also Mart. 5.24.12. Junkelmann, Das Spiel, 85.

193 Junkelmann, 'Familia Gladiatoria', in Köhne and Ewigleben (eds), The Power of Spectacle, 51.

194 14.213.

195 9.68.7–8.

196 Calig. 55.2.

197 Ibid. 54.1.

198 Suet. Ner. 30.2; 47.3. See Ville, La Gladiature, 444.

199 Suet. Tit. 8.2.

200 He referred to himself as dominus et deus ('lord and god') (Suet. Dom. 13.2).

201 Pan. 33.3–4. See Ville (La Gladiature, 445) on charges of impiety and treason.

202 Suet. Dom. 10.1. These dogs were a regular part of the venatio and were used to chase down and kill deer and the like.

203 For the thraex vs a hoplomachus, see figure 43 in Junkelmann, 'Familia Gladiatoria', in Köhne and Ewigleben (eds), The Power of Spectacle, 51.

204 Spect. 31.

205 I adopt the reading of parma ('small shield') for palma ('the palm of victory') in Mart. Spect. 31.5 proposed by P. Wagner and accepted by D. R. Shackleton Bailey, ibid. 34, note ad loc.

206 Mart. *Spect.* 31.9. There will be further discussion of this match later in this chapter.
207 *Med.* 1.5.1.
208 *CIL* VI.9719. See Allen Guttman, 'Sports Spectators from Antiquity to the Renaissance', *Journal of Sport History*, 8.2 (1981) 11.
209 The word *retiarius* is derived from the Latin word for net (*rete*), one of the gladiator's primary weapons.
210 There is one basic difference between the gladiator and the soldier: the soldier wears a cuirass, while most gladiators fought with a bare torso.
211 The *Oxford Latin Dictionary* says that the *retiarius* was also called a *pinnirapus* ('a feather snatcher'), but no source I know of connects the *retiarius* specifically with this name. *Pinnirapus* may be just a generic term for a gladiator, as Juvenal uses the word. The name may come from the custom of a gladiator taking a decorative feather from the helmet of his opponent as a trophy, either in the midst of battle or after the fight was over. Scholiasts on Juv. 3.158 and Varro (*LL* 5.142) say that Samnite gladiators wore feathers on their helmets, which opponents seized, probably as trophies. See Lucilius (fr. 3.121–2) for a gladiator who had taken seven feathers in combat. Barbara Levick ('The Senatus Consultum from Larinum', *JRS* 73 (1983) 102) believes that *pinnirapus* is a gladiator in training (*tiro*) whose job was to collect helmet feathers from dead gladiators to give to the victors, I do not think that this interpretation is supported by the evidence in Juvenal, who speaks of the *pinnirapus* as a full-fledged gladiator.
212 As Junkelmann '*Familia Gladiatoria*', in Köhne and Ewigleben (eds), *The Power of Spectacle*, 61, explains: 'The equipment of the *murmillo* and the *secutor* differed only in the shape of their helmets'.
213 2.144; 8.206.
214 *ILS* 5118; 5119.
215 Juvenal describes the ordinary *retiarius* as *nudus*, which in this case means 'almost naked' (6. Ox 12).
216 See A. E. Houseman, '*Tunica Retiarii*', *CR* 18.8 (1904), 397, his edition of Juvenal's *Satires* (Cambridge, 1931) 50, n. 10–13) and Cerutti and Richardson, '*Retiarius Tunicatus*', 589–91.
217 6. Ox. 9–10.
218 The *munus* sometimes also featured group fights among boxers (*pugiles catervarii*). See Suet. *Aug.* 45.2; *Calig.* 18.1 and *CIL* X.1074d.
219 Suet. *Calig.* 30.3.
220 Owen ('Tunica Retiarii', 354–6) rejects the connection between the tunic and effeminacy. The garment was commonly used in everyday life without any hint of disgrace. He (357) also suggests that in the case of Gracchus, the tunic was part of his outfit as a Salian priest. Susanna Braund (*Juvenal and Persius* (Cambridge, MA, 2004) 341, n. 51) agrees. J. Colin ('Les Baladins et les rétiaires d'après le manuscrit d'Oxford', *Atti della Accademia delle scienze di*

Torino, 87 (1952–53) 352) argues that the shame of the tunic is derived from the fact that convicted criminals wore them. Thus, *retiarii* who were convicts would wear the tunic, while volunteer *retiarii* would not. The problem is that there is no evidence that, among gladiators, dress was used to differentiate between slave and free status.

221 2.117–42. If the wedding with another man were not bad enough in the eyes of the Romans, Gracchus' husband was a man from the lowest level of society: a horn player, probably a slave or at best a freedman.

222 8.203–6.

223 8.209–10. Seneca points out that gladiators felt shame if they were matched with inferior fighters (*Prov.* 3.4).

224 Juv. 6. Ox. 9–13.

225 See *CIL* VI.631.

226 See Robert, *Les Gladiateurs*, 72; 106; plate xiii.46.

227 Junkelmann, '*Familia Gladiatoria*', in Köhne and Ewigleben (eds), *The Power of Spectacle*, 61–2.

228 *Orig.* 18.57.

229 *Bell. Gall.* 4.33.1.

230 Petronius has one of his characters mention the appearance of a female chariot fighter (*essedaria*) in an upcoming *munus* (45.7). Since only one *essedaria* is mentioned, it is not clear whom she was supposed to fight. The usual assumption is that *essedarii* fought opponents of the same category.

231 'Gladiator', in Dar.–Sag., *Dictionnaire*, 1589.

232 *Orig.* 18.56.

233 *Das Spiel*, 127.

234 *Fam.* 7.10.2.

235 Lafaye, 'Gladiator', in Dar.–Sag., *Dictionnaire*, 1589.

236 *ILS* 5126.

237 Suet. *Calig.* 26.5. See Junkelmann, *Das Spiel*, 128.

238 *ILS* 5083a.

239 See Junkelmann, *Das Spiel*, 127.

240 4.42.

241 It is not clear in the Florence relief whether the legs of the two archers are bare or have leg protectors.

242 For the *dimachaerus*, see Robert, *Les Gladiateurs*, 130–1.

243 Lafaye, 'Gladiator' in Dar.–Sag., *Dictionnaire*, 1586.

244 Junkelmann, '*Familia. Gladiatoria*', in Köhne and Ewigleben (eds), *The Power of Spectacle*, 60–1.

245 *CIL* X.1074d.

246 *Les Gladiateurs*, 72–3; *Das Spiel*, 127.

247 Tac. *Ann.* 3.43; 46.

248 See paragraphs 17–18 of the decree (both Latin and English translation) in Barbara Levick, '*Senatus Consultum*', 98–9.

249 *Ibid.* 98.12–13.

250 Jane Gardner, *Women in Roman Law and Society* (Bloomington, IN, 1986) 248. Gladiators were denied burial in the town of Sassina (modern Sarsina). The author of an inscription prohibits gladiators, suicides by hanging, and prostitutes from burial in a cemetery, which he has given to his fellow citizens for their use (*ILS* 7846).

251 *Ann.* 15.32.

252 Cass. Dio 61.17.3.

253 *Ibid.* 63.3.1.

254 45.7.

255 1.22–3.

256 6.246–67.

257 66.25.2.

258 *Dom.* 4.1.

259 *Silv.* 1.6.57–64. If D. R. Shackleton Bailey's plausible reading of *pumilos* ('dwarfs') for *pugiles* ('boxers') is correct (*Silvae* (Cambridge, MA, 2003) 92–3 n. 12), dwarf gladiators also fought cranes in the arena, their traditional enemies in folktale. See Hom. *Il.* 3.3–7; Plin. *HN* 7.26; Juv. *Sat.* 13.168–73. This battle was a popular subject in Roman art (J. M. C. Toynbee, *Animals*, 244. See Alex Scobie, 'The Battle of the Pygmies and the Cranes in Chinese, Arab and North American Indian Sources', *Folklore*, 86.2 (1975) 123.

260 Cass. Dio 67.8.4. Newlands (*Statius's Silvae and the Poetics of Empire* (Cambridge, 2002) 244) thinks that the female and dwarf gladiators may have been convicted criminals given the task of executing each other.

261 We also should consider the possibility that traditional pairings were ignored for female gladiators.

262 See Kathleen Coleman, '*Missio* at Halicarnassus', *Harv. Stud.* 100 (2000), 500.

263 Amy Zoll, *Gladiatrix* (New York, 2002) 37.

264 Shelby Brown, 'Death as Decoration: Scenes from the Arena on Roman Domestic Mosaics', in Amy Richlin (ed.), *Pornography and Representation in Greece and Rome* (Oxford, 1992) 188; 207–8 and Marilyn Skinner, *Sexuality*, 187–8.

265 Coleman, '*Missio*', 495–6. Amy Zoll's book (*Gladiatrix*) is based on the premise that the recent discovery (2000) of the bones of a woman buried with some lamps decorated with gladiator figures are those of a female gladiator. Hopkins and Beard (*The Colosseum*, 75), however, have cast doubt on this assumption, claiming that objects in the grave prove only that the woman was a fan of gladiatorial combat, rather than a participant.

266 Cass. Dio 75.16.1. The *Senatus Consultum* of AD 19, which had banned upper-class women from fighting as gladiators had probably had fallen into disuse.

267 *CIL* XIV.4616; 5381. *Munerarii* were very proud of any 'firsts' they were able to present. For example, see *CIL* IX.2237 and X.1795.

268 'Revisions et nouveautés pour trios inscriptions d'Ostie', *MEFRA*, 88.2 (1976) 614.

269 Cebeillac-Gervasoni and Zevi, 'Revisions', 615 and Mark Vesley, 'Gladiatorial Training for Girls in the *Collegia Iuvenum* of the Roman Empire', *Echos du Monde Classique/Classical Views* XLII NS 17 (1998) 88–91.

270 *ILS* 6635.

271 Cebeillac-Gervasoni and Zevi, 'Revisions', 615–16.

272 '*Missio*', 498, n. 34. Coleman rejects the dating of this inscription by Cebeillac-Gervasoni and Zevi to before AD 200, because they ignored 'criteria of letter-forms and phraseology'.

273 See Junkelmann, *Das Spiel*, 146.

274 Freedmen often had three names because it was the custom to take the *praenomen* and *nomen* of their former master, but retain their slave name as a *cognomen*, e.g., L. Sextius Eros. This, however, was not an attempt to fool any-one, because the foreign third name (in this case, Greek) gave a freedman away immediately.

275 Ville (*La Gladiature*, 308) notes that sometimes free gladiators (*auctorati*) took stage names to keep their family name free from the *infamia* associated with being a gladiator.

276 Robert, *Les Gladiateurs*, 211.245.

277 Ap. Rhod. *Argon.* 2.1–97.

278 Stat. *Theb.*, 8.751–66.

279 One might argue that these mythological names indicate the homosexuality of gladiators who adopted them, but more likely they were just meant to convey the image of masculine beauty.

280 *SHA Div. Claud.* (Trebellius Pollio) 5.5.

281 Ville (*La Gladiature*, 309–10) notes that gladiators often adopted pseudonyms that associated them with great gladiators of the past like Triumphus, Myrinus and Columbus.

282 5.24.

283 *Spect.* 17 and 32. For discussion and commentary of these two poems, see Coleman, *M. Valerii Martialis Liber Spectaculorum* (Oxford, 2006) 140–7 and 235–43.

284 See Dunbabin, *Mosaics*, 73.

285 29.3.9.

286 See Plass, *Game of Death*, 10; 22.

287 See Tert. *De spect.* 21.4.

288 Pirates were the terrorists of the ancient world, notorious for kidnapping victims at sea. As a young man Julius Caesar was kidnapped by pirates and ran-somed himself. After his release, he eventually captured them and, annoyed by the provincial governor's delay in applying punishment, had them all crucified (Plut. *Caes.* 2).

289 Ps. Quint. *Decl. Mai.* 9.6.1–14. Libitina was a goddess of death and her 'couch' was a stretcher for the removal of seriously injured and dead gladiators (Figure 11).

290 Junkelmann, '*Familia Gladiatoria*', in Köhne and Ewigleben (eds), *The Power of Spectacle*, 64.

291 Petron. 34.4; Mart 2.75.5–6; Suet. *Ner.* 12.1.

292 It took considerable time to find a worthy (and available) troupe of gladiators. It was perhaps even more difficult to assemble a good collection of wild beasts for the *venatio*. This, however, was not true in every case. One of the Metelli won for himself and his descendants the cognomen of *Celer* ('swift') because of the astonishing speed with which he was able to organize a *munus* within a few days after the death of his father. (Plut. *Cor.* 11.4).

293 60.

294 For the first alternative, see Ps. Quint. *Decl. Mai.* 9.9.

295 Sen. *Ep.* 37.2.

296 *ILS* 5113.

297 The letters or word in the brackets supply what was missing from the full word or phrase in the Latin abbreviations.

298 *Spect.* 31.

299 K. Coleman (*Liber Spectaculorum*, 226–9), however, argues for the reading of *palma* instead of *parma*. Her most telling argument points out that ordering the two gladiators to fight without their shields, 'would . . . reduce professional combat to the status of a blood-bath'. She explains her reading of *posita . . . palma*, 'with the palm having been placed' as follows: 'a palm was placed in a prominent position to symbolize that the fight had to continue until there was a clear winner'. My problem with this interpretation is that it does not seem necessary for the emperor to use the palm in this way to inform the crowd of his decision. Even if a herald could not have made himself heard or placards could not be read clearly by the crowd in a large amphitheatre like the Colosseum (as Coleman suggests), would the spectators not have realized the nature of Titus' decision when the two gladiators resumed their fight, even without the placement of a palm?

300 *Spect.* 31.8.

301 *Ibid.* 31.9.

302 '*Missio*', 493–5.

303 See Ville, *La Gladiature*, 415–16.

304 Helen Lovatt, *Statius and Epic Games: Sport, Politics, and Poetics* in the *Thebaid* (Cambridge, 2005). 285.

305 Cass. Dio 72.19.5–6.

306 *Ibid.* 77.19.3–4.

307 *CIL* V.5933. In his epitaph (Robert, *Les Gladiateurs*, 131.79), a gladiator named Diodorus expresses a similar sentiment, but he also blames 'destructive Destiny and the dire treachery of the referee'.

308 Robert, *Les Gladiateurs*, 115.56. See also 85.20; 113–14.55.

309 *ILS* 5134. See Junkelmann, '*Familia Gladiatoria*', in Köhne and Ewigleben (eds), *The Power of Spectacle*, 68.

310 Mart. 12.28.7–8 and 13.99.

311 Plin. *HN* 28.25. See A. Corbeill, *Nature Embodied: Gesture in Ancient Rome* (Princeton, NJ, 2004) 52–62.

312 Quint. *Inst.* 11.3.119.

313 415 (413 Shackleton Bailey), 27–8.

314 *Nature Embodied*, 49–50.

315 3.36.

316 3.37.

317 *CIL* IV.2508.

318 Cass. Dio 60.28.2.

319 *CIL* X.6012.

320 *Pont.* 2.8.53. In the Greek east, a provincial governor overturned the decision of an *editor* and granted *missio* to a gladiator named Idomeneus (Robert, *Les Gladiateurs*, 169.155).

321 45.6.

322 Suet. *Aug.* 45.3.

323 *Nero* 4.1.

324 45.6.

325 Tac. *Ann.* 1.76.

326 Cass. Dio 57.13.1. These 'sharp' swords were also known in the Greek east. See Robert, *Les Gladiateurs*, 258.

327 Cass. Dio 71.29.3.

328 'Gladiators and Blood Sport', in Winkler (ed.), *Gladiator: Film and History*, 76–7.

329 *Claud.* 34.1 See Ville, *La Gladiature*, 416.

330 Suet. *Claud.* 21.5.

331 Corbeill, *Nature Embodied*, 56–8.

332 Cic. *Tusc.* 2.41.

333 Cic. *Mil.* 92; Sen. *Tranq.* 11.4.

334 *Ep.* 30.8.

335 *Ep.* 93.12.

336 Suet. *Claud.* 34.2.

337 *ad loc. Sat.* 1.7.20. For other double deaths see Robert, *Les Gladiateurs*, inscriptions 122–3.66; 153–4.122; 155.124; 191.191; 208–9.239; 223–4.285. In inscription 191, the gladiator Kinyras was declared winner before he died of his wounds. See also *ILS* 5118.

338 48.19.31.pr.

339 *Spect.* 33. Martial also refers to a possible release of a gazelle (13.99).

340 See Richard Saller, 'The Family and Society', in John Bodel (ed.), *Epigraphic Evidence: Ancient History from Inscriptions* (London, 2001) 100.

341 *La Gladiature*, 318.

342 *The Colosseum*, 89

343 *La Gladiature*, 319.

344 *ILS* 5062.

345 *La Gladiature*, 320–1.

346 *Ibid.* 321.

347 *Ibid.*, 325.

348 *The Colosseum*, 87.

349 *Emperors*, 120.

350 B. Frier, 'Roman Life-Expectancy: Ulpian's Evidence', *Harv. Stud.* 86 (1982) 213–51.

351 *ILS* 5113.

352 *ILS* 5090.

353 Tert. *De spect.* 21.4.

354 *FIRA* 2.572.4–5. According to Ulpian, Hadrian's decree also emphasized that the penalty for cattle rustling was not the same everywhere.

355 See Cic. *Phil.* 2.74.

356 Ps. Cic. *Ad. Oct.* 9; Suet. *Calig.* 26.5; Petron. 45.11.

357 *CIL* VI.10189; VI.10184; VI.10178; XIII.1997. See *La Gladiature*, 323–4.

358 *The Colosseum*, 88; 'Contagion', 70.

359 *La Gladiature*, 325.

360 *ILS* 5088.

361 Ville, *La Gladiature*, 311.

362 *Ibid.* 324–5.

363 For another example of gladiators fighting twice in the same *munus*, see Plin. *HN* 36.120 (Curio's show in 52 BC).

364 Suet. *Calig.* 35.2; Cass. Dio 77.6.2.

365 See Suet. *Calig.* 32.2. A similar celebration takes place today when the Wimbledon champion carries his/her trophy around Centre Court. Likewise, Olympic gold medal winners do a victory lap, carrying the flag of their country around the stadium.

366 See Ville, *La Gladiature*, 315.

367 *Claud.* 21.5.

368 Mart. *Spect.* 31.6.

369 Oliver and Palmer, *Aes Italicense*, 332, 45–6. Michael Carter ('Gladiatorial Ranking', 104), however, believes that this money was a percentage of the lease fee, amounting to a wage of the gladiator, and not of the victor's cash reward. The difficulty is with the word *mercedis* in *ILS* 5163.45, which can mean either 'lease fee' or 'reward'.

370 'Fighting for Identity', in Alison Cooley (ed.), 97.

371 See Robert, *Les Gladiateurs*, 174.171.

372 9–10. The numbers here and in endnotes 373, 376, 378–81 are references to the lines of inscription 171 in Robert, *Les Gladiateurs*.

373 18.

374 *Les Gladiateurs*, 177.

375 *HN* 33.53.

376 15–16.

377 See Dunbabin, *Mosaics*, 69, plate XXII.54. (Le Kef = *Sicca Veneria*); 71, plate XXIV.57 (Carthage).

378 17.

379 1–2.

380 7; 14.

381 18.

382 For two other honorific inscriptions dedicated to a *munerarius*, see *CIL* VIII.5276 and 7969.

383 Stat. *Silv.* 1.6.48–50.

384 *Silv.* 1.6.28–33.

385 45.10.

386 Suet. *Ner.*11.2 and Sen. *Ep.* 74.6–7.

387 Cass. Dio 66.25.5.

388 *Ep.* 74.7.

389 *Q Nat.* 2.9.2.

390 Mart. 11.8.2. See See Alex Scobie, 'Spectator Security and Comfort at Gladiatorial Games', *Nikephoros* 1 (1988) 223–4 and Robert, *Les Gladiateurs*, 86.22.

391 Tert. *De spect.* 16.7.

392 Suet. *Calig.* 35.2.

393 Suet. *Dom.* 10.1.

394 Servius (*ad Aen.* 12.296) explains that '*hoc habet!*' was shouted by crowds in the past, but in his day (fourth century AD) '*peractum est!*' was favoured. There is, however, evidence that the two shouts were used as early as the first century AD. See Sen. *Ag.* 901 and *Herc. O.* 1457).

395 Sen. *Dial.* 3.2.4.

396 Macrob. *Sat.* 2.6.1.

397 *Ep.* 7.3.

398 Seneca comments on the great din of crowds at gladiator shows at Rome (*Tranq.* 2.13).

399 August. *Conf.* 6.8.

400 *De spect.* 27.2–4.

401 Joyce Salisbury, *Perpetua's Passion*, 134.

402 7.

403 Ps. Quint. *Decl. Mai.* 9.9.

404 16.323-5.

405 *C. Symm.* 2.1096–101. These lines might have been the inspiration for Jean-Léon Gérôme's depiction of the Vestal Virgins demanding the death of a fallen *retiarius* in his famous painting *Pollice Verso* (see Figure 24).

406 Plut. *Marius* 17.3.

407 Stat. *Silv.* 2.5.25–7.

408 See Auguste Audollent, *Defixionum tabellae. Quotquot innotuerunt tam in Graecis orientis quam in totius occidentis partibus praeter Atticas in corpore inscriptionum Atticarum editas*, reprint of Paris 1904 edition (Frankfurt 1967) 348–50.252; 354.254. I have chosen the example of a *defixio* targeting a *venator*, because the two surviving *defixiones* considered to be gladiatorial are untranslatable in any meaningful way. For the use of *defixiones* in Roman sports, see Florent Heintz, 'Circus Curses and their Archaeological Contexts', *JRA* 11 (1998) 337–442.

409 Audollent (*Defixionum tabellae*, 336.247) suggests a hybrid divinity: Greek Typhon/Egyptian Seth.

410 *ILS* 8755. For other *defixiones* targeting *venatores*, see Audollent, *Defixionum tabellae*, 348–50.248–251.

411 Procop. *De bell.* 1.24.1–58. See Alan Cameron, *Circus Factions: Blues and Greens at Rome and Byzantium* (Oxford, 1976) 278–80 and J. P. V. D. Balsdon, *Life and Leisure in Ancient Rome* (London, 1969) 265–6.

412 *Dig.* 1.12.1.12; Tac. *Ann.* 13.24. Coleman (*Contagion*, 80) says that violence in the amphitheatre was 'exquisitely controlled' by confining it to the arena. See Scobie, 'Spectator Security', 219; W. Nippel, *Public Order in Ancient Rome* (Cambridge, 1995) 93–4; and Balsdon, *Life and Leisure*, 266.

413 'Spectator Security', 232.

414 Nippel, *Public Order*, 93.

415 'Security at the Games in the Early Imperial Period, *Echos du monde classique* 18 (1999) 370–1; 375–6.

416 61.8.1–3. Tacitus (*Ann.* 13.24) gives three different reasons for Nero's removal of soldiers from the games: (1) to allow greater freedom for the spectators, (2) that soldiers might not be degraded by the licence of the theatre, and (3) to see whether spectators would behave themselves in the absence of a military guard.

417 Scobie, 'Security and Comfort', 220.

418 Tac. *Ann.* 14.17. Roman authorities believed that *collegia* were often instigators of violence (Cic. *Sest*, 34; *Pis.* 9; Suet. *Iul.* 42.3; *Aug.* 32.1). Livienus Regulus was a man of dubious reputation who had been expelled from the Senate. Edmondson ('Dynamic Arenas', 101) suggests that seating by *collegia* may have contributed to the riot. Bomgardner (*Story*, 50) suggests a plot by military veterans in Pompeii organized into *collegia* against their neighbours.

419 *ILS* 5084; 5084a and Dessau's notes on these two inscriptions in *ILS*. See Cameron, *Circus Factions*, 77–8.

420 Plin. *HN* 35.52.

421 *Ibid.*

422 Petron. 52.3.

423 2.7.96–100.

Chapter 4 A Brief History of Gladiator Games

1 Livy 23.30.15. The office of augur required knowledge of the 'science' of interpreting the flight of birds to determine the will of the gods. Augury was taken
so seriously that no important political business was undertaken without the magistrate consulting a member of this board. This Lepidus was an ancestor of the
man with the same name who was a member of the second triumvirate (along with
Marc Antony and Octavian) that lasted from the late 40s to the middle 30s BC.

2 Livy 41.20.11.

3 *Spectacles of Death*, 47–9. For recruitment of slaves, see Livy 22.57.9–12 and Val.
Max. 7.6.1.

4 41.28.11.

5 See Edmondson, 'Dynamic Arenas', 76.

6 Sen. *Dial.* 10.20.5; Cic. *Sull.* 54.

7 *Sat.* 2.3.84–99.

8 Petronius' Trimalchio expresses a desire to be admired posthumously for his
generosity (71.3).

9 Livy 23.30.16.

10 The *Ludi Romani* were often called the 'Great' (*Magni*) or the 'Greatest' games
(*Maximi*). The *Ludi Romani* and other annually celebrated *ludi* such as the
Ludi Plebeii (Plebeian Games), *Ludi Cereales* (for Ceres), *Ludi Apollinares* (for
Apollo), the *Ludi Florales* (for Flora) and the *Ludi Megalenses* (for Cybele) were
the oldest of these religious festivals. Other *ludi* continued to be added to
Rome's religious calendar throughout the Republic and well into the empire.

11 Livy 31.50.4.

12 Livy 39.46.1.

13 Ville (*La Gladiature*, 396) estimates that thirteen combats was the maximum
number that could be accommodated comfortably in a single day.

14 Livy 41.28.11

15 Plin. *HN.* 35.52.

16 See R. C. Beacham, *Spectacle Entertainment of Early Imperial Rome* (New
Haven, CT, 1999) 14–15. On the other hand, Futrell (*Blood*, 24) claims that
seventy-four pairs were presented in the *munus* for Flamininus in 174 BC. Unfortunately, she did not notice that Livy was referring to the total number of
gladiators in this *munus* and not pairs.

17 31.28.1–6.

18 A talent is a Greek monetary unit. Polybius wrote for a Greek audience and thus
gives monetary sums in terms of Greek currency. See R. C. Beacham, *Spectacle
Entertainment*, 258, n. 26 for a fuller discussion of the problem of estimating
the modern value of ancient sums of money.

19 *Bread and Circuses: Historical Sociology and Political Pluralism*, abridged with
an introduction by Oswyn Murray, trans. Brian Pearce (London, 1990) 223;
271, n. 92.

20 Polyb. 31.28.3.

21 Paullus could have been a fabulously rich man. His restraint after his victory over Perseus was remarkable. He gave the great amounts of gold and silver he found in Perseus' palaces to the Roman treasury. The only spoils he took were Perseus' books, which he gave to his sons, Fabius and Scipio (Plut. *Aem.* 28.10).

22 Ter. *Hecyra* 39–41. This information comes from the prologue of the play's third presentation a little later in the same year as Paullus' *munus*, perhaps during the *Ludi Romani* in September. In the early empire, Horace reports that even in his day drama fared no better with the common people who preferred boxing or bear baiting in the *venatio* (*Epist.* 2.1.185–6).

23 See Holt Parker, 'Plautus vs Terence: Audience and Popularity Re-examined', *AJP* 117.4 (1996) 593.

24 *Off.* 2.55–6.

25 *Ibid.* 2.56.

26 *Ep.* 6.34.

27 Ps. Quint. *Decl. Mai.* 9.6.

28 *Caes.* 5.9. On the other hand, the giving of lavish spectacles was not itself an absolute guarantee of public favour, which was also influenced by the personality of the giver. Julius Caesar and Pompey both gave extravagant spectacles, but the former enjoyed great public goodwill whereas the latter did not. See Z. Yavetz, *Plebs and Princeps* (Oxford, 1969) 49.

29 *Fam.* 2.3.1.

30 *HN* 36.120.

31 Suet. *Caes.* 29.2; Cass. Dio 40.60.1–3. See Beacham, *Spectacle Entertainment*, 72.

32 Ville (*La Gladiature*, 86) points out that all the Republican *munera* of which we have record were given by members of the senatorial class, for whom the only career was politics. There is no record of a *munus* given by a member of the equestrian class, which included men of considerable wealth. Equestrians did not pursue a political career.

33 See Lily Ross Taylor, *Party Politics in the Age of Caesar* (Berkeley, CA, 1964) 30–1.

34 Suet. *Tib.* 37.3.

35 *Public Order*, 41.

36 Ath. *Deipnosoph.* 4.39.

37 Paul J. J. Vanderbroeck, *Popular Leadership and Collective Behavior in the Late Roman Republic (c. 80–50 B.C.)* (Amsterdam, 1987) 79–80.

38 Lily Ross Taylor, *Roman Voting Assemblies from the Hannibalic War to the Dictatorship of Caesar* (Ann Arbor, MI, 1966) 56–7.

39 Veyne (*Bread and Circuses*, 224–5) points out that spectacles were only one important factor in elections.

40 *Off.* 2.59. Cicero was a special case. His enormous oratorical skills and political acumen no doubt freed him from the need to give extravagant spectacles.

41 Plut. *Sull.* 5.1.

42 Plut. *Caes.* 5.9.

43 *La Gladiature*, 82. The way Caesar threw himself so wholeheartedly into the production of this *munus* (even owning a large gladiator school in Capua) makes evident that his spectacles were not just a means to a political end, but truly a passion of his.

44 *Caesar* 5.9.

45 Plutarch puts Caesar's debt at 1,300 talents (31,200,000 sesterces), an appallingly huge sum.

46 Plut. *Crass.* 7.6 and *Caes.* 11.1–2. For accession to power through deliberate bankruptcy, see Veyne, *Bread and Circuses*, 14.

47 *Iul.* 10.2.

48 Cic. *Att.* 7.14.2.

49 Sall. *Cat.* 30.7.

50 Cic. *Sest.* 9.

51 Caes. *B Civ.* 1.14.4–5.

52 During the civil wars of AD 69, Otho incorporated two thousand gladiators into his army, most of whom did not perform well in battle (Tac. *Hist.* 2.11; 2.34–5; 3.76–7.) A century or so later, Marcus Aurelius employed a unit of gladiators in his war against the Marcomanni, whom he called the *Obsequentes* ('the obedient ones') perhaps a reference to the traditional loyalty of gladiators. Didius Julianus (briefly emperor in AD 193) armed the gladiators of Capua at the approach of Septimus Severus (*SHA Marc.* (Julius Capitolinus) 21.7 and *Did. Jul.* (Aelius Spartianus) 8.3).

53 Cic. *Att.* 7.14.2.

54 *Att.* 8.2.1.

55 The practice of naming gladiator troupes after their owners prefigures the names given to imperial gladiatorial troupes (*Iuliani* and *Neroniani*).

56 Lintott, *Violence*, 84.

57 Plut. *Cato Min.* 27.1–8.

58 Asc. *ad loc. Scaur.* 18, *ad loc. Mil.* 26; Lintott, *Violence*, 84.

59 Cic. *Cat.* 3.5.10.

60 Besides gladiators, the gangs, sponsored by Roman politicians, consisted of slaves, clients (dependants attached to wealthy patrons) and hired hooligans. See Cic. *Dom.* 6 and Lintott, *Violence*, 83–5.

61 Cass. Dio, 39.7.2.

62 The reason for the different spelling of the names of the two brothers is that Clodius, who had himself transferred to the plebeian class, spelled his name in accordance with how the lower classes pronounced the name *Claudius*.

63 77.

64 78.

65 Cass. Dio 39.8.2–3.

66 *Dom.* 6.

67 Asc. *ad loc. Mil.* 27.

68 *Ibid.* 28.

69 *Q Fr.* 2.5.3; Cass. Dio. 39.8.1. A chance meeting of the gangs of Clodius and Milo resulted in deadly violence, in which Clodius was killed. Milo was prosecuted for the murder of Clodius, but went into exile before he could be convicted.

70 44.16.2. See also App. *B Civ.* 2.17.118.

71 App. *B Civ.* 2.17.122; Plut. *Brut.* 12.5.

72 *Brut.* 12.5.

73 2.58.2. See also App. *B Civ.* 2.17.120.

74 Cic. *Sull.* 54.

75 *Ibid.*

76 The proposer of a law gave his name to the bill, an adjectival form of his surname which modified the feminine noun *lex.* Thus a law proposed by M. Tullius Cicero was known as a *Lex Tullia.*

77 Cic. *Mur.* 67.

78 See Marsh, *A History of the Roman World from 146 to 30 B.C.,* 374–77 (Revised with additional notes by H. H. Scullard (London, 1957)). The thirty-five tribes also provided the structure of the Tribal Assembly, which elected lower magistrates and voted on the passage of laws.

79 133.

80 37.

81 Curio had originally planned to run for the aedileship of 50 BC, but instead became a candidate for the tribunate of the plebs and was elected to that office for the same year.

82 *La Gladiature,* 83.

83 In fact, it is not a full two-year period, but a year and a half because elections took place in July. Once a candidate had been elected, it did not matter whether he gave *munus* or not.

84 *Sest.* 134

85 *Vat.* 37.

86 Suet. *Iul.* 26.2.

87 See Yavetz, *Plebs,* 44.

88 Cass. Dio 43.19.2.

89 Veyne, *Bread and Circuses,* 251; 259.

90 *Principia Historiae* 2.18. See Yavetz, *Plebs,* 47.

91 43.22.4.

92 Suet. *Iul.* 26.3.

93 Suetonius mentions letters of Caesar begging equestrians and senators to undertake this training.

94 During the Republic, Roman aristocrats commonly began their careers by serving as officers in the army. See Cicero's reference to his own military training in the *Pro Caelio* (11).

95 Cass. Dio 43.23.5; Suet. *Iul.* 39.1.

96 Cass. Dio 43.23 5. From the time of Sulla (early first century), attaining the quaestorship, the lowest office in the *cursus honorum* ('sequence of major magistracies available to a Roman politician') entitled the holder of this office to a permanent seat in the Senate. A senator's son had equestrian standing until he was elected to the quaestorship.

97 Cass. Dio 48.43.2–3.

98 *Ibid.* 51.22.4.

99 *Ibid.* 54.2.5.

100 *Ibid.* 56.25.7.

101 *Ibid.* 56.25.7–8.

102 *Ibid.* 56.25.8.

103 Ville, *La Gladiature* 252 and 262.

104 45.4.

105 This fictional *munus* was to take place not in Rome but in an unidentified southern Italian town. In the imperial period, when gladiator shows at Rome were controlled by the emperor and supervised by his procurators, it was in the towns like this that independent small-time gladiatorial troupes run by a *lanista* were able to find work.

106 Suet. *Aug.* 43.3.

107 Cass. Dio 59.8.3. See Ville, *La Gladiature*, 258.

108 Suet. *Ner.* 21.3.

109 Tac. *Hist.* 2.62; Cass. Dio 65.6.3.

110 *SHA Marc.* (Julius Capitolinus) 12.3.

111 *Princeps* was commonly used to refer to the emperor.

112 Cass. Dio 53.21.6. See Yavetz, *Plebs*, 103.

113 See Beacham, *Spectacle Entertainment*, 13–14.

114 2.3.2. Ennodius, a fifth century AD author, claims that Rutilius and his colleague gave a government-sponsored *munus* to allow the people of Rome to experience warfare (*Panegyricus. dictus clementissimo regi Theodorico.* 19). I, however, agree with Ville (*La Gladiature*, 46) that this claim is a distortion of Valerius Maximus' information and actually a bit of late propaganda in favour of gladiatorial combat to counter the increasing objections of Christian polemicists.

115 *ILS* 6087.70. See Welch, 'Roman Arena', 62.

116 *CIL* IV.7991.

117 *CIL* XIV.3014.

118 *CIL* X.6240; 6243.

119 53.27.6. Balsdon (*Life and Leisure*, 307) calls this spectacle 'the last great show of animals given by a private individual'.

120 Cass. Dio 54.2.3–4.

121 *Ibid.* 59.14.2.

122 *Ibid.* 54.2.3–4. See Ville, *La Gladiature*, 120.

123 *Ibid.* 54.17.4. These rules did not apply to the emperor and members of his family, who were not limited in their spending on spectacles.

124 *Ibid.* 59.14.1–5.

125 *Ibid.* 60.5.6. See Ville, *La Gladiature*, 164–5.

126 Wiedemann, *Emperors*, 8. The organization of *munera* given by the emperor was taken care of by an imperial official entrusted with this duty. We hear of a superintendent (*curator*) of *munera* and animal hunts under Caligula, who seems to have seriously disappointed the emperor. Caligula had him beaten with chains for a number of consecutive days as he watched until the smell of his decaying brains led the emperor to have him put of his misery (Suet. *Calig.* 27.4).

127 Petron. 45.13.

128 Tac. *Ann.* 13.31.

129 *Emperors*, 43.

130 Cassius Dio (54.2.4) assigns these restrictions to the praetorian *munus*, but I agree with Ville (*La Gladiature*, 121), who believes that these limitations belong more logically to private citizens than to the praetors. Cass. Dio 59.14.1–5.

131 22. Augustus paid for these *munera* that were not given in his own name. At these games, his stepsons and grandsons sat in the *editor*'s place of honour in the amphitheatre during the games. The purpose of this practice was to promote the careers of younger men, a kind of survival of the primary political function of the Republican *munus*. It was by this means that the emperor gave a visible sign of his support and hope for their political advancement and general popularity. See Cass. Dio 54.19.5 for Augustus' promotion of his two stepsons Tiberius and Drusus in this manner.

132 Augustus realized their importance both to the people and to the effectiveness of his rule. On the other hand, Cassius Dio tells us that Augustus was frequently not present in the amphitheatre during his shows (54.29.6). In the case of his absence, he sent a representative to act as *munerarius* in his place.

133 The second of these two *munera* (7 BC) consisted of gladiators fighting individual duels and in groups (*gregatim*) with an equal number of gladiators on both sides (Cass. Dio 55.8.5). Augustus seems to have enjoyed group fights.

134 Cass. Dio 55.27.3; Suet. *Tib.* 7.1; *Claud.* 2.2.

135 Cass. Dio 61.17.3.

136 *Ibid.* 59.14.2.

137 *Ann.* 1.76.

138 Suet. *Tib.* 7.2. See Beacham, *Spectacle Entertainment*, 157.

139 Tac. *Ann.* 1.76.

140 57.14.3.

141 Two other emperors disliked gladiatorial combat: Vespasian for unspecified reasons and Marcus Aurelius because of his distaste for bloodshed (Cass. Dio 71.29.3).

142 Suet. *Tib.* 47.1; Tac. *Ann.* 4.62.

143 *Dial.* 1.4.4.
144 Tac. *Ann.* 4.63. During the reign of Augustus, the property qualification for the senatorial class had been raised to 1 million sesterces.
145 *Ann.* 4.62.
146 *Mur.* 77.
147 See Ward-Perkins, *From Classical Antiquity*, 105.
148 See Nippel, *Public Order*, 87. Ville ("Les Jeux', 312) explains that when the common people lost their political power in the fall of the Republic, 'the *munera* [became] one of the principal compensations that were offered to them . . .' to maintain 'equilibrium among the classes'.
149 *Sest.* 125–7.
150 *Ibid.* 106.
151 *Ibid.* 124.
152 Cicero, who could not resist a pun, sarcastically refers to Appius' path to his seat as 'the Appian Way', Rome's most famous road, built by a prominent ancestor of Appius in the late fourth century BC.
153 *Sest.* 126.
154 *AJ* 19.24.
155 Cass. Dio 57.11.5. See J. C. Edmondson, 'Dynamic Arenas', 84. The spectacles that Tiberius did attend early in his reign were in all probability not gladiator shows.
156 Suet. *Aug.* 45.1.
157 Suet. *Claud.* 21.5.
158 Normally, the emperor could be counted on to give a *munus* of the highest quality, but this was not always true. For example, Caligula in a bad mood deliberately gave a *munus* with gladiators who were the cheapest he could find and wild animals on their last legs (Suet. *Calig.* 26.5).
159 Millar, *The Emperor*, 373–5 and Nippel, *Public Order*, 87.
160 43.22.3.
161 22. See Ville, *La Gladiature*, 126.
162 See Plin. *HN* 8. 4–5.
163 *Claud.* 21.4.
164 See Ville, *La Gladiature*, 119–20.
165 *Fasti*, 3.813–14.
166 Cass. Dio 54.28.3.
167 The introduction of gladiator shows at Antioch in 175 BC by Antiochus Epiphanes (discussed in Chapter 1) was successful after a shaky beginning, but its success was only temporary. See Robert, *Les Gladiateurs*, 239–54; 264). Wiedemann (*Emperors*, 42), however, believes that gladiatorial combat 'became a regular institution at Antioch', but his reliance on Livy's account (41.20.13) for this claim seems to me unjustified.
168 Cass. Dio 47.40.6.

169 *Ibid.* 54.2.3–4.

170 Tac. *Ann.* 11.22. See Ville, *La Gladiature*, 164–6.

171 Mart., 7.37. See Ville, *La Gladiature*, 166–8, n. 55. The emperor Alexander Severus (AD 222–235) introduced a distinction between quaestors with a political future and those without. The former were called *quaestores candidati* and were required to give *munera* completely at their own expense with the promise that they would later be chosen praetor and govern a province. The latter, called *quaestores arcarii* (from *arca*, 'treasury') also gave *munera* but less lavishly and received money from the treasury to help them pay for the shows (*SHA Alex. Sev.* (Aelius Lampridius) 43.3–4).

172 Wiedemann (*Emperors*, 47) believes that Augustus decreed two annual *munera*, one taking place in March and the other in December. Both in his book and in a later article ("Das Ende der Gladiatorenspiele', *Nikephoros* 8 (1995) 151), Wiedemann attaches elaborate symbolism for the pairing of the well-attested December *munus* and his alleged March *munus*. He sees these two annual *munera*, given during the winter and spring solstices, as symbols of renewal. The December *munus* marks the end of the old year and the March *munus* celebrates spring regeneration. Ville (*La Gladiature*, 159–60), in fact, believes that there was only one annual *munus*, which in the time of Augustus took place in March and was later moved to December by Caligula. I would side with Ville in this matter. There is no further mention of the March *munus* in the sources after the reign of Augustus and no reference at all to a December *munus* during his reign. The fourth century AD calendar of Philocalus mentions only the December *munus*.

173 It is true that by the fourth century, the celebration of the Saturnalia had been extended several days, but the December gladiator games were only suspended for the traditional date of the festival. See R. M. Ogilvie, *The Romans and Their Gods* (London and Toronto, 1969) 98.

174 *La Gladiature*, 160–1.

175 *CIL* IV.9969.

176 Suet. *Ner.* 7.2.

177 *CIL* IV.1181; 3822; 7988b; 7989a.

178 *CIL* IV.1180; 1196; 1197; 1198; 7986a; 9964; 9971a.

179 *CIL* IV.1180.

180 *CIL* X.4893.

181 Cass. Dio 59.8.3.

182 *Calig.* 14.2.

183 *SHA Max. & Balb.* (Julius Capitolinus) 8.5–6. Ville ("Les Jeux', 288) calls this passage 'propaganda in favor of *munera*' that were coming under attack by Christianity.

184 Cass. Dio 51.22.4; 54.19.4–5; 55.10.6.

185 Suet. *Ner.* 12.1; Cass. Dio 66.25.1–3.

186 Suet. Claud. 21.4; Cass. Dio 60.17.9.

187 Tac. *Hist.* 2.95. The *venatio*, however, seems to have been a more common way of celebrating the emperor's birthday. For example, see Cass. Dio 54.26.2 and *Pass. Perpet. et Felic.* 7.9.

188 Cass. Dio 51.7.2–3; 53.1.4–6.

189 *Ibid.* 67.8.4; 68.15.1.

190 Suet. *Ner.* 12.1. See Ville, *La Gladiature*, 138–9.

191 Suet. *Ner.* 12.1.

192 This, however, is not to say that nobles always fought with harmless weapons. When Drusus, the son of Tiberius, allowed two equestrians to fight as gladiators in his *munus*, they must have fought with regular swords because one of them was killed (Cass. Dio 57.14.3).

193 Suet. *Ner.* 31.3.

194 *La Gladiature.*, 138.

195 28.21.1–4. Livy cites other reasons for participation: a love of competition and the need to settle disputes (4–6).

196 'Ideology', 140.

197 *Ibid.* 141.

198 Yavetz (*Plebs*, 115) in speaking of Caligula's humiliation of the upper classes says that 'it was a source of particular gratification to the masses'.

199 *Ann.* 14.14. See Edwards, 'Unspeakable Professions', 85–8.

200 Cass. Dio 66.25.4.

201 *Spect.* 4; 5. Titus, probably wanting not to appear harsh at the beginning of his reign, chose the lesser of two punishments that he could have imposed on these informers, who were no doubt citizens. The other harsher penalty was death by the sword.

202 See Ville, *La Gladiature*, 147.

203 See K. M. Coleman, 'Contagion', 77.

204 Cass. Dio 66.25.2.

205 Tac. *Ann.* 15.32; Suet. *Dom.* 4.1; Stat. *Silv.* 1.6.57–62.

206 Cass. Dio 68.15.1.

207 Caligula: Suet. *Calig.* 32.2; Hadrian: *SHA Hadr.* (Aelius Spartianus) 14.11; Lucius Verus: *SHA Marc.* (Julius Capitolinus) 8.12; Didius Julianus: *SHA Did.* (Aelius Spartianus) 9.1.

208 *Ner.* 53.1.

209 Cass. Dio 72.20.1.

210 72.19.3 Aurelius Victor (*Caes.* 17.4) says that Commodus was able to kill many gladiators because he used a real dagger while they were limited to one with a dulled point.

211 Aur. Vict. *De Caes.* 17.5–6. Herodian (1.15.8) mentions that when Commodus stopped wanting to be called Hercules, he took the name of a dead gladiator, which may have been Scaeva, in as much as Commodus was left-handed. See C. R. Whittaker's *Loeb Classical Library* translation of *Herodian* (Cambridge, MA, 1969) I, 105, n. 4.

212 Cass. Dio 72.17.2; *SHA Comm.* (Aelius Lampridius) 5.5).

213 Cass. Dio 72.19.2–6.

214 *Ibid.* 72.21.3 and *SHA Comm.* (Aelius Lampridius) 16.8. It is likely that the *Porta Libitiensis* ('Gate of Death') and its opposite, the *Porta Sanivivaria* ('Gate of Life') were standard features of amphitheatres throughout the empire. The Gate of Life in an amphitheatre in Carthage is mentioned twice in the *Passion of Perpetua and Felicity* (10.13; 20.7). See also Kyle, *Spectacles*, 156.

215 Cass. Dio 72.22.5.

216 *Iul.* 39.3.

217 'Launching into History: Aquatic Displays in the Early Empire', *JRS* 83 (1993) 49.

218 43.23.3.

219 *HN* 8.22.

220 Lucr. 5.1302; Juv. 12.110.

221 Suet. *Iul.* 39.3. The turning posts were called *metae*, which consisted of three cones topped with egg-shaped objects on a high foundation.

222 Cass. Dio 51.22.6–8.

223 Suet. *Claud.* 21.6.

224 Coleman, 'Launching', 71.

225 The lake was filled in after Caesar's death because of the suspicion that it had caused a plague (Cass. Dio 45.17.8).

226 'Launching', 70.

227 *Ibid.* 67–8.

228 Suet. *Iul.* 39.4.

229 These events with mutual 'executions' by the participants performed the same function as the *meridianum spectaculum*, but on a much larger scale.

230 Suet. *Iul.* 39.4.

231 2.100.2.

232 Aug. *RG* 23.

233 *Ibid.*

234 Ov. *Ars. am.* 1.171–2.

235 Cass. Dio 55.10.8.

236 See Coleman, 'Launching,' 70.

237 *The Power of Images in the Age of Augustus*, trans. Allan Shapiro (Ann Arbor, MI, 1990) 84.

238 *Ibid.* 72. There had already been a triumphal celebration for his victory over Cleopatra, a foreign enemy.

239 Caligula seems to have given *naumachiae*, but we know nothing specific about them. We have only one puzzling reference to his excavation of the *Saepta* and filling it with water. After all this effort, only one ship could be accommodated, which hardly qualifies as a *naumachia*. Cassius Dio says enigmatically that he transferred his spectacles 'to another place', which involved demolishing many large buildings (50.10.5). We may presume, however, that if Caligula had given a notable *naumachia* elsewhere, it would have been recorded.

240 H. J. Leon, 'Morituri Te Salutamus', *TAPA* 70 (1939) 46–7. Cass. Dio 60.11.5.

241 Suet. *Claud.* 21.6.

242 *Ann.* 12.56.

243 Suet. *Claud.* 21.6.

244 *Ann.* 12.56.

245 60.33.4.

246 See *OCD*, 'Trireme'.

247 Cass. Dio 60.33.4. Suetonius reports these words in third person: 'Hail, emperor, those who are about to die salute you' (Suet. *Claud.* 21.6).

248 Cass. Dio 60.33.4.

249 The Praetorian Guard was a small army which protected the emperor.

250 *Ann.* 13.31.1. See Wistrand, *Entertainment*, 26–7.

251 *Ann.* 12.56.

252 61.9.5.

253 Suet. Ner. 12.1.

254 *Ibid.*

255 As Coleman ('Launching', 56) points out, although aquatic shows ideally required a structure built specifically for this purpose, the Romans were in the habit of flooding existing structures such as the *Saepta* and the Circus Flaminius.

256 'Launching', 57.

257 62.15.1. Cassius Dio (writing in Greek) regularly refers to the Roman amphitheatre as a 'theatre' or 'hunting theatre' probably because the *venatio* took place there. For example see 66.25.2 and 66.21.2.

258 Cass. Dio 62.15.1–5. Tacitus (*Ann.* 15.37), describes a similar water party, also hosted by Tigellinus, but locates the brothels (no mention of taverns), on the banks of the *stagnum Agrippae*, an artificial lake built by Augustus' chief naval commander. Ville (*La Gladiature*, 140) assumes that the two aquatic dinner parties are one and the same and argues that, contrary to Cassius Dio's assignment of Nero's show to an '[amphi]theatre', the spectacle had really taken place on the *stagnum Agrippae*. Locating the show on an artificial lake, however, creates a problem. The trick of flooding, draining and flooding again, would not have been possible with an artificial lake. It is better to take the aquatic party in Tacitus as an event separate from the one described by Cassius Dio. See Coleman, 'Launching', 51; 53–4.

259 See 'The great Colosseum debate', in Ronald Ridley, *The Eagle and the Spade*: *Archeology in Rome during the Napoleonic Era* (Cambridge, 1992) 217–37.

260 'Launching', 58–60. See also Golvin, *L'Amphithéâtre Romain*, 335; Connolly, *Colosseum*, 139–51; Hazel Dodge, 'Amusing the Masses: Buildings for Entertainment and Leisure in the Roman World', in D. S. Potter and D. J. Mattingly (eds), *Life, Death, and Entertainment in the Roman Empire* (Ann Arbor, MI, 1999) 236.

261 Coleman, 'Launching', 61.

262 66.25.2–3.

263 *Spect.* 27.

264 *Ibid.* 28–30. See Coleman, 'Launching', 62–5. The legend re-enacted in this spectacle told of a young man named Leander, guided by the lamp of the beautiful Hero, who swam every night across the Hellespont to be with her. One stormy night when the wind blew out the lamp out, Leander lost his way and drowned. In despair, Hero then jumped from her tower into the sea and drowned.

265 *Spect.* 34.9–10.

266 Cass. Dio 66.25.2–4. The monument may have been dedicated to the two grandsons of Augustus, Gaius and Lucius Caesar, designated as his heirs, who died before Augustus. The name of the area in which the lake was located was 'Grove of the Caesars' (*Nemus Caesarum*), named in their honour. See Coleman, 'Launching', 54.

267 Coleman ('Launching', 53) notes that draining a lake the size of this one would have taken seventeen days.

268 *Spect.* 34.5–6.

269 *Ibid.* 34.11–12. See Coleman, 'Launching', 67–8.

270 *Dom.* 4.1.

271 *Dom.* 4.2.

272 Cass. Dio 48.19.1.

273 Hor., *Epist.* 1.18.61–4. See Coleman, 'Launching', 61–2.

274 Aur. Vict. *Caes.* 28.1. See Coleman, 'Launching', 54.

275 *De spect.* 12. See Ps. Cyprian, *Spect.* 4.

276 For example, Cass. Dio 47.40.7; Tert. *Apol.* 9; Prudent. *C. Symm.* 1.407; Auson. *De feriis romanis* 33.37.

277 *C. Symm.* 2.1091–1132.

278 See Wiedemann, *Das Ende*, 146.

279 *Serm.* 199.3.

280 *Conf.* 6.8.

281 See Ramsay MacMullen, *Changes in the Roman Empire: Essays in the Ordinary* (Princeton, NJ, 1990) 148.

282 *Ep.* 7.3. For similar thoughts on this matter from another pagan author, see Plut. *Mor.* 997 c.

283 'Das Ende', 148. Wiedemann (*Emperors*, 92 and 'Das Ende', 156; 159) explains the incompatibility of the Church and gladiatorial combat differently. He sees the main theme of the gladiatorial experience as the conquest of death through martial virtue in the arena, providing an earthly 'salvation' granted by the Roman people when they persuaded the *editor* to grant *missio* and, on rare occasions, a permanent release from the arena. This process resulted in a 're-surrection' from the status of non-person to that of freedman in the Roman community. Thus gladiatorial combat came into direct competition with the Church, which jealously claimed to be the sole instrument of salvation and re-surrection in the conquest of death. Wiedemann claims that gladiatorial combat disappeared because it became superfluous. This is an interesting and ingenious theory, but as I see it, unlikely.

284 *Apost. Const.* 2.61. As Ville ('Les Jeux', 294, n. 1) points out, Tertullian's *De Spectaculis* was intended as a warning for Christians not to attend the amphitheatre.

285 See Ville, 'Les Jeux', 297.

286 *Cod. Theod.* 15.12.1. Wiedemann ('Das Ende', 159) suggests that this decree may have been motivated by a need for new workers in the mines, rather than compassion for convicts. MacMullen (*Changes*, 148) writes of an 'unwilling-ness to feed the amphitheater through the law courts' and adds that 'exactly why the courts should not be used for that purpose, we have no hint or infor-mation' but this legislation was not a matter of 'any general tenderness towards one's fellow beings'.

287 Gian Luca Gregori, 'Legislation on the Arena Shows', in Ada Gabucci (ed.), *The Colosseum*, trans. Mary Becker (Los Angeles, 2001) 95. If convicts could no longer be forced to become gladiators, the only remaining source was voluntary gladiators (*auctorati*), whose price must have gone up dramatically, thereby posing a further economic barrier to the frequent presentation of glad-iator games.

288 Ville ('Les Jeux', 317) calls the effect of Constantine's edict 'ephemeral', say-ing that the law may have been ignored or revoked. He points out that in this period an *editor* set up an epitaph at Tergesta for two gladiators in which he congratulates them for having made his *munus* such a great success (*CIL* V.563). See also 315–16.

289 See MacMullen, *Changes*, 148. Could this comment have anything to do with the claim of Julius Capitolinus that in the mid-third century AD a *munus* was given before a war to habituate the soldiers to the sight of blood (*SHA Max. & Balb.* 8.7)?

290 *CIL* XI. 5283. See Gian Luca Gregori, 'Constantine's Reply to the Umbrians', in Gabucci (ed.), *The Colosseum*, 90.

291 *Med.* 1.5.1; 6.46.1.

292 Cass. Dio 71.29.3.

293 *SHA Marc.* (Julius Capitolinus) 21.6–8; 23.4–5.

294 *Changes*, 147. Ward-Perkins (*From Classical Antiquity*, 113) points out that the Church never pursued the elimination of gladiatorial combat aggressively and, moreover, emperors probably were not able to enforce a legal ban.

295 For the role of economics in the decline of gladiatorial combat, see Ramsay MacMullen, *Changes*, 147 and Gregori, 'The End of the Gladiators', in Gabucci (ed.), *The Colosseum*, 96. Ward-Perkins (*From Classical Antiquity*, 112) bases his argument on the fact that chariot races and *venationes*, both expensive spec-tacles, continued after the disappearance of gladiators in the second half of the fifth century.

296 'Gladiatorial Ranking', 111.

297 *SHA Alex. Sev.* (Aelius Lampridius) 43.4.

298 *SHA Gord. Tres* (Julius Capitolinus) 3.5.

299 Hopkins and Beard, *The Colosseum*, 54 and Gregori, 'The End of the Gladiators', in Gabucci (ed.), *The Colosseum*, 97.
300 28.4.33.
301 See Ville, 'Les Jeux', 331.
302 *Hist. Eccles.* 5.26.
303 'Les Jeux', 326–9.
304 *Cod. Theod.* 15.12.3. Gregori, 'Legislation on the Arena Shows', in Gabucci (ed.), *The Colosseum*, 95 suggests that this measure was to prevent senators from using gladiators as bodyguards.
305 A. Chastagnol, *Le Sénat romain*, (Bonn, 1966) 22. See Bomgardner, *Story*, 207, 257, n. 47.
306 'Les Jeux', 316. See also Rossella Rea, 'The Colosseum through the Centuries', in Gabucci (ed.), *The Colosseum*, 181.
307 Gregori, 'The End of the Gladiators', in Gabucci (ed.), *The Colosseum*, 97.
308 For example, Tert. *Apol.* 39. See Veyne, *Bread and Circuses*, 23–6; 28.
309 Cameron, *Circus factions*, 217. Ward-Perkins (*From Classical Antiquity*, 112) complains that Cameron's suggestion is 'too vague and difficult . . . to accept' and cites 'the absence of any firm evidence to support it'. I too would have liked some specific evidence, but sometimes the historian must fall back on intuition and informed conjecture.

Chapter 5 A Brief History of the Arena Hunt

1 39.22.1–2.
2 44.18.8. The sources tend to refer to large African cats simply as 'African beasts'.
3 Plin. *HN* 8.64. Ville (*La Gladiature*, 55) suggests various motives that the Senate might have had for this ban: (1) fear of the danger that these wild animals posed in Rome, (2) concern that purchases of animals would enrich a powerful North African enemy (Carthage), and (3) an attempt to restrict the political ambition of magistrates who gave *venationes*.
4 *Sest.* 116.
5 Plin. *HN* 36.114–5.
6 22.15.24.
7 See Friedländer, *Roman Life*, II, 63.
8 Plin. *HN* 8.96. *Euripus* is the Greek word meaning 'a strait', specifically the one between Boeotia and the island of Euboea in Greece.
9 *HN* 9.11.
10 17.1.44.
11 See Sen. *Ep.* 88.22.
12 Plin. *HN* 8.53.
13 *Ibid.* 8.17.
14 *Ibid.* 8.18.

15 *Ibid.* 8.4.
16 Cic. *Fam.* 7.1.3.
17 Plin. *HN* 8.20.
18 *Dial.* 10.13.6.
19 *HN* 8.21.
20 39.38.3–4. Cassius Dio refuses to accept or reject this story.
21 *Fam.* 7.1.3.
22 *Animals*, 23.
23 Subjecting animals to violence as entertainment is a practice that survived the ancient world in the form of bull- and bear-baiting, bullfights, dog- and cockfights, etc. Dog- and cockfights, although illegal, are enjoying a renaissance in contemporary America.
24 *Fam.* 7.1.3.
25 *Dial.* 10.13.6.
26 *Ibid.* 10.13.7.
27 *HN* 8.22. *La Gladiature*, 394.
28 12.106–7.
29 *SHA Aurel.* (Flavius Vopiscus) 5.6.
30 Caesar surrounded the racecourse of the Circus Maximus with a moat to keep dangerous animals away from the spectators. In addition to the four hundred lions in the *venatio*, twenty elephants were involved in the infantry and cavalry battle that Caesar presented in the Circus Maximus (Suet. *Iul.* 39.2–3; Plin. *HN* 8.22). Caesar had obviously learned a lesson from the debacle of Pompey's *venatio* in 55 BC.
31 Cassius Dio (39.38.2) says that five hundred lions were slaughtered at Pompey's *venatio*, while Pliny the Elder says six hundred (*HN* 8.53).
32 Suet. *Iul.* 75.3.
33 Plut. *Brut.* 8.5–7.
34 *NA* 5.14.7.
35 *HN* 8.182.
36 Cass. Dio 61.9.1; Suet. *Claud.* 21.3. This event was also popular in the Greek east. See Robert, *Les Gladiateurs*, 318–19.
37 43.23.1–2. This translation by E. Cary and H. Foster is from the *Loeb Classical Library* edition of Cassius Dio's *History of Rome*.
38 *Spect* 20.
39 *NA* 2.11.
40 One is reminded of the dancing elephants and hippos in Walt Disney's *Fantasia*.
41 *HN* 8.4–5.
42 Pliny may be mistaken about the tightrope walking. Suetonius says that Galba (later emperor briefly in AD 69) first presented this trick in the early 30s. Elephant tightrope walking was again seen in a *munus* given by Nero for his mother Agrippina. A Roman equestrian rode an elephant walking on a tightrope from the highest point of a theatre's seating to the floor to the stage (Cass. Dio 61.17.2;

Suet. *Ner.* 11.2). Seneca says that tiny Ethiopian trainers taught elephants to kneel and to walk on a tightrope (*Ep.* 85.41).

43 Musurillo, *Acts*, 10–13 (12). See Ville, *La Gladiature*, 235–40. Note that the *editor* was not entirely free to do whatever he wanted.

44 When the flames failed to finish Polycarp off, he was dispatched by a *confector*, whose job it was to put dying animals out of their misery (Suet. *Aug.* 43.2; *Ner.* 12.1). See Musurillo, *Acts*, 14–15 (16).

45 Val. Max. 2.7.14.

46 Livy, *Per.* 51. See also Val. Max. 2.7.13.

47 Tac. *Hist.* 2.61.

48 *Dig.* 48.19.8.11.

49 Shaw, 'The Passion of Perpetua', 6.

50 Musurillo, *Acts*, 4–5 (3).

51 Martial's list of crimes eligible for this penalty varies only slightly: the murder of his father or master, robbing a temple, or arson (*Spect.* 9.8–10).

52 *Dig.* 48.10.8.pr. It should also be noted that slaves guilty of counterfeiting received even worse punishments. They were burned alive or crucified. This is in accordance with the Roman legal principle: the lower the status of the criminal, the harsher the penalty.

53 9.18.1.

54 *Dig.* 48.13.7. pr.

55 Crucifixion is not mentioned in this passage, but this too was an extreme punishment that involved an even slower death with much suffering. Crucifixion, which required the victim to hang on the cross sometimes for days before death came, also laid him open to frequent mockery from passers-by.

56 48.19.28.15. See Coleman, 'Fatal Charades', 46–7.

57 *Dig.* 48.8.11.1. The *Digest* specifically mentions the possibility of delay involved in the carrying out the *ad bestias* penalty, but gives a different reason: the authorities sometimes wanted to question the condemned further for evidence against their associates, although it is hard to see why this would not be true of other methods of capital punishment (48.19.29.pr).

58 *Ep.* 70.20.

59 *Ep.* 70.23.

60 *Dig.* 48.8.11.1.

61 *La Gladiature*, 239.

62 45.7–8.

63 *De spect.* 19.4.

64 Cic. *Fam.* 10.32.3. This was not the only outrage that Balbus committed in this province (of which he was a native). C. Asinius Pollio gives a full listing of his offences in the same letter (2–3).

65 *Pis.* 89.

66 Cass. Dio 59.10.3. See Suet. *Calig.* 27.4, which may refer to the same incident.

67 Suet. *Calig.* 27.1.
68 Tac. *Ann.* 15.44.
69 See Shaw, 'The Passion of Perpetua', 3, n. 3.
70 From the beginning of the imperial period it became common practice to add an amphitheatre to a military installation in the provinces for the purpose of training and entertainment for the soldiers. Some camps even had their own gladiator troupe (Futrell, *Blood*, 150–2). The remains of this Carthaginian military amphitheatre have not yet been discovered. As Shaw ('The Passion of Perpetua', 3, n. 3) points out, there is evidence of only one amphitheatre in Carthage, but this was a large venue with a capacity of *c.* 30,000 spectators, not a small military structure. See Bomgardner, 'Carthage Amphitheatre', 86. There was even a military amphitheatre in Rome, built during the reign of Elagabalus (AD 218–222), perhaps for the use of the Praetorian Guard. The emperor Aurelian may have intended to use the upper seating area as part of Rome's fortifications. See Lawrence Richardson, *A New Topographical Dictionary of Ancient Rome* (Baltimore, 1992) 7 ('Amphitheatrum Castrense').
71 The *venatio* was a traditional form of celebration of the birthday of the emperor and members of his family (Ville, *La Gladiature*, 124). It should be noted that the date, which I have taken from Shaw ('The Passion', 3, n. 2), is by no means certain. Shaw calls AD 203 'conjectural' and the month and day 'probable'.
72 Cass. Dio 76.15.2.
73 *Pass. Perpet. et Felic.* 2.1; 4.5.
74 Perpetua never mentions Felicitas; the anonymous author of the *Passion* tells her story. See Shaw, 'The Passion', 25.
75 This arrest was not part of an official persecution of all Christians by the government, but may have been the result of a decree by the emperor Septimius Severus forbidding conversion to Judaism or Christianity (Eus. *Hist. Eccl.* 6.1.1; *SHA Sever.* (Aelius Spartianus) 17.1). James Rives ('The Piety of a Persecutor', *Journal of Early Christian Studies* 4.1 (1996) 19), however, argues that the *Historia Augusta* is unreliable on this point and that Eusebius is talking about only Alexandria.
76 *Pass. Perpet. et Felic.* 3.5–6. The soldiers were guards in the military prison, who probably extorted either sex or money from female prisoners in return for privileges.
77 *Pass. Perpet. et Felic.* 3.8; 6.7. Eventually she gave her baby to her family.
78 *Ibid.* 16.2–4.
79 Neither Perpetua nor the anonymous author of this work ever mentions her husband. Shaw ('The Passion', 25, n. 56) suggests that her husband may have found Christianity not to his taste and disowned his wife for embracing it.
80 *Pass. Perpet. et Felic.* 6.1–3.
81 See Robin Lane Fox, *Pagans and Christians* (New York, 1987) 434.
82 *HE* 5.1.11.

83 Eus. *De martyribus Palaestrinae*. 3.3–4. For other volunteer martyrs, see Eus. *Hist. Eccl.* 7.12 and Tert. *Ad Scap.* 5. See also Salisbury, *Perpetua's Passion*, 135; Fox, *Pagans*, 457–8 and Coleman, 'Fatal Charades', 57.

84 *Med.* 11.3.

85 See Symm. *Relat.* 3; Prudent. *C. Symmachum* 2.23–44; and R. H. Barrow, *Prefect and Emperor: The Relationes of Symmachus AD 384* (Oxford, 1973) 32–3.

86 'The Martyrdom of Polycarp', 46.

87 Hilarianus here was following the policy established in the previous century by Trajan (AD 98–117) with regard to treatment of the Christians: 'the one who denies that he is a Christian and proves it unequivocally, that is by praying to our gods, even if he has been under suspicion in the past, should receive pardon as a result of his repentance (Plin. *Ep.* 10.97)'.

88 'Martyrdom as Spectacle', in Ruth Scodel (ed.), *Theater and Society in the Classical World* (Ann Arbor, MI, 1993) 64–5.

89 *Pass. Perpet. et Felic.* 6.4–6. Perpetua's use of the word *hilares* to express the Christians' joy after being condemned must be intended as a mocking pun on the name Hilarianus.

90 Rives, 'Piety', 20–4.

91 *Pass. Perpet. et Felic.* 15.1–6.

92 *Ibid.* 17.1–3.

93 Shaw ('The Passion', 5) describes the worship of Saturn and Ceres as 'the great non-Christian religious cults of North Africa'.

94 *Pass. Perpet. et Felic.* 18.1–9.

95 See Bomgardner, *Story*, 142.

96 *Pass. Perpet. et Felic.* 19.1–3. See Coleman, 'Fatal Charades', 59.

97 It is clear that, when wild beasts were roaming the arena, more lives were at risk than just those who were the intended objects of their animal fury. Martial tells the story of a performing lion whose trainer could insert his hand in the animal's mouth with no danger. On one occasion, the lion's savagery returned suddenly and he killed two young arena attendants (*harenarii*) whose job it was to rake the bloody sand (Mart. 2.75).

98 See Coleman, 'Fatal Charades', 59, nn. 135, 136.

99 *Pass. Perpet. et Felic.* 19.4–6.

100 Lions and leopards were still used in Italy as public executioners in the late Middle Ages (Friedländer, *Roman Life*, II, 64).

101 Christian writers often see the cause of this behaviour as the martyr's sanctity.

102 Eus. *Hist. Eccl.* 5.1.41; 56. See also 8.7.2. Being tossed by a bull was another of the typical punishments for sexually promiscuous women. See Petron. 45.8.

103 Salisbury (*Perpetua's Passion*, 143) points out that a feral cow could be as ferocious as a bull and that, even today, matadors in Spain fight wild cows to add variety to the show.

104 *Pass. Perpet. et Felic.* 20.1.

105 See Shaw, 'The Passion', 8. Punishing a woman by exposing her to a bull seems to have been considered appropriate for an adulteress, as a character in Petronius' *Satyricon* says of the mistress who he claims forced her husband's steward to have sex with her (45.8).

106 Blandina, like Perpetua, was wrapped in a net, before she was exposed to a bull (Eus. *Hist. Eccl.* 5.1.56).

107 She pinned up her hair to avoid giving a wrong impression to the crowd (unkempt hair in women was a sign of mourning). Perpetua wanted to avoid any sign of sorrow, preferring to show her joy at her entrance into eternal life.

108 *Pass. Perpet. et Felic.* 20.1–7.

109 Cf. Suet. *Claud.* 34.2.

110 *Pass. Perpet. et Felic.* 21.1–10. Louis Robert ('Une Vision de Perpetue martyre a Carthage en 203', *Comptes rendus des séances – Académie des inscriptions et belles-lettres* (1982) 238–43) argues that the gladiator in training who was assigned to dispatch Perpetua and her two friends was a *retiarius*. Robert notes that it would have been beneath the dignity of a veteran gladiator to perform this menial task in the *venatio*. He then goes on to claim that the apprentice *retiarius* would have been the choice among the *tirones* of the various gladiatorial categories, since the lightly armed and nearly naked *retiarius* was the most despised of gladiators.

111 *HN* 8.56.

112 Arthur Gilchrist Brodeur, 'The Grateful Lion', *PMLA* 39.3 (1924), 485–524. See also Campbell Bonner, 'Eros and the Wounded Lion', *AJA*, 49.4 (1945) 443.

113 *NA* 5.14.5–30.

114 *NA* 7.48.

115 Along with the announcements of stentorian heralds, this was a normal method of providing information to the crowd. We know that Claudius used them for this purpose (Cass. Dio 60.13.5). Arena placards are also mentioned in a rhetorical exercise attributed to Quintilian (Quint. *Decl. Min.* 302, pr.). When a placard was displayed to the crowd announcing that one of the gladiators about to take part in combat was a freeman who had sold himself to pay for his father's burial, the crowd requested that he be released from further service as a gladiator, a request that the *munerarius* granted.

116 Gell. *NA* 5.14.30.

117 *Ben.* 2.19.1.

118 The love of a lion for his carer has been vividly demonstrated by a videotape from an animal shelter in Cali, Colombia: http://www.local6.com/news/10726779/detail.html.

119 Brodeur ('The Grateful Lion', 503) believes that Apion's story in Gellius was the inspiration for all other extant tales of the grateful lion, which is possible, but, I think, unlikely. Apion's tale seems to me a later development of the stories recorded by Pliny the Elder.

120 Shaw's play was brought to the screen in 1952 in a film of the same name star-
    ring Alan Young, Victor Mature and Jean Simmons (dir. Chester Erskine).
    Shaw changes Androcles from a pagan runaway slave to a Christian freeman.
121 'Fatal Charades', 49.
122 App. *B Civ.* 5.13.131.
123 *Ibid.* 5.13.132.
124 Coleman ('Fatal Charades', 53) suggests that this execution took place in the
    late 30s BC. In this spectacular execution, Octavian may have been inspired by
    the showmanship of his adoptive father, Julius Caesar.
125 6.2.6.
126 For the representation of Mt Aetna, see Coleman, 'Fatal Charades', 54: 'the
    offender is humiliated by the expedient of associating the instrument of his
    execution with the symbol of his power'.
127 10.104–107.
128 *Met.* 4.13.
129 Apuleius' description of this contraption is no doubt based on something he
    had seen in an amphitheatre. Although Apuleius' *Metamorphoses* is a work of
    fiction, it has been shown to be based on fact. See Fergus Millar, 'The World of
    the Golden Ass', *JRS* 71 (1981) 63. A collapsing device in the form of ship was
    employed in a *venatio* given by Septimius Severus, but not in order to execute
    noxii. This 'ship' was used to provide a spectacular entry of hundreds of ani-
    mals (bears, lionesses, panthers, lions, ostriches, wild asses, bison), which
    spilled out into the arena and were slaughtered by arena hunters (Cass. Dio
    76.1.5).
130 Coleman (*Liber Spectaculorum*, 83) notes that he could be historical or fictitious.
131 Josephus *AJ* 19.94; Juv. 8.187–8; Suet. *Cal.* 57.4. The word 'mime' in its
    ancient usage is not to be confused with the modern. The Romans used the
    word of both a dramatic genre and its actors. The Roman mime was a short
    dramatic performance with dialogue, depicting a slice of life, with an emphasis
    on comedy. With its lack of sophistication and literary pretension, it may be
    compared to modern situation comedy on television.
132 See Coleman, 'Fatal Charades', 64.
133 Mart. *Spect.* 9.3.
134 *Ibid.* 24.7.
135 *Ibid.* 10. There is no extant account of the death of Daedalus.
136 Cf. the device called the *deus ex machina* used in ancient drama to depict gods
    arriving on earth from the sky.
137 Mart. *Spect.* 19.
138 In the myth, the product of this union was the Minotaur.
139 *Spect.* 6.
140 'Fatal Charades', 64. In support of her suggestion of a covering of cowhide for
    Pasiphae, Coleman points to Nero's having Christians wrapped in animal skins
    when he set dogs on them.

141 10.28. The ass is actually a human being named Lucius, who has been transformed into this animal. Thus the title of Apuleius' work: *Metamorphoses* ('Changes'). Coleman gives modern examples of bestiality as public entertainment (though not judicial punishments) in North Africa, Mexico and the Middle East ('Fatal Charades', 64, n. 173).

142 *Epistle to Corinthians*, 6.2.

143 Coleman, 'Fatal Charades', 66; Potter, 'Martyrdom', in Scodel (ed.), *Theater and Society*, 67.

144 The story of Mucius Scaevola was told in Chapter 1.

145 10.25.

146 8.30.

147 10.25.3.

148 'Fatal Charades', 61–2.

149 Tert. *Apol.* 15.5.

150 Coleman ('Fatal Charades', 61) gives an example of a similar option offered to convicts in seventeenth century England: self-mutilation or starvation.

151 *Anth. Pal.* 11.184.

152 Coleman, 'Fatal Charades', 61.

153 Cass. Dio 72.20.3.

154 *Fam.* 8.2.2.

155 Christopher Epplett ('The Capture of Animals by the Roman Military', *Greece & Rome* 2nd Ser. 48.2. (2001) 210) points out that although it is likely that Cicero used soldiers to hunt for animals in Cilicia, there is no specific evidence that this practice existed in the Republic. Epplett, however, presents ample evidence that in the imperial period, army trackers (*vestigatores*) and hunters (*venatores*) worked together in the capture of animals (217–19). The official title of the hunters seems to have been *venatores immunes* ('exempt hunters'), referring to their exemption from regular soldierly duties in compensation for their hunting activities (212).

156 *Fam.* 8.4.5.

157 *Fam.* 8.9.3.

158 *Fam.* 8.6.5. Caelius calls the leopards he wants Cicero to send from Cilicia 'Greek' because Asia Minor in which Cilicia was located was a hellenized area. See *Cicero's Letters to His Friends*, I, trans. D. R. Shackleton Bailey (New York, 1978) 189, n. 354.

159 *Fam.* 2.11.2.

160 *Fam.* 8.9.3.

161 See Plin. *Ep.* 6.34.3, discussed in Chapter 1.

162 15.11.2.

163 *Met.* 4.14. See Kyle's chapter, 'Arenas and Eating: Corpses and Carcasses as Food?' in his *Spectacles of Death*, 184–212.

164 App. *B Civ.* 3.3.23.

165 *Att.* 15.18.2.

166 Cic. *Phil.* 1.36; *Att.* 16.5.3.
167 Plut. *Brut.*, 21.5.
168 *Phil.* 10.7.
169 *Ibid.* 1.36; 10.8.
170 *Att.* 16.2.3.
171 App. 3.3.24.
172 *Ecl.* 7.65–6.
173 G. B. Townend ('Calpurnius Siculus and the *Munus Neronis*', *JRS* 70 (1980) 171–2) claims that there is no evidence of polar bears at Rome up through the 3rd century AD. He does point out, however, that arctic hares, elk and possibly even polar bears could have been brought back to Rome by the Roman equestrian sent to northern Europe to get amber for Nero's *munus* (Plin. *HN* 37.45). I would like to point out that Martial describes a bear killed in a *venatio* in AD 80 as having dwelt 'under the vault of the Arctic skies' (*Spect.* 17.4).
174 Calp. *Ecl.* 7.69–73. The strawberry tree is so called not because it produces actual strawberries, but owing to its colour, although its fruit only vaguely resembles strawberries.
175 *Spect.* 24.3.
176 *SHA Prob.* (Flavius Vopiscus) 19.4.
177 See *SHA Gord. Tres* (Julius Capitolinus) 3.6.
178 Poems 6 through 26 and 32–3. D. R. Shackleton Bailey (*Martial: Epigrams* I (Cambridge, MA, 1993) 39, note *a*) notes that since the earliest manuscripts do not include poems 35–37, they 'probably (certainly in the case of 37) do not belong to this book'. They have nothing to do with the Colosseum or the inaugural shows there and poem 37 was clearly written after the death of Domitian (AD 96).
179 Cass. Dio 66.25.4. The one hundred days refer to how much time elapsed from the first event of the inauguration to the last. It does not mean that events were held on every one of the hundred days. See Ville, *La Gladiature*, 144.
180 Cass. Dio 66.25.1. I am not sure how cranes could be induced to fight each other. Perhaps, males were tied together as large animals like bulls and bears were (and even, on at least one occasion, gladiators).
181 Poems 6, 9, 10, 18, 19, 24, 25.
182 The numbers in parentheses refer to the order of the poems in Shackleton Bailey's *Loeb Classical Library* edition of Martial's *Book of Spectacles*.
183 Another example of an offence to modern sensibilities is the tastelessness (from our point of view) of the owner of a villa at Silin in Libya, who adorned one of his bedrooms with a mosaic depicting *damnati* being killed by a bull. See Coleman, 'Contagion', 79.
184 Europa was an Asian princess carried off over the sea to Crete by Zeus (Jupiter) in the form of a bull. She became the mother of Minos, a king of Crete. Alcides is a patronymic of Hercules derived from his grandfather Alcaeus.
185 1.15.2.

186 Cass. Dio 72.18.1. Domitian also was fond of playing the arena hunter, but not in public. At his Alban private retreat he would kill up to a hundred animals with his bow and arrows for invited friends. He had a reputation for accuracy with the bow. It was said that he could shoot two arrows into the heads of his animal victims so that they resembled horns. It was also reported that he could shoot arrows into the spaces between the fanned out fingers of a boy's hand (Suet. *Dom.* 19).

187 Cass. Dio 72.18.1–2.

188 *SHA, Comm.* (Aelius Lampridius) 11.9.

189 Cass. Dio 73.20.1–3.

190 *Ibid.* 72.19.1.

191 1.15.5–6.

192 72.21.1–2.

193 *SHA Gord. Tres* (Julius Capitolinus) 3.6.

194 *SHA Probus* (Flavius Vopiscus) 19.5–6.

195 *SHA Gord. Tres* (Julius Capitolinus) 33.1.

196 *Ibid.* 3.7–8.

197 *SHA Prob.* (Flavius Vopiscus) 19.4.

198 *SHA Elagab.* (Aelius Lampridius) 8.3.

199 8.78.10.

200 Mart. 8.78.11–12. See J. R. Killeen, 'What Was the Linea Dives (Martial, VIII, 78,7)? *AJP* 80.2 (1959) 187–8. According to Killeen, birds distributed in this way included guinea fowl, turtle doves, pigeons and ducks. At a December *munus* under Domitian, the birds were more exotic; they were from Egypt, eastern Black Sea area and northern Africa (Statius, *Silvae* 1.6.77–8).

201 Sen. *Ep.* 74.7.

202 See David Potter, 'Gladiators and Blood Sport', in Winkler (ed.), *Gladiator: Film and History*, 74; Wiedemann, *Emperors*, 154.

203 Cassiod. *Var.* 5.42.1–2; 11. See also Rea, 'The Colosseum through the Centuries', in Gabucci (ed.), *The Colosseum*, 182 and Hopkins and Beard, *The Colosseum*, 153.

204 Bomgardner, 'Carthage Amphitheater', 103 and *Story*, 225–6.

Chapter 6 The Roman Amphitheatre and the Colosseum

1 Gian Luca Gregori, 'The Dedication of the Amphitheatre in Pompeii', in Gabucci (ed.), *The Colosseum*, 30.

2 *ILS* 5627. In the towns of Italy, two men were elected every fifth year to the prestigious position of *duoviri quinquennales*, which required them to administer the census and check the worthiness of members of the local senate (*decuriones*).

3 The settlement of veterans was Pompeii's punishment for opposing the Romans in the Social War (Nicholas Purcell, 'Pompeii' in the *OCD*). See Katherine Welch, *The Roman Amphitheatre: From Its Origins To The Colosseum* (Cambridge, 2007) 76–7.

4 Connolly, *Colosseum*, 35–6 and Welch, *Roman Amphitheatre*, 192–4. Another early technique of amphitheatre construction was to cut out the seating area from surrounding bedrock, as at Sutrium (modern Sutri in north Italy) and Corinth.

5 The historian Velleius Paterculus calls this resistance an example of 'the outstanding strictness (*severitas*) of the state' (1.15.3).

6 There is mention of two earlier theatrical structures built in 179 BC and in 174 BC but it is not clear that these were permanent stone theatres. See Constance Campbell, 'The Uncompleted Theatres of Rome', *Theatre Journal* 55.1 (2003) 67–8.

7 *Ann.* 14.20.

8 2.4.2.

9 Appian, *B Civ.* 1.4.28. See also E. Gruen, *Culture and Identity in Republican Rome* (Ithaca, NY, 1992) 209–10. Campbell, 'Uncompleted Theatres', 76–7) suggests that defective concrete may have also contributed to the decision to destroy this theatre.

10 Val. Max 2.4.2.

11 Campbell, 'Uncompleted Theatres', 68–9.

12 See Golvin, *L'Amphithéâtre romain*, 19 and Welch, 'Roman arena', 69–79.

13 See Livy's account of the origins of drama at Rome in the fourth century BC, beginning in 364 (7.2.3–7). Welch (*Roman Amphitheatre*, 34) suggests another purpose of the balconies was for viewing triumphal processions as they proceeded through the Forum (Plut. *Aem.* 32.1).

14 Fest. *Gloss. Lat.* 134.7–9.

15 Basilica Porcia (184 BC), Basilica Aemilia et Fulvia (179 BC) and the Basilica Sempronia (170 BC).

16 Welch, *Roman Amphitheatre*, 34–5.

17 Isid. *Orig.* 51.3.11.

18 E. J. Jory, 'Gladiators in the Theatre', *CQ* NS 36.2 (1986) 538.

19 *C. Gracch.* 33.5–6.

20 72.19.1.

21 Welch, *Roman Amphitheatre*, 50.

22 *Sest.* 124. See Edmondson, 'Dynamic Arenas', 87.

23 *HN* 36.115.

24 Cic. *Fam.* 8.2.1.

25 Plin. *HN* 36.5.

26 *Ibid.* 36.117. See Golvin's thorough discussion of this architectural novelty (*L'Amphithéâtre romain*, 30–2).

27 *HN* 36.118.

28 Cass. Dio. 43 22.3.

29 P. Connolly and H. Dodge, *The Ancient City: Life in Classical Athens and Rome* (Oxford, 1998) 190–2; Dodge, 'Amusing the Masses', in Potter and Mattingly (eds), *Life, Death, and Entertainment*, 225; Scobie, 'Security and Comfort', 199.

30 Scobie, 'Spectator Security', 198–99.

31 *ad Martyr.* 6.1.

32 Welch, *Roman Amphitheatre*, 39.

33 Dodge, 'Amusing the Masses', 230.

34 For example, the plebeian aediles gave gladiatorial matches in the Circus Maximus in 42 BC. (Cass. Dio 47.40.6–7).

35 Cass. Dio 43.23.3.

36 Vitr. *De arch.* 5.1.1.

37 Suet. *Tib.* 7.1.

38 Bomgardner, *Story*, 59.

39 'The Arena', 77–80. Some of these amphitheatres were located in areas that had strong military ties with Rome, e.g. Pompeii (a military colony founded by Sulla for his veterans).

40 For a detailed discussion of amphitheatres in the west, see Futrell, *Blood*, 53–76.

41 See Golvin, *L'Amphithéâtre romain*, 175–7.

42 Bomgardner, *Story*, 60; Welch, *Roman Amphitheatre*, 255–9.

43 Welch, *Roman Amphitheatre*, 259–63.

44 Thompson, 'The Martyrdom of Polycarp', 30.

45 See Robert, *Les Gladiateurs*, 33–6.

46 Philostr. *VA* 4.22.

47 *Or.* 31.121.

48 Val. Max. 1.7.8

49 Cass. Dio 51.23.1; Suet. *Aug.* 29.5. The Campus Martius covered an area of about 600 acres bordered on the west by the Tiber.

50 *Roman Amphitheatre*, 116.

51 Tac. *Ann.* 3.72.

52 *ILS* 5156.

53 *ILS* 5157.

54 Cass. Dio 51.23.1.

55 See Zanker, *Power of Images*, 70; Diane Favro, *The Urban Image of Augustan Rome* (Cambridge, 1996) 164; Edmondson, 'Dynamic Arenas', 78.

56 59.10.5.

57 *Roman Amphitheatre*, 113.

58 Suet. *Calig.* 21.1.

59 Cic. *Att.* 4.16.8.

60 Cass. Dio 53.23.1–3.

61 See Claridge, *Rome*, 207. Seneca lists the *Saepta* with the Forum and the Circus Maximus as locations that could accommodate very large crowds (*Dial.* 4.8.1).

The footprint of the Saepta was nearly two acres larger than that of the later Colosseum.

62 *Ecl.* 7.45–6. It is likely that Corydon's two references to 'sheepfolds' (*ovilia*, 11, 15) in his home town are allusions to the *Saepta*, popularly called 'the sheep pen' (*ovile*). This interpretation is made even more plausible by Corydon's scornful comparison of these sheep pens with what he had seen in Rome: 'Let Stimicon [a winner of a local musical contest in Corydon's absence] carry off all the sheepfolds which Thyrsis [sponsor of contest] purifies; he will still not equal my joys, not if someone presented me with all the herds of the Lucanian [in southern Italy] forest' (*Ecl.* 7.15–17).

63 *Ann.* 13.31.

64 *Ecl.* 7.23–4.

65 Claridge, *Rome*, 276.

66 *Ecl.* 7.47–8. In an amphitheatre, the *balteus* ('belt') was one of the walls running around the whole building that divided the seating area into different levels (*maeniana*).

67 *Ecl.* 7.53–4. *HN* 37.45.

68 Suet. *Iul.* 39.2.

69 *Ecl.* 7.48–53.

70 *Ibid.* 7.53–5. Pliny the Elder also mentions the nets, the purpose of which he describes as 'protecting the podium' (*HN* 37.45), but oddly omits any reference to the cylinder mentioned by Calpurnius and discussed below.

71 See Townend, 'Calpurnius Siculus', 171–3.

72 See Bomgardner, *Story*, 20–1; Junkelmann, *Familia Gladiatoria*, in Köhne and Ewigleben (eds), *The Power of Spectacle*, 35.

73 'Spectator Security', 210.

74 *Ibid.* 210; 238, n. 113.

75 Suetonius (*Ner.* 12.1–2) calls these enactments *pyrrhicae*. The term *pyrrhica*, borrowed from the Greek, is usually translated as pyrrhic dancing, i.e., 'a war dance in armour' in accordance with its original meaning, but its application here indicates that the word during the empire had acquired a wider connotation including dramatic performances. See Coleman, 'Fatal Charades', 68, n. 200.

76 Townend ('Calpurnius Siculus', 173) argues that the enclosed box was in place on the first day of the *munus* because Nero was afraid of an attack by wild animals, but was afterwards removed when he saw that the nets had been effective. David Woods ('Pliny, Nero, and the "Emerald", (*NH* 37, 64)', *Arctos* 40 (2006) 195) takes a different tack altogether. He claims that the purpose of Nero's enclosed box was to allow him to spy on the spectators unobserved.

77 The saffron mist must have been produced by the same device that shot a saffron spray into the seating area to refresh the crowd (*Q Nat.* 2.9.2.).

78 *Spect.* 1.

79 Amm. Marc. 16.10.14.

80 Claridge, *Rome*, 271. See Plin. *HN* 34.45; Suet. 31.1; and Cass. Dio 66.15.1. As a point of comparison, the Statue of Liberty is (not including the base) 152 feet, 2 inches high. Nero indeed had megalomaniac tendencies. He had a painting made of himself on canvas, 120 (Roman) feet high (= 114 modern feet). Soon after it was displayed publicly, it was set on fire by lightning (Plin. *HN* 35.51).

81 See 'Domus Aurea' in the *OCD*, 3rd edn, and Suet. *Ner.* 31.1–2.

82 H. V. Canter ('The Venerable Bede and the Colosseum', *TAPA* 61 (1930) 162–5) supports this interpretation.

83 See Hopkins and Beard, *The Colosseum*, 35 and Claridge, *Rome*, 271.

84 'Signs of Continued Use after Antiquity', in Gabucci (ed.), *The Colosseum*, 197.

85 *Spect*, 2. Coleman (*Liber Spectaculorum*, 20) claims that Vespasian erased Nero's features from the face of the statue, but that was actually the work of Hadrian, who had the statue converted to a representation of the Sun god (*SHA Hadrian*. (Aelius Spartianus) 19.13).

86 Cass. Dio 66.15.2.

87 The use of money acquired from the sale of *manubiae* for gifts to the Roman people was a regular practice of victorious generals. For example, Augustus often financed gifts to the Roman people (including public buildings) from his *manubiae* (*RG* 15; 21). See Coleman, 'Contagion', *Hermathena* 164 (1998) 67.

88 *CIL* VI.40454a.

89 Hopkins and Beard (*Colosseum*, 34) are dubious about this reconstruction: 'A skeptical reader is likely to feel (as we do) that there is an uncomfortably long distance between the scatter of holes and the suspiciously appropriate solution to "joining the dots" '. Nevertheless, Hopkins and Beard do not go so far as to deny the overall accuracy of the reconstruction.

90 Silvia Orlandi, 'The Bronze-Lettered Inscription of Vespasian and Titus', in Gabucci (ed.), *The Colosseum*, 165.

91 Ramsay MacMullen ('Some Pictures in Ammianus Marcellinus', *The Art Bulletin* 46.4. (1964) 443) points out that for the Romans, when it came to amphitheatres, money was no object. See also Richard Duncan-Jones, *The Economy of the Roman Empire: Quantitative Studies* (Cambridge, 1974) 75.

92 *AE* 1961, 140; 1969–70, 183.

93 'Contagion', 76 (*CIL* X.5183).

94 See Bomgardner, *Story*, 30. A fourth century chronicle (354 AD) attributes the completion of the attic story, at that time decorated with shields, to Domitian. The depiction of the Colosseum on the tomb of the Haterii has only three stories.

95 Only arches numbered 31 to 54 on the northern side have survived.

96 Scobie, 'Security and Comfort', 204.

97 Claridge, *Rome*, 266, fig. 128; 271–2.

98 Hopkins and Beard, *The Colosseum*, 133–4. See also Rea and Orlandi, 'The Interior', in Gabucci (ed.), *The Colosseum*, 132–4; 138–9 and P. Connolly, *The*

Colosseum, 59–60. Bomgardner (*Story*, 9) oddly places the passageway of Commodus and the emperor's box on the north side, but he may have been misled by a schematic from Golvin (*L'Amphithéâtre romain*, plate XXXVII), reproduced in his text (10), which appears to have its directional arrows reversed.

99 Cass. Dio 72.4.4.
100 *Aug.* 44.3.
101 Connolly and Dodge, *The Ancient City*, 194.
102 'The Interior', in Gabucci (ed.), *The Colosseum*, 132–4.
103 Cic. *Har. Resp.* 24. See also Val. Max 2.4.3 and Livy 34.44.5.
104 Cic. *Mur.* 40 and Vell. Pat. 2.32.3.
105 See Elizabeth Rawson, '*Discrimina Ordinum*: The *Lex Julia Theatralis*', PBSR 55 (1987) 102, n. 110.
106 Sen. *Ben.* 7.12.4. Seneca also says that he does not have the right to sell or rent his place. This is probably the result not of a legal prohibition but of convention. It was obviously considered *déclassé* to sell a seating privilege that one had been awarded because of one's elite status.
107 Quint. *Inst.* 6.3.63.
108 Epict. *Dissertationes* 1.25.26–9.
109 Tac, *Ann.* 3.31.
110 '*Discrimina*', 108.
111 Suet. *Aug.* 14.1.
112 Suet. *Dom.* 8.3.
113 5.14. Martial gives the name of this usher (Leitus) here and in 5.8.12. Martial refers by name to one other usher (Oceanus) in 3.95.10 and 5.23.4.
114 3.95.9–10. See Tac. *Ann.* 16.12 and Rawson, '*Discrimina*' (1987) 100. Martial apparently was peeved because Naevolus would never say hello to him, unless he spoke first.
115 5.23.
116 Rawson, '*Discrimina*', 102, n. 112.
117 Rawson (*Ibid.* 86) notes that the seating assignments in the Colosseum followed the requirements of the *lex Julia Theatralis*.
118 Suet. *Aug.* 44.1 See Edmondson, 'Dynamic Arenas', 102–3.
119 Suet. *Aug.* 44.1.
120 *Ibid.* 44.2.
121 *Silvae* 1.6.44.
122 Rawson, '*Discrimina*', 84.
123 Augustus believed that men who remained unmarried and did not produce children were not performing their duty as Roman citizens (Cass. Dio 56.5.7). He backed up this belief with legislation that encouraged marriage. See Rawson, '*Discrimina*', 98–9.
124 Florence Dupont (*Daily Life in Ancient Rome*, trans. Christopher Woodall (Cambridge, MA, 1993) 223) suggests that the *toga praetexta* was a symbol of

inviolability, which applied to both magistrates, young boys and young girls, who wore the *praetexta* until they were married.

125 There is no reference in the sources to any other seating area for slaves. Perhaps the Romans still followed the policy that was in effect during the Republic. The prologue speaker in Plautus' *Poenulus* warns slaves to stand in the theatre in order not to deprive freeborn Romans of a seat, although they could purchase one if they could afford it (23–4). In the Colosseum, perhaps slaves found empty seats in the upper reaches of the stands.

126 Suet. *Aug.* 44.2–3. These people were called *pullati* ('clad in dark clothing').

127 Calp. Sic. *Ecl.* 7.29. Following van Berchem and Bollinger, I read *tribules* ('citizens belonging to tribes', 'commoners') instead of the perplexing *tribuni* ('tribunes') in line 29. *Tribules*, if correct, would be a reference to the *plebs* divided into their tribes (politican divisions of the Roman people). See Rawson, '*Discrimina*', 95. I believe that *nivei* ('snow white') modifying *tribules* implies an understood *niveus* qualifying *eques* ('equestrians').

128 *Aen.* 1.282.

129 Cass. Dio 60.7.4.

130 3.171–2.

131 14.135.

132 4.2.

133 Suet. *Aug.* 44.2–3. Wives, no matter what their status, were not permitted to sit with their husbands. See Rawson, '*Discrimina*', 91.

134 Calp. Sic. *Ecl.* 7.25–7.

135 Plut. *Sull.* 35.3–5.

136 *Ars am.* 1.167–8. Since this poem was written long after the passage of Augustus' *Lex Julia Theatralis*, one might wonder why Ovid has men and women sitting together in the amphitheatre. (Rawson ('*Discrimina*', 98) gives 26 to 17 BC as the most likely time frame for the issuing of the *lex Julia Theatralis*.) There are as many different opinions as scholars. Edmondson ('Dynamic Arenas', 88–90) suggests that there might have been a lag in the application of the seating rules to the amphitheatre in comparison with the theatre, but eventually they were applied equally to both structures. Rawson ('*Discrimina*', 108) notes that in the early principate there were some occasions when Augustus' seating rules were not observed. Ville (*La Gladiature*, 436, n. 157) argues that all these seating rules probably were not established at the same time, but in a piecemeal fashion. Cassius Dio says that the rules about separate seating for the senators and the equestrians were not put into effect in the Circus Maximus until AD 5 (55.22.4).

137 *Ars. am.* 1.165–6; 169–70.

138 4.8.76–7.

139 *Am.* 2.7.1–6.

140 Tac. *Ann.* 4.16.

141 Cass. Dio 59.3.4; 60.22.2.

142 *ILS* 5049. See Silvia Orlandi, 'Seating Inscriptions for the Fratres Arvales', in Gabucci (ed.), *The Colosseum*, 126.

143 Edmondson, 'Dynamic Arenas', 91, n. 93.

144 Hopkins and Beard, *The Colosseum*, 109.

145 Arval Brothers who were members of the senatorial order no doubt sat on the podium among their senatorial colleagues to enjoy the better vantage point.

146 Jerzy Kolendo, 'La répartition des places aux spectacles et la stratification social dans l'empire romain, *Ktema: civilizations de l'Orient, de la Grèce et de Rome antiques* 6 (1981) 304–5. Kolendo, however, ignoring Augustus' rule that women sit in the upper regions of the amphitheatre, seems to include them in his mention of the family members sitting with the Arvals in the *maenianum primum*.

147 Arnob. *Ad. Nat.* 4.35.4.

148 Kolendo, 'La répartition', 304.

149 Rawson, '*Discrimina*', 92.

150 The Frisians were a Germanic tribe, ancestors of the Dutch.

151 Tac. *Ann.* 13.54.

152 *Spect.* 3.

153 Catherine Edwards and Greg Woolf, 'Cosmopolis: Rome as World City', in Catharine Edwards and Greg Woolf (eds), *The Cosmopolis* (Cambridge, 2003) 1.

154 Cass. Dio 61.17.5.

155 The award could only be given if testimony was given by the person saved.

156 Plin. *HN* 16.12–13. See Rawson, '*Discrimina*', 106.

157 *Phil.* 9.16. How long this honour for the Sulpician family remained in effect is not known. See Rawson, '*Discrimina*', 110.

158 'Roman arena', 76–7, n. 42.

159 Welch (*Roman Amphitheatre*, 32–5) gives an account of the scholarly debate over whether the *maeniana* were invented by the fourth century Maenius or the second century Maenius. She notes that the sources for the earlier Maenius are more reliable than those for the later Maenius and rightly points out that this question is not crucial and that what is significant for the topic at hand is (1) *maeniana* existed in the Forum as early as 184 BC and (2) by this date gladiator shows had become so popular that more viewing space was necessary.

160 Ps. Asc. 201.15; Porphyr. *ad loc.* Hor. *Sat.* 1.3.21.

161 *AE* 1927 58. See Rawson, '*Discrimina*', 110, n. 162. The reason for this honour is unknown.

162 See Hopkins and Beard, *The Colosseum*, 109. Roman patronage involved assistance, both financial and legal, that was provided by a well-to-do patron of higher status to a man of lower status with whom he had a long-standing relationship, for example (e.g. a slave freed by the patron). Some patrons had many such

clients. In return, the client supported his patron in various ways and gave him respect by greeting him early in the morning at his house.

163 See Bomgardner, *Story*, 6; Paul J. J. Vanderbroeck, *Popular Leadership*, 79–80; Futrell, *Blood*, 164.

164 '*Discrimina*', 97.

165 Cic. *Att.* 2.1.5.

166 73.

167 '*Discrimina*', 97.

168 Futrell, *Blood*, 164.

169 5.24.9.

170 See Gunderson, 'Ideology', 123; 125.

171 Balsdon, *Life*, 268.

172 Edmondson, 'Dynamic Arenas', 91.

173 *Ner.* 12.2.

174 Suet. *Aug.* 44.1.

175 Cass. Dio 59.7.8.

176 Edmondson ('Dynamic Arenas', 91, n. 97) says there is no convincing evidence that the equestrians sat in the *maenianum primum*. He suggests that their seats were immediately behind the podium with no walkway (*praecinctio*) separating them. The more common interpretation is that there were three concentric walkways backed by a balustrade (*balteus*) which divided the *cavea* into the four main sections noted in Figure 30. The lowest walkway would have been just behind the podium; the highest was immediately behind the *maenianum imum secundum*.

177 *Ibid.* 92.

178 Connolly, *Colosseum*, 61.

179 Rea and Orlandi, 'The Underground Chambers', in Gabucci (ed.), *The Colosseum*, 129 and Connolly, *Colosseum*, 56.

180 *Story*, 12.

181 Suet. *Aug.* 44.3.

182 Calp. Sic. *Ecl.* 7.27. Golvin (*L'Amphithéâtre romain*, 36, n. 85) has suggested that the *cathedrae* were box seats. See also Edmondson, 'Dynamic Arenas', 93.

183 Suet. *Calig.* 26.5.

184 Plin. *HN* 19.23.

185 *Ibid.*

186 *Ibid.*

187 Cass. Dio 53.31.3.

188 4.75–80. The translation is by Cyril Bailey with adjustments made by the author (*Titi Lvcreti Cari De Rerum Natura: Edited with Prolegomena, Critical Apparatus, Translation and Commentary*, I (Oxford 1947) 367).

189 Plin. *HN* 19.24; Cass. Dio 63.6.2.

190 Claridge, *Rome*, 271 and Coleman, *Liber Spectaculorum*, 21. See *SHA Hadrian* (Aelius Spartianus) 19.13.

191 *SHA Comm.* (Aelius Lampridius) 15.6. See Connolly and Dodge, *Ancient City*, 198; Claridge, *Rome*, 269; and Ville, *La Gladiature*, 282. Misenum on the Bay of Naples was Rome's most important naval base.

192 Mart. 4.2.5; 11.21.6. The sailors may have used a device called an anemoscope to determine the direction of the wind. One of these wind indicators was found on the Esquiline Hill not far from the Colosseum. See Silvia Orlandi, 'The Anemoscope', in Gabucci (ed.), *The Colosseum*, 119.

193 'Reconstructing the Roman Colosseum Awning', *Archaeology* 35.2 (1982) 62.

194 *SHA Comm.* (Aelius Lampridius) 15.5–8.

195 14.28.

196 Scobie, 'Security and Comfort', 222; Hopkins and Beard, *The Colosseum*, 110–11.

197 Cass. Dio 59.7.8; Mart. 14.29.

198 Connolly, *Colosseum*, 64.

199 *HN* 19.24.

200 Connolly and Dodge, *Ancient City*, 199.

201 Claridge, *Rome*, 280–2.

202 Connolly and Dodge, *Ancient City*, 208.

203 Connolly, *Colosseum*, 196 and Bomgardner, *Story*, 30.

204 Claridge, *Rome*, 281.

205 *Ibid.* 280–1.

206 Connolly and Dodge, *Ancient City*, 206–7.

207 *Ibid.* 208.

208 Cass. Dio 78.25.2–4. The 'stadium' mentioned by Dio was probably the one built by Domitian, the shape of which is now evident in the Piazza Navona (Claridge, *Rome*, 209–11).

209 Rea, 'Original Use from A.D. 80 to 523', in Gabucci (ed.), *The Colosseum*, 176.

210 *Ibid.*

211 The colonnade may also have fallen during an earthquake in the fifth century. See Rea, 'Original Use', in Gabucci (ed.), *The Colosseum*, 181 and Connolly, *Colosseum*, 158.

212 Hopkins and Beard, *The Colosseum*, 154–5 and Rea, 'Ludwig the Bavarian', in Gabucci (ed.), *The* Colosseum, 200.

213 *History of the Decline and Fall of the Roman Empire*, ch. 71.

214 Connolly, *Colosseum*, 158.

215 Claridge, *Rome*, 276.

216 Connolly, *Colosseum*, 158.

217 Cassiod. *Var.* 3.49.3

218 The other two owners were the Capitoline Senate (the government of the city of Rome) and the religious order of Santissimo Salvatore ad Sancta Sanctorum.

219 Rea and Orlandi, 'From Ruins to Monument', in Gabucci (ed.), *The Colosseum*, 203–4.

220 *Ibid.* 208; 212.

221 Rea, 'Myth and Legends', in Gabucci (ed.), *The Colosseum*, 205. Pope Sylvester presided over the dedication of St John Lateran in 324.

222 See Tert. *De spect.* 7.3.

223 *The Autobiography of Benvenuto Cellini*, ch. 64.

224 See Rea, 'Virgil the Magician', in Gabucci (ed.), *The Colosseum*, 207.

225 Rea, 'From Arena of Death to Place of Prayer', in Gabucci (ed.), *The Colosseum*, 209.

226 Hopkins and Beard, *The Colosseum*, 103. The article 'The Coliseum' in the online version of the *Catholic Encyclopedia* (http://www.newadvent.org/cathen/04101b.htm, 1913 edition) points out that it is just as likely that Christian martyrs in Rome were executed in other entertainment buildings such as the Circus Flaminius, the *Amphitheatrum Castrense* and the stadium of Domitian. This article also expresses doubt about the Colosseum as the location of Ignatius of Antioch's martyrdom.

227 Rea, 'From Ruins to Monument', in Gabucci (ed.), The *Colosseum*, 204.

228 Clement XI (1700–1721) revived the plan of his seventeenth century namesake to build a substantial church in the arena, but plans for this monument also were abandoned. See Connolly, *Colosseum*, 164–6.

229 Hopkins and Beard, *The Colosseum*, 167.

230 Rea, 'From Ruins to Monument', in Gabucci (ed.), *The Colosseum*, 213 and Beard and Hopkins, *The Colosseum*, 6 (figure 2). The ritual of the Stations ('stopping places') of the Cross involves a procession of the devout, who stop before depictions of various scenes of Christ's passion from his condemnation to his death, meditating on each scene. The tradition of the Stations of the Cross in the Colosseum was revived in the twentieth century and is still performed by the Pope every Good Friday.

231 Hopkins and Beard, *The Colosseum*, 172.

232 Rea, 'From Ruins to Monument', in Gabucci (ed.), *The Colosseum*, 214.

233 Connolly, *Colosseum*, 166.

234 Rea, 'From Ruins to Monument', in Gabucci (ed.), *The Colosseum* 219–27.

235 See Hopkins and Beard, *The Colosseum*, 3–12 for the less romantic views of Dickens, de Staël and Mark Twain.

236 *Ibid.* 19–20.

Chapter 7 Gladiators in Film

1 As Martin Winkler ('*Gladiator* and the Traditions of Historical Cinema', in Winkler (ed.), *Gladiator: Film and History*, 16–24) ably explains, films need not limit themselves to what actually happened but can fill in gaps in the historical record by inserting what might have happened, provided that these 'fill-ins' have sufficient plausibility in the context of the extant evidence.

2 See Junkelmann, *Das Spiel*, 7.

3 'The Pedant Goes to Hollywood: The Role of the Academic Consultant', in Winkler (ed.), *Gladiator: Film and History*, 51. Junkelmann (*Das Spiel*, 7) sees historical films as educators of the public and every such film, whether it portrays the past accurately or not, becomes 'a factoid'.

4 Even scholars (e.g., myself) can be led into error by a film. Junkelmann (*Das Spiel*, 7) cites the scene in William Wyler's *Ben Hur* (1959) in which chained slaves and convicts ply the oars in a Roman galley as a prime example of a film perpetuating an historical error (rowers were normally freemen). It never occurred to me to question the accuracy of that scene when I first saw the film soon after its release and even when I saw it for a second time a few years ago.

5 In *Sign*, Nero's *munus* takes place in a large stone amphitheatre, which is given no name. It could not be the Colosseum, which was built twelve years after Nero's death. The stone amphitheatre of Statilius Taurus was available during the first ten years of Nero's reign, but was burned down (along with Nero's famous wooden amphitheatre) in the great fire of AD 64.

6 Shaw, however, does include in his play the error of gladiators addressing the 'we who are about to die' speech to the emperor.

7 For example, *CIL* IV.1194.

8 The Romans used the adverb *gregatim* ('in a group') to describe these *mêlées* among gladiators.

9 See Suet. *Calig.* 30.3. The legislation of AD 177–180 required that outside Rome every gladiator show present a number of gladiators who fought *gregatim* equal to the number of gladiators who fought in individual duels (*ILS* 5163.37–40). This, however, is an emergency measure inspired by the outrageous costs of gladiators. Before this legislation, we do not often hear of *gregatim* fights; they were not a regular feature of the *munus*.

10 Suet. *Ner.* 12.1; Cass. Dio 59.10.1 and 61.9.5.

11 A herm is a column usually topped by a head of the Greek god Hermes (thus the name). The indication seems to be that the gorilla is going to rape the woman. Perhaps this scene was inspired by the punishment of a convicted woman in a *venatio*, who was raped by a bull as a mythical enactment of the Pasiphae myth (Mart. *Spect.* 6). Did DeMille think that gorilla rape was more palatable than bull rape?

12 *CIL* IV.1189 (*edictum*). *A(uli) Suetti Certi | aedilis familia gladiatorial pugnab(it) Pompeis | pr(idie) kalendas Iunias: venatio et vela erunt* [letters in parentheses complete abbreviations]. 'The gladiatorial troupe of the aedile A. Suettius Certus will fight at Pompeii on the day before the calends of June (31 May): there will be an animal hunt and awnings'. Unfortunately, *ERUNT*, which means 'there will be', is spelled erroneously in the film as *FRUNT*. The graphic artist apparently left off the bottom horizontal bar of the 'E'.

13 Suet. *Claud.* 21.5.

14 It would have been unusual for a member of the imperial family other than the emperor to own a gladiator school.

15 As the camera looks across the arena from the emperor's box, the Vestal Virgins sitting together are clearly visible. Although the evidence is unclear, this is one of the possible locations of the Vestal Virgin's box.

16 This pairing of a black and a white gladiator is a precursor of the Woody Strode (Draba)/Kirk Douglas fight in *Spartacus*. In both cases, the black fighter shows goodwill towards his white opponent. Glycon tries to save the life of the inexperienced Demetrius by faking the duel, while Draba does not attack when Spartacus is helpless, but instead throws his trident at the aristocratic Roman guests in the viewing box. The emphasis on black/white friendship must be understood as a product of the contemporary American civil rights movement in the 1950s. The friendship between Juba and Maximus in *Gladiator* is an echo of this theme, but the two do not fight.

17 The reason that Glycon gives to Strabo for forcing Demetrius to fight more opponents is to give the emperor a truly worthy birthday show. It does seem somewhat out of character for Glycon to force Demetrius to risk his life further, especially since Demetrius had spared his life the day before.

18 Earlier in the film, the same topic comes up in a conversation between Spartacus and Draba, in which the latter preferred not to know the name of a potential opponent in the arena. In Howard Fast's novel *Spartacus*, although he is enrolled in Batiatus' school, never fights as a gladiator.

19 *Das Spiel*, 10.

20 *The Gladiators*, 224. In the film *Fabiola* (dir. Blasetti, 1949), an Italian production dubbed into English and released in the United States, a banquet scene features a contest between the hero Rual (Henri Vidal), a *retiarius*, and a *thraex*, clearly identified by his helmet with a griffin finial. Like Spartacus, the *thraex* uses a small round shield instead of the rectangular shield of the historical *thraex*. The end of this contest illustrates why the *secutor* with his smooth fishbowl helmet was a more appropriate opponent for the *retiarius*. Clearly, any gladiator who wore a helmet with a prominent crest was at a significant disadvantage against a *retiarius'* trident. Rual catches his trident on the thin finial of his opponent's helmet and uses it as a lever keep him at a distance. Rual eventually is able to wrap him up in his net, but, as a Christian, spares his life.

21 Note that Russell Crowe in *Gladiator* also fights on occasion without a helmet, probably for the same reason.

22 The film uses the amphitheatre in Verona for its gladiatorial scenes. The DVD version identifies it as the Colosseum, but that building did not exist during Nero's reign. This, however, is a forgivable error, especially in comparison with the solecisms that follow.

23 The Scandinavian name Torvald seems out of place in ancient Italy, but movies have never been very careful about giving historically appropriate names to gladiators. For example, the programmes (*libelli*) for gladiator shows that list opponents in *The Last Days of Pompeii* include names that are at best medieval: Laurentius, Gulielmus, Gregorus, Carolus and Ludovicius and misunderstands the terms

Iulianus and *Neronianus,* presenting them as if they were names of individual gladiators and not indications of their special status. The history of the character Torvald, however, has a solid basis in the real world of gladiators. We are told he had already won his freedom, but still returned to the arena three times. This was a common phenomenon among retired star gladiators. *Editores* paid large sums to these returning retired gladiators because of their popularity with spectators. Tigris in *Gladiator* is another retiree who has returned to the arena.

24 Balsdon (*Life and Leisure,* 294–5) mentions a contest between an *essedarius* and a *retiarius,* but gives no primary or even secondary source. In any case, Barrabas and his two colleagues, although wearing only a *subligaculum* like a *retiarius,* do not use the trident as a weapon. In fact, it is the *essedarius* Torvald who uses a net, one of the *retiarius'* weapons.

25 See Kathleen M. Coleman, 'The Pedant' 45–52 and Allen M. Ward, 'Gladiator in Historical Perspective', 31, both in *Gladiator: Film and History,* Winkler (ed.). One should be especially wary of the information provided in the documentary (*Gladiator Games: Roman Blood Sport*) on the special features disc included with the DVD of the film. The words of excellent scholars like Kathleen Coleman, David Potter and Andrew Wallace Hadrill can be trusted, but there is an 'archaeologist' who says that gladiators on horseback were called *andabatae* and were blindfolded along with their horses. This nonsense confuses the *andabatae,* who were blindfolded, with the *equites,* who were not, as ancient depictions clearly demonstrate. Her Latin is also inaccurate. The crowd's cry for release of a gladiator is not *missa,* but *missum* or *missos.* The commentary provided by the voiceover runs the gamut of informational quality from erroneous to acceptable.

26 He also gave permission to a wealthy citizen to present a *munus* in the town of Avella (southern Italy), where this kind of spectacle had been long forgotten (*CIL* X.1211). He did ban all spectacles (including gladiatorial contests) in Antioch (Syria), but that was only because the city had supported his rival to the throne, Avidius Cassius (*SHA Marc.* (Julius Capitolinus) 9.1).

27 Zucchabar was not a Roman province but an Augustan colony in Mauretania (modern Algeria).

28 *Das Spiel,* 8.

29 Could the film be suggesting here the savage animal nature of gladiators? This seems to be a recurring theme in the film. Later on, a gladiator wears a helmet with a lion mask and another, a mask with two horns and two tusks. These helmets, of course, are the fantasy of the modern designers, as is the futuristic design of Maximus' helmet in the re-creation of the battle of Zama and that of Tigris of Gaul in his duel with Maximus, with a visor representing the mask of Tragedy. As unhistorical as Tigris' helmet is, I cannot help liking the design and the idea.

30 The most striking misrepresentation in this contest is that of a *retiarius* (identified by his trident, net and shoulder protector (*galerus*) – on the wrong shoulder). He wears a skull-like helmet enclosing the whole head, another example of the

fantasy armour in this film. It would be interesting to know why the *retiarius*, after being depicted accurately in the gladiator films of the 1930s, suddenly acquires a helmet in *Demetrius* (1954). *Spartacus* corrected this error, but *Gladiator* fell right back into it.

31 The television series *Rome* (co-produced by the BBC, HBO (USA) and RAI (Italy)) imitates this scene but ups the ante. Pullo kills seven opponents in a row.

32 In reality, Commodus and his representatives would never have bothered importing gladiators of a minor *lanista* all the way from North Africa. The emperor had the greatest gladiators in the empire in the *Ludus Magnus* adjacent to the Colosseum. Considerations of the plot have prevailed over historical accuracy in this instance.

33 *Das Spiel*, 9. Similar *metae* appear in the amphitheatre scene of George Lucas's *Attack of the Clones* (2002). Their presence is probably due to the influence of *Gladiator.* Obviously, film makers watch each other's films.

34 The film first guilty of the anachronism of medieval weapons is Richard Lester's *A Funny Thing Happened on the Way to the Forum* (1966) in which a gladiator apprentice practises on victims with a flail. This anachronism may have been deliberate for comic effect, but *Gladiator* and *Rome* (n. 31 above) apparently took it seriously. In *Rome*, a huge gladiator employs a flail, at the other end of which is a sword blade. I am not sure that this concoction ever existed, even in medieval times. It is interesting to note that in the background of a gladiatorial school scene in *Demetrius and the Gladiators*, a trainee is swinging a battleaxe at a *palus*, but at least the gladiators in the film's combat scenes never use this weapon.

35 '*Gladiator* in Historical Perspective', in Winkler (ed.), *Gladiator: Film and History*, 40.

36 After killing Commodus, Livius declines the throne.

37 See Wiedemann, *Emperors*, 92–3 and 102–4. Junkelmann (*Das Spiel*, 10), who has few kind words for *Gladiator*, praises the solidly historical depiction of Proximo, the *lanista*.

38 The historical Commodus served as co-ruler with Aurelius for the last three years of his father's life and, after his death, was his choice to succeed him.

Bibliography

Anderson, J. K., *Hunting in the Ancient World* (Berkeley, CA, 1985).

Arendt, Hannah, *Eichmann in Jerusalem: A Report on the Banality of Evil* (New York, 1963).

Audollent, Auguste, (*Defixionum tabellae. Quotquot innotuerunt tam in Graecis orientis quam in totius occidentis partibus praeter Atticas in corpore inscriptionum Atticarum editas*) reprint of Paris 1904 edition (Frankfurt, 1967).

Auguet, Roland, *Cruelty and Civilization: The Roman Games* (London, 1994).

Aurigemma, Salvatore, *I Mosaici di Zliten* (Rome, 1926).

Bailey, Cyril, *Titi Lvcreti Cari De Rerum Natura: Edited with Prolegomena, Critical Apparatus, Translation and Commentary* (Oxford, 1947).

Baldwin, Barry, 'The Sports Fans of Rome and Byzantium', *Liverpool Classical Monthly* 9 (1984) 28–30.

Balsdon, J. P. V. D., *Life and Leisure in Ancient Rome* (London, 1969).

Barnish, S. J. B. (trans.), *The Variae of Magnus Aurelius Cassiodorus Senator* (Liverpool, 1992).

Barrow, R. H., *Prefect and Emperor: The Relationes of Symmachus AD 384* (Oxford, 1973).

Barton, C., 'The Scandal of the Arena', *Representations* 27 (Summer 1989) 1–36.

Barton, C., *The Sorrows of the Ancient Romans: The Gladiator and the Monster* (Princeton, NJ, 1993).

Barton, C., 'Savage Miracles: The Redemption of Lost Honor in Roman Society and the Sacrament of the Gladiator and the Martyr', *Representations* 45 (Winter 1994) 41–71.

Bateman, Nick, *Gladiators at the Guildhall: The Story of London's Roman Amphitheatre and Medieval Guildhall* (London, 2000).

Beacham, R. C., *Spectacle Entertainment of Early Imperial Rome* (New Haven, CT, 1999).

Bingham, S., 'Security at the Games in the Early Imperial Period', *Echos du monde classique/Classical Views* 18 (1999) 369–79.

Bomgardner, David, 'The Carthage Amphitheater: A Reappraisal', *AJA*, 93.1 (1989) 85–103.

Bomgardner, David, *The Story of the Roman Amphitheatre* (London, 2000).

Bonner, Campbell, 'Eros and the Wounded Lion', *AJA* 49.4 (1945) 441–4.

Boyarin, Daniel, 'Martyrdom and the Making of Christianity and Judaism', *Journal of Early Christian Studies* 6.4 (1998) 577–627.

Braund, Susanna (ed. and trans.), *Juvenal and Persius* (Cambridge, MA, 2004).

Braund, Susanna, *Juvenal Satires: Book I* (Cambridge, 1996).

Brettler M. Z. and Poliakoff, M., 'Rabbi Simeon ben Lakish at the Gladiator's Banquet: Rabbinic Observations on the Roman Arena', *Harv. Theol. Rev.* 83.1 (1990) 93–8.

Brodeur, Arthur Gilchrist, 'The Grateful Lion', *PMLA* 39.3 (1924) 485–524.

Brown, Peter, *The World of Late Antiquity AD 150–750* (London, 1971).

Brown, Shelby, 'Death as Decoration: Scenes from the Arena on Roman Domestic Mosaics', in Amy Richlin and Marilyn Skinner (eds), *Pornography and Representation in Greece and Rome* (Oxford, 1992) 180–211.

Cagniart, P., 'The Philosopher and the Gladiator', *CW* 93 (2000) 607–18.

Cameron, Alan, *Circus Factions: Blues and Greens at Rome and Byzantium* (Oxford, 1976).

Cameron, Alan, *Porphyrius the Charioteer* (Oxford, 1973).

Campbell, Constance, 'The Uncompleted Theatres of Rome', *Theatre Journal* 55.1 (2003) 67–79.

Canter, H. V., 'The Venerable Bede and the Colosseum', *TAPA* 61 (1930) 150–64.

Capps, Jr., Edward, 'Observations on the Painted Venatio of the Theatre at Corinth and on the Arrangements of the Arena' *Hesperia Supplements, 8, Commemorative Studies in Honor of Theodore Leslie Shear* (1949) 64–70, 444–5.

Caron, Beaudoin, 'Note sur une lampe représentant deux gladiateurs', *Phoenix* 57.1/2 (2003) 139–43.

Carter, Michael, Review of A. Futrell, *Blood in the Arena: The Spectacle of Roman Power*, *Phoenix* 53. 1/2 (1999) 155–7.

Carter, Michael, 'Gladiatorial Ranking and the *SC de Pretiis Gladiatorum Minuendis* (*CIL* II 6278 = *ILS* 5163)', *Phoenix* 57.1/2 (2003) 83–114.

Catholic Encyclopedia (1913 edition) available at http://www.newadvent.org/cathen/04101b.htm.

Cebeillac-Gervasoni, M. and Zevi, F., 'Revisions et nouveautés pour trois inscriptions d'Ostie', *MEFRA* 88.2 (1976) 612–18.

Cellini, Benvenuto, *The Autobiography of Benvenuto Cellini*, available at http://www.gutenberg.org/dirs/etext03/7clln10h.htm.

Cerutti, Steven and Richardson, L. ('The *Retiarius Tunicatus* of Suetonius, Juvenal, and Petronius', *AJP* 110. 4 (1989) 589–94.

Chastagnol, A., *Le Sénat romain sous le règne d'Odacre: recherches sur l'epigraphie du Colisée au Vᵉ siècle* (Bonn, 1966).

Claridge, Amanda, *Rome: An Oxford Archaeological Guide* (Oxford, 1998).

Clavel-Lévêque, M., *L'Empire en jeux: espace symbolique et pratique sociale dans le monde romain* (Paris, 1984).

Coleman, K. M., 'Fatal Charades: Roman Executions Staged as Mythological Enactments', *JRS* 80 (1990) 44–73.

Coleman, K. M., 'Launching into History: Aquatic Displays in the Early Empire', *JRS* 83 (1993) 48–74.

Coleman, K. M., 'The Contagion of the Throng: Absorbing Violence in the Roman World', *Hermathena* 164 (1998) 65–88.

Coleman, K. M., 'Missio at Halicarnassus', *Harv. Stud.* 100 (2000) 487–500.

Coleman, K. M., 'The Pedant Goes to Hollywood: The Role of the Academic Consultant', in Winkler, Martin (ed.), *Gladiator: Film and History* (Malden, MA, 2004) 45–52.

Coleman, K. M., *M. Valerii Martialis Liber Spectaculorum* (Oxford, 2006)

Colin, J., 'Juvenal, les baladins et les rétiaires d'apres le manuscrit d'Oxford', *Atti della Accademia delle Scienze di Torino. Tomo 1, Classe di scienze fisiche, matematiche e naturali*, 87 (1952–53) 315–86.

Connolly, P. and Dodge, H., *The Ancient City: Life in Classical Athens and Rome* (Oxford, 1998).

Connolly, P., *Colosseum: Rome's Arena of Death* (London, 2003).

Corbeill, A., *Nature Embodied: Gesture in Ancient Rome* (Princeton, NJ, 2004).

Crook, J. A., *Law and Life of Rome* (Ithaca, NY, 1967).

Curtis, Robert I., 'A Slur on Lucius Asicius, the Pompeian Gladiator', *TAPA* 110 (1980) 51–61.

Den Boeft, Jan and Bremmer, Jan, 'Notiunculae Martyrologicae II', *Vigiliae Christianae* 36.4 (1982) 383–402.

Dill, Samuel, *Roman Society from Nero to Marcus Aurelius* (New York, 1956).

Dodge, Hazel, 'Amusing the Masses: Buildings for Entertainment and Leisure in the Roman World', in D. S. Potter and D. J. Mattingly (eds), *Life, Death, and Entertainment in the Roman Empire* (Ann Arbor, MI, 1999) 205–55.

Dronke, Peter, *Women Writers of the Middle Ages: A Critical Study of Texts from Perpetua (+203) to Marguerite Porete (+1310)* (Cambridge, 1984).

Duff, J. D., *Fourteen Satires of Juvenal* (Cambridge, 1957).

Dunbabin, Katherine, *The Mosaics of Roman North Africa: Studies in Iconography and Patronage* (Oxford, 1978).

Duncan-Jones, Richard, *The Economy of the Roman Empire: Quantitative Studies* (Cambridge, 1974).

Dupont, Florence, *Daily Life in Ancient Rome*, trans. Christopher Woodall (Malden, MA, 1993).

Edmondson, J. C., 'Dynamic Arenas: Gladiatorial Presentations in the City of Rome and the Construction of Roman Society during the Early Empire', in W. J. Slater (ed.), *Roman Theater and Society* (Ann Arbor, MI, 1996) 69–112.

Edwards, Catharine, 'Unspeakable Professions: Public Performance and Prostitution in Ancient Rome', in Amy Richlin and Marilyn Skinner (eds), *Pornography and Representation in Greece and Rome* (Oxford, 1992) 66–95.

Edwards, Catharine, *The Politics of Immorality in Ancient Rome* (Cambridge, 1993).

Edwards, Catharine and Woolf, Greg (eds) *The Cosmopolis* (Cambridge, 2003).

Epplett, Christopher, 'The Capture of Animals by the Roman Military', *Greece and Rome*, 2nd Ser., 48.2 (2001) 210–22.

Fast, Howard, *Spartacus* (Armonk, NY, 1951).

Favro, Diane, *The Urban Image of Augustan Rome* (Cambridge, 1996).

Fora, Maurizio, *I Munera Gladiatoria in Italia. Considerazioni sulla loro Documentazione Epigrafica* (Naples, 1996).

Fox, Robin Lane, *Pagans and Christians* (New York, 1987).

Friedländer, Ludwig, *Roman Life and Manners under the Early Empire*, seventh enlarged and revised edition of *Sittengeschichte Roms*, trans. J. H. Freese and Leonard A. Magnus, II (London and New York, 1908–13).

Frier, B., 'Roman Life-Expectancy: Ulpian's Evidence', *Harv. Stud.* 86 (1982) 213–51.

Futrell, Alison, *Blood in the Arena: The Spectacle of Roman Power* (Austin, TX, 1997).

Gardner, Jane, *Women in Roman Law and Society* (Bloomington, IN, 1986).

Garnsey, Peter and Saller, Richard, *The Roman Empire: Economy, Society and Culture* (Berkeley, CA, 1987).

Golden, Mark, *Sport and Society in Ancient Greece* (Cambridge, 1998).

Goldman, N., 'Reconstructing the Roman Colosseum Awning', *Archaeology* 35.2 (1982) 57–65.

Golvin, Jean-Claude, *L'Amphithéâtre romain: essai sur la théorisation de sa forme et de ses functions* (Paris, 1988).

Grant, Michael, *Gladiators: The Bloody Truth* (New York, 1967).

Gregori, Gian Luca, 'Constantine's Reply to the Umbrians', in Ada Gabucci (ed.), Mary Becker (trans.), *The Colosseum* (Los Angeles, 2001) 90.

Gregori, Gian Luca, 'Legislation on the Arena Shows', in Ada Gabucci (ed.), Mary Becker (trans.), *The Colosseum* (Los Angeles, 2001) 89–95.

Gregori, Gian Luca, 'The Dedication of the Amphitheatre in Pompeii', in Ada Gabucci (ed.), Mary Becker (trans.), *The Colosseum* (Los Angeles, 2001) 30.

Gregori, Gian Luca, 'The End of the Gladiators', in Ada Gabucci (ed.), Mary Becker (trans.), *The Colosseum* (Los Angeles, 2001) 96–8.

Gruen, E., *Culture and Identity in Republican Rome* (Ithaca, NY, 1992).

Gunderson E., 'The Ideology of the Arena', *Cl. Ant.* 15 (1996) 113–51.

Guttman, Allen, 'Sports Spectators from Antiquity to the Renaissance', *Journal of Sport History*, 8.2 (1981) 5–27.

Guttman, Allen, 'Roman Sports Violence', in Jeffrey Goldstein (ed.), *Sports Violence* (New York, 1983) 7–19.

Hallett, J. and Skinner, M. (eds), *Roman Sexualities* (Princeton, NJ, 1997).

Heintz, F., 'Circus Curses and their Archaeological Contexts', *JRA* 11 (1998) 337–42.

Hoffman, Carl, 'The Evolution of a Gladiator: History, Representation, and Revision in *Spartacus*', *Journal of American Culture* 23.1 (2000) 63–70.

Hope, Valerie M., 'Negotiating Identity and Status: The Gladiators of Roman Nîmes', in J. Berry and Ray Laurence (eds), *Cultural Identity in the Roman Empire* (London, 1998) 179–95.

Hope, Valerie M., 'Fighting for Identity: The Funerary Commemoration of Italian Gladiators', in Alison Cooley (ed.), *The Epigraphic Landscape of Roman Italy* (London, 2000) 93–113.

Hopkins, Keith, *Conquerors and Slaves* (Cambridge, 1978).

Hopkins, Keith, *Death and Renewal* (Cambridge, 1983).

Hopkins, Keith and Beard, Mary, *The Colosseum* (Cambridge, MA, 2005).

Houseman, A. E., 'Tunica Retiarii', *CR* 18.8 (1904) 395–98.

Huizinga, Johan, *Homo Ludens: A Study of the Play Element in Culture* (New York, 1970).

Jacobelli, Luciana, *Gladiators at Pompeii* (Los Angeles, 2003).

Jennison, George, 'Polar Bears at Rome. Calpurnius Siculus, Ecl. VII.65–6', *CR* 36.3/4 (1922) 73.

Jennison, George, *Animals for Show and Pleasure in Ancient Rome* (Manchester, 1937).

Jory, E. J., 'Gladiators in the Theatre', *CQ*, NS., 36.2 (1986) 537–39.

Junkelmann, Marcus, *Das Spiel mit dem Tod: So Kämpften Roms Gladiatoren* (Mainz am Rhein, 2000).

Junkelmann, Marcus, '*Familia Gladiatoria*: The Heroes of the Amphitheatre', in Eckart Köhne and Cornelia Ewigleben (eds), *The Power of Spectacle in Ancient Rome: Gladiators and Caesars* (Berkeley, CA, 2000) 31–74.

Junkelmann, Marcus, Review of Wiedemann's *Emperors and Gladiators*, *Plekos* 4 (2002) 33–44.

Kanz, F. and Grossschmidt, K., 'Head Injuries of Roman Gladiators', *Forensic Science International* 160.2/3 (2006) 207–16.

Kelly, Christopher, 'Corruption', in Simon Hornblower and Antony Spawforth (eds), *Oxford Classical Dictionary*, 3rd edn (Oxford, 1996).

Kiefer, Otto, *Sexual Life in Ancient Rome* (New York, 1993).

Killeen, J. F., 'What Was the Linea Dives (Martial, VIII, 78, 7)?' *AJP* 80.2 (1959) 185–8.

Kleijvegt, M., 'The Social Dimensions of Gladiatorial Combat in Petronius' *Cena Trimalchionis*', in H. Hofmann and M. Zimmermann (eds), *Groningen Colloquia on the Novel*, 9 (Groningen, 1998) 75–96.

Kolendo, Jerzy, 'La répartition des places aux spectacles et la stratification social dans l'Empire Romain', *Ktema: civilizations de l'Orient, de la Grèce et de Rome antiques* 6 (1981) 301–15.

Kyle, Donald, *Spectacles of Death in Ancient Rome* (London, 1998).

Lafaye, G., 'Gladiator', in C. Daremberg, E. Saglio and M. Pottier (eds), *Dictionnaire des antiquités greques et romaines d'après les textes et les monuments*, 2 (Paris, 1896) 1563–99.

Lendon, J. E., 'Gladiators', *CJ* 95 (Apr./May 2000) 399–406.

Leon, H. J., 'Morituri Te Salutamus', *TAPA* 70 (1939) 46–50.

Lepore, Jill, 'Goodbye Columbus', *The New Yorker*, 8 May 2006, 74–8.

Levick, Barbara, 'The *Senatus Consultum* from Larinum', *JRS* 73 (1983) 97–115.

Lintott, A. W., *Violence in Republican Rome* (Oxford, 1968).

Lovatt, Helen, *Statius and Epic Games: Sport, Politics, and Poetics in the Thebaid* (Cambridge, 2005).

MacDonald, Dennis R., 'A Conjectural Emendation of 1 Cor 15:31–32: Or the Case of the Misplaced Lion Fight', *Harv. Theol. Rev.* 73.1/2, *Dedicated to the Centennial of the Society of Biblical Literature* (Jan./Apr. 1980) 265–76.

MacMullen, Ramsay, 'Some Pictures in Ammianus Marcellinus', *The Art Bulletin* 46 (Dec. 1964) 435–56.

MacMullen, Ramsay, *Roman Social Relations 50 BC to AD 284* (New Haven, CT, 1974).

MacMullen, Ramsay, *Changes in the Roman Empire: Essays in the Ordinary* (Princeton, NJ, 1990).

Magie, David, *Roman Rule in Asia Minor, to the End of the Third Century after Christ*, I (Princeton, NJ, 1950).

Malamud, Margaret, 'Roman Entertainments for the Masses in Turn-of-the-Century New York', *CW* 95 (Fall 2001) 49–57.

Marsh, Frank, *A History of the Roman World from 146 to 30 B.C.* (revised with additional notes by H. H. Scullard, (London, 1957).

Matthews, J. F., Review of A. Birley's *Marcus* Aurelius, *JRS* 58.1/2 (1968) 262–3.

Meijer, Fik, *The Gladiators: History's Most Deadly Sport*, trans. Liz Waters (New York, 2005).

Meuli, Karl, *Der griechische Agon: Kampf und Kampfspiele in Totenbrauch, Totentanz, Totenklage, und Totenlob* (Cologne, 1968).

Millar, Fergus, *The Emperor in the Roman World (31 BC–AD 337)* (Ithaca, NY, 1977).

Millar, Fergus, 'The World of the Golden Ass', *JRS* 71 (1981) 63–75.

Muellner, Leonard, 'The Simile of the Cranes and Pygmies: A Study of Homeric Metaphor', *Harv. Stud.* 93 (1990) 59–101.

Mumford, Lewis, *The City in History: Its Origins, Its Transformations and its Prospects* (New York, 1961).

Musurillo, Herbert, *The Acts of the Christian Martyrs* (Oxford, 1972).

Newlands, C., *Statius's Silvae and the Poetics of Empire* (Cambridge, 2002).

Nippel, Wilfred, *Public Order in Ancient Rome* (Cambridge, 1995).

Nutton, Vivian, 'The Chronology of Galen's Early Career', *CQ* NS 23.1 (1973) 158–71.

O'Donnell, James, *Cassiodorus* (Berkeley, CA, 1979).

Oakley, S. P., 'Single Combat in the Roman Republic', *CQ* NS 35.2 (1985) 392–410.

Oliver, James H. and Palmer, Robert E. A., 'Minutes of an Act of the Roman Senate', *Hesperia* 24.4 (1955) 320–49.

Orlandi, Silvia, 'Il Colosseo nel V secolo', *The Transformations of Vrbs Roma in Late Antiquity* 33 (1999) 249–63.

Orlandi, Silvia, 'Seating Inscriptions for the Fratres Arvales', in Ada Gabucci (ed.), Mary Becker (trans.), *The Colosseum* (Los Angeles, 2001) 126.

Orlandi, Silvia, 'The Anemoscope', in Ada Gabucci (ed.), Mary Becker (trans.), *The Colosseum* (Los Angeles, 2001) 119.

Orlandi, Silvia, 'The Bronze-Lettered Inscription of Vespasian and Titus', in Ada Gabucci (ed.), Mary Becker (trans.), *The Colosseum* (Los Angeles, 2001) 165.

Owen, S. G., 'On the Tunica Retiarii. (Juvenal II. 143 ff.; VIII. 199 ff.; VI. Bodleian Fragment 9 ff.)', *CR* (Oct. 1905) 354–7.

Parker, Holt, 'Plautus vs. Terence: Audience and Popularity Re-examined', *AJP* 117.4 (1996) 585–617.

Patterson, Orlando, *Slavery and Social Death: A Comparative Study* (Cambridge, MA, 1982).

Pauly, A., Wissowa, G. and Kroll, W., *Real-Encyclopädie der klassischen Altertumswissenschaft* (1893–).

Plass, Paul, *The Game of Death in Ancient Rome: Arena Sport and Political Suicide* (Madison, WI, 1995).

Poliakoff, M., *Combat Sports in the Ancient World: Competition, Violence, and Culture* (New Haven, CT, 1987).

Potter, D. S., 'Entertainers in the Roman Empire' in D. S. Potter and D. J. Mattingly (eds), *Life, Death, and Entertainment in the Roman Empire* (Ann Arbor, MI, 1999) 256–325.

Potter, David, 'Martyrdom as Spectacle', in Ruth Scodel (ed.), *Theater and Society in the Classical World* (Ann Arbor, MI, 1983) 53–88.

Potter, David, 'Gladiators and Blood Sport', in Martin Winkler (ed.), *Gladiator: Film and History* (Malden, MA, 2004) 73–86.

Prettejohn, Elizabeth, 'The Monstrous Diversion of a Show of Gladiators: Simeon Solomon's Habet!' in Catharine Edwards (ed.), *Roman Presences: Receptions of Rome in European Culture, 1789–1945* (Cambridge, 1999) 157–72.

Price, Simon, *Rituals and Power: Roman Imperial Cult in Asia Minor* (Cambridge, 1984).

Purcell, Nicholas, 'Pompeii', in Simon Hornblower and Antony Spawforth (eds), *Oxford Classical Dictionary*, 3rd edn (Oxford, 1996).

Rawson, Beryl, 'Family Life among the Lower Classes at Rome in the First Two Centuries of the Empire', *C. Phil.* 61.2 (1966) 71–83.

Rawson, E., '*Discrimina Ordinum*: The *Lex Julia Theatralis*', *Papers of the British School in Rome* 55 (1987) 83–114.

Rea, Rossella, 'From Arena of Death to Place of Prayer', in Ada Gabucci (ed.), Mary Becker (trans.), *The Colosseum* (Los Angeles, 2001) 209.

Rea, Rossella, 'Ludwig the Bavarian', in Ada Gabucci (ed.), Mary Becker (trans.), *The Colosseum* (Los Angeles, 2001) 200.

Rea, Rossella, 'Myth and Legends', in Ada Gabucci (ed.), Mary Becker (trans.), *The Colosseum* (Los Angeles, 2001) 205.

Rea, Rossella, 'Original Use from A.D. 80 to 523', in Ada Gabucci (ed.), Mary Becker (trans.), *The Colosseum* (Los Angeles, 2001) 161–90.

Rea, Rossella, 'Signs of Continued Use after Antiquity', in Ada Gabucci (ed.), Mary Becker (trans.), *The Colosseum* (Los Angeles, 2001) 192–200.

Rea, Rossella, 'Virgil the Magician', in Ada Gabucci (ed.), Mary Becker (trans.), *The Colosseum* (Los Angeles, 2001) 207.

Rea, Rossella and Orlandi, Silvia, 'From Ruins to Monument', in Ada Gabucci (ed.), Mary Becker (trans.), *The Colosseum* (Los Angeles, 2001) 202–27.

Rea, Rossella and Orlandi, Silvia, 'The Interior', in Ada Gabucci (ed.), Mary Becker (trans.), *The Colosseum* (Los Angeles, 2001) 127–45.

Rea, Rossella and Orlandi, Silvia, 'The Underground Chambers', in Ada Gabucci (ed.), Mary Becker (trans.), *The Colosseum* (Los Angeles 2001) 148–59.

Reeve, M. D., 'Gladiators in Juvenal's Sixth Satire', *CR* NS 23.2 (1973) 124–5.

Riccobono, Salvatore, *Fontes iuris romani antejustiniani* (Florence, 1940–43).

Richardson, Lawrence, *Pompeii: An Architectural History* (Baltimore, 1988).

Richardson, Lawrence, *A New Topographical Dictionary of Ancient Rome* (Baltimore, 1992).

Ridley, Ronald, *The Eagle and the Spade: Archeology in Rome during the Napoleonic Era* (Cambridge, 1992).

Rives, James, 'The Piety of a Persecutor', *Journal of Early Christian Studies*, 4.1 (1996) 1–25.

Robert, Louis, *Les Gladiateurs dans l'orient grec* (Amsterdam, 1971, reprint of 1940 edition).

Robert, Louis, 'Une vision de Perpetue martyre a Carthage en 203', *Comptes rendus des séances – Académie des inscriptions et belles-lettres* (1982) 228–76.

Rousselle, Robert, 'The Dreams of Vibia Perpetua: An Analysis of a Female Christian Martyr', *The Journal of Psychohistory* 14 (1987) 193–206.

Runciman, W. G., 'The Sociologist and the Historian', *JRS* 76 (1986) 259–65.

Salisbury, Joyce, *Perpetua's Passion: The Death and Memory of a Young Roman Woman* (New York, 1997).

Saller, Richard, 'The Family and Society', in John Bodel (ed.), *Epigraphic Evidence: Ancient History from Inscriptions* (London, 2001) 95–117.

Scarborough, John, 'Galen and the Gladiators', *Episteme* 5 (1971) 98–111.

Schnurr, C., 'The Lex Julia Theatralis of Augustus: Some Remarks on Seating problems in Theatre, Amphitheatre and Circus', *Liverpool Classical Monthly* 17.10 (1992) 147–60.

Scobie, Alex, 'The Battle of the Pygmies and the Cranes in Chinese, Arab and North American Indian Sources', *Folklore* 86.2 (1975) 122–32.

Scobie, Alex, 'Spectator Security and Comfort at Gladiatorial Games', *Nikephoros* 1 (1988) 191–243.

Shackleton Bailey, D. R. (ed.), *Cicero's Letters to Atticus* (Cambridge, 1968).

Shackleton Bailey, D. R. (trans.), *Martial, Epigrams. I: Spectacles, Books 1–5* (Cambridge, MA, 1993).

Shaw, Brent, 'The Passion of Perpetua', *Past and Present* 139 (May 1993) 3–45.

Shaw, Brent, *Spartacus and the Slave Wars: A Brief History with Documents* (Boston, 2001).

Skinner, Marilyn, *Sexuality in Greek and Roman Culture* (Malden, MA, 2005).

Smith, William, *A Dictionary of Greek and Roman Antiquities* (1875) available at http://penelope.uchicago.edu/Thayer/E/Roman/Texts/secondary/SMIGRA/home.html.

Sturtevant, E. H., *The Pronunciation of Greek and Latin: The Sounds and Accents* (Chicago, 1920).

Taylor, L. R., *Roman Voting Assemblies From the Hannibalic War to the Dictatorship of Caesar* (Ann Arbor, MI, 1966).

Taylor, L. R., *Party Politics in the Age of Caesar* (Berkeley, CA, 1964).

Thompson, James W., 'The Alleged Persecution of the Christians at Lyons in 177', *American Journal of Theology*, 16.3 (1912) 359–84.

Thompson, James W., 'The Alleged Persecution of the Christians at Lyons in 177: A Reply to Certain Criticisms', *American Journal of Theology*, 17.2 (1913), 249–58.

Thompson, Leonard, 'The Martyrdom of Polycarp: Death in the Roman Games, *Journal of Religion*, 82.1 (2002) 27–52.

Toner, J. P., *Leisure and Ancient Rome* (Cambridge, MA, 1995).

Townend, G. B., 'Calpurnius Siculus and the *Munus Neronis*', *JRS*, 70 (1980) 166–74.

Toynbee, J. M. C., *Animals in Roman Life and Art* (Ithaca, NY, 1973).

Vanderbroeck, Paul J. J., *Popular Leadership and Collective Behavior in the Late Roman Republic (c. 80–50 B.C.)* (Amsterdam, 1987).

Vesley, Mark, 'Gladiatorial Training for Girls in the *Collegia Iuvenum* of the Roman Empire', *Echos du monde classique/Classical Views* XLII, NS 17 (1998) 85–93.

Veyne, Paul, *Bread and Circuses: Historical Sociology and Political Pluralism*, abridged with an introduction by Oswyn Murray, trans. Brian Pearce (London, 1990).

Ville, Georges, 'Les jeux de gladiateurs dans l'empire chrétien', *Mélanges d'archéologie et d'histoire* 72 (1960) 273–335.

Ville, Georges, *La Gladiature en occident des origines à la mort de Domitien* (Rome, 1981).

Ward, Allen, '*Gladiator* in Historical Perspective', in Martin Winkler (ed.), *Gladiator: Film and History* (Malden, MA, 2004) 31–44.

Ward-Perkins, Bryan, *From Classical Antiquity to the Middle Ages: Urban Public Building in Northern and Central Italy AD 300–850* (Oxford, 1984).

Warmington, E. H. (ed. and trans.), *Remains of Old Latin*, 3 (Cambridge, MA, 1938).

Welch, Katherine, Review of Carlin Barton's The *Sorrows of the Ancient Romans*, *Journal of Social History* 27.2 (1993), 430–3.

Welch, Katherine, 'The Roman Arena in Late-Republican Italy: A New Interpretation', *JRA*, 7 (1994) 59–80.

Welch, Katherine, *The Roman Amphitheatre: From its Origins to the Colosseum* (Cambridge, 2007).

Whittaker, C. R. (trans.), *Herodian I, Books 1–4* (Cambridge, MA, 1969).

Wiedemann, Thomas, 'Das Ende der Gladiatorenspiele', *Nikephoros* 8 (1995) 145–59.

Wiedemann, Thomas, *Emperors and Gladiators* (London, 1995).

Winkler, Martin, '*Gladiator* and the Traditions of Historical Cinema', in Martin Winkler (ed.), *Gladiator: Film and History* (Malden, MA, 2004) 16–30.

Wistrand, Magnus, *Entertainment and violence in Ancient Rome: The Attitudes of Roman Writers of the First Century A.D.* (Gothenburg, 1992).

Woods, David, 'Pliny, Nero, and the "Emerald" (*NH* 37, 64)', *Arctos* 40 (2006) 189–96.

Woodward, Christopher, *In Ruins* (New York, 2001).

Wyke, Maria, *Projecting the Past: Ancient Rome, Cinema and History* (New York, 1997).

Yavetz, Z., *Plebs and Princeps* (London, 1969).

Zanker, Paul, *The Power of Images in the Age of Augustus*, trans. Allan Shapiro (Ann Arbor, MI, 1990).

Zanker, Paul, *Pompeii: Public and Private Life*, trans. Deborah Lucas Schneider (Cambridge, MA, 1998).

Zoll, Amy, *Gladiatrix* (New York, 2002).

Index